Adobe® Photoshop® 7.0

Classroom in a Book®

Adobe®

www.adobe.com/adobepress

Adobe® Photoshop® 7.0 Classroom in a Book®

Written and designed at Adobe Systems Incorporated, 345 Park Avenue, San Jose, California 95110, USA

Printed in the U.S.A.

ISBN 0-321-11562-7
9 8 7 6 5 4 3

Contents

Basic Photo Corrections

Lesson 3

Working with Selections

Lesson 4

Layer Basics

Lesson 5

Getting Started

Adobe® Photoshop® 7.0 delivers powerful, industry-standard image-editing tools for professional designers who want to produce sophisticated graphics for the Web and for print. Included with Photoshop 7.0 is ImageReady™ 7.0 and its powerful set of Web tools for optimizing and previewing images, batch-processing images with droplets in the Actions palette, and creating rollovers and GIF animations. Photoshop and ImageReady combined offer a comprehensive environment for designing graphics for the Web.

About Classroom in a Book

Adobe Photoshop 7.0 Classroom in a Book® is part of the official training series for Adobe graphics and publishing software developed by experts at Adobe Systems. The lessons are designed to let you learn at your own pace. If you're new to Adobe Photoshop or ImageReady, you'll learn the fundamental concepts and features you'll need to master the programs. And if you've been using Adobe Photoshop or ImageReady for a while, you'll find that Classroom in a Book teaches many advanced features, including tips and techniques for using the latest version of these applications and for preparing images for the Web.

The lessons in this edition include new information on using the File Browser, defining custom workspaces, and working with the powerful new painting engine. In addition, existing lessons have been updated to incorporate new commands and tools, such as the new healing brush, patch tool, and pattern maker.

Although each lesson provides step-by-step instructions for creating a specific project, there's room for exploration and experimentation. You can follow the book from start to finish or do only the lessons that correspond to your interests and needs. Each lesson concludes with a review section summarizing what you've covered.

Prerequisites

Before beginning to use *Adobe Photoshop 7.0 Classroom in a Book*, you should have a working knowledge of your computer and its operating system. Make sure that you know how to use the mouse and standard menus and commands, and also how to open, save, and close files. If you need to review these techniques, see the printed or online documentation included with your Windows® or Mac® OS documentation.

Installing Adobe Photoshop and Adobe ImageReady

Before you begin using *Adobe Photoshop 7.0 Classroom in a Book*, make sure that your system is set up correctly and that you've installed the required software and hardware. You must purchase the Adobe Photoshop 7.0 software separately. For system requirements and complete instructions on installing the software, see the *InstallReadMe* file on the application CD.

Photoshop and ImageReady use the same installer. You must install the applications from the Adobe Photoshop 7.0 application CD onto your hard disk; you cannot run the program from the CD. Follow the on-screen instructions.

Make sure that your serial number is accessible before installing the application; you can find the serial number on the registration card or CD sleeve.

Starting Adobe Photoshop and Adobe ImageReady

You start Photoshop and ImageReady just as you would any software application.

To start Adobe Photoshop or ImageReady in Windows:

1 Choose Start > Programs > Adobe > Photoshop 7.0 > Adobe Photoshop 7.0 or ImageReady 7.0.

In Photoshop, if you have deleted the preferences file, the Adobe Color Management Assistant appears.

2 Click Cancel to close the Assistant without adjusting the monitor.

For instructions on how to calibrate a monitor, see Lesson 17, "Setting Up Your Monitor for Color Management," in this book.

To start Adobe Photoshop or Adobe ImageReady in Mac OS:

1 Open the Adobe Photoshop folder, and double-click the Adobe Photoshop or Adobe ImageReady program icon. (If you installed the program in a folder other than Adobe Photoshop, open that folder.)

In Photoshop, if you have deleted the preferences, the Adobe Color Management Assistant appears.

2 Click Cancel to close the Assistant without adjusting the monitor. For instructions on how to calibrate a monitor, see Lesson 17, "Setting Up Your Monitor for Color Management," in this book.

The Adobe Photoshop or Adobe ImageReady application window appears. You can now open a document or create a new one and start working.

Installing the Classroom in a Book fonts

To ensure that the lesson files appear on your system with the correct fonts, you may need to install the Classroom in a Book font files. The fonts are in the Fonts folder on the *Adobe Photoshop 7.0 Classroom in a Book* CD. If you already have these on your system, you do not need to install them.

If you have ATM® (Adobe Type Manager®), see its documentation on how to install fonts.

If you do not have ATM, you can install it from the *Adobe Photoshop 7.0 Classroom in a Book* CD. This process automatically installs the necessary fonts.

Please read the instructions carefully, because you do not need to install ATM if you are running Windows XP or Mac OS 10.

Installing fonts from the Adobe Photoshop 7.0 Classroom in a Book CD

Use the following procedure to install the fonts on your hard drive.

1 Insert the *Adobe Photoshop 7.0 Classroom in a Book* CD in your CD-ROM drive.

2 Install the font files using the procedure for the version of your operating system:

- Windows (other than Windows XP). Open the ATM installer files on the CD, which are located in the Fonts/ATM folder. Double-click the installer file (Setup), and follow the on-screen instructions for installing ATM and the fonts.

- Windows XP. Do not use the ATM font installer to install the fonts. Instead, simply drag the fonts from the CD to your hard disk and place them in your Adobe common fonts folder (typically in C:\Program Files\Common Files\Adobe\Fonts).

- Mac OS 9. Open the Fonts folder on the CD. Double-click the ATM® 4.6.1 + Fonts Installer to install the fonts.

- Mac OS 10. Open the Fonts folder on the CD. Select all of the fonts in the Fonts folder and drag them into the Library/Fonts folder on your hard disk. You can select and drag multiple fonts to install them, but you cannot drag the entire folder to install the fonts.

Copying the Classroom in a Book files

The *Adobe Photoshop 7.0 Classroom in a Book* CD includes folders containing all the electronic files for the lessons. Each lesson has its own folder, and you must copy the folders to your hard drive to do the lessons. To save room on your drive, you can install only the necessary folder for each lesson as you need it, and remove it when you're done.

To install the Classroom in a Book files:

1 Insert the *Adobe Photoshop 7.0 Classroom in a Book* CD into your CD-ROM drive.

2 Create a folder named PS70_CIB on your hard drive.

3 Copy the lessons you want to the hard drive:

- To copy all of the lessons, drag the Lessons folder from the CD into the PS70_CIB folder.

- To copy a single lesson, drag the individual lesson folder from the CD into the PS70_CIB folder.

If you are installing the files in Windows, you need to unlock them before using them. You don't need to unlock the files if you are installing them in Mac OS.

4 In Windows, unlock the files you copied:

• If you copied all of the lessons, double-click the unlock.bat file in the PS70_CIB/Lessons folder.

• If you copied a single lesson, drag the unlock.bat file from the Lessons folder on the CD into the PS70_CIB folder. Then double-click the unlock.bat file in the PS70_CIB folder.

Note: *As you work through each lesson, you will overwrite the Start files. To restore the original files, recopy the corresponding Lesson folder from the* Adobe Photoshop 7.0 Classroom in a Book *CD to the PS70_CIB folder on your hard drive.*

Restoring default preferences

The preferences files store palette and command settings and color-calibration information. Each time you quit Adobe Photoshop or Adobe ImageReady, the positions of the palettes and certain command settings are recorded in the respective preferences file. When you use the Adobe Color Management Assistant, monitor-calibration and color-space information is stored in the Photoshop preferences files as well.

Before you begin working on the *Adobe Photoshop 7.0 Classroom in a Book* lessons, save your initial preferences file. This enables you to restore any custom settings you have when you are done with the book. (If you are using a fresh installation of Photoshop 7.0 that has not yet been opened, you can skip saving the initial preferences file.)

You should restore the default preferences for Photoshop or ImageReady each time you begin a lesson. This ensures that the tools and palettes function as described in this book. When you finish all the lessons, you can restore your saved settings. Instructions for each of these processes are shown.

Important: *If you have adjusted your color-display and color-space settings, be sure to move the preferences file rather than delete it, so that you can restore your settings when you are done with the lessons in this book.*

To save your current Photoshop preferences:

1 Exit Adobe Photoshop.

2 Locate and open the Adobe Photoshop 7.0 Settings folder.

Note: *The default location of the Adobe Photoshop 7.0 Settings folder varies by operating system; use your operating system's Find command to locate this folder.*

3 Drag the Adobe Photoshop 7.0 Prefs.psp file from the Adobe Photoshop 7.0 Settings folder to your desktop.

To restore preferences to their default settings before each lesson:

1 Press and hold Shift+Alt+Control (Windows) or Shift+Option+Command (Mac OS) *immediately after* launching Photoshop or ImageReady.

2 When message appears, click Yes to delete the existing preferences file.

New preferences files will be created the next time you start Photoshop or ImageReady.

3 If Photoshop asks whether you want to set custom color settings, click No.

To restore your saved settings after completing the lessons:

1 Exit Photoshop.

2 Drag the preferences file from the desktop back into the Adobe Photoshop 7.0 Settings folder.

3 In the warning dialog box that appears, confirm that you want to replace the existing version of the file.

Additional resources

Adobe Photoshop 7.0 Classroom in a Book is not meant to replace documentation that comes with the program. Only the commands and options used in the lessons are explained in this book. For comprehensive information about program features, refer to these resources:

• The *Adobe Photoshop 7.0 User Guide*. Included with the Adobe Photoshop 7.0 software, this guide contains a complete description of all features.

• Online Help, an online version of the user guide, which you can view by choosing Help > Contents (Windows) or Help > Help Contents (Mac OS). (For more information, see Lesson 1, "Getting to Know the Work Area.")

• The Adobe Web site (www.adobe.com), which you can view by choosing Help > Adobe Online if you have a connection to the World Wide Web.

Adobe Certification

The Adobe Training and Certification Programs are designed to help Adobe customers improve and promote their product-proficiency skills. The Adobe Certified Expert (ACE) program is designed to recognize the high-level skills of expert users. Adobe Certified Training Providers (ACTP) use only Adobe Certified Experts to teach Adobe software classes. Available in either ACTP classrooms or on-site, the ACE program is the best way to master Adobe products. For Adobe Certified Training Programs information, visit the Partnering with Adobe Web site at http://partners.adobe.com.

Lesson 1

1 Getting to Know the Work Area

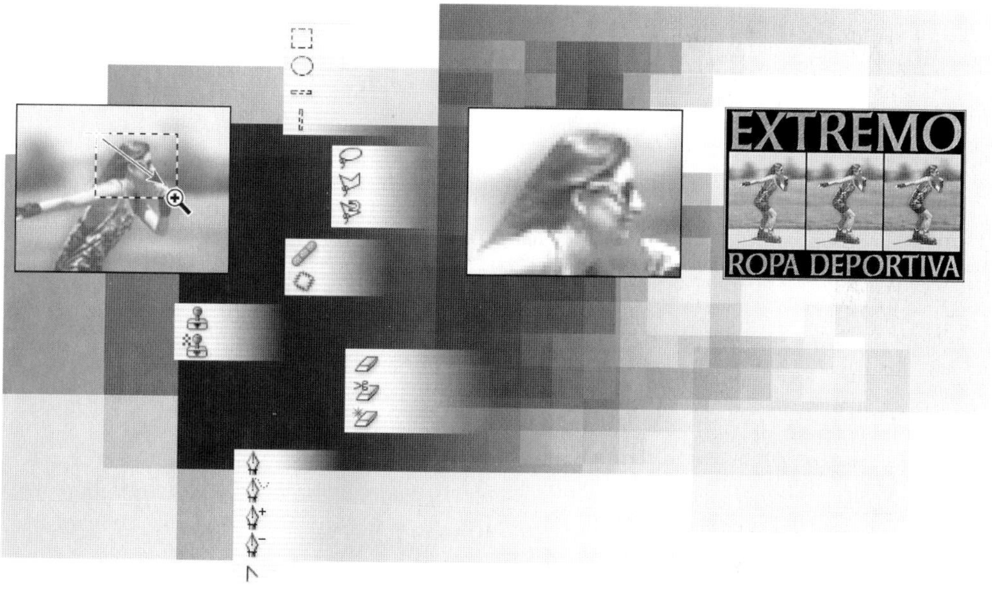

As you work with Adobe Photoshop and Adobe ImageReady, you'll discover that there is often more than one way to accomplish the same task. To make the best use of the extensive editing capabilities in these programs, you first must learn to navigate the work area.

In this lesson, you'll learn how to do the following:

- Open an Adobe Photoshop file.
- Select tools from the toolbox.
- Use viewing options to enlarge and reduce the display of an image.
- Work with palettes.
- Use online Help.

This lesson will take about 60 minutes to complete. The lesson is designed to be done in Adobe Photoshop, but information on using similar functionality in Adobe ImageReady is included where appropriate.

Before starting Adobe Photoshop, locate the Lesson01 folder on the *Adobe Photoshop 7.0 Classroom in a Book* CD, and copy the folder into the Lessons folder on your hard drive. As you work on this lesson, you'll overwrite the start files. If you need to restore the start files, copy them from the *Adobe Photoshop 7.0 Classroom in a Book* CD.

Before beginning this lesson, restore the default application settings for Adobe Photoshop. See "Restoring default preferences" on page 5.

Note: *Windows users need to unlock the lesson files before using them. For more information,* *see "Copying the Classroom in a Book files" on page 4.*

Starting Adobe Photoshop and opening files

The Adobe Photoshop and Adobe ImageReady work areas include the command menus at the top of your screen and a variety of tools and palettes for editing and adding elements to your image. You can also add commands and filters to the menus by installing third-party software known as *plug-in modules*.

In this part of the lesson, you'll familiarize yourself with the Adobe Photoshop work area and open a file in Adobe Photoshop.

Both Photoshop and ImageReady work with bitmapped, digitized images (that is, continuous-tone images that have been converted into a series of small squares, or picture elements, called *pixels*). In Photoshop, you can also work with vector graphics, which are shapes made up of smooth lines that retain their crispness when scaled. In ImageReady, you can create moving elements, such as animations and rollovers, for on-screen viewing.

You can create original artwork in both Photoshop and ImageReady, or you can bring images into the program by scanning a photograph, a transparency, a negative, or a graphic; by capturing a video image; or by importing artwork created in drawing programs. You can also import previously digitized images—such as those produced by a digital camera or by the Kodak® Photo CD process.

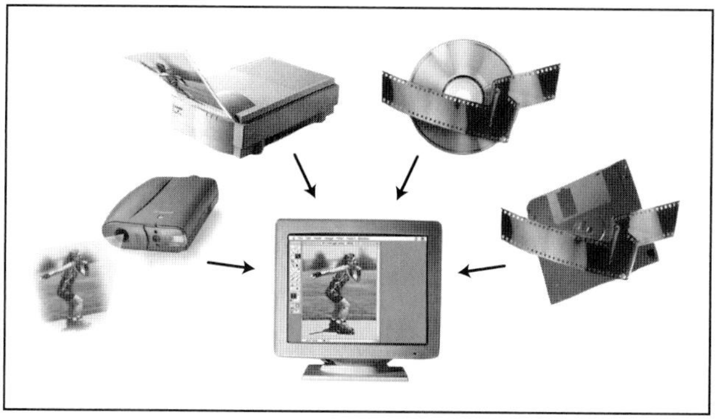

For information on the kinds of files you can use with Adobe Photoshop, see "About file formats" in Adobe Photoshop 7.0 online Help.

1 On the desktop, double-click the Adobe Photoshop icon to start Adobe Photoshop. If you do not see the Photoshop icon on your desktop, look for it on the Start/Programs/Adobe menu (Windows), in the Applications folder in the Finder (Mac OS 9 and Mac OS 10), or in the dock (Mac OS 10).

2 Choose File > Open, and open the file 01Start.psd from the Lessons/Lesson01 folder that you copied to your hard drive.

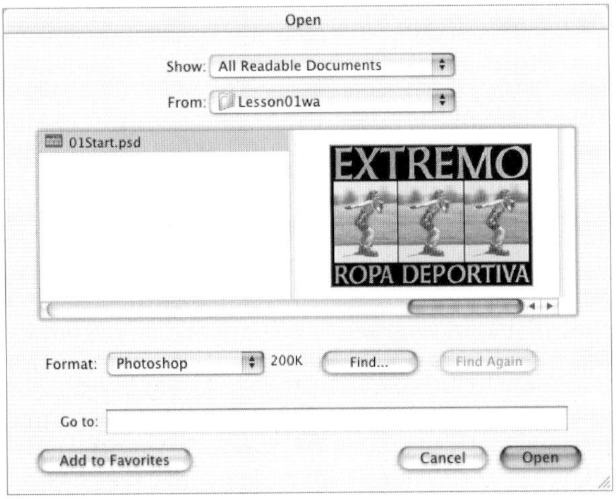

Using the tools

Together, Photoshop and ImageReady provide a consistent and integrated set of tools for producing sophisticated graphics for print and online viewing. ImageReady includes many tools that will already be familiar to users of Photoshop.

Finding tools in the work area

The default work areas of Photoshop and ImageReady consist of a menu bar at the top of the work area, a floating toolbox on the left, a tool options bar below the menu bar, floating palettes, and one or more image windows, which you open separately. In Photoshop, the four default palette groups appear along the right of the work area. In ImageReady, additional palettes appear in the lower left part of the work area.

The tools are located in the toolbox but are also controlled by options you select in the tool options bar and, in some cases, in the various palettes.

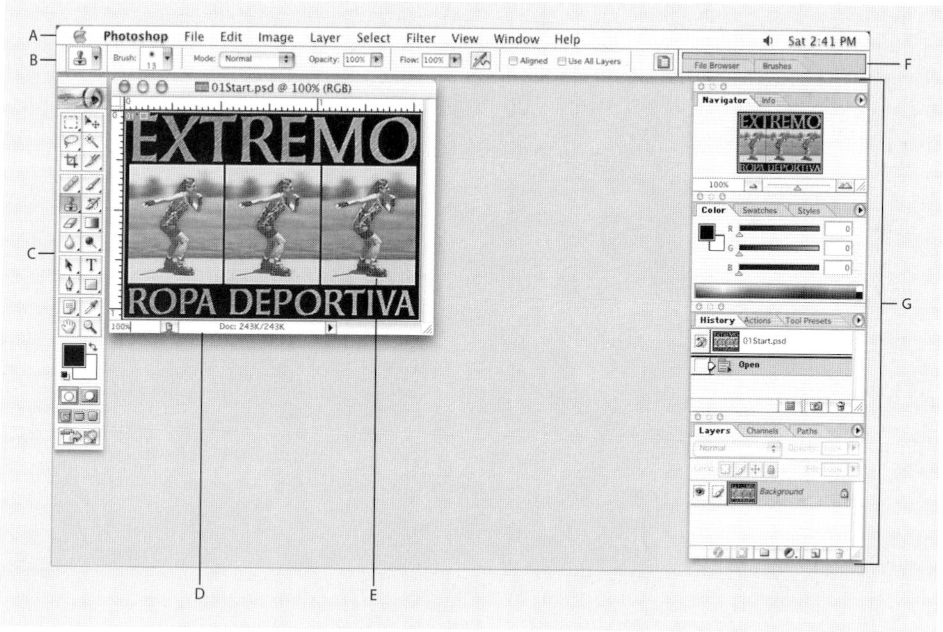

A. Menu bar B. Tool options bar C. Toolbox D. Info bar E. Image window F. Palette well G. Palettes

Selecting tools in the toolbox

The toolbox contains selection tools, painting and editing tools, foreground- and background-color selection boxes, and viewing tools. This section introduces the toolbox and shows you how to select tools. As you work through the lessons, you'll learn more about each tool's specific function.

1 To select a tool, click the tool in the toolbox, or you can press the tool's keyboard shortcut.

For example, to use the keyboard shortcut to select the zoom tool, press Z. Then, you can press M to switch back to the marquee tool. Selected tools remain active until you select a different tool.

If you don't know the keyboard shortcut for a tool, position the pointer over the tool until a tooltip appears, displaying the tool name and shortcut. All keyboard shortcuts are also listed in the Quick Reference section of online Help. You'll learn how to use online Help later in this lesson.

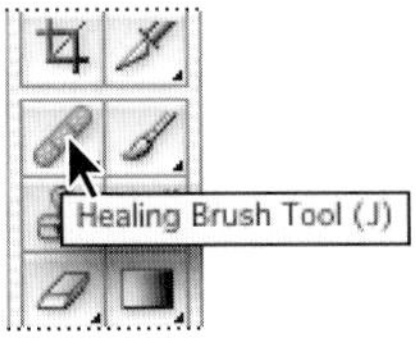

Photoshop and ImageReady use the same keyboard shortcut keys for corresponding keys, with the exceptions of A, P, Q, and Y:

- *In Photoshop, press A for the selection tools; in ImageReady, press A to show or hide image maps.*
- *In Photoshop, press P for the pen tools; in ImageReady, press P for the image map tools.*
- *In Photoshop, press Q to switch between Quick Mask mode and Standard mode; in ImageReady, press Q to show or hide slices.*
- *In Photoshop, press Y for the history brush tools; in ImageReady, press Y for rollover preview.*

Some of the tool buttons in the toolbox include a small triangle at the bottom right corner, indicating the presence of additional tools hidden behind the selected tool.

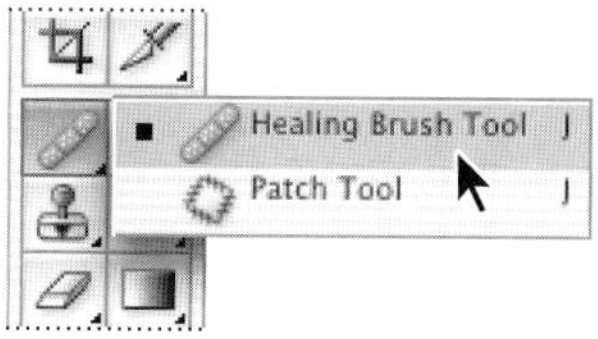

2 Select hidden tools in any of the following ways:

• Hold down the mouse button on a tool with a small triangle symbol (such as the rectangular marquee tool, which is the default tool selection) to open a pop-up menu of the additional hidden tools. Drag the pointer to the tool you want to use, and release the mouse button.

• Hold down Alt (Windows) or Option (Mac OS), and click the tool in the toolbox to toggle through the hidden tools in sequence until the tool you want to use is selected.

• Press Shift + the tool's keyboard shortcut repeatedly until the tool you want is selected.

Photoshop 7.0

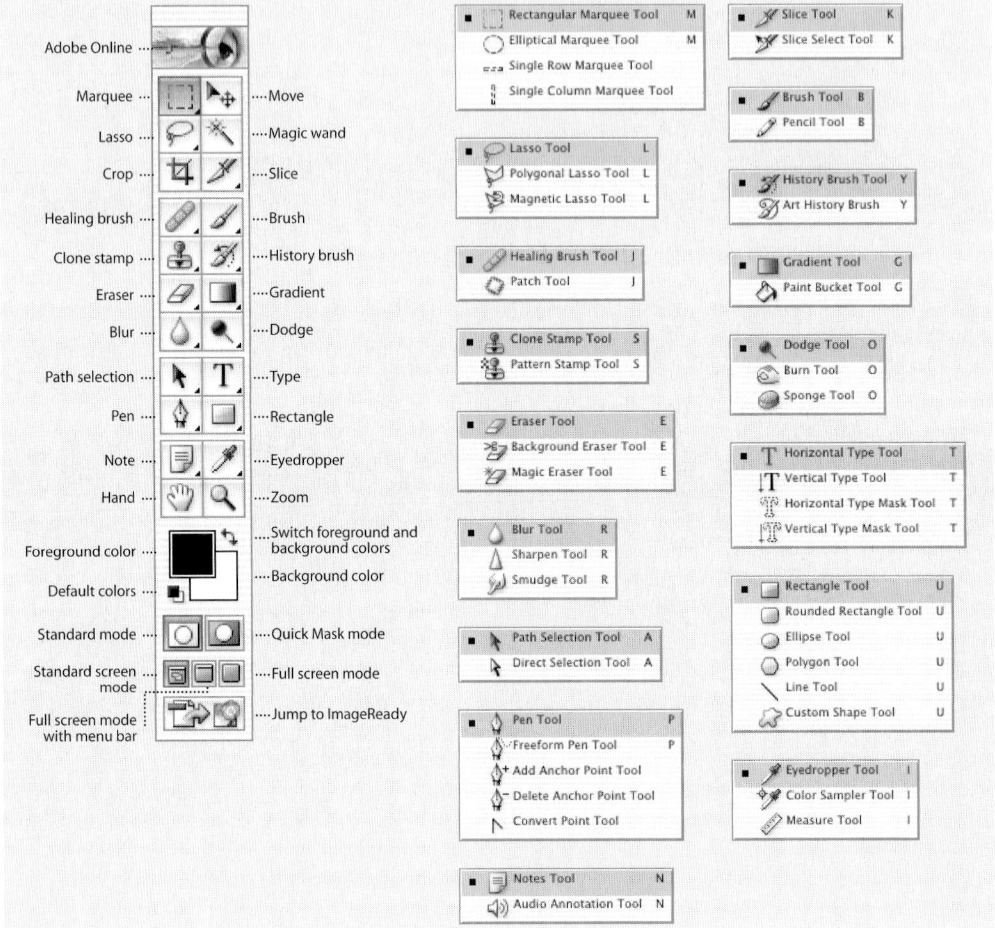
Adobe Online
Marquee
Move
Lasso
Magic wand
Crop
Slice
Healing brush
Brush
Clone stamp
History brush
Eraser
Gradient
Blur
Dodge
Path selection
Type
Pen
Rectangle
Note
Eyedropper
Hand
Zoom
Foreground color
Switch foreground and background colors
Background color
Default colors
Standard mode
Quick Mask mode
Standard screen mode
Full screen mode
Full screen mode with menu bar
Jump to ImageReady
Rectangular Marquee Tool M
Elliptical Marquee Tool M
Single Row Marquee Tool
Single Column Marquee Tool
Lasso Tool L
Polygonal Lasso Tool L
Magnetic Lasso Tool L
Healing Brush Tool J
Patch Tool J
Clone Stamp Tool S
Pattern Stamp Tool S
Eraser Tool E
Background Eraser Tool E
Magic Eraser Tool E
Blur Tool R
Sharpen Tool R
Smudge Tool R
Path Selection Tool A
Direct Selection Tool A
Pen Tool P
Freeform Pen Tool P
Add Anchor Point Tool
Delete Anchor Point Tool
Convert Point Tool
Notes Tool N
Audio Annotation Tool N
Slice Tool K
Slice Select Tool K
Brush Tool B
Pencil Tool B
History Brush Tool Y
Art History Brush Y
Gradient Tool G
Paint Bucket Tool G
Dodge Tool O
Burn Tool O
Sponge Tool O
Horizontal Type Tool T
Vertical Type Tool T
Horizontal Type Mask Tool T
Vertical Type Mask Tool T
Rectangle Tool U
Rounded Rectangle Tool U
Ellipse Tool U
Polygon Tool U
Line Tool U
Custom Shape Tool U
Eyedropper Tool I
Color Sampler Tool I
Measure Tool I

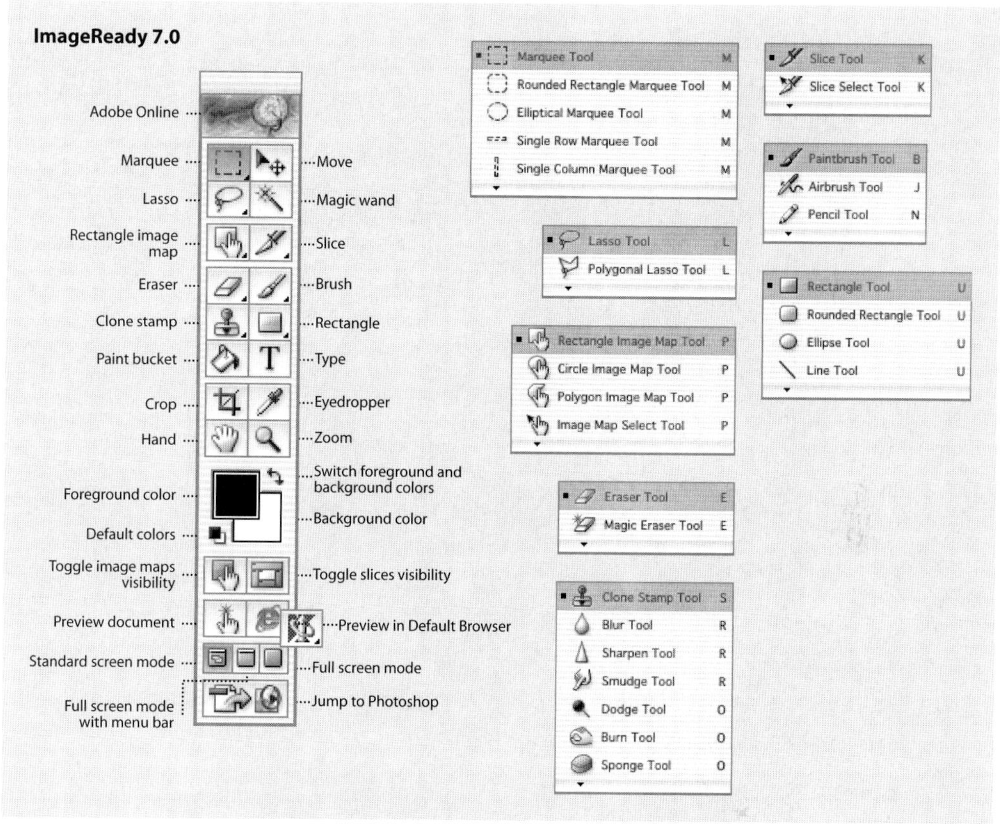

For an overview of the tools that describes their functions, see figure 1-1 in the color section.

Using the tool options bar

Most tools have options that are displayed in the tool options bar. The tool options bar is context-sensitive and changes as different tools are selected. Some settings in the tool options bar are common to several tools (such as painting modes and opacity), and some are specific to one tool (such as the Auto Erase setting for the pencil tool).

You can move the tool options bar anywhere in the work area. In Photoshop, you can also dock it at the top or bottom of the screen.

The Photoshop tool options bar includes a palette well for storing palettes without closing them entirely. The palette well is available only when the work area is greater than 800 pixels x 600 pixels (a setting of at least 1024 x 768 is recommended).

The following steps demonstrate the interactions between the tools and the tool options bar.

1 To see options for a tool, select the tool (such as the rectangular marquee tool (⬚), which is selected by default) in the toolbox and then notice the display in the tool options bar.

***Note:** If the tool options bar does not appear, open the Window menu and make sure that the Options command has a check mark, or select it now to display the tool options bar.*

2 Select a different tool in the toolbox, and notice how the tool option bar changes.

3 To move the tool options bar, drag the left edge of the tool options bar to a new location. In Photoshop, the left edge appears as a gripper bar when the tool options bar is docked under the menu bar or at the bottom of the work area.

Note: *In Photoshop (Windows, Mac OS 10) and ImageReady (all platforms), you can double-click the gripper bar at the left end of the tool options bar to collapse it, so that only the tool icon appears.*

4 To dock the Photoshop tool options bar again under the menu bar or at the bottom of your screen, drag the tool options bar by its left edge until it snaps into position.

After you select options for a tool, those options remain selected until you change them again, even if you select other tools and work with them. You can easily reset your tool options back to the default settings.

5 To reapply default settings for a tool, click the tool in the tool options bar to open a pop-up palette, and then open the palette menu and choose Reset Tool. (Then click anywhere outside the pop-up palette to close it.)

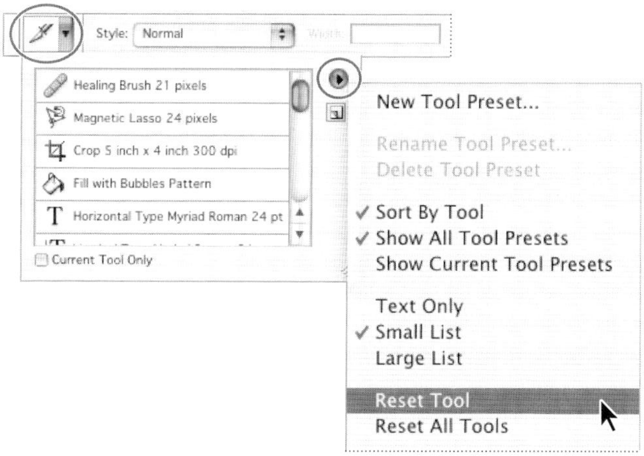

Notice that you can also choose Reset All Tools from that same palette menu to restore the default settings for all tools.

Entering values

Some tool options bars, palettes, and dialog boxes contain options that you enter as values. There are various methods for entering values: sliders, angle controls, arrow buttons, and text boxes. As you do each lesson, whenever you're asked to enter a value, use one of the methods listed below. In many cases, you may have a choice of techniques that you can use to enter the value.

• Type a value in the text box. To apply your entry, do one of the following: select a different option or text box in the palette; press Tab to go to a different text box in the palette; click the background in the composition; or press Enter or Return.

Note: *For certain options, you can use numeric shortcuts for entering percentages. For instance, typing 1 enters 10%, 2 enters 20%, 3 enters 30%, and so on.*

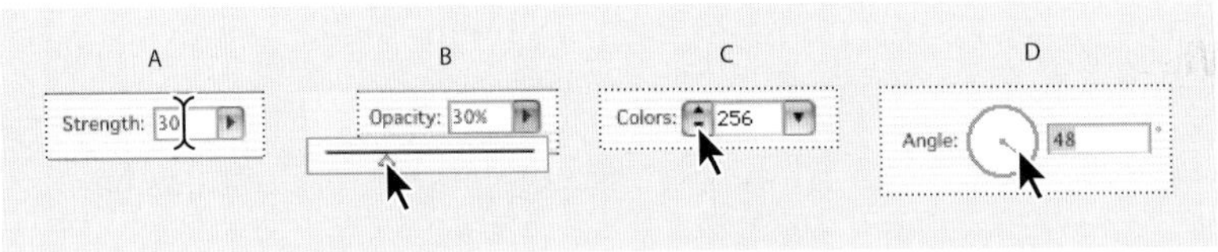

A. *Text Box* ***B.*** *Slider* ***C.*** *Up and Down arrows* ***D.*** *Angle control*

• Drag the slider to change the value. In many cases, you must first click a down arrow button next to the text box to open the slider. If you shift-drag a slider, the values change in increments of 10 units.

• Click the up arrow and down arrow buttons to increase and decrease values.

• Drag an angle control to change the value. Shift-drag to change the angle in 15-degree increments.

• (Windows, Mac OS 10 only) Click in the text field and then press the Up Arrow or Down Arrow key on the keyboard to increase or decrease the value. Hold down Shift as you click an arrow key to change the value in increments of 10 units.

• (Windows only) Use the mouse wheel to increase or decrease the value.

To cancel values before you apply them, press the Escape key.

Viewing images

You can view your image at any magnification level from 0.29% (Photoshop) or 12.5% (ImageReady) to 1600% of the image's actual size. Adobe Photoshop displays this percentage in the image window title bar. When you use any of the viewing tools and commands, you affect the *display* of the image, not the image dimensions or file size.

Using the View menu

To enlarge or reduce the view of an image using the View menu, do one of the following:

- Choose View > Zoom In to enlarge the display of the image.
- Choose View > Zoom Out to reduce the display of the image.
- Choose View > Fit on Screen. The size of the image and the size of your monitor determine how large the image appears on-screen.

Note: *You can also double-click the hand tool ( ) in the toolbox to fit the image on your screen.*

Each time you choose a Zoom command, the view of the image is resized. The percentage at which the image is viewed is displayed in the Title bar and in the lower left corner of the image window.

Using the zoom tool

In addition to the View commands, you can use the zoom tool to magnify and reduce the view of an image.

1 Select the zoom tool (🔍) and move the tool pointer onto the 01Start image. Notice that a plus sign appears at the center of the zoom tool.

2 Position the zoom tool over one of the skater images in the 01Start image, and click once to magnify the image to the next largest preset percentage.

3 With the zoom tool selected and positioned in the image area, hold down Alt (Windows) or Option (Mac OS). A minus sign appears at the center of the zoom tool (🔍).

4 Click once; the magnification of the image is reduced to the next lower preset percentage.

You can also draw a marquee with the zoom tool to magnify a specific area of an image.

5 Draw a marquee around the head of one of the skaters using the zoom tool.

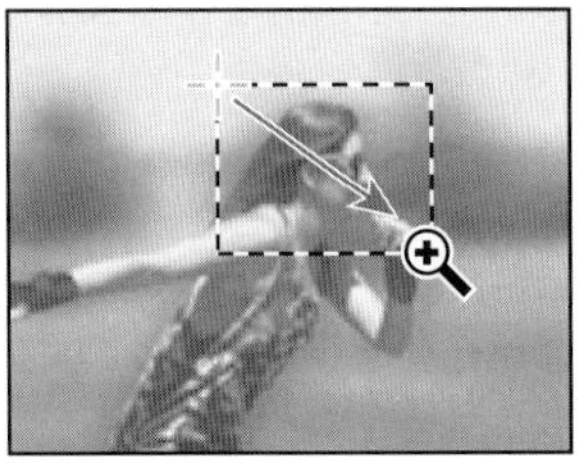

Area selected

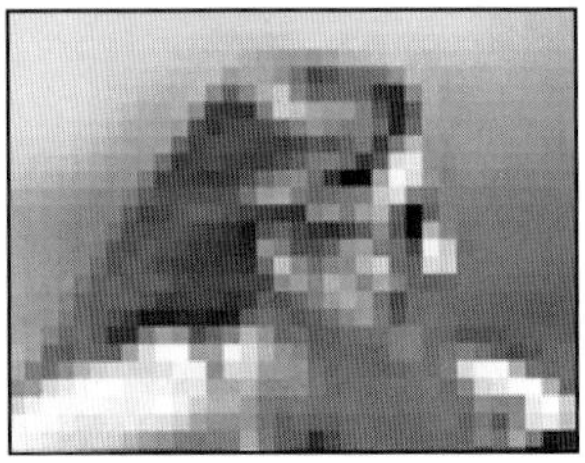

Resulting view

The percentage at which the area is magnified is determined by the size of the marquee you draw with the zoom tool. (The smaller the marquee you draw, the larger the level of magnification will be.)

Note: *You can draw a marquee with the zoom-in tool to enlarge the view of an image, but you cannot draw a marquee with the zoom-out tool to reduce the view of an image.*

You can use the zoom tool to return quickly to a 100% view, regardless of the current magnification level.

6 In the toolbox, double-click the zoom tool button to return the 01Start file to a 100% view.

Because the zoom tool is used frequently during the editing process to enlarge and reduce the view of an image, you can select it from the keyboard at any time without deselecting the active tool.

7 Select another tool, such as the hand tool (✋).

8 Use the keyboard to temporarily select the zoom-in tool by holding down spacebar+Ctrl (Windows) or spacebar+Command (Mac OS). Click to zoom in on an area of the image, and then release the keys.

9 To select the zoom-out tool from the keyboard, hold down spacebar+Alt (Windows) or spacebar+Option (Mac OS). Click the image to reduce the magnification, and then release the keys.

Scrolling an image

You use the hand tool to scroll through an image that does not fit in the active window. If the image fits in the active window, the hand tool has no effect when you drag it in the image window.

1 Drag the lower right corner of the image window inward to reduce the window size so that only part of the image fits in the window.

2 Select the hand tool (✋) and drag different directions in the image window to bring another skater into view. As you drag, the image moves with the hand tool pointer.

Like the zoom tool, you can select the hand tool from the keyboard without deselecting the active tool.

3 Select any tool but the hand tool.

4 Hold down the spacebar to select the hand tool from the keyboard. Drag to reposition the image. Then release the spacebar.

5 Double-click the zoom tool to return the image to 100% magnification.

Note: *To return the window to its original size at 100% view, select Resize Windows to Fit in the zoom tool options bar, and then double-click the zoom tool.*

Using the Navigator palette

The Photoshop Navigator palette lets you scroll an image at different magnification levels without scrolling or resizing an image in the image window. (ImageReady does not have a Navigator palette.)

1 If you don't see the Navigator palette, choose Window > Show Navigator to display it.

2 In the Navigator palette, drag the slider to the right to about 300% to magnify the view of the skater. As you drag the slider to increase the level of magnification, the red outline in the Navigator window decreases in size.

3 In the Navigator palette, position the pointer inside the red outline. The pointer becomes a hand.

Dragging slider to 200%

200% view of image

View in Navigator palette

4 Drag the hand to drag the red outline to different parts of the image. In the image window, notice that the area of the image that is visible also changes as you drag in the Navigator palette.

You can also draw a marquee in the Navigator palette to identify the area of the image you want to view.

5 With the pointer still positioned in the Navigator palette, hold down Ctrl (Windows) or Command (Mac OS), and draw a marquee over an area of the image. The smaller the marquee you draw, the greater the magnification level in the image window will be.

Using the Info bar

In Photoshop, the Info bar is positioned at the lower border of the application window (Windows) or the lower border of the image window (Mac OS). This area displays the current magnification, an area for specific choices of information types, and context-sensitive information about the currently selected tool. In ImageReady, the Info bar appears at the lower border of the image window.

You can click an arrow button on the Info bar to open a pop-up menu of different categories of information. Your selection from the menu determines what kind of information appears next to that arrow on the Info bar.

Note: *The pop-up menu on the Info bar is not available if the window is too small.*

Photoshop Info bar

ImageReady Info bar

By default, the file size for the active image appears in the Info bar. The first value indicates the size if saved as a flattened file with no layer data; the second value indicates the size if saved with all layers and channels.

In ImageReady, you can use the percentage pop-up menu in the Info bar to change the view of an image by a preset zoom percentage. For complete information on the ImageReady Info bar options, see "Looking at the Work Area" in ImageReady 7.0 online Help.

Working with palettes

Palettes help you monitor and modify images. By default, they appear in stacked groups. To show or hide a palette as you work, choose the appropriate Window > *[palette name]*. A checkmark by a palette name on the Window menu indicates that the palette is shown now in the front of its palette group. No checkmark means that the palette is either closed or hidden behind another palette in its palette group.

Changing the palette display

You can reorganize your work space in various ways. Experiment with several techniques:

- To hide all open palettes, the toolbox, and the tool options bar, press Tab. Then press Tab again to reopen them.
- To hide or display the palettes only (but not change the toolbox or tool options bar displays), press Shift+Tab.
- To make a palette appear at the front of its group, click the palette tab.

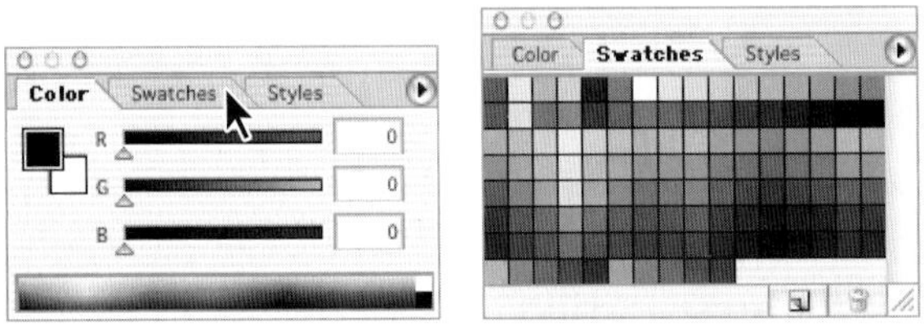

- To move an entire palette group, drag the title bar to another location.
- To separate a palette from its palette group, drag the palette tab beyond the existing group.

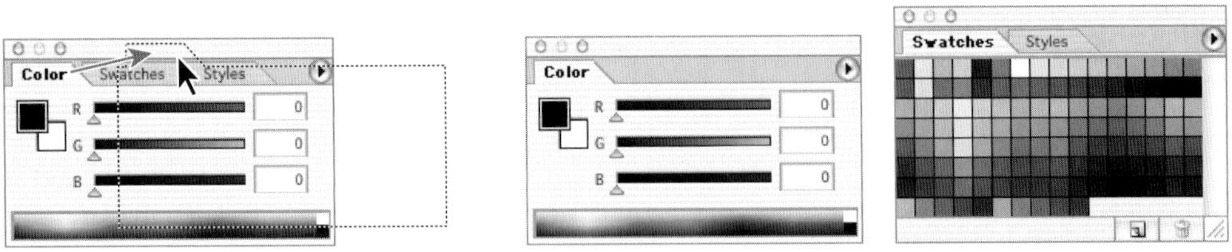

• To move a palette to another group, drag the palette tab inside that palette group so that a black highlight appears inside the group, and then release the mouse button.

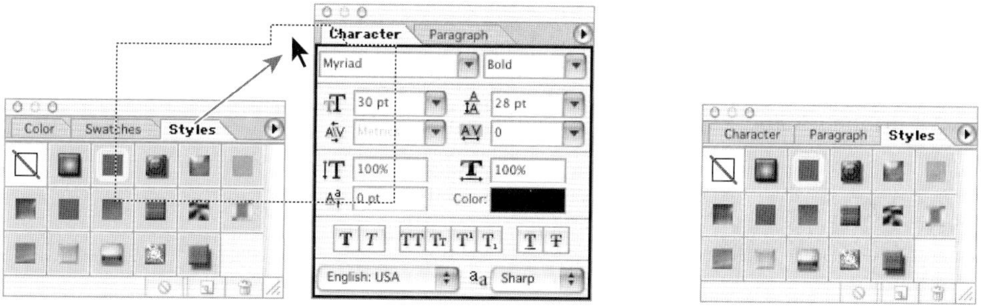

• To dock a palette in the palette well on the Photoshop tool options bar, drag the palette tab into the palette well so that the palette well is highlighted.

***Note:** Palettes are considered hidden when stored in the palette well. Clicking on the title of a palette stored in the well temporarily opens the palette until you click outside the palette or click the palette tab a second time.*

Using palette menus

Most palettes (including pop-up palettes), pickers, and a few dialog boxes have attached menus with commands that affect the available options or related options for that palette or dialog box. These menus are sometimes referred to as *fly-out menus* because of the way they open out from the palettes. (However, this book consistently refers to these as *palette menus.*)

To display a palette menu, click the round arrow button in the upper right corner of the palette. You can then move the pointer to the command you want to choose.

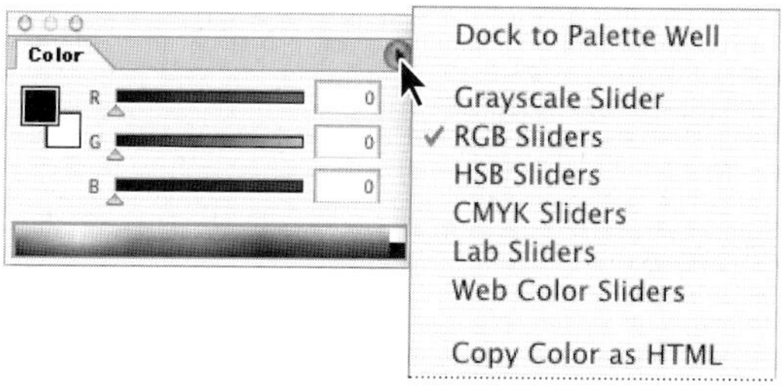

Expanding and collapsing palettes

You can also resize a palette to see more or fewer of the available options it contains, either by dragging or by clicking to toggle between preset sizes.

- To change the height of a palette, drag its lower right corner.
- To return a resized palette to its default size, click the minimize/maximize box (Windows) or the resize box (Mac OS). (A second click collapses the palette group.)

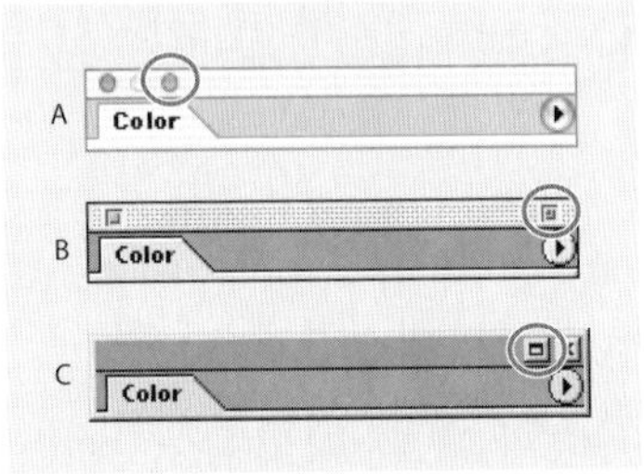

***A.** Mac OS 10* ***B.** Mac OS* ***C.** Windows*

Note: *You cannot resize the Info, Color, Character, and Paragraph palettes in Photoshop, or the Optimize, Info, Color, Layer Options, Character, Paragraph, Slice, and Image Map palettes in ImageReady.*

- To collapse a group to palette titles only, Alt-click the minimize/maximize box (Windows) or click the resize box (Mac OS). Or, double-click a palette tab.

Notice that the tabs for the various palettes in the palette group and the button for the palette menu remain visible after you collapse a palette.

Setting the positions of palettes and dialog boxes

The positions of all open palettes and movable dialog boxes are saved by default when you exit the program. However, you can always start with default palette positions or restore default positions at any time:

- To reset palettes to the default positions, choose Window > Workspace > Reset Palette Locations.
- To always start with the preset palette and dialog box positions, choose Edit > Preferences > General (Windows, Mac OS 9) or Photoshop > Preferences > General (Mac OS 10), and deselect the Save Palette Locations check box. The change takes effect the next time you start Adobe Photoshop or Adobe ImageReady.

Using context menus

In addition to the menus at the top of your screen, context menus display commands relevant to the active tool, selection, or palette.

• To display a context menu, position the pointer over the image or over an item in a palette and right-click (Windows) or Control-click (Mac OS).

• To try this out, select the eyedropper tool (), move it over the image window, and right-click or Control-click. A context menu appears, showing options you can set for the eyedropper tool, including a palette menu with additional options. You can also access these options by clicking the Brush option arrow in the tool options bar.

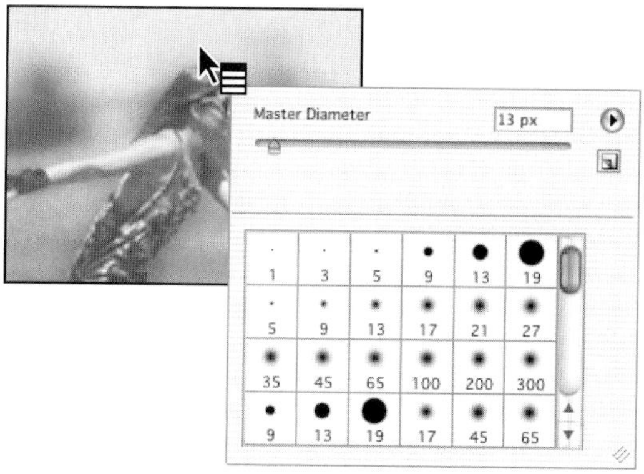

Using online Help

For complete information about using palettes, tools, and the application features, you can use online Help. Photoshop Help includes all the same topics and information as in the printed *Adobe Photoshop 7.0 User Guide*.

Adobe Photoshop and Adobe ImageReady each include complete documentation in online Help, plus keyboard shortcuts, full-color galleries of examples, and more detailed information about some procedures.

Online Help is easy to use, because you can look for topics in several ways:

- Scanning a table of contents.
- Searching for keywords.
- Using an index.
- Jumping from topic to topic using related topic links.

First you'll try looking for a topic using the Contents screen.

1 Display online Help, choose Help > Photoshop Help (Photoshop) or Help > ImageReady Help (ImageReady).

Note: *In Windows, you can also open Photoshop Help by pressing F1.*

Your browser opens. The topics for the Photoshop 7.0 online Help system appear in the left frame of your browser window.

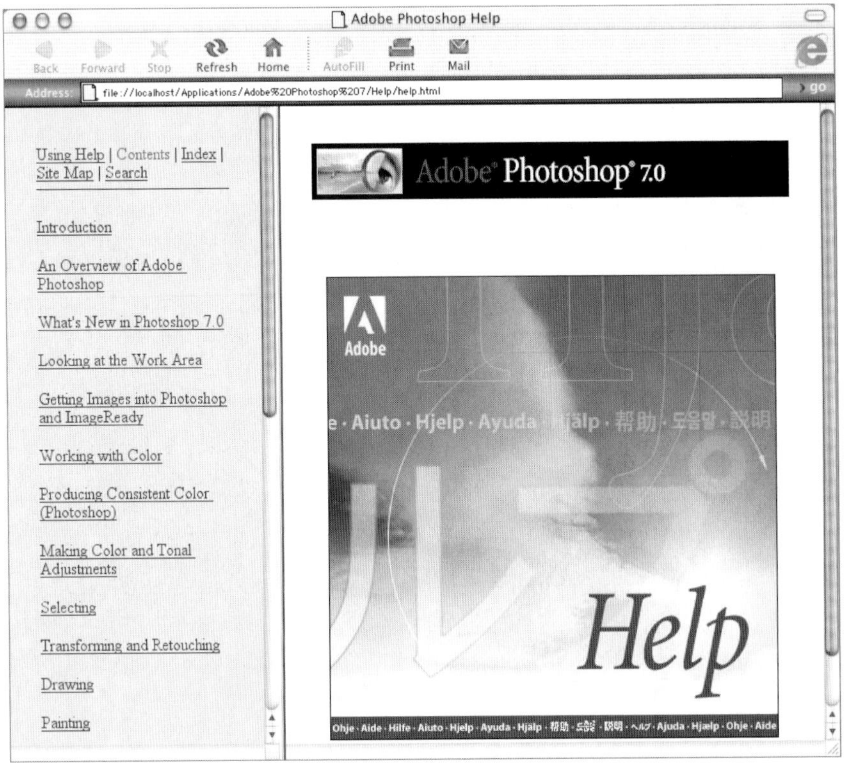

2 In the left frame of the Help window, scroll down to skim through the Help contents. The contents are organized in a hierarchy of topics, just like the chapters of a book.

3 Near the top of the list of topics in the left pane, click *Looking at the Work Area*. The "Looking at the Work Area" Help topic appears in the right pane.

4 In the right pane, click *Using the toolbox* to open that topic.

5 Near the bottom of the "Using the toolbox" topic, click *Toolbox overview (1 of 3)* to open that topic. An illustration of various tools appears with brief descriptions of each tool.

The online Help topics are interactive. You can click any text link to jump to another topic. Whenever you move the mouse pointer over a link or a hotspot, the mouse pointer changes to a pointing-finger icon (☝).

Using the Help system keywords, links, and the index

If you can't find the topic you are interested in by scanning the Contents page, you can try searching using a keyword.

1 At the top of the left pane, click the word *Search.*

A search text box appears in the left pane.

2 Type a keyword in the text box, such as **lasso**, and click the Search button. After a brief pause, a list of topics based on your keyword search appears below the text box in the left pane. To see any of these topics, click the topic name.

You can also search for a topic using the index.

3 At the top of the left pane, click the word *Index.* An alphabetical list of letters appears across the top of the left pane, followed by the listings for the letter A.

4 Click another letter, such as T, to display index entries for that letter.

These entries appear alphabetically by topic and subtopic, like the index of a book.

5 Click the number [1] next to an entry to open the first topic about that entry. (If there is more than one number, clicking the number [2] or [3] opens a second or third topic about the same entry.)

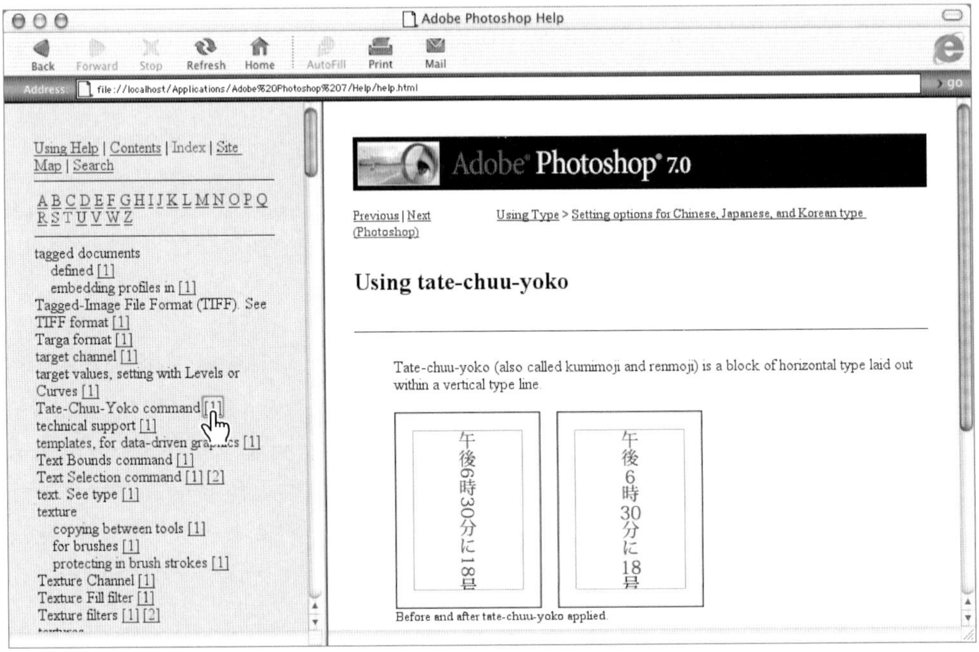

6 When you have finished browsing, click the Close box to close the Photoshop online Help window, or quit your browser application.

Using Adobe online services

Another way to get information on Adobe Photoshop or on related Adobe products is to use the Adobe online services. If you have an Internet connection and a Web browser installed on your system, you can access the U.S. Adobe Systems Web site (www.adobe.com) for information on services, products, and tips pertaining to Photoshop.

Adobe Online also provides access to up-to-the-minute information about services, products, and tips for using Photoshop and other Adobe applications.

1 In Photoshop or ImageReady, choose Help > Adobe Online, or click the icon ( ) (Photoshop) or ( ) (ImageReady) at the top of the toolbox.

2 Choose Edit > Preferences > Adobe Online (Windows, Mac OS 9) or Photoshop > Preferences > Adobe Online (Mac OS 10) and enter the preferences you want to use, including settings in the Update Options pop-up menu for updating Adobe Online.

When you set up Adobe Online to connect to your Web browser, Adobe can either notify you whenever new information is available or automatically download that information to your hard disk. If you choose not to use the Adobe automatic download feature, you can still view and download new files whenever they are available from within the Adobe Online window.

3 If you use Netscape as your browser, click the bookmark button ( ) in the Adobe Online dialog box to view Web pages related to Photoshop and Adobe. These bookmarks are automatically updated as new Web sites become available.

4 Click Close to return to Photoshop or ImageReady.

Using Adobe Online, you can find information specifically on Photoshop and ImageReady—including tips and techniques, galleries of artwork by Adobe designers and artists around the world, the latest product information, and troubleshooting and technical information. Or, you can learn about other Adobe products and news.

Jumping to ImageReady

Now you'll switch to ImageReady. Jumping between the applications lets you use the full feature sets of both applications when preparing graphics for the Web or other purposes, yet still maintain a streamlined workflow.

1 In the Photoshop toolbox, click the Jump To ImageReady button ( ).

The 01Start.psd file opens in ImageReady.

You can jump between Photoshop and ImageReady to transfer an image between the two applications for editing, without closing or exiting the originating application. In addition, you can jump from ImageReady to other graphics-editing applications and HTML-editing applications installed on your system. For more information on jumping to other applications in ImageReady, see Photoshop 7.0 online Help.

2 In ImageReady, click the Jump To Photoshop button ( ) in the toolbox to return to Photoshop, or choose File > Jump To > Adobe Photoshop 7.0.

Each time an image in Photoshop or ImageReady is updated with changes made in a jumped-to application, a single history state is added to the Photoshop or ImageReady History palette. You'll learn more about how to use the History palette later; see "About snapshots and History palette states" on page 203 of this book.

3 Close the file.

Now that you're acquainted with the basics of the Photoshop 7.0 work area, you're ready to explore the new File Browser feature or to begin learning how to create and edit images. Once you know the basics, you can do the *Adobe Photoshop 7.0 Classroom in a Book* lessons in sequential order or you can jump ahead to the subject matter that most interests you.

Review questions

1 Describe two ways to change your view of an image.

2 How do you select tools in Photoshop or ImageReady?

3 What are two ways to get more information about Photoshop and ImageReady?

4 Describe two ways to create images in Photoshop and ImageReady.

5 How do you switch between Photoshop and ImageReady?

Review answers

1 You can choose commands from the View menu to zoom in or out of an image, or to fit it to your screen; you can also use the zoom tools and click or drag over an image to enlarge or reduce the view. In addition, you can use keyboard shortcuts to magnify or reduce the display of an image. You can also use the Navigator palette to scroll an image or change its magnification without using the image window.

2 To select a tool, you can select the tool in the toolbox, or you can press the tool's keyboard shortcut. A selected tool remains active until you select a different tool. To select a hidden tool, you can use either a combination keyboard shortcut to toggle through the tools or you can hold down the mouse button on the tool in the toolbox to open a pop-up menu of the hidden tools.

3 Adobe Photoshop contains online Help, with all the information in the *Adobe Photoshop 7.0 User Guide*, plus keyboard shortcuts and some additional information and full-color illustrations. Photoshop also includes a link to the Adobe Systems home page for additional information on services, products, and tips pertaining to Photoshop. ImageReady 7.0 also contains online Help and a link to the Adobe home page.

4 You can create original artwork in Adobe Photoshop or ImageReady, or you can get images into the program by scanning a photograph, a transparency, a negative, or a graphic; by capturing a video image; or by importing artwork created in drawing programs. You can also import previously digitized images—such as those produced by a digital camera or by the Kodak Photo CD process.

5 You can click the Jump To button in the toolbox or choose File > Jump To to switch between Photoshop and ImageReady.

1-1: **Toolbox overview**

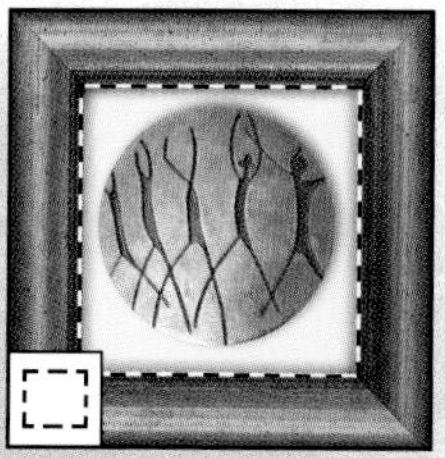

The marquee tools *make rectangular, elliptical, single row, and single column selections.*

The move tool *moves selections, layers, and guides.*

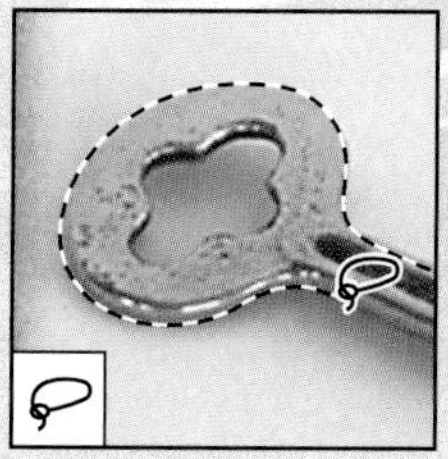

The lasso tools *make freehand, polygonal (straight-edged), and magnetic* (snap-to) selections.*

The magic wand tool *selects similarly colored areas.*

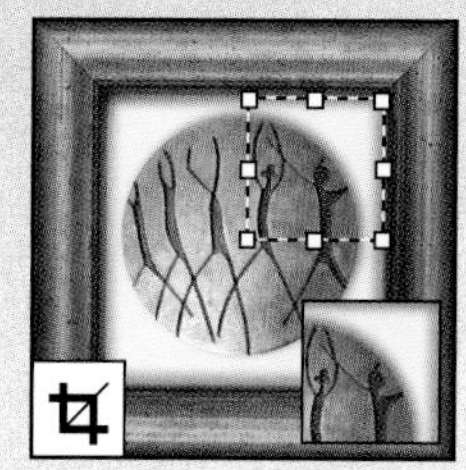

The crop tool *trims images.*

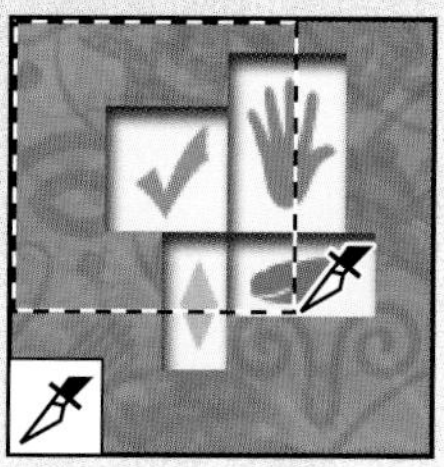

The slice tool *creates slices.*

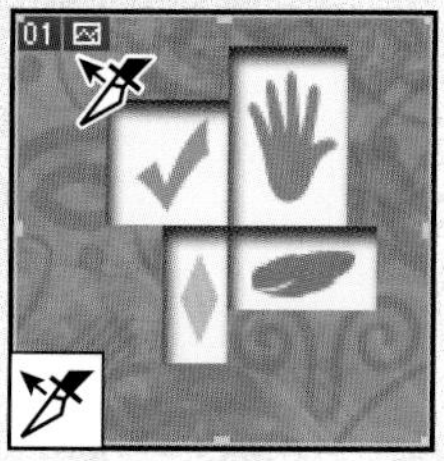

The slice selection tool *selects slices.*

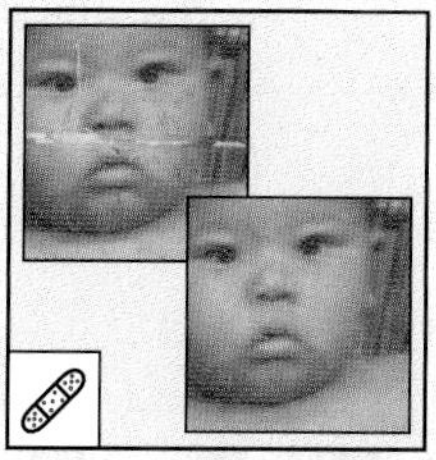

The healing brush tool* *paints with a sample or pattern to repair imperfections in an image.*

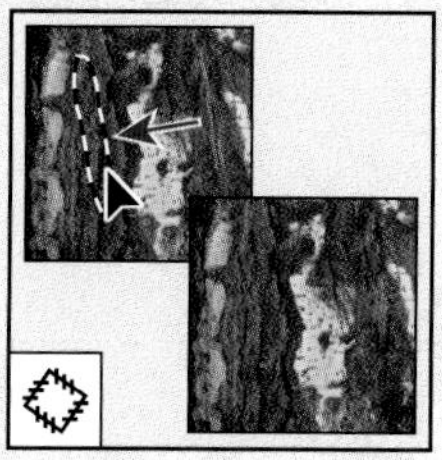

The patch tool* *repairs imperfections in a selected area of an image using a sample or pattern.*

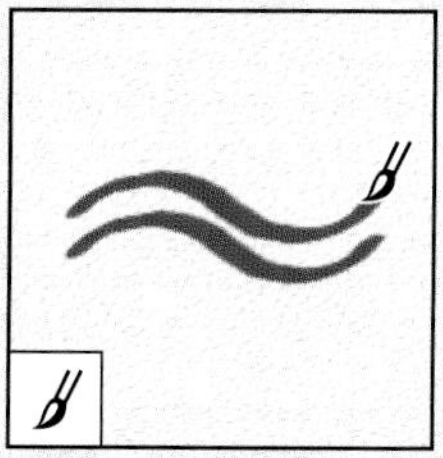

The brush tool *paints brush strokes.*

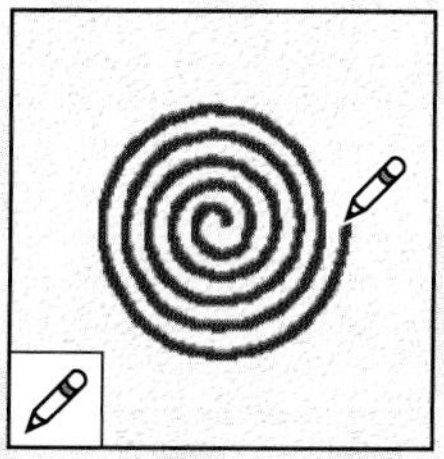

The pencil tool *paints hard-edged strokes.*

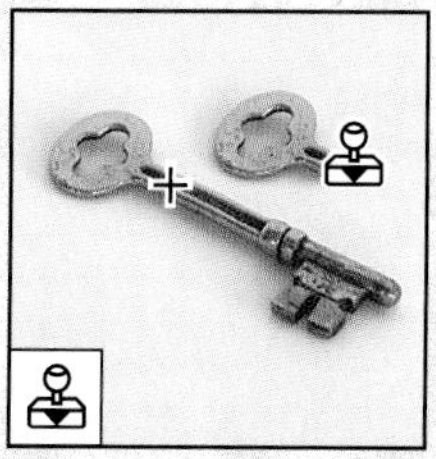

The clone stamp tool *paints with a sample of an image.*

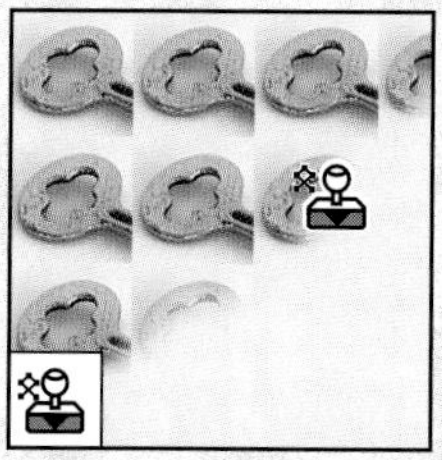

The pattern stamp tool* *paints with a part of an image as a pattern.*

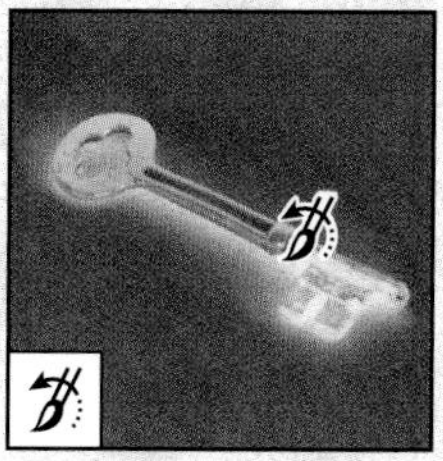

The history brush tool* *paints a copy of the selected state or snapshot into the current image window.*

The art history brush tool* *paints with stylized strokes that simulate the look of different paint styles, using a selected state or snapshot.*

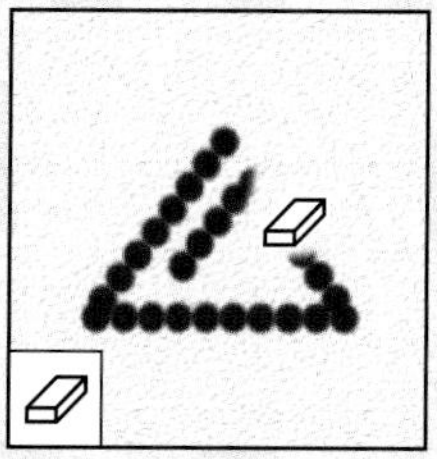

The eraser tool *erases pixels and restores parts of an image to a previously saved state.*

* *Photoshop only*
§ *ImageReady only*

1-1: **Toolbox overview (cont.)**

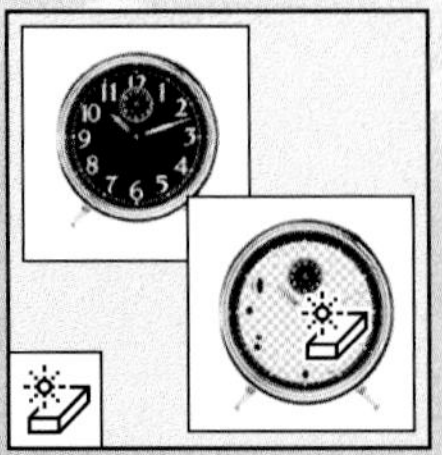

The magic eraser tool *erases solid-colored areas to transparency with a single click.*

The background eraser tool erases areas to transparency by dragging.*

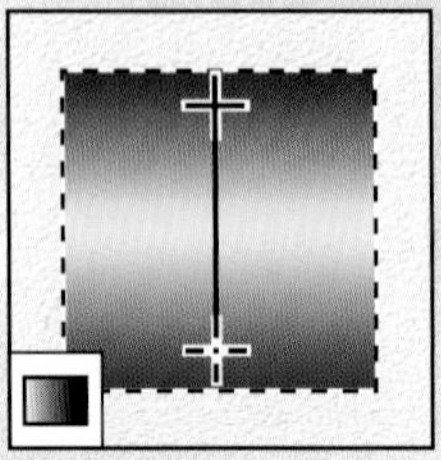

The gradient tools *create straight-line, radial*, angle*, reflected*, and diamond* blends between colors.*

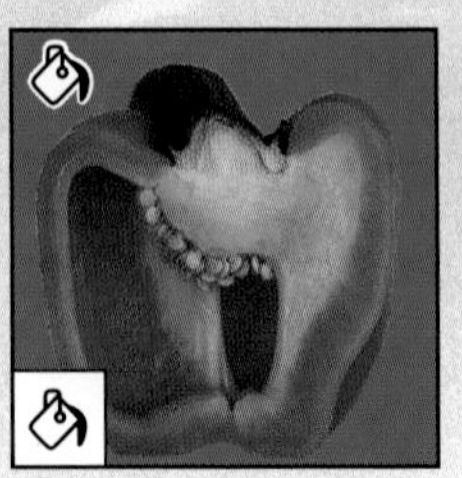

The paint bucket tool fills similarly colored areas with the foreground color.*

The blur tool *blurs hard edges in an image.*

The sharpen tool *sharpens soft edges in an image.*

The smudge tool *smudges data in an image.*

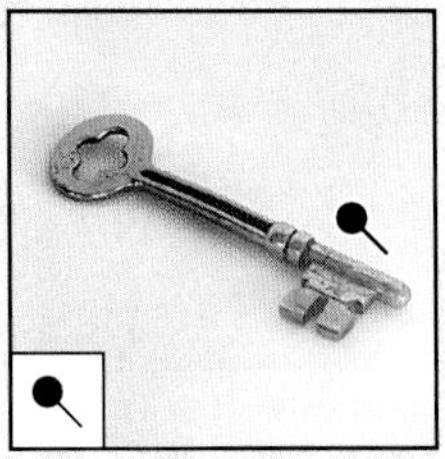

The dodge tool *lightens areas in an image.*

The burn tool *darkens areas in an image.*

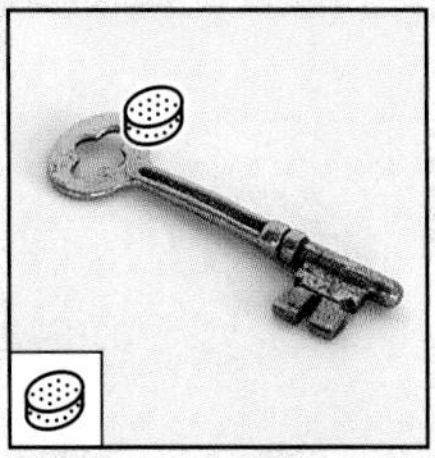

The sponge tool *changes the color saturation of an area.*

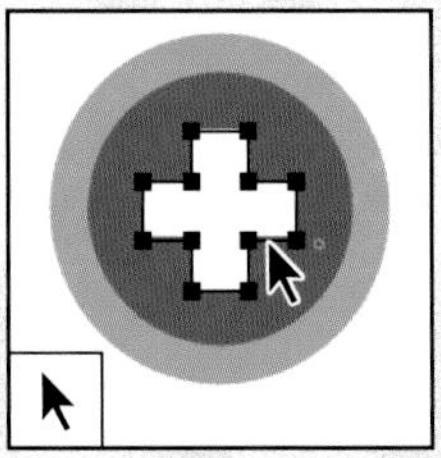

The path selection tools make shape or segment selections showing anchor points, direction lines, and direction points.*

The type tool *creates type on an image.*

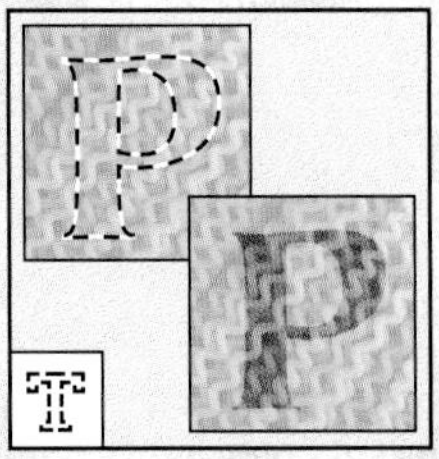

The type mask tools create a selection in the shape of type.*

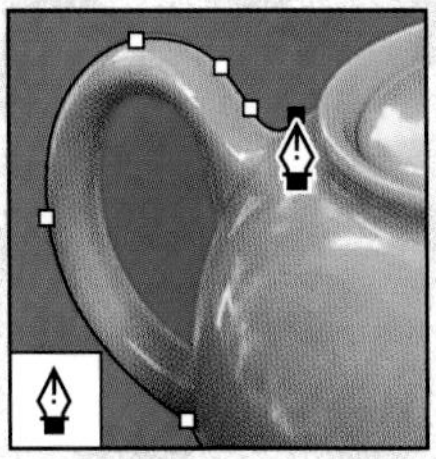

The pen tools let you draw smooth-edged paths.*

The custom shape tool makes customized shapes selected from a custom shape list.*

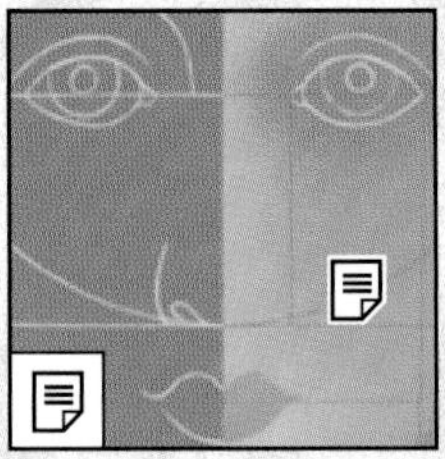

The annotations tool makes notes and audio annotations that can be attached to an image.*

* *Photoshop only*
§ *ImageReady only*

1-1: **Toolbox overview (cont.)**

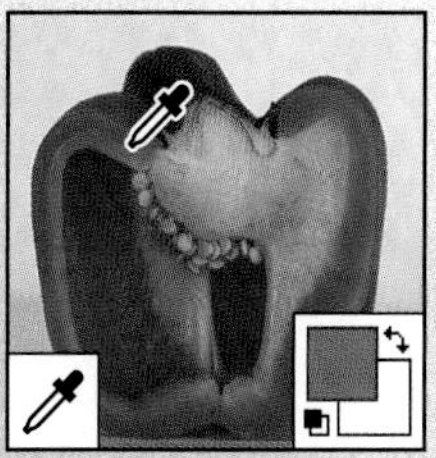

The eyedropper tool *samples colors in an image*

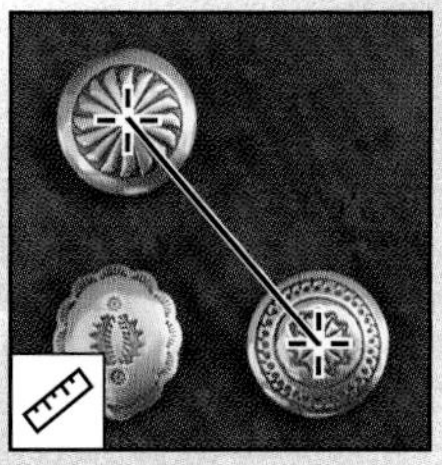

The measure tool measures distances, locations, and angles.*

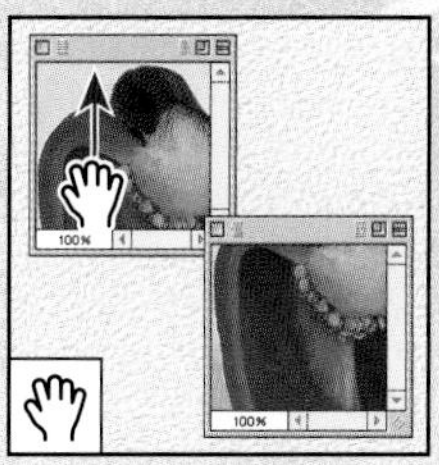

The hand tool *moves an image within its window.*

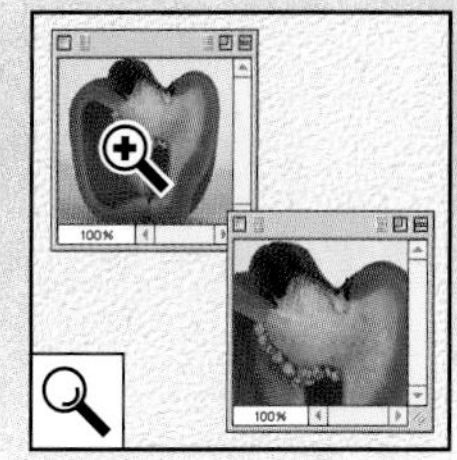

The zoom tool *magnifies and reduces the view of an image.*

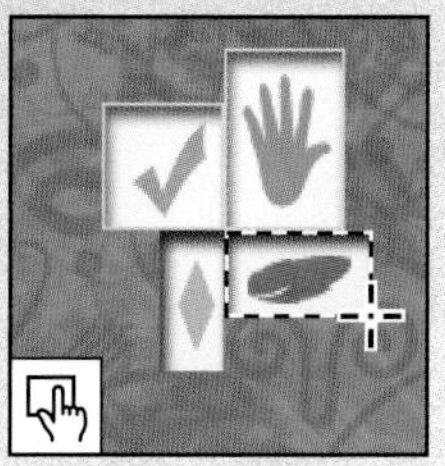

***The image map tools**§ define image map areas in an image.*

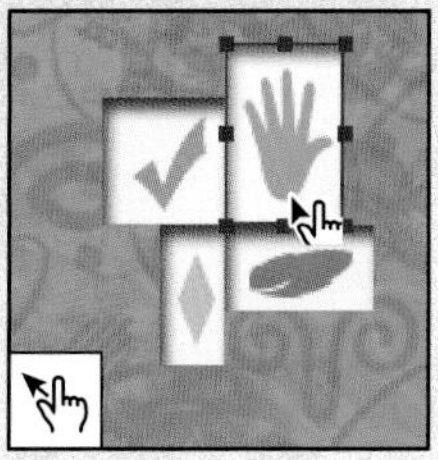

***The image map select tool**§ selects image maps.*

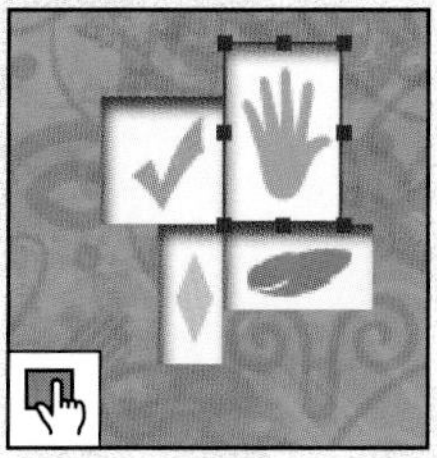

***The toggle image map visibility tool**§ toggles between showing and hiding image maps.*

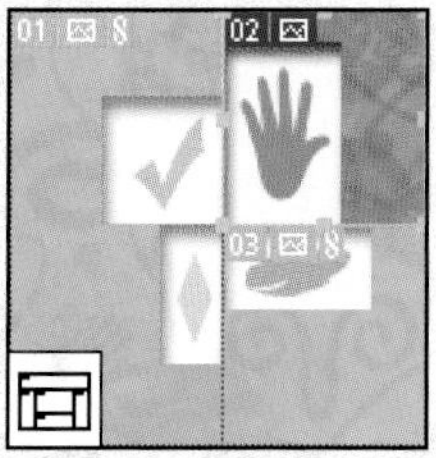

***The toggle slices visibility tool**§ toggles between showing and hiding slices in an image.*

***The preview document tool**§ previews rollover effects directly in ImageReady.*

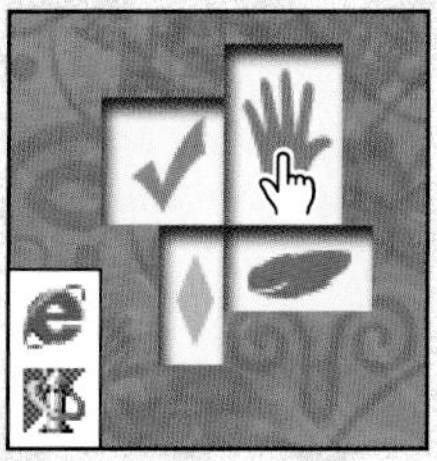

***The preview in default browser tool**§ previews animations in a Web browser.*

* *Photoshop only*
§ *ImageReady only*

3-1: **Removing a color cast**

Before Auto Color command

After Auto Color command

3-2: **Adjusting saturation with the sponge tool**

Before Sponge tool

After Sponge tool

6-1: **Selecting in Standard mode and Quick Mask mode**

Lesson 5 start file

Standard mode

Quick Mask mode
A. Selected areas
B. Hidden areas

6-2: **Painting in Quick Mask mode**

Quick Mask mode

Painting with white

Resulting selection

Painting with black

Resulting selection

6-3: **Extracting an object from its background**

Highlighting edges of foxtail tip

Filling highlighted tip area

6-4: **Extracting an intricate image**

Highlighting weed edges

Selecting top third of weeds

8-1: **Layer blending mode samples**

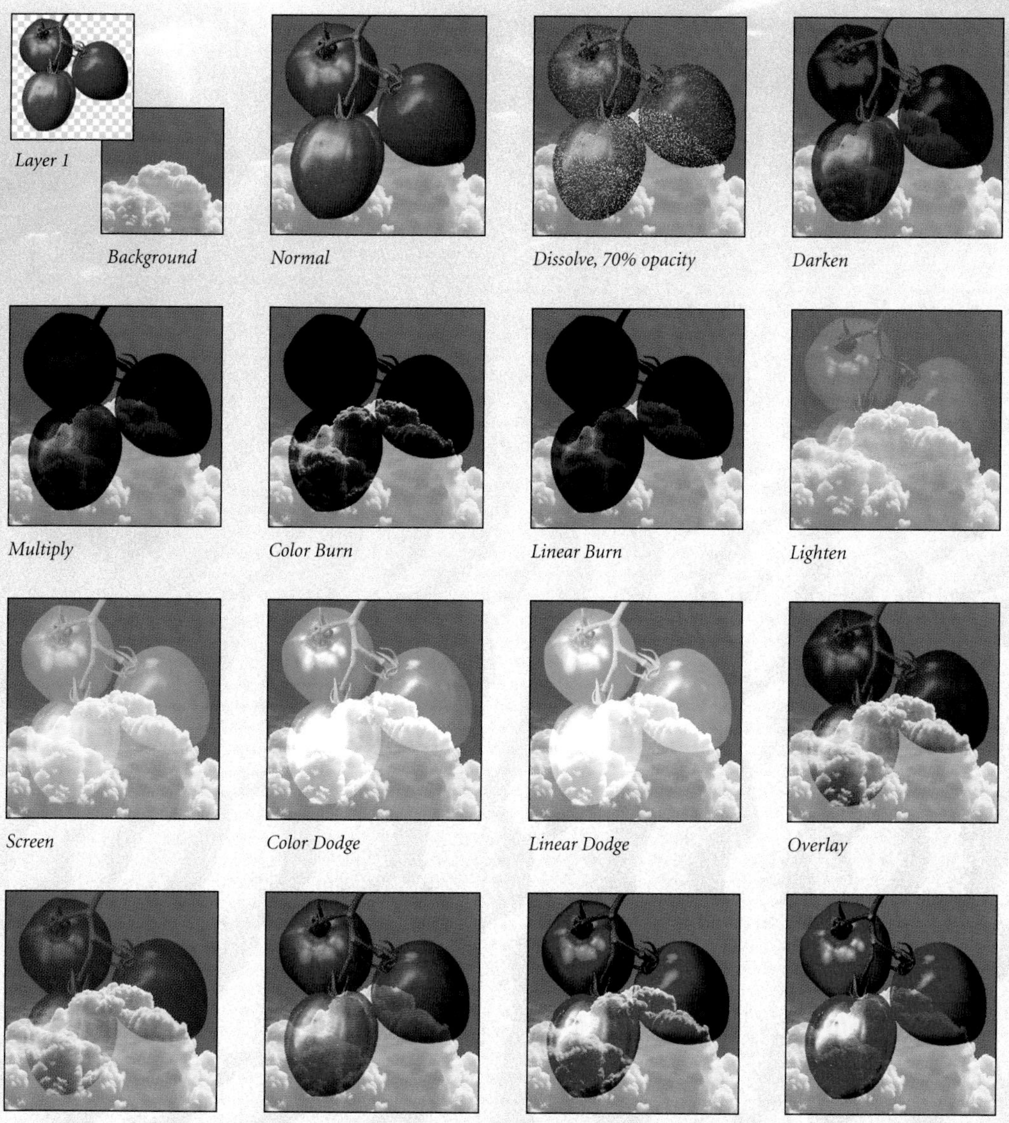

Layer 1

Background

Normal

Dissolve, 70% opacity

Darken

Multiply

Color Burn

Linear Burn

Lighten

Screen

Color Dodge

Linear Dodge

Overlay

Soft Light

Hard Light

Vivid Light

Linear Light

8-1: **Layer blending mode samples (cont.)**

Pin Light

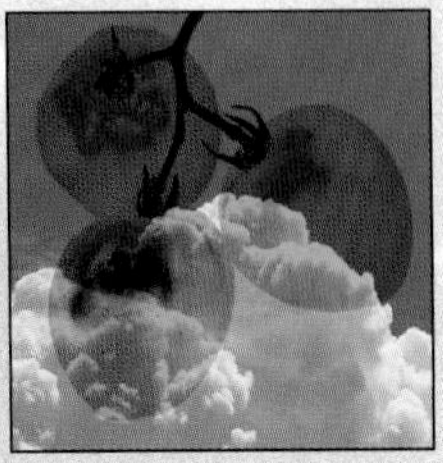

Difference

Exclusion

Hue

Saturation

Color

Luminosity

8-2: **Application of brush strokes to background using blending modes**

Original

Normal

Dissolve, 70% opacity

Darken

Multiply

Color Burn

Linear Burn

Lighten

Screen

Color Dodge

Linear Dodge

Overlay

Soft Light

Hard Light

Vivid Light

Linear Light

8-2: **Application of brush strokes to background using blending modes (cont.)**

Pin Light

Difference

Exclusion

Hue

Saturation

Color

Luminosity

Original

Behind

Clear

12-1: **Hand-coloring selections on a layer**

Original

After desaturating a selection

After hand-painting the selection

After adding a gradient fill to a selection

14-1: **Optimized continuous-tone images**

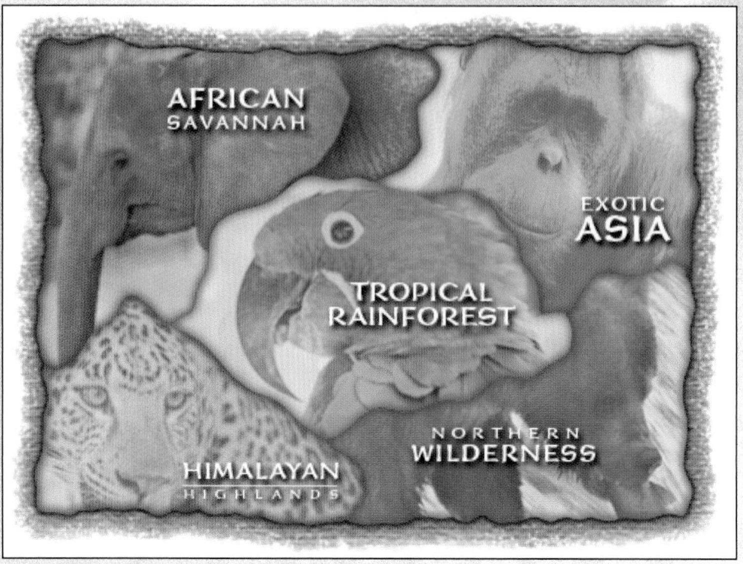

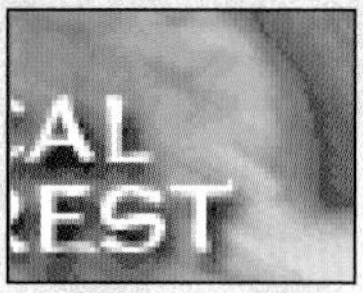

GIF, 128 colors, 88% dither

GIF, 128 colors, No dither

GIF, 32 colors, 88% dither

GIF, 32 colors, No dither

GIF, 64 colors, 88% dither

GIF, 64 colors, No dither

GIF, Web palette, auto colors

JPEG, Quality 60

JPEG, Quality 10

14-2: **Optimized solid graphics**

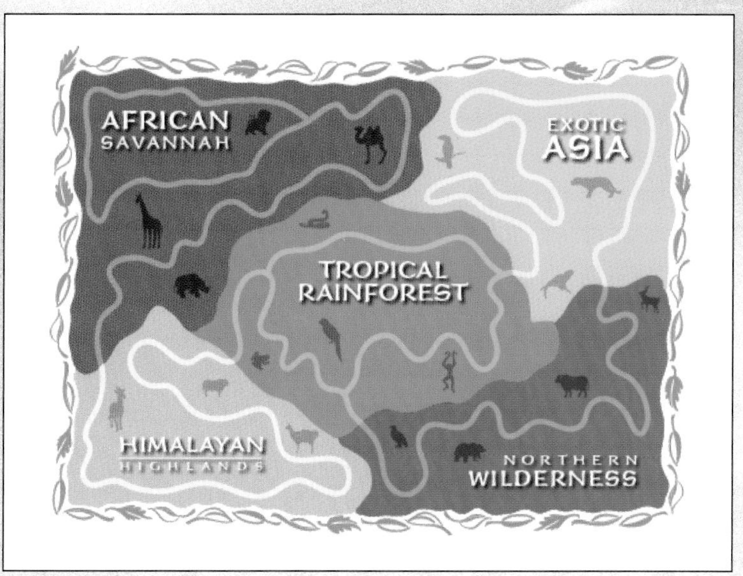

GIF, 128 colors,
88% dither

GIF, 128 colors,
No dither

GIF, 32 colors,
88% dither

GIF, 32 colors,
No dither

GIF, 64 colors,
88% dither

GIF, 64 colors,
No dither

GIF, Web palette,
auto colors

JPEG, Quality 60

JPEG, Quality 10

17-1: **Setting the monitor's white point**

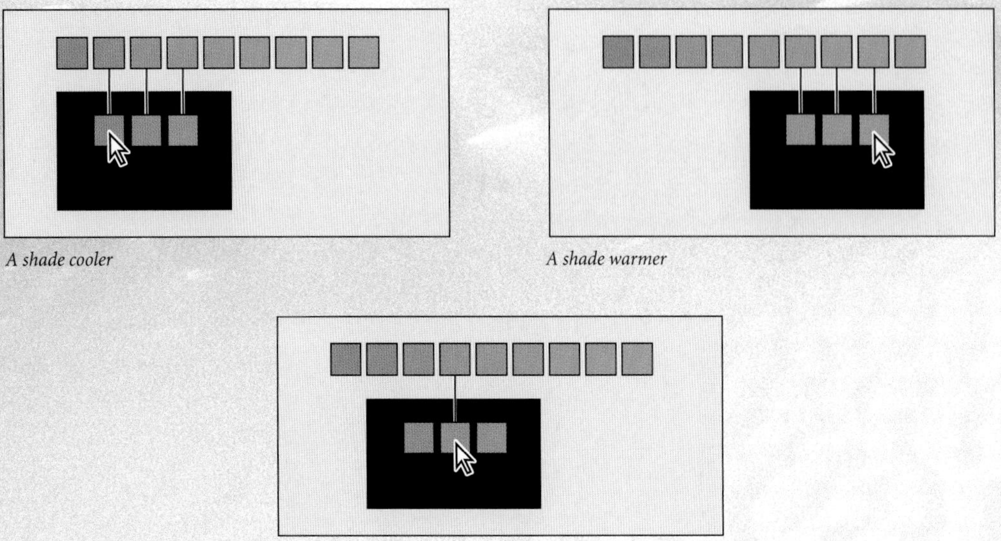

A shade cooler

A shade warmer

A neutral gray

18-1: **RGB image with red, green, and blue channels**

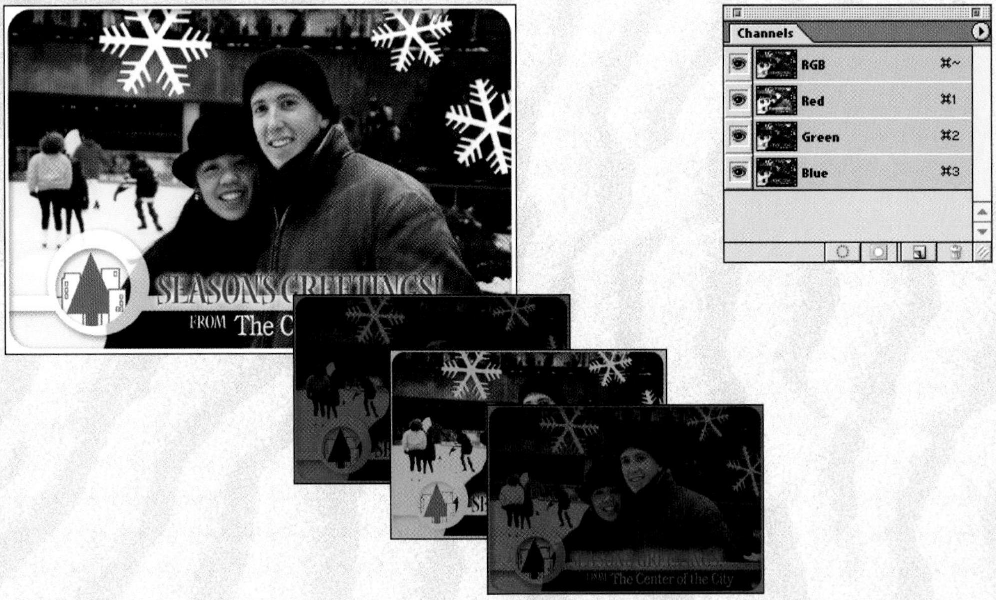

18-2: **CMYK image with cyan, magenta, yellow, and black channels**

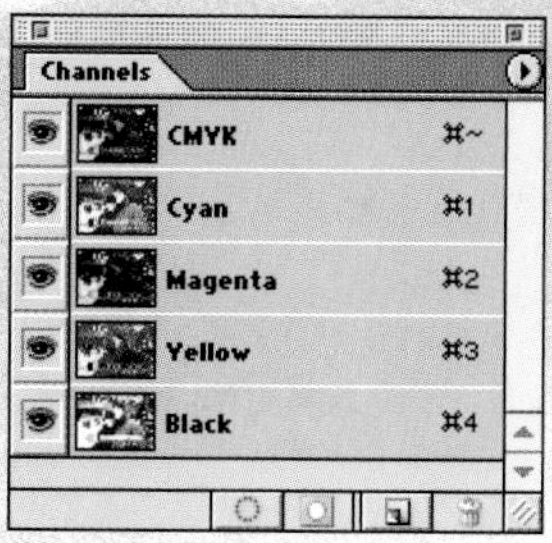

18-3: **Color gamuts**

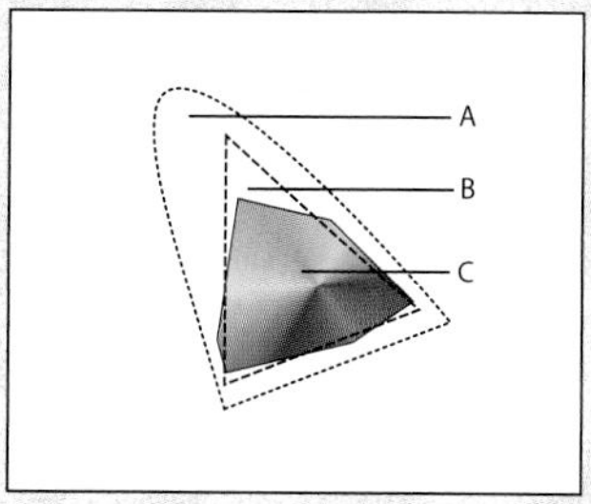

A. Natural color gamut
B. RGB color gamut
C. CMYK color gamut

18-4: **RGB color model**

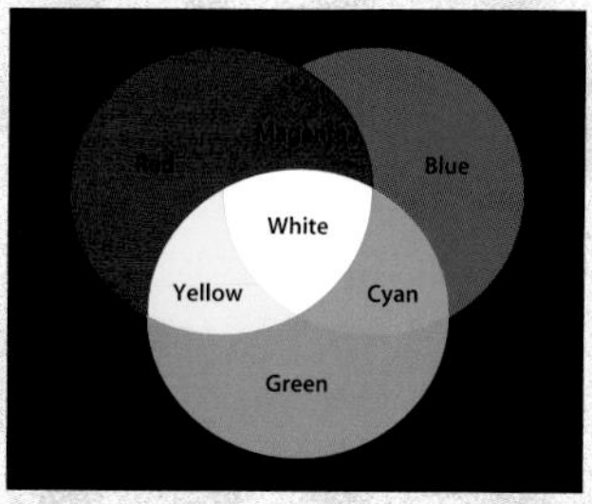

18-5: **CMYK color model**

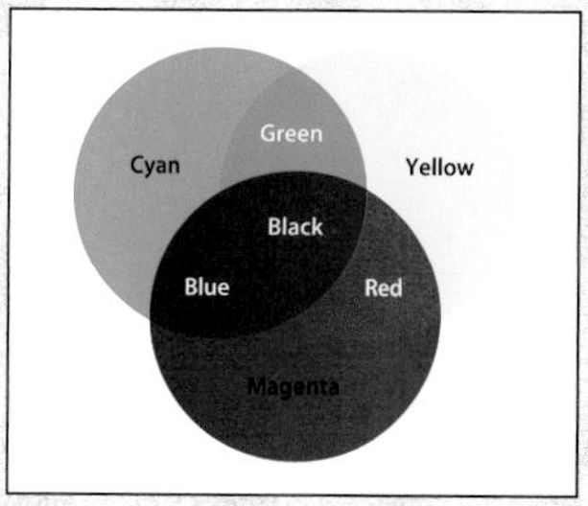

Lesson 2

2 Using the File Browser

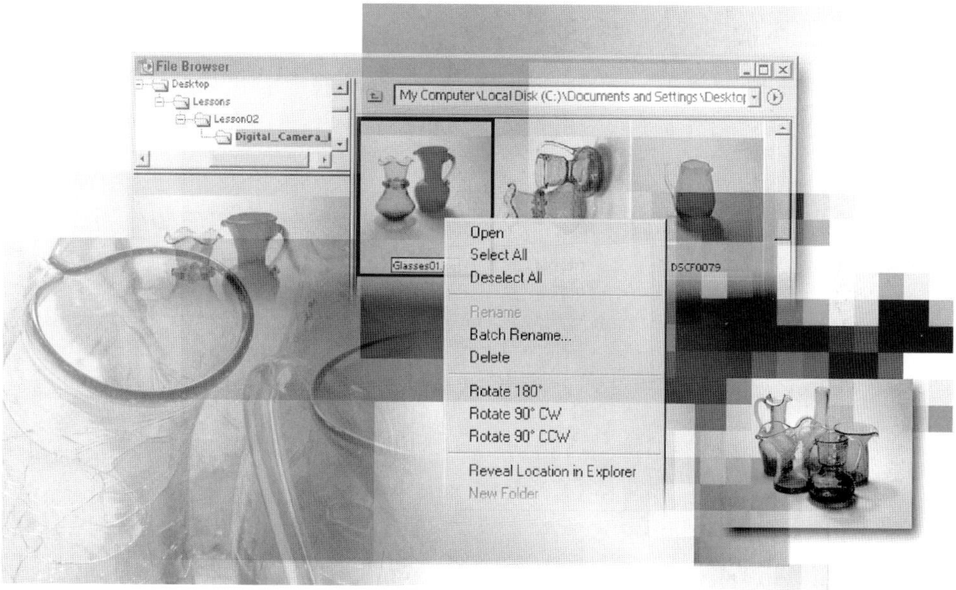

You can use the new File Browser as a time-saver for many tasks, including creating new folders, renaming files, moving files, and deleting them from your hard disk. But the unique power of the File Browser is its ability to display thumbnails and metadata for unopened files, making it extremely easy to find and open just the files you need. You can even rotate images in the File Browser.

In this lesson, you'll learn how to do the following:

- Open, close, and dock the File Browser.
- Identify and resize the four panes in the File Browser.
- Delete, rename, and batch-rename files from the File Browser.
- Assign rankings to files and sort files by rank.
- Rotate images without opening them in Photoshop.

This lesson will take about 30 minutes to complete. The File Browser is not available in ImageReady, so you must do this lesson in Photoshop.

If needed, remove the previous lesson folder from your hard drive, and copy the Lesson02 folder onto it. As you work on this lesson, you'll overwrite the start files. If you need to restore the start files, copy them from the *Adobe Photoshop 7.0 Classroom in a Book* CD.

Before beginning the lesson, restore the default application settings for Adobe Photoshop. See "Restoring default preferences" on page 5.

Getting Started

In this lesson, you'll become familiar with one of the new features in the Photoshop 7.0 work area: the File Browser. The File Browser looks and works in ways similar to other Photoshop palettes. It also shares some functions with ordinary folders on the desktop, Explorer (Windows), and Finder (Mac OS). Beyond both desktop folders and Photoshop palettes, the File Browser has unique features and displays that are not available elsewhere.

1 Start Photoshop.

If a notice appears asking whether you want to customize your color settings, click No.

2 Choose File > Browse to open the Photoshop File Browser.

3 The File Browser expands open from the palette well in the upper right work area. Drag the File Browser tab to the center of the work area to pull it away from the palette well.

Note: *If the size of the Photoshop work area on your monitor is less than 800 pixels x 600 pixels, the palette well does not appear, and the File Browser opens in its separated state.*

4 Resize the File Browser, either by dragging the lower right corner or by clicking the maximize button (on the right end of the File Browser title bar).

If you click the maximize button, the File Browser fills the entire work area.

5 (Optional) Press Tab to hide the toolbox and all the other palettes, leaving the File Browser open. Then choose Window > Options to reopen the tool options bar.

Exploring the File Browser

To begin, you'll learn to identify the different areas of the File Browser and their uses. Notice the four panes in the File Browser, three on the left and one on the right side of the window.

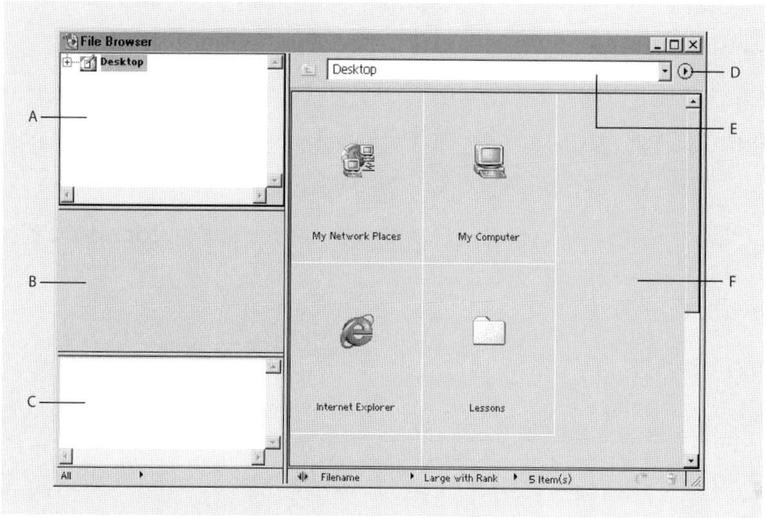

***A.** Navigation ("tree") pane **B.** Preview pane **C.** Information (metadata) pane*
***D.** Palette menu button **E.** Address display **F.** Thumbnails pane*

1 In the upper pane on the left, click the plus sign to expand the Desktop icon. Then continue opening folders down to the Lessons/Lesson02 folder, and select the Digital_Camera_Images folder.

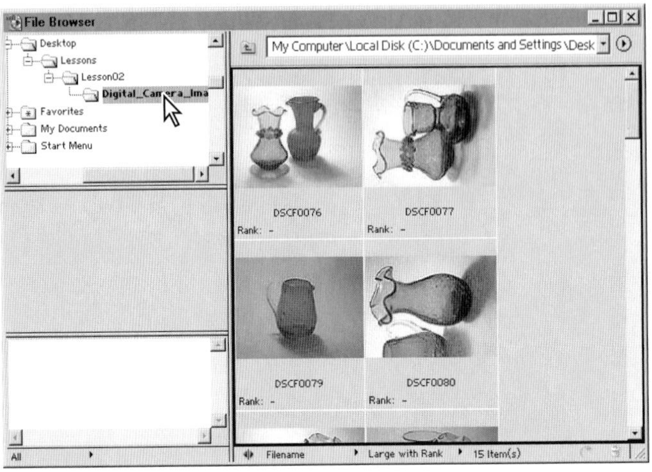

On the right side of the File Browser, thumbnails appear, showing the contents of the Digital_Camera_Images folder.

2 At the bottom of the File Browser, click the arrow after the Large With Rank option to open the View By pop-up menu, and select some of the other commands, one by one.

- The Small, Medium, and Large options change the size of the thumbnails.
- The Details option displays additional information about the image file.

You will work with the Large with Rank option later in this lesson. For now, select the Medium or Large view option.

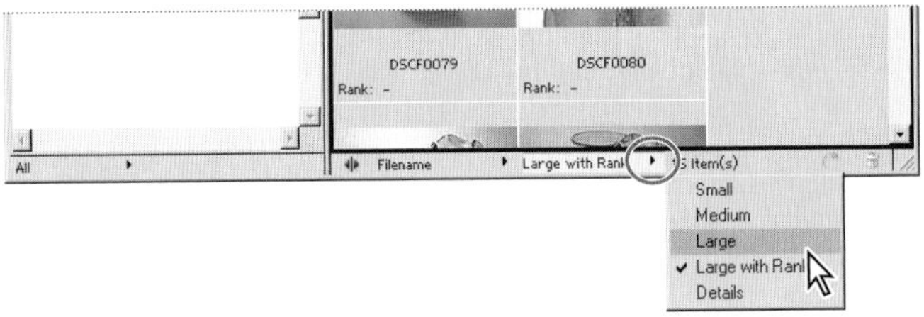

2 Right-click (Windows) or Ctrl-click (Mac OS) one of the thumbnails to open the context menu, and choose Rank A.

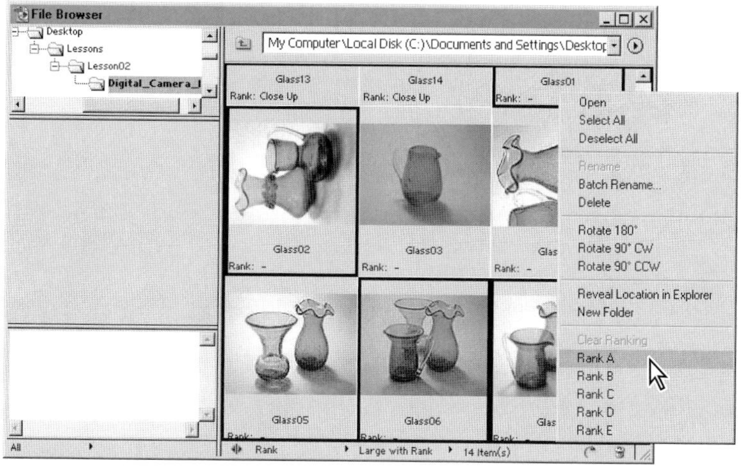

3 Using the same techniques as in step 2, select several other thumbnails and assign Rank B to those images. Then assign Rank C to any remaining unranked image thumbnails.

4 In the Sort By pop-up menu at the bottom of the File Browser, choose Rank again.

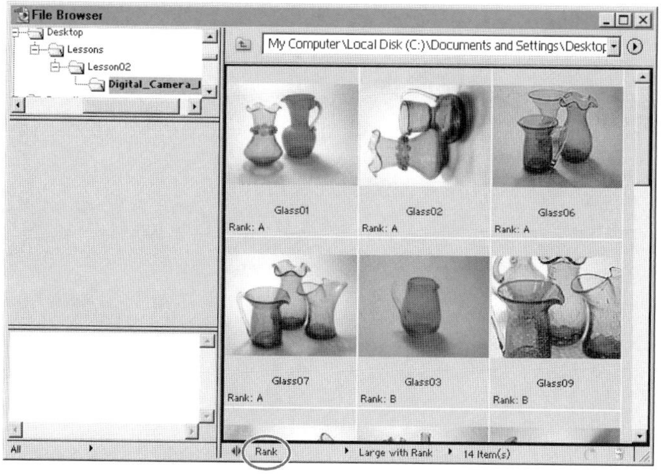

The thumbnails are now displayed according to the order that you assigned.

Rotating images in the File Browser

Another feature of the File Browser that goes far beyond the capabilities of a desktop folder is the ability to rotate thumbnail images. Unlike the Rename option, this feature does not alter the actual files until you open them. When you open a rotated thumbnail, Photoshop automatically rotates the image file according to the rotation you assigned in the File Browser.

1 Ctrl-click (Windows) or Command-click (Mac OS) to select the three thumbnails that are oriented sideways with the open edge of the vase or pitcher on the left side of the image.

(Do not select the thumbnail that is sideways with its open end on the right side of the image. You'll use a slightly different procedure to straighten that file.)

2 Click the Rotate button (↻) at the bottom right of the File Browser.

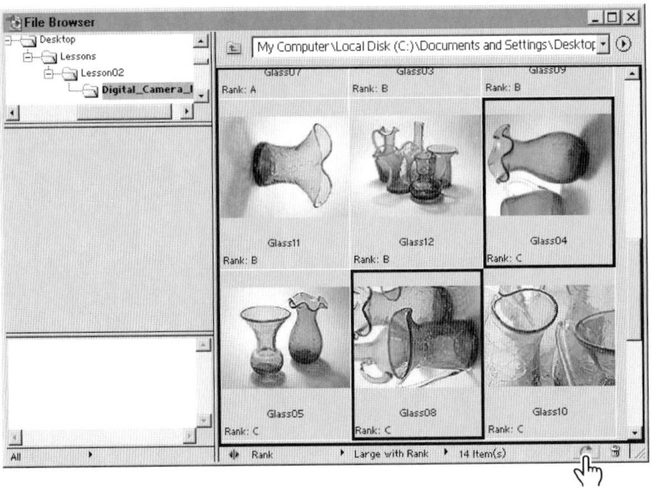

3 When an alert message appears, click OK.

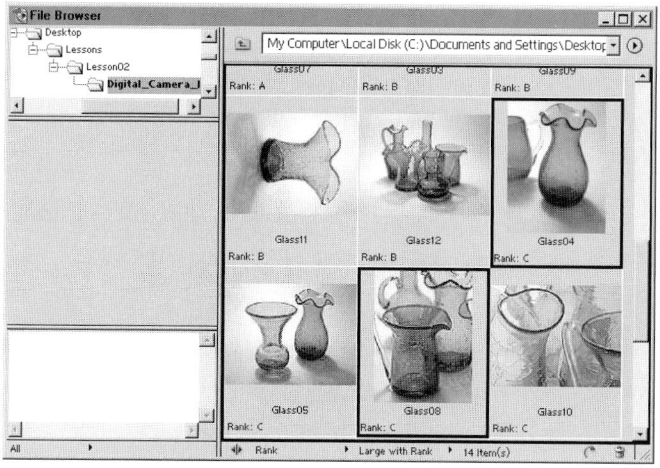

The three images are rotated clockwise in the thumbnails pane. If you select one of the thumbnails, its image also appears rotated in the preview pane.

The Rotate button rotates images clockwise. Although you could rotate images counter-clockwise by clicking the rotate button three times or by holding down Alt and clicking, you'll use a different technique for the next image.

4 Select the image that is still sideways, with the top of the vase on the right side of the image. Right-click (Windows) or Ctrl-click (Mac OS) the thumbnail to open the context menu, and choose Rotate 90° CCW.

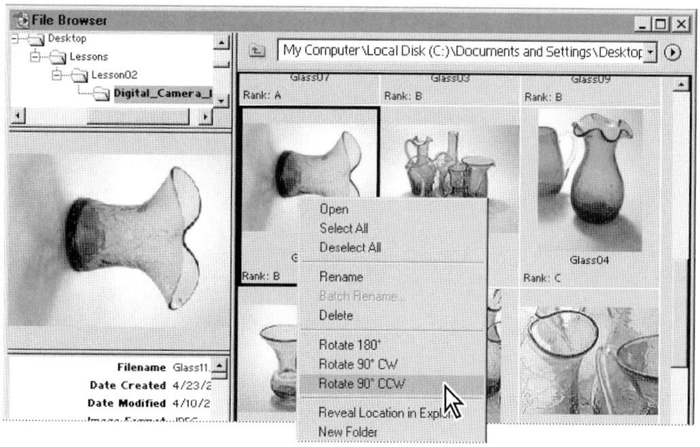

5 Click OK to dismiss the alert message.

The image is rotated counterclockwise.

6 With the rotated image still selected, press Enter (Windows) or Return (Mac OS).

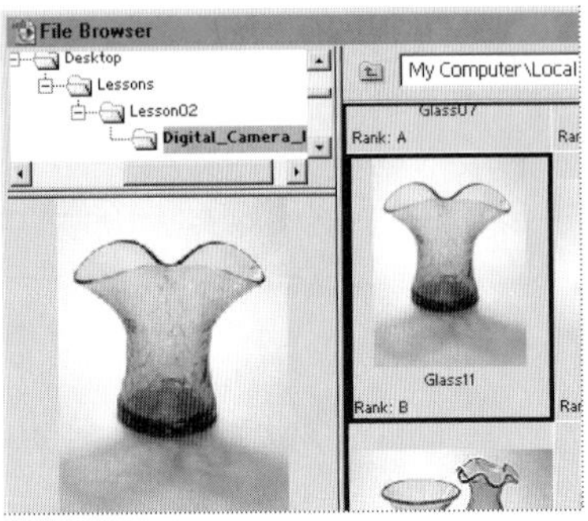

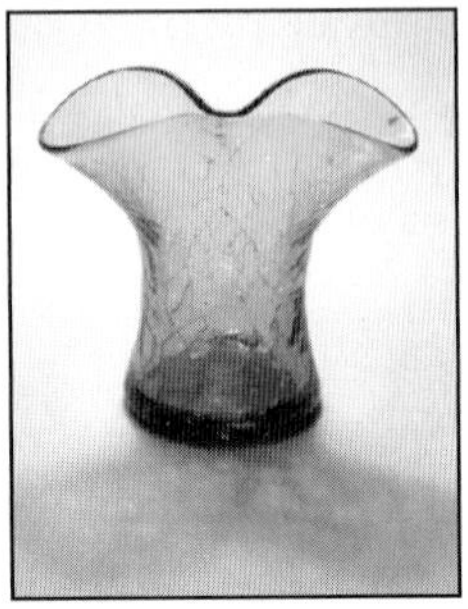

The image opens in Photoshop rotated to the proper orientation.

You've finished this introductory lesson on the File Browser. As you work through this book, you'll have other opportunities to use the File Browser in lessons in which its advantages are particularly helpful.

Review questions

1 Describe two ways to open the File Browser as a window.

2 What are some of the similarities between working with folders and files on the desktop and working with them in the Photoshop File Browser?

3 What are the advantages of using the File Browser instead of a desktop folder?

4 In what ways is the File Browser like other palettes? Are there differences?

5 Describe two ways to rotate an image from the File Browser.

Review answers

1 You can open the File Browser by choosing File > Browse or, if your work area is larger than 800 x 600 pixels, by dragging the File Browser tag out of the palette well.

2 You can use either the File Browser or a desktop folder—such as the Explorer (Windows) or the Finder (Mac OS)—to rename files, delete files from your hard disk, move files and folders from one location to another, and to create new folders.

3 Unlike desktop folders, the File Browser shows a thumbnail of each item within a selected folder and a preview of the selected item, plus information or *metadata* about the selected item, including EXIF information for images captured by a digital camera. This makes it easier to identify files without going to the trouble of opening them. This is especially useful for images you create with a digital camera and have auto-generated names rather than descriptive names. You can also use the File Browser to assign rankings to files, sort by those rankings, and batch-name items in a folder, and you can rotate images so that they open in Photoshop with the orientation you assigned in the File Browser.

4 The File Browser, like any other palette, has a palette menu and can be docked in the palette well. Unlike other palettes, when you drag the File Browser from the palette well, it appears with a title bar but no tab. To dock the File Browser, you must choose a command from the palette menu, but you can just drop other palettes into the palette well by dragging them by the tab. On the menus, you can open the File Browser from the File menu (File > Browse), whereas you open other palettes by selecting the palette name from the Window menu.

5 You can click the Rotate button at the lower right of the File Browser to rotate the selected image. Each click advances the rotation clockwise by 90°. You can right-click (Windows) or Ctrl-click (Mac OS) an image thumbnail to open a context menu and then select one of the rotation commands: Rotate 180°, Rotate 90° CW, or Rotate 90° CCW.

Lesson 3

3 Basic Photo Corrections

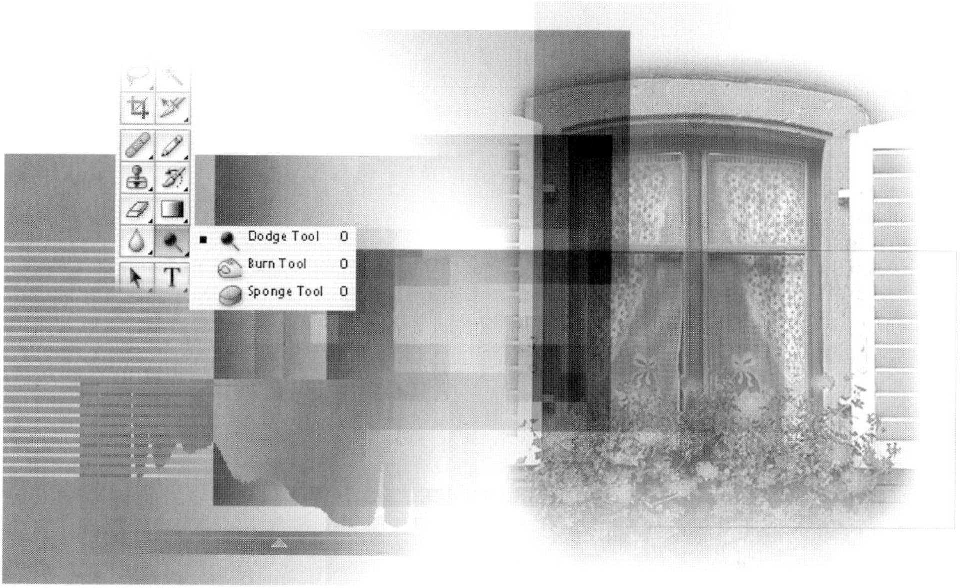

Adobe Photoshop and Adobe ImageReady include a variety of tools and commands for improving the quality of a photographic image. This lesson steps you through the process of acquiring, resizing, and retouching a photo intended for a print layout. The same workflow applies to Web images.

In this lesson, you'll learn how to do the following:

- Choose the correct resolution for a scanned photograph.
- Crop an image to final size.
- Adjust the tonal range of an image.
- Remove a color cast from an image Auto Color correction.
- Adjust the saturation and brightness of isolated areas of an image using the sponge and dodge tools.
- Apply the Unsharp Mask filter to finish the photo-retouching process.
- Save an Adobe Photoshop file in a format that can be used by a page-layout program.

This lesson will take about 45 minutes to complete. The lesson is designed to be done in Adobe Photoshop, but information on using similar functionality in Adobe ImageReady is included where appropriate.

If needed, remove the previous lesson folder from your hard drive, and copy the Lesson03 folder onto it. As you work on this lesson, you'll overwrite the start file. If you need to restore the start files, copy them from the *Adobe Photoshop 7.0 Classroom in a Book* CD.

Note: *Windows users need to unlock the lesson files before using them. For more information, see "Copying the Classroom in a Book files" on page 4.*

Strategy for retouching

You can retouch photographic images in ways once available only to highly trained specialists. You can correct problems in color quality and tonal range created during the original photography or during image scanning. You can also correct problems in composition and sharpen the overall focus of the image.

Photoshop provides a comprehensive set of color-correction tools for adjusting the color and tone of individual images. ImageReady has a more basic set of color-correction tools, including Levels, Auto Levels, Brightness/Contrast, Hue/Saturation, Desaturation, Invert, Variations, and the Unsharp Mask filter.

Organizing an efficient sequence of tasks

Most retouching follows these six general steps:

- Checking the scan quality and making sure that the resolution is appropriate for the way you will use the image.
- Cropping the image to final size and orientation.
- Adjusting the overall contrast or tonal range of the image.
- Removing any color casts.
- Adjusting the color and tone in specific parts of the image to bring out highlights, midtones, shadows, and desaturated colors.
- Sharpening the overall focus of the image.

Usually, you should complete these processes in the order listed above. Otherwise, the results of one process may cause unintended changes to other aspects of the image, making it necessary for you to redo some of your work.

Adjusting your process for intended uses

The retouching techniques you apply to an image depend in part on how you will use the image. Whether an image is intended for black-and-white publication on newsprint or for full-color Internet distribution affects everything from the resolution of the initial scan to the type of tonal range and color correction that the image requires. Photoshop supports the CMYK color mode for preparing an image to be printed using process colors, as well as RGB and other color modes. ImageReady supports only RGB mode, used for on-screen display.

To illustrate one application of retouching techniques, this lesson takes you through the steps of correcting a photograph intended for four-color print publication.

For more information about CMYK and RGB color modes, see Lesson 18, "Producing and Printing Consistent Color."

Original image

Image cropped and retouched

Image placed into page layout

For the Web: The printed page versus on-screen display

Although you can create publications for both paper and on-screen use, remember that a computer screen and a printed page are very different. Keep these differences in mind when you create publications for either medium—or for both media:

- *Text can be small and still very legible on paper, because the dots of ink on paper are much finer than the dots of light used in a monitor. Therefore, avoid small text and finely detailed graphics on-screen. This means that it is more difficult to effectively use formatting such as multiple columns on-screen.*
- *Computer monitors come in all sizes, and you can rarely guarantee that your online readers all have the same monitor size. You should design for the smallest monitor you expect people to have—typically a 15-inch monitor. By contrast, when you print to paper, you know what size the paper is and can design the publication accordingly. However, a page in an HTML or PDF publication can be any length.*
- *The larger dimension of a computer screen is horizontal ("landscape"), while in most printed pages, the larger one is vertical ("portrait"). This fact fundamentally affects the format of your pages.*
- *A printed publication is usually read sequentially—even to flip through the publication the reader must turn from one page to the next. In an online publication, the reader can go anywhere any time, either by indicating what page to go to or by clicking on a link that goes to somewhere else, such as to an entirely different publication.*

Resolution and image size

The first step in retouching a photograph in Photoshop is to make sure that the image is the correct resolution. The term *resolution* refers to the number of small squares known as *pixels* that describe an image and establish its detail. Resolution is determined by *pixel dimensions*, or the number of pixels along the width and height of an image.

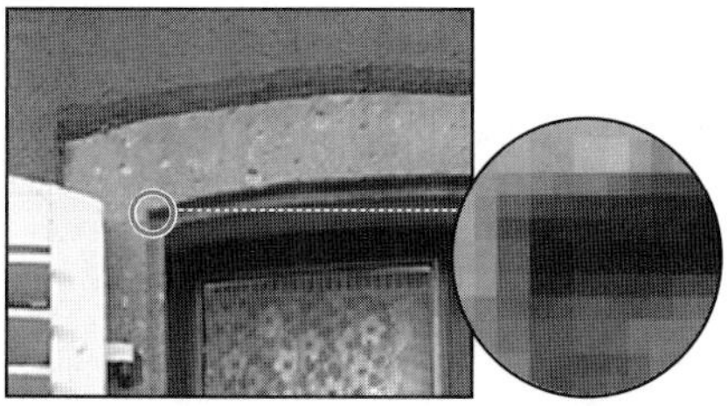

Pixels in a photographic image

Types of resolution

In computer graphics, there are different types of resolution:

The number of pixels per unit of length in an image is called the *image resolution*, usually measured in pixels per inch (ppi). An image with a high resolution has more pixels (and therefore a larger file size) than an image of the same dimensions with a low resolution. Images in Photoshop can vary from high resolution (300 ppi or higher) to low resolution (72 ppi or 96 ppi), whereas images in ImageReady are fixed at 72 ppi.

The number of pixels per unit of length on a monitor is the *monitor resolution*, usually measured in dots per inch (dpi). Image pixels are translated directly into monitor pixels. In Photoshop, if the image resolution is higher than the monitor resolution, the image appears larger on-screen than its specified print dimensions. For example, when you display a 1-inch-by-1-inch, 144-ppi image on a 72-dpi monitor, the image fills a 2-inch-by-2-inch area of the screen. ImageReady images have a consistent image resolution of 72 ppi and display at the monitor resolution.

4 in. x 6 in. at 72 ppi; file size 342K

100% on-screen view

4 in. x 6 in. at 200 ppi; file size 2.48 MB

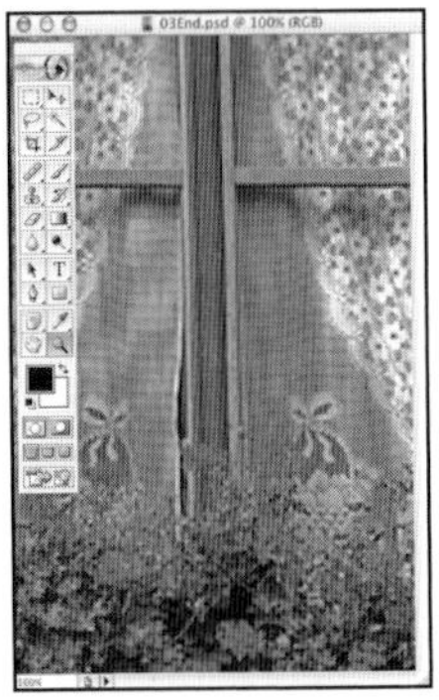

100% on-screen view

Note: *It is important to understand what "100% view" means when you work on screen. At 100%, 1 image pixel = 1 monitor pixel. Unless the resolution of your image is exactly the same as the resolution of the monitor, the image size (in inches, for example) on screen may be larger or smaller than the image size will be when printed.*

The number of ink dots per inch produced by an imagesetter or laser printer is the *printer* or *output resolution*. Of course, higher-resolution printers combined with higher-resolution images generally produce the best quality. The appropriate resolution for a printed image is determined both by the printer resolution and by the *screen frequency* or lines per inch (lpi) of the halftone screens used to reproduce images.

Keep in mind that the higher the image resolution, the larger the file size and the longer the file takes to download from the Web.

Resolution for this lesson

To determine the image resolution for the photograph in this lesson, we followed the computer graphics rule of thumb for color or grayscale images intended for print on large commercial printers: Scan at a resolution 1.5 to 2 times the screen frequency used by the printer. Because the magazine in which the image will be printed uses a screen frequency of 133 lpi, the image was scanned at 200 ppi (133 x 1.5).

For complete information on resolution and image size, see Adobe Photoshop 7.0 online Help.

Getting started

Before beginning this lesson, restore the default application settings for Adobe Photoshop. See "Restoring default preferences" on page 5.

The image you'll work on in this lesson is a scanned photograph. In this scenario, you'll prepare the image to be placed in an Adobe InDesign® layout for a fictitious magazine. The final image size in the print layout will be 2 inches by 3 inches.

You'll start the lesson by viewing the finished image. The picture you'll work on shows an interesting window with a window box that is overflowing with blooming red geraniums.

1 Start Adobe Photoshop.

If a notice appears asking whether you want to customize your color settings, click No.

2 Choose File > Open, and open the file 03End.psd from the Lessons/Lesson03 folder.

3 When you have finished viewing the file, either leave the file open for reference or close it without saving changes.

For some color illustrations of the artwork for this lesson, see the color section.

Now you'll open the start file and begin the lesson by viewing the photograph you will be retouching.

4 Choose File > Open, and open the file 03Start.psd from the Lessons/Lesson03 folder.

The start image shows the same window, but the colors are dull, the scan is crooked, and the dimensions are larger than needed for the requirements of the magazine. These are the qualities that you'll fix in this lesson using Photoshop retouching techniques.

Straightening and cropping an image

You'll use the crop tool to trim and scale the photograph for this lesson so that it fits the space designed for it. You can use either the crop tool or the Crop command to crop an image.

You can decide whether to delete or discard the area outside of a rectangular selection, or whether to hide the area outside of the selection. In ImageReady, the Hide option is useful when creating animations with elements that move from off-screen into the live image area.

1 In the toolbox, select the crop tool (crop tool icon). Then, in the tool options bar (at the top of the work area), enter the dimensions (in inches) of the finished image: For Width, type **2** and for Height type **3**.

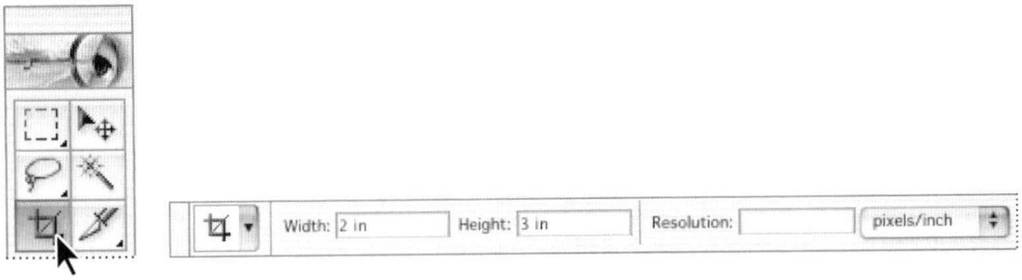

Note: *If you are working in ImageReady, select the Fixed Size option in the tool options bar before entering the dimensions.*

2 Draw a marquee around the image. Don't worry about whether or not the entire image is included, because you'll adjust the marquee size later.

As you drag, the marquee retains the same proportion as the dimensions you specified for the target size (2 x 3).

When you release the mouse button, a *cropping shield* covers the area outside the cropping selection, and the tool options bar now displays choices about the cropping shield.

3 In the tool options bar, make sure that the Perspective check box is *not* selected.

4 In the image window, move the pointer outside the crop marquee, so that it appears as a curved double arrow (curved double arrow icon). Drag clockwise to rotate the marquee until it is parallel with the edges of the pictured window frame.

5 Place the pointer inside the crop marquee, and drag the marquee until it contains all the parts of the picture you want shown to produce an artistically pleasing result. If you also want to adjust the size of the marquee, drag one of the corner handles.

Initial crop marquee

Marquee rotated

Marquee moved

Marquee resized

6 Press Enter (Windows) or Return (Mac OS). The image is now cropped, and the cropped image now fills the image window, straightened, sized, and cropped according to your specifications.

Image cropped

In Photoshop and ImageReady, you can use the Image > Trim command to discard a border area around the edge of the image, based on transparency or edge color.

7 Choose File > Save to save your work.

Adjusting the tonal range

The tonal range of an image represents the amount of *contrast*, or detail, in the image and is determined by the image's distribution of pixels, ranging from the darkest pixels (black) to the lightest pixels (white). You'll now correct the photograph's contrast using the Levels command.

1 Choose Image > Adjustments > Levels, to open the Levels dialog box.

2 Make sure that the Preview check box is selected, and then move the dialog box aside, as needed, so that you can also see the image window as you work.

In the middle area of the dialog box, the three triangles directly beneath the histogram represent the shadows (black triangle), highlights (white triangle), and midtones or gamma (gray triangle). If your image had colors across the entire brightness range, the graph would extend across the full width of the histogram, from black triangle to white triangle. Instead, the graph is clumped somewhat toward the center, indicating there are no very dark or very light colors.

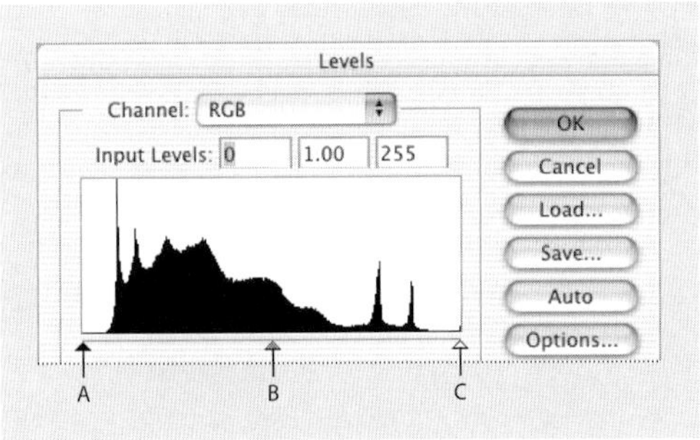

***A.** Shadows **B.** Midtones or gamma **C.** Highlights*

You can adjust the black and white points of the image to extend its tonal range and then adjust the midtones.

3 Drag the left triangle to the right to the point where the histogram indicates that the darkest colors begin.

As you drag, the first Input Levels value (above the histogram) changes and so does the image itself.

4 Drag the right triangle to the left to the point where the histogram indicates that the lightest colors begin. Again, notice the changes in the third Input Levels value and in the image.

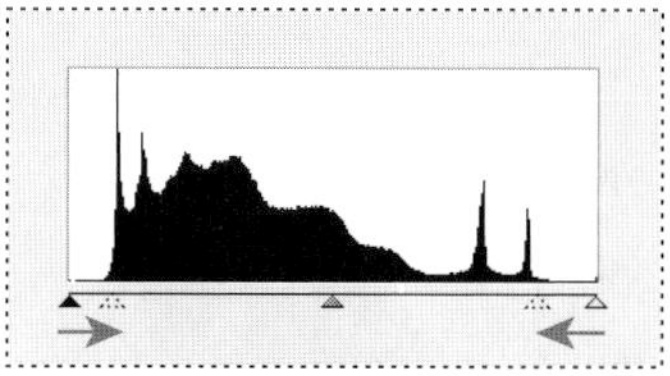

Increasing shadows (black triangle) and adding highlights (white triangle)

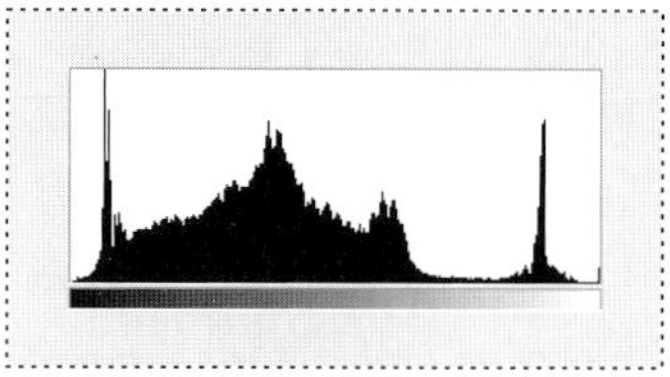

Result

5 Drag the middle triangle a short distance toward the left side to lighten the midtones. Watch the image updates in the image window to determine how far to drag the middle triangle.

6 When the image looks good to you (the sample uses Input Levels values of 18, 1.30, and 232), click OK to apply the changes.

7 Choose Image > Histogram to view the new histogram. The tonal range now extends throughout the entire range of the histogram. Click OK to close the histogram, and then save your work.

Note: *ImageReady does not have a Histogram command. To adjust and view a histogram, use the Levels command.*

About Auto Contrast

You can also adjust the contrast (highlights and shadows) and the overall mix of colors in an image automatically using the Image > Adjustments > Auto Contrast command. Adjusting the contrast maps the darkest and lightest pixels in the image to black and white.

This remapping causes the highlights to appear lighter and the shadows to appear darker and can improve the appearance of many photographic or continuous-tone images. (The Auto Contrast command does not improve flat-color images.)

The Auto Contrast command clips white and black pixels by 0.5%—that is, it ignores the first 0.5% of either extreme when identifying the lightest and darkest pixels in the image. This clipping of color values ensures that white and black values are representative areas of the image content rather than extreme pixel values.

For this project, you won't use the Auto Contrast feature, but it's a feature you should know about so that you can use it in your own projects.

Removing a color cast

Some images contain color casts (imbalanced colors), which may occur during scanning or which may have existed in the original image. This photograph of the window has a blue cast. You'll use the Auto Color feature in Photoshop 7.0 to correct this. (ImageReady does not include the Auto Color command, so this task must be done in Photoshop.)

Note: *To see a color cast in an image on your monitor, you need a 24-bit monitor (one that can display millions of colors). On monitors that can display only 256 colors (8 bits), a color cast is difficult, if not impossible, to detect.*

For an illustration of color casting, see figure 3-1 in the color section.

1 Choose Image > Adjustments > Auto Color.

Notice that the blue color cast is gone.

2 Choose File > Save.

> ***Using the Auto Color command (Photoshop)***
>
> *The Auto Color command adjusts the contrast and color of an image by searching the actual image rather than the channels' histograms for shadows, midtones, and highlights. It neutralizes the midtones and clips the white and black pixels based on the values set in the Auto Correction Options dialog box.*
>
> ***Setting auto correction options (Photoshop)***
>
> *The Auto Correction Options dialog box lets you automatically adjust the overall tonal range of an image, specify clipping percentages, and assign color values to shadows, midtones, and highlights. You can apply the settings during a single use of the Levels dialog box or Curves dialog box, or you can save the settings for future use with the Levels, AutoLevels, Auto Contrast, Auto Color, and Curves commands.*
>
> *To open the Auto Correction Options dialog box, click Options in the Levels dialog box or Curves dialog box.*
>
> –From Adobe Photoshop 7.0 online Help

Replacing colors in an image

With the Replace Color command, you can create temporary *masks* based on specific colors and then replace these colors. (A mask isolates an area of an image, so that changes affect just the selected area and not the rest of the image.) The Replace Color dialog box contains options for adjusting the hue, saturation, and lightness components of the selection: *Hue* is color, *saturation* is the purity of the color, and *lightness* is how much white or black is in the image.

You'll use the Replace Color command to change the color of the wall at the top of the image. The Replace Color command is not available in ImageReady.

1 Select the rectangular marquee tool (⬚), and draw a selection border around the blue wall at the top of the image. Don't worry about making a perfect selection, but be sure to include all of the blue wall.

2 Choose Image > Adjustments > Replace Color to open the Replace Color dialog box.

By default, the Selection area of the Replace Color dialog box displays a black rectangle, representing the current selection.

Notice the three eyedropper tools in the Replace Color dialog box. One selects a single color; another selects additional colors and adds them to the color selection; the third selects colors that it removes from a selection.

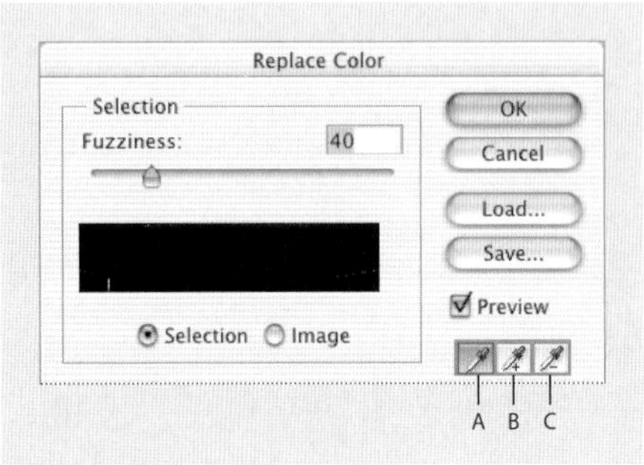

A. *Single-color eyedropper tool*
B. *Eyedropper plus tool*
C. *Eyedropper minus tool*

3 Select the first (single-color) eyedropper tool (✗) in the Replace Color dialog box and click anywhere in the blue-wall area of the image window to select all of the area with that color.

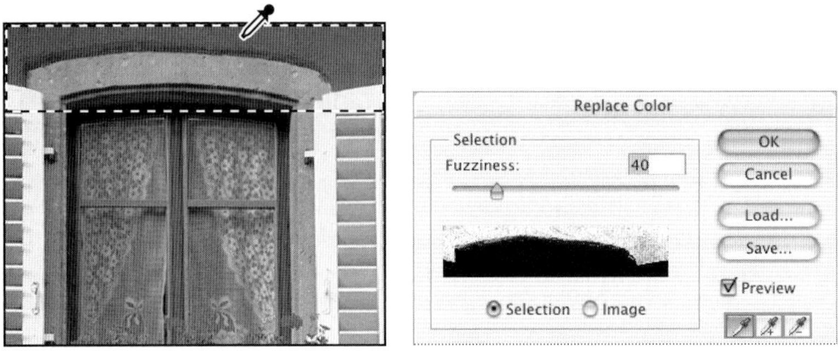

4 In the Replace Color dialog box, select the eyedropper-plus tool (), and drag over the other areas of the blue wall until the entire wall shape is highlighted in white in the dialog box.

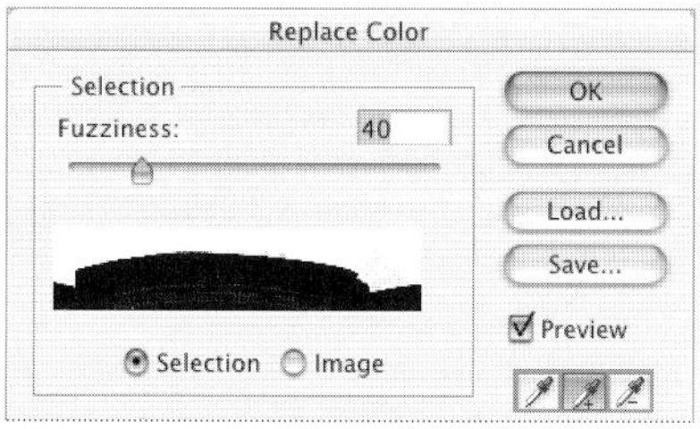

5 Adjust the tolerance level of the mask by dragging the Fuzziness slider or typing **80**.

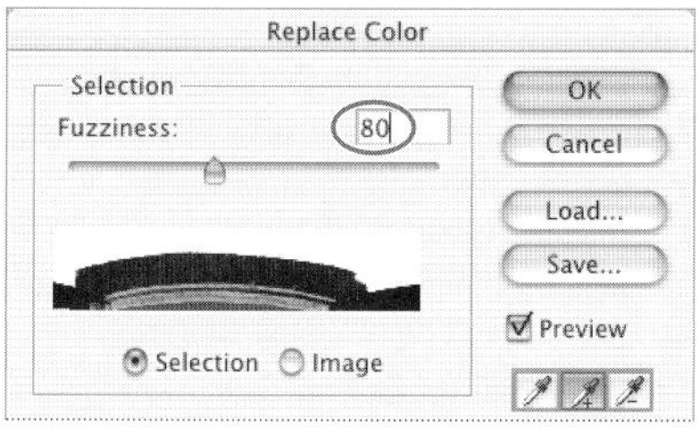

Fuzziness controls the degree to which related colors are included in the mask.

6 If there are any white areas of the mask display in the dialog box that are not part of the wall, select the eyedropper-minus tool () and click in the black area around the selection in the Replace Color dialog box to remove most of the white. (It's OK if a few pixels in the shadowed window inset remain in the selection.)

7 In the Transform area of the Replace Color dialog box, drag the Hue slider to **–40**, the Saturation slider to **–45**, and the Lightness slider to **0**.

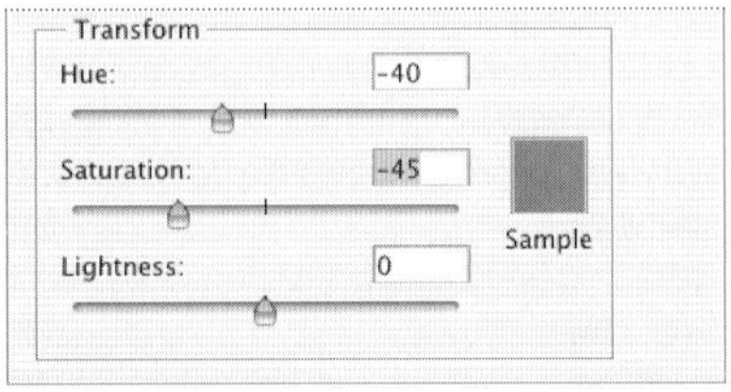

As you change the values, the color of the wall changes in hue, saturation, and lightness, so that the wall is now a slaty green color.

8 Click OK to apply the changes.

9 Choose Select > Deselect, and then choose File > Save.

Adjusting lightness with the dodge tool

You'll use the dodge tool to lighten the highlights and bring out the details of the curtains behind the window. The dodge tool is based on a traditional photographer's method of holding back light during an exposure to lighten an area of the image.

1 In the toolbox, select the dodge tool ().

In ImageReady, the dodge tool is hidden under the clone stamp tool ().

2 In the tool options bar, select the following settings:

- For Brush, select a fairly large feathered brush on the Brush pop-up palette, such as 27. Then click outside the palette to close it.
- In the Range pop-up menu, select Highlights.
- For Exposure, type or use the pop-up slider to enter **15%**.

3 Using vertical strokes, drag the dodge tool over the window curtains to bring out the details. You don't always need to use vertical strokes with the dodge tool, but they work well with this particular image. If you make a mistake or don't like the results, choose Edit > Undo and try again until you are satisfied with the results.

Original

Result

4 Choose File > Save.

Adjusting saturation with the sponge tool

Next you'll use the sponge tool to saturate the color of the geraniums. When you change the saturation of a color, you adjust its strength or purity. The sponge tool is useful for making subtle saturation changes to specific areas of an image.

For an illustration of saturating with the sponge tool, see figure 3-2 in the color section.

1 Select the sponge tool ( ), hidden under the dodge tool ( ).

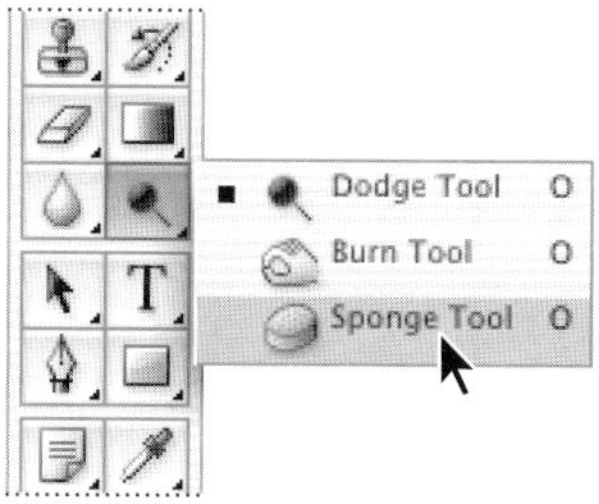

ImageReady also has a sponge tool hidden under the clone stamp tool ( ).

2 In the tool options bar, select the following settings:

- In the Brush pop-up palette, again select a large, feathered brush, such as 27.
- In the Mode pop-up menu, select Saturate.
- In Flow, type **90** to set the intensity of the saturation effect.

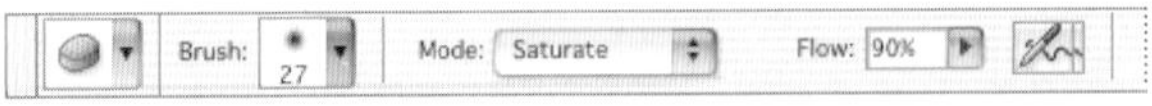

3 Drag the sponge back and forth over the flowers and leaves to saturate their color. The more you drag over an area, the more saturated the color becomes.

Original

Result

4 Save your work.

Applying the Unsharp Mask filter

The last step you take when retouching a photo is to apply the Unsharp Mask filter, which adjusts the contrast of the edge detail and creates the illusion of a more focused image.

1 Choose Filter > Sharpen > Unsharp Mask.

2 In the Unsharp Mask dialog box, make sure that the Preview option is selected so that you can see the results in the image window.

You can drag inside the preview window in the dialog box to see different parts of the image or use the plus (+) and minus (–) buttons below the thumbnail to zoom in and out.

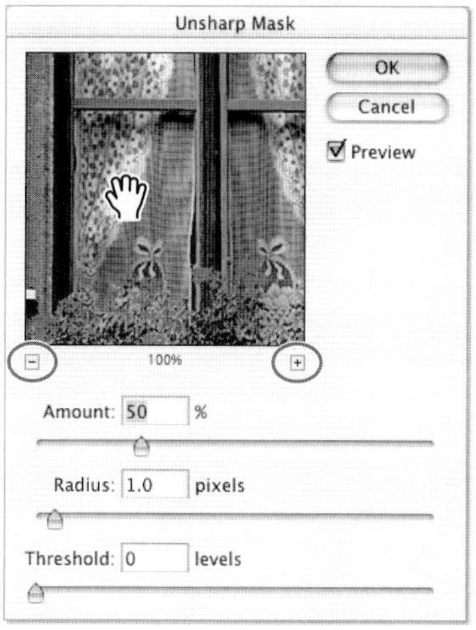

3 Drag the Amount slider until the image is as sharp as you want (we used 75%).

As you try different settings, toggle the Preview check box off and on to see how your changes affect the image in the image window. Or, you can just click the image in the dialog box to toggle the filter off and on. If your image is large, using the display in the dialog box can be more efficient because only a small area is redrawn.

4 Drag the Radius slider to determine the number of pixels surrounding the edge pixels that will affect the sharpening. The higher the resolution, the higher the Radius setting should be. (We used the default value, 1.0 pixel.)

5 (Optional) You can adjust the Threshold slider. This determines how different the sharpened pixels must be from the surrounding area before they are considered edge pixels and subsequently sharpened by the Unsharp Mask filter. The default Threshold value of 0 sharpens all pixels in the image.

6 Click OK to apply the Unsharp Mask filter.

Sharpening the image

Unsharp masking, or USM, is a traditional film compositing technique used to sharpen edges in an image. The Unsharp Mask filter corrects blurring introduced during photographing, scanning, resampling, or printing. It is useful for images intended for both print and online viewing.

The Unsharp Mask locates pixels that differ from surrounding pixels by the threshold you specify and increases the pixels' contrast by the amount you specify. In addition, you specify the radius of the region to which each pixel is compared.

The effects of the Unsharp Mask filter are far more pronounced on-screen than in high-resolution output. If your final destination is print, experiment to determine what dialog box settings work best for your image.

–From Adobe Photoshop 7.0 online Help

Saving the image for four-color printing

Before you save a Photoshop file for use in a four-color publication, you must change the image to CMYK color mode in order to print your publication correctly in four-color process inks. You'll use the Mode command to change the image color mode.

For more information on color modes, see "Converting between color modes" in Adobe Photoshop 7.0 online Help.

You can perform these tasks only in Photoshop. ImageReady does not have printing capability and uses only one color mode, RGB, for on-screen display.

1 Choose Image > Mode > CMYK Color.

• If you are using Adobe InDesign to create your publication, you can skip the rest of this process and just choose File > Save. InDesign can import native Photoshop files, so there is no need to convert the image to TIFF format.

• If you are using another layout application, you must save the photo as a TIFF file.

2 Choose File > Save As.

3 In the Save As dialog box, choose TIFF from the Format menu.

4 Click Save.

5 In the TIFF Options dialog box, select the correct Byte Order for your system and click OK.

The image is now fully retouched, saved, and ready for placement in the publication layout.

Review questions

1 What does resolution mean?

2 How can you use the crop tool in photo retouching?

3 How can you adjust the tonal range of an image?

4 What is saturation, and how can you adjust it?

5 Why would you use the Unsharp Mask filter on a photo?

Review answers

1 The term *resolution* refers to the number of pixels that describe an image and establish its detail. The three different types of resolution include *image resolution*, measured in pixels per inch (ppi); *monitor resolution*, measured in dots per inch (dpi); and *printer* or *output resolution*, measured in ink dots per inch.

2 You can use the crop tool to trim, scale, and straighten an image.

3 You can use the black, white, and gray triangles below the Levels command histogram to control the midpoint and where the darkest and lightest points in the image begin, thus extending its tonal range.

4 Saturation is the strength or purity of color in an image. You can increase the saturation in a specific area of an image with the sponge tool.

5 The Unsharp Mask filter adjusts the contrast of the edge detail and creates the illusion of a more focused image.

Lesson 4

4 Working with Selections

Learning how to select areas of an image is of primary importance—you must first select what you want to affect. Once you've made a selection, only the area within the selection can be edited. Areas outside the selection are protected from change.

In this lesson, you'll learn how to do the following:

- Select parts of an image using a variety of tools.
- Reposition a selection marquee.
- Deselect a selection.
- Move and duplicate a selection.
- Constrain the movement of a selection.
- Choose areas of an image based on proximity or color of pixels.
- Adjust a selection with the arrow keys.
- Add to and subtract from selections.
- Rotate a selection.
- Use multiple selection tools to make a complex selection.
- Crop an image.
- Erase within a selection.

This lesson will take about 30 minutes to complete. The lesson is designed to be done in Adobe Photoshop, but information on using similar functionality in Adobe ImageReady is included where appropriate.

If needed, remove the previous lesson folder from your hard drive, and copy the Lesson04 folder onto it. As you work on this lesson, you'll overwrite the start files. If you need to restore the start files, copy them from the *Adobe Photoshop 7.0 Classroom in a Book* CD.

Note: *Windows users need to unlock the lesson files before using them. For more information, see "Copying the Classroom in a Book files" on page 4.*

Getting started

Before beginning this lesson, restore the default application settings for Adobe Photoshop. See "Restoring default preferences" on page 5.

You'll start the lesson by viewing the finished lesson file to see the image that you'll create as you explore the selection tools in Photoshop.

1 Start Adobe Photoshop.

If a notice appears asking whether you want to customize your color settings, click No.

2 Choose File > Open, and open the 04End.psd file, located in the Lessons/Lesson04 folder on your hard drive.

The project is a collage of symbolic objects, including a writing journal, a pen, globes, a number, a flower, and a padlock. Your own placement of the objects can be subject to your personal sense of artistic composition and balance rather than in a prescribed arrangement that you must match exactly. There is no "right" or "wrong" placement here.

3 When you have finished viewing the file, either leave the 04End.psd file open for reference, or close it without saving changes.

Practicing making selections

In this section, you'll experiment with making selections before you begin working in earnest on your sample files. By working with the tools in a practice session, you'll understand better how the basic tools work and how to use them.

You'll also learn about selecting and moving as a two-step process. In Photoshop, you first select the part of an image you want to move with one of the selection tools. After you select it, you can then use another tool to move the selected pixels to another location.

Selection tools overview

In Adobe Photoshop, you can make selections based on size, shape, and color, using four basic sets of tools—the marquee, lasso, magic wand, and pen tools. You can also use the magic eraser tool to make selections in much the same way as you use the magic wand tool.

Note: *In this lesson, you will use only the marquee, lasso, magic wand, and move tools. You'll learn about the pen tools later in a chapter entirely devoted to them (Lesson 9, "Basic Pen Tool Techniques").*

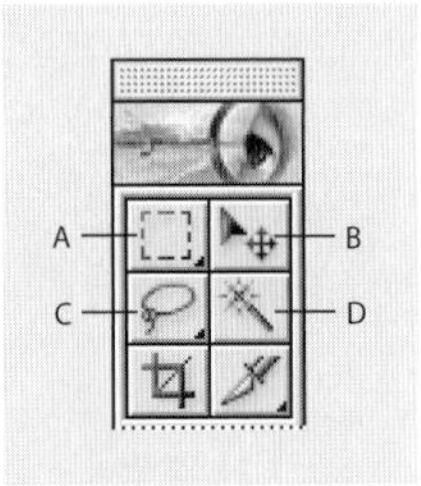

A. *Marquee tool*
B. *Move tool*
C. *Lasso tool*
D. *Magic wand tool*

The marquee and lasso tool icons are among those that contain hidden tools. You can select a hidden tool by holding down the mouse button on the displayed tool icon and then dragging to the desired tool in the pop-up menu.

To create a selection, you drag a selection tool around the area you want to select. The shape of the selection depends on the tool you use to create it.

Geometric selections You use the *rectangular marquee tool* (⬚) to select a rectangular area in an image. The *elliptical marquee tool* (◯) selects elliptical areas. The *single row marquee tool* (⋯) and *single column marquee tool* (⋮) let you select either a 1-pixel-high row or a 1-pixel-wide column.

***Note:** You can make another type of rectangular selection using the crop tool (⌗). You'll get a chance to use the crop tool later in this lesson.*

Freehand selections You can drag the *lasso tool* (ᑭ) around an area to make a freehand selection. Using the *polygonal lasso tool* (ᑭ), you can make a straight-line selection around an area. The *magnetic lasso tool* (ᑭ) in Photoshop works in a similar manner as the lasso tool, but your freehand border snaps to the edges of an area when you use the magnetic lasso tool.

Color-based selections The *magic wand tool* (✱) selects parts of an image based on the similarity in color of adjacent pixels. This tool is useful for selecting odd-shaped areas without having to trace a complex outline using the lasso tool.

ImageReady includes the basic marquee selection tools, the lasso and polygonal lasso tools, and the magic wand tool familiar to users of Photoshop. For more convenience in working with common shapes, ImageReady adds an extra marquee selection tool, the rounded-rectangle marquee tool (⬚).

Selecting and deselecting an area of an image

You'll start practicing selection techniques using the rectangular marquee tool.

1 Choose File > Open, and open the 04Start.psd file, located in the Lessons/Lesson04 folder on your hard drive.

2 In the toolbox, select the rectangular marquee tool (⬚), if it is not already selected.

3 Drag diagonally from the upper left corner to the lower right corner of the book to create a rectangular selection.

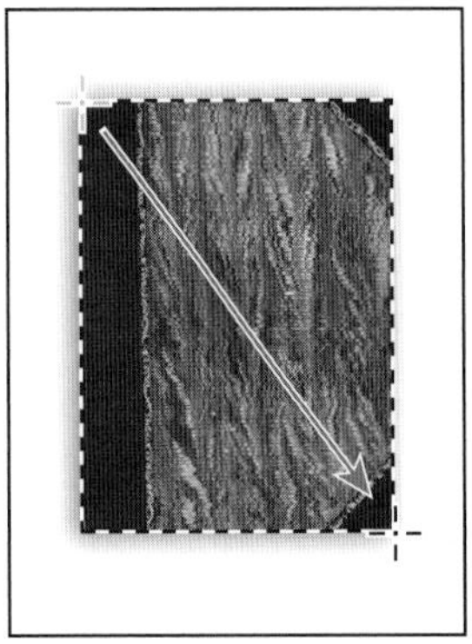

You can move a selection border after you've drawn it.

4 Position the pointer anywhere inside the selection. The pointer becomes an arrow with a small selection icon next to it (), but the pointer will change shape again when you start to drag.

5 Drag from the book to a different area of the image window. Notice that this technique changes the location of the selection border; it does not affect the size or shape of the selection. Also, it does not move any of the pixels—the image itself remains as it was.

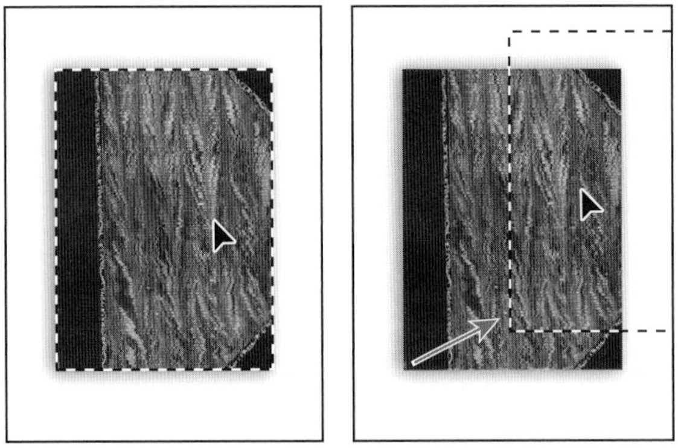

***Note:** Repositioning techniques for selection borders work with any of the marquee, lasso, and magic wand tools.*

6 Choose Edit > Deselect. Or, you can deselect by clicking another area in the window, outside the selection border.

To go back one step at any point in the lesson, choose Edit > Undo. In ImageReady, you can set the number of undos in the ImageReady preferences. (The default is 32.)

Repositioning a selection border while creating it

You saw in the previous topic that you can move a selection border after you release the mouse button, but that you cannot change the size or shape of the selection. In this procedure, you'll use the elliptical marquee tool to select the black oval and learn how to adjust the position of the selection border as you create it.

1 Select the zoom tool (), and click the black oval on the right side of the image window as needed to zoom in to at least 100% view (use 200% view if the entire oval will fit in the image window on your screen).

2 Select the elliptical marquee tool () hidden under the rectangular marquee tool.

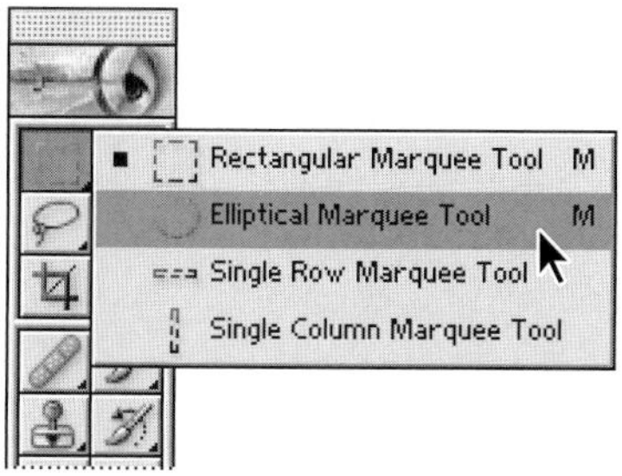

3 Move the pointer over the oval, and drag diagonally across the oval to create a selection, but do not release the mouse button. It's OK if your selection does not match the oval shape yet.

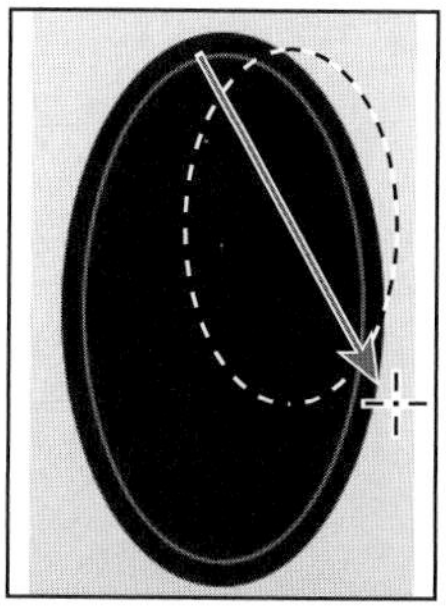

If you accidently release the mouse button, draw the selection again. In most cases—including this one—the new selection replaces the previous one.

4 Still holding down the mouse button, hold down the spacebar on your keyboard and drag the selection. The border moves as you drag.

5 Carefully release the spacebar (but not the mouse button), and continue to drag, trying to make the size and shape of the selection match the oval as closely as possible. If necessary, hold down the spacebar and drag to move the selection marquee into position around the black oval.

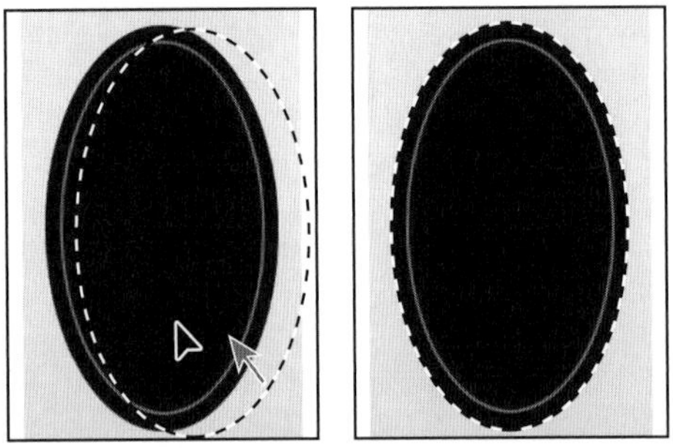

6 When the selection border is positioned and sized correctly, release the mouse button.

You won't be using this selection because you've just been practicing so far. However, you can either leave the oval selected for now or choose Select > Deselect to deselect it.

Moving selection contents

Now that you've had some experience with a couple of methods of making selections, you're ready to start using selections to make changes in your image. In the previous procedures, you made selections with various tools and used different keyboard combinations to help you make them, but you did not change the image.

One of the basic reasons for making a selection is to move the pixels located within that selection to another area of the image. In the following topics, you'll get plenty of practice doing just that. But first, you have to make a selection.

Selecting from a center point

Sometimes it's easier to make elliptical or rectangular selections by drawing a selection from the center point of the object to the outside edge. Using this method, you'll select the globe.

1 In the toolbox, select the zoom tool ( ).

2 Scroll to the globe in the lower left area of the image, and click the zoom tool to increase the magnification to about 300%. Make sure you can see the entire globe in your image window.

3 In the toolbox, select the elliptical marquee tool ( ).

4 Move the pointer to the approximate center of the globe. You can use the pivot points holding the globe and line of the equator as visual guides to help you locate the center.

5 Click and begin dragging. Then without releasing the mouse button, hold down Alt (Windows) or Option (Mac OS) and continue dragging the selection to the outer edge of the globe.

Notice that the selection is centered over its starting point.

To ensure that your ellipse is a perfect circle, you can also hold down Shift as you drag. If you held down Shift while using the rectangular marquee tool, you'd constrain the marquee shape to a perfect square.

6 When you have the entire globe selected, release the mouse button first and then release Alt or Option (and the Shift key, if you used it, too). Do not deselect, because you'll use this selection in the next topic.

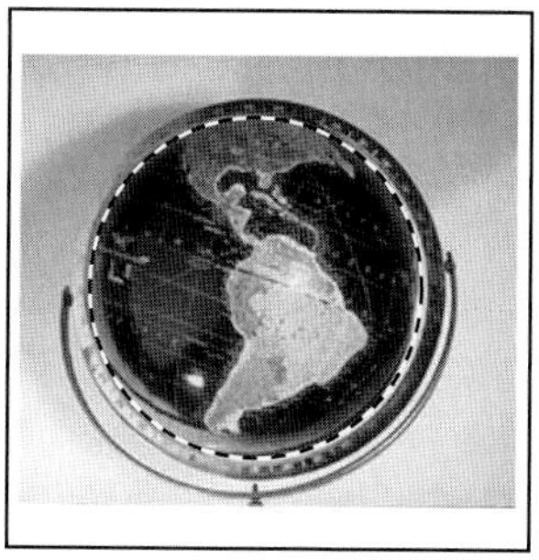

If necessary, adjust the selection border using one of the methods you learned earlier. If you accidentally released the Alt or Option key before you release the mouse button, try selecting the globe again.

Moving and changing the pixels in a selection

Now you'll use the move tool to move the globe to the upper right area of the book image. Then you'll do a completely different kind of change by altering the color of the globe for a dramatic effect.

Before you begin, make sure that the globe is still selected. If it is not, reselect it, following the procedure in the previous topic.

1 Choose View > Fit on Screen to adjust the magnification so that the entire image fits within the image window.

2 In the toolbox, select the move tool (). Notice that the globe remains selected.

3 Position the pointer within the globe selection. The pointer becomes an arrow with a pair of scissors () to indicate that dragging the selection will cut it from its present location and move it to the new location.

4 Drag the globe above the book image, somewhat close to the right edge. If you want to adjust the position after you stop dragging, simple start dragging again. The globe remains selected throughout the process.

5 Choose Image > Adjustments > Invert.

The colors making up the globe are inverted, so that it is now effectively a color negative of the original.

6 Leaving the globe selected, choose File > Save to save your work.

Moving and duplicating simultaneously

Next you'll move and duplicate a selection simultaneously. If your globe image is no longer selected, reselect it now, using the techniques you learned earlier.

1 Using the move tool (▸✥), hold down Alt (Windows) or Option (Mac OS), and position the pointer within the globe selection. The pointer becomes a double arrow, which indicates that a duplicate will be made when you move the selection.

2 Continue holding down Alt or Option, and drag a duplicate of the globe down and to the right, so that it is near the upper right corner of the book image. You can allow the duplicate globe to partially overlap the original one. Release the mouse button and Alt or Option, but do not deselect the duplicate globe.

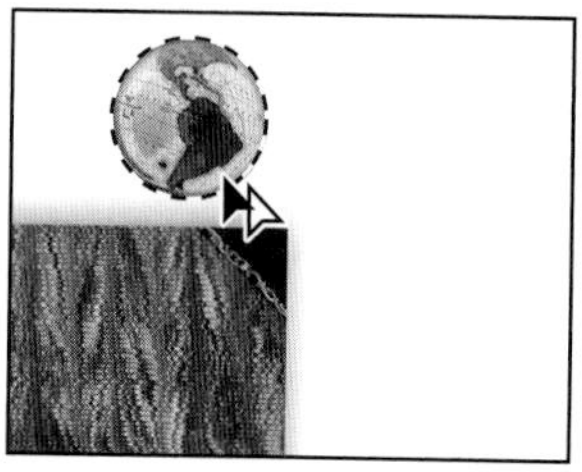

3 Choose Edit > Transform > Scale to activate a bounding box around the selection.

4 Hold down Shift and drag one of the corner points to enlarge the globe so that it is larger than the original by about half. Then press Enter to commit the transformation and hide the bounding box.

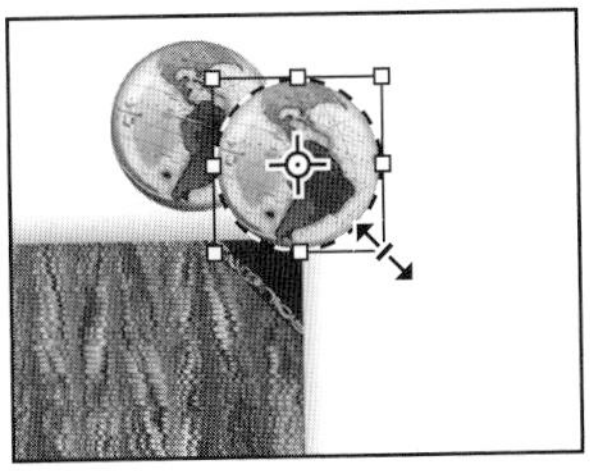

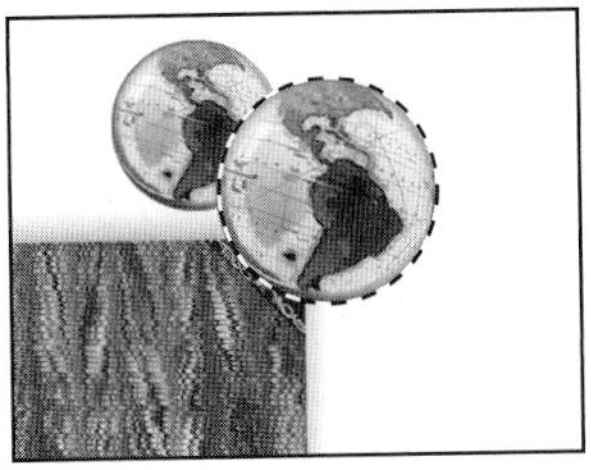

Notice that the selection marquee also resizes and that the resized, copied globe remains selected.

5 Hold down Shift+Alt (Windows) or Shift+Option (Mac OS), and drag a new copy of the second globe down and to the right.

Holding down Shift when you move a selection constrains the movement horizontally or vertically in 45° increments.

6 Repeat steps 3 and 4 for the third globe, making it about twice the size of the first one.

7 When you are satisfied with the size and position of the third globe, choose Select > Deselect, and then choose File > Save.

Moving with a keyboard shortcut

Next you'll select the black oval and then move it onto the book using a keyboard shortcut. The shortcut enables you to temporarily access the move tool instead of selecting it from the toolbox.

1 Select the elliptical marquee tool (◌).

2 Drag a selection around the black oval using the techniques you learned earlier. (To review those steps, see "Repositioning a selection border while creating it" on page 107.)

***Note:** You do not have to include absolutely all of the black oval, but make sure that the shape of your selection has the same proportions as the oval and that the thin yellow line is contained symmetrically within the selection. As long as the selection marquee is between the yellow line and the outer edge, you're fine.*

3 With the elliptical marquee tool selected, hold down Ctrl (Windows) or Command (Mac OS), and move the pointer within the selection. A pair of scissors appears with the pointer to indicate that the selection will be cut from its current location.

4 Drag the oval onto the book so that it is only roughly centered. (You'll use another technique to nudge the oval into the exact position wanted.) Do not deselect.

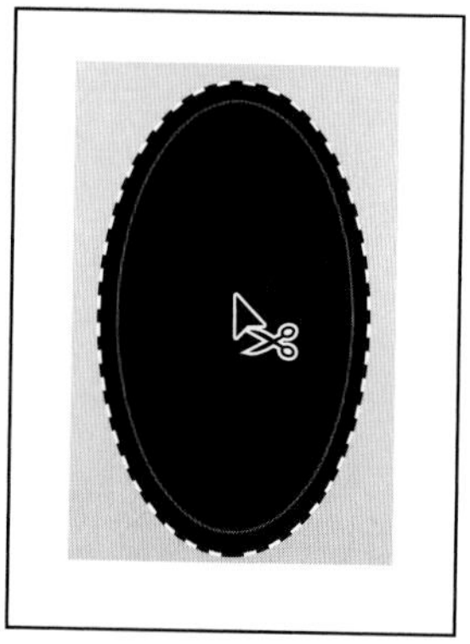

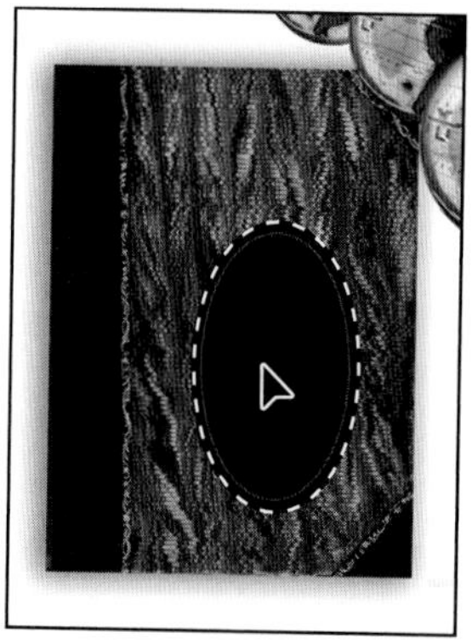

Moving with the arrow keys

You can make minor adjustments to the position of selected pixels, using the arrow keys to nudge the oval in increments of either 1 pixel or 10 pixels.

When your selection tool is active in the toolbox, the arrow keys nudge the selection border, but not the contents. When the move tool is active, the arrow keys move the selection border and its contents.

Before you begin, make sure that the black oval shape is still selected in the image window.

1 In the toolbox, select the move tool (▶✥) and press the Up Arrow key (↑) on your keyboard a few times to move the oval upward.

Notice that each time you press the arrow key, the oval moves in 1-pixel increments. Experiment by pressing the other arrow keys to see how they affect the selection.

2 Hold down Shift, and press an arrow key.

Notice that the selection now moves in 10-pixel increments.

Sometimes the border around a selected area can distract you as you make adjustments. You can hide the edges of a selection temporarily without actually deselecting and then display the selection border once you've completed the adjustments.

3 Choose View > Show > Selection Edges or View > Extras.

The selection border around the oval disappears.

4 Use the arrow keys to nudge the oval until it is positioned where you want it. Then choose View > Show > Selection Edges or View > Extras.

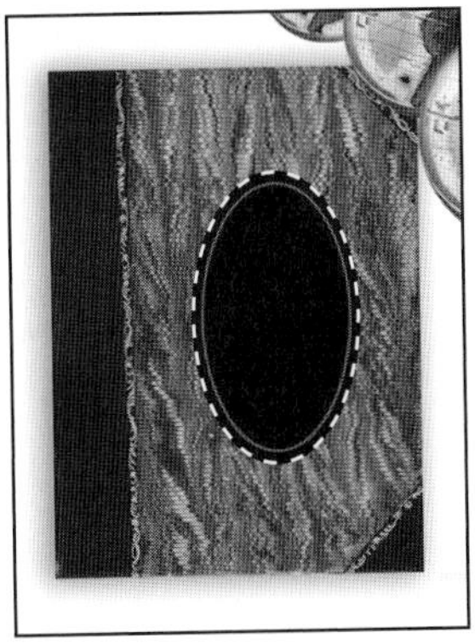

5 Choose File > Save.

Copying selections or layers

You can use the move tool to copy selections as you drag them within or between images, or you can copy and move selections using the Copy, Copy Merged, Cut, and Paste commands. Dragging with the move tool saves memory because the Clipboard is not used as it is with the Copy, Copy Merged, Cut, and Paste commands.

Photoshop and ImageReady contain several copy and paste commands:

- *The Copy command copies the selected area on the active layer.*
- *The Copy Merged command makes a merged copy of all the visible layers in the selected area.*
- *The Paste command pastes a cut or copied selection into another part of the image or into another image as a new layer.*
- *(Photoshop) The Paste Into command pastes a cut or copied selection inside another selection in the same image or different image. The source selection is pasted onto a new layer, and the destination selection border is converted into a layer mask.*

Keep in mind that when a selection or layer is pasted between images with different resolutions, the pasted data retains its pixel dimensions. This can make the pasted portion appear out of proportion to the new image. Use the Image Size command to make the source and destination images the same resolution before copying and pasting.

–From Adobe Photoshop 7.0 online Help

Selecting with the magic wand tool

The magic wand tool selects adjacent pixels in an image based on their similarity in color. You'll use the magic wand tool to select the large number "5."

1 Select the magic wand tool ( ).

The tool options bar contains settings you can change to alter the way a tool works. In the tool options bar for the magic wand tool, the Tolerance setting controls how many similar tones of a color are selected when you click an area. The default value is 32, indicating that 32 similar lighter tones and 32 similar darker tones will be selected.

2 In the tool options bar, enter **70** in the Tolerance text box to increase the number of similar tones that will be selected.

3 Using the magic wand tool, click what looks like the surface of the large number "5" image. Most of it will be selected.

4 To select the remaining area of the number "5," hold down Shift, so that a plus sign appears with the magic wand pointer, indicating that whatever you click will be added to the current selection. Then click one of the unselected areas of the blue number "5."

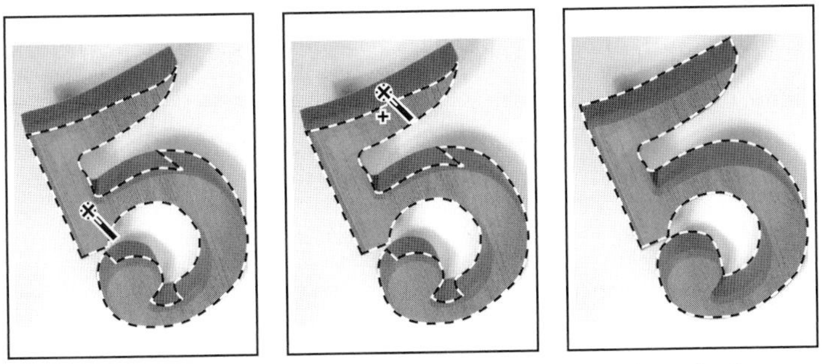

Initial selection *Adding to selection (Shift key depressed)* *Complete selection*

***Note:** When you use other selection tools, such as a marquee tool or lasso tool, you can also use the Shift key to add to a selection. Later in this lesson, you'll learn how to subtract from a selection.*

5 Continue adding to the selection until all the blue areas are selected. If you accidentally select an area outside the blue number, choose Edit > Undo, and try again.

6 With all of the "5" selected, hold down Ctrl (Windows) or Command (Mac OS) and drag the number to the area to the upper left of the book image.

7 Choose Select > Deselect.

8 Choose File > Save.

Selecting with the lasso tool

You can use the lasso tool to make selections that require both freehand and straight lines. You'll select the fountain pen for the collage using the lasso tool this way. It takes a bit of practice to use the lasso tool to alternate between straight-line and freehand selections—if you make a mistake while you're selecting the fountain pen, simply deselect and start again.

1 Select the zoom tool (🔍), and click the fountain pen image as needed until the view enlarges to 100%. Make sure that you can see the entire pen image in the window.

2 Select the lasso tool (lasso icon). Starting at the lower left of the image, drag around the rounded end of the fountain pen, tracing the shape as accurately as possible. Do not release the mouse button.

3 Hold down Alt (Windows) or Option (Mac OS) and then release the mouse button so that the lasso pointer changes to the polygonal lasso shape (polygonal lasso icon).

4 Begin clicking along the top side of the cap and barrel of the pen to place anchor points, using long or short lines as needed to match the contours of the fountain pen. Be sure to keep the Alt or Option key held down throughout this process.

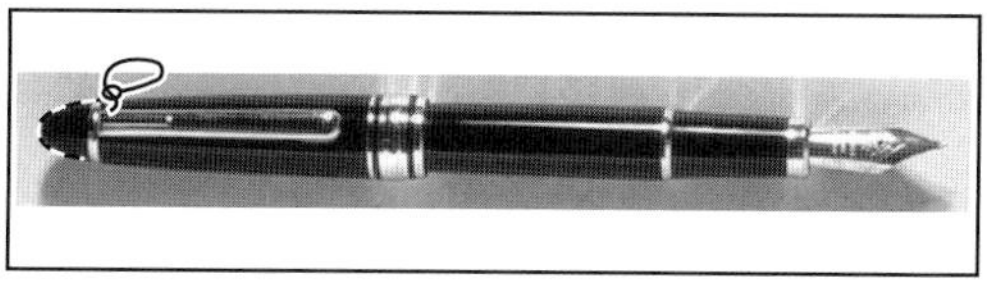

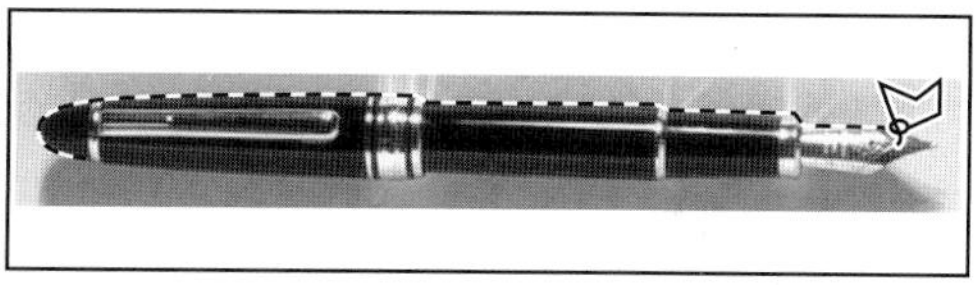

5 When you reach the curved edge of the nib, keep the mouse button held down and then release the Alt or Option key. The pointer again appears as the lasso icon.

6 Carefully drag around the nib of the pen, keeping the mouse button down.

7 When you finish tracing the nib and reach the lower side of the barrel, first hold down Alt or Option again, and then release the mouse button and start clicking along the lower side of the pen. Continue to trace the pen until you arrive back at the starting point of your selection near the left end of the image.

8 Make sure that the last straight line crosses the start of the selection, release Alt or Option, and then release the mouse button. The pen is now entirely selected. Go on to the next procedure without deselecting the fountain pen.

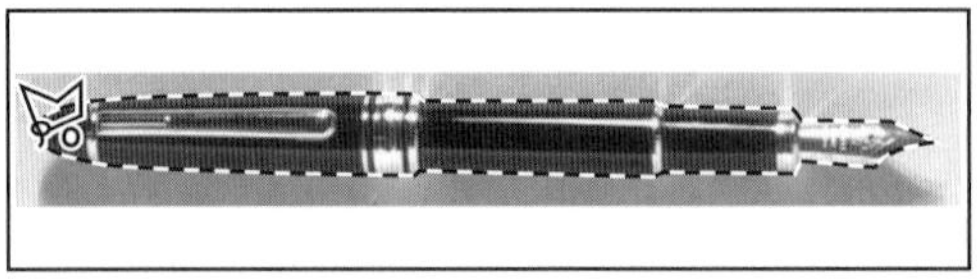

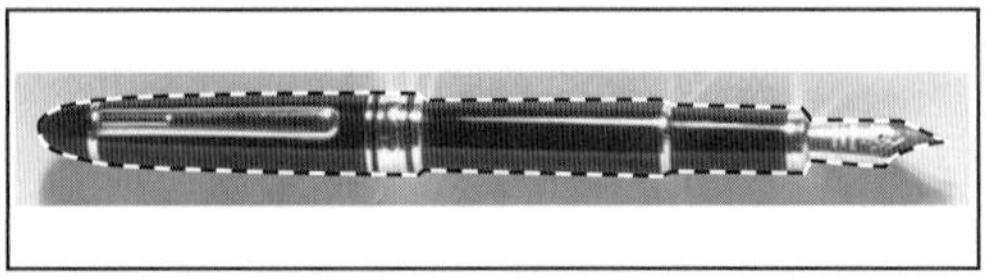

Transforming a selection

So far you've moved selected images and inverted the color of a selected area. But there are many more things you can do with a selection. In the following steps, you'll see how easy it is to rotate a selected object.

Before you begin, make sure the fountain pen is selected.

1 Choose View > Fit on Screen to resize the document to fit on your screen.

2 Hold down Ctrl (Windows) or Command (Mac OS), and drag the fountain-pen selection to the area just below the book and off center to the left of the book.

3 Choose Edit > Transform > Rotate. The pen and selection marquee are enclosed in a bounding box and the pointer appears as a double-headed arrow (↰).

4 Move the pointer outside the bounding box and drag to rotate the pen to a jaunty angle. Then press Enter to commit the transformation.

5 If necessary, select the move tool (▸✥) and drag to change the position of the pen. When you are sure that you're satisfied with the pen position, choose Select > Deselect.

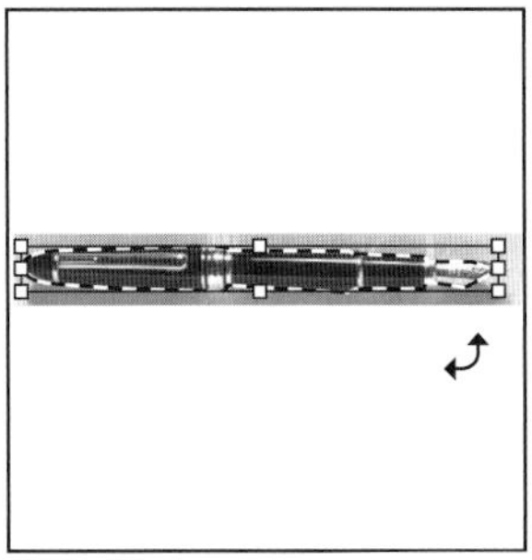

6 Choose File > Save.

Selecting with the magnetic lasso

You can use the magnetic lasso tool in Photoshop to make freehand selections of areas with high-contrast edges. When you draw with the magnetic lasso, the border automatically snaps to the edge you are tracing. You can also control the direction of the tool's path by clicking the mouse to place occasional fastening points in the selection border. (There is no magnetic lasso tool in ImageReady.)

You'll now move the padlock to the center of the black oval you placed on the book cover earlier in this lesson, using the magnetic lasso to select the padlock.

1 Select the zoom tool (🔍), and click the padlock to zoom in to a 300% view.

2 Select the magnetic lasso tool ( ) hidden under the lasso tool ( ).

3 Click once along the left edge of the padlock, and begin tracing the outline of the padlock by moving the magnetic lasso pointer around the outline of the padlock, staying fairly close to the edge of the padlock as you move.

Even though you're not holding down the mouse button, the tool snaps to the edge and automatically adds fastening points.

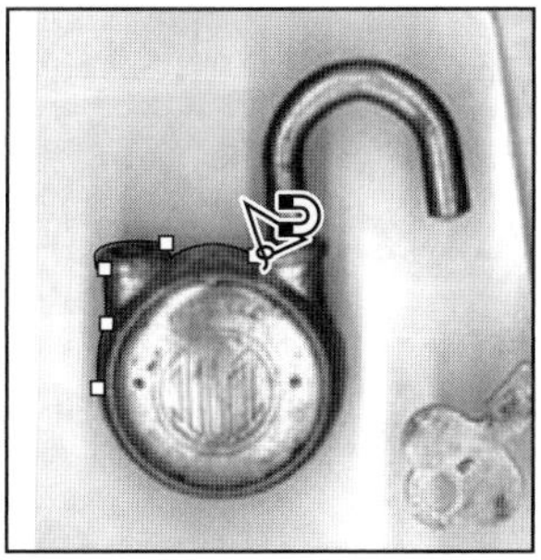

If you think the tool is not following the edge closely enough (such as in low-contrast areas), you can place your own fastening points in the border by clicking the mouse button. You can add as many fastening points as you feel are necessary. You can also remove fastening points and back up in the path by pressing Delete and then moving the mouse back to the last remaining fastening point.

4 When you reach the left side of the padlock again, double-click the mouse button to make the magnetic lasso tool return to the starting point, closing the selection.

5 Double-click the hand tool () to fit the image on-screen.

6 Select the move tool (), and drag the padlock to the middle of the black oval in the center of the notebook.

7 Choose Select > Deselect, and then choose File > Save.

Softening the edges of a selection

You can smooth the hard edges of a selection by anti-aliasing and by feathering.

Anti-aliasing *Smooths the jagged edges of a selection by softening the color transition between edge pixels and background pixels. Since only the edge pixels change, no detail is lost. Anti-aliasing is useful when cutting, copying, and pasting selections to create composite images.*

Anti-aliasing is available for the lasso, polygonal lasso, magnetic lasso, rounded rectangle marquee (ImageReady), elliptical marquee, and magic wand tools. (Select the tool to display its tool options bar.) You must specify the anti-aliasing option before using these tools. Once a selection is made, you cannot add anti-aliasing.

Feathering *Blurs edges by building a transition boundary between the selection and its surrounding pixels. This blurring can cause some loss of detail at the edge of the selection.*

You can define feathering for the marquee, lasso, polygonal lasso, or magnetic lasso tool as you use the tool, or you can add feathering to an existing selection. Feathering effects become apparent when you move, cut, or copy the selection.

- *To use anti-aliasing, select the lasso, polygonal lasso, magnetic lasso, rounded rectangle marquee (ImageReady), elliptical marquee, or magic wand tool. Select Anti-aliased in the options bar.*
- *To define a feathered edge for a selection tool, select any of the lasso or marquee tools. Enter a Feather value in the options bar. This value defines the width of the feathered edge and can range from 1 to 250 pixels.*
- *To define a feathered edge for an existing selection, choose Select > Feather. Enter a value for the Feather Radius, and click OK.*

–From Adobe Photoshop 7.0 online Help

For information on working with the center point in a transformation, see "Transforming objects in two dimensions" in Adobe Photoshop 7.0 online Help.

Combining selection tools

As you already know, the magic wand tool makes selections based on color. If an object you want to select is set against a differently colored background, it can be much easier to select the object and the background and then use the magic wand tool to subtract the background color, leaving the desired object selected.

You'll see how this works by using the rectangular marquee tool and the magic wand tool to select the water lily.

1 Select the rectangular marquee tool ( ) hidden under the elliptical marquee tool ( ).

2 Drag a selection around the water lily. Make sure your selection includes a margin of white background between the tips of the petals and the sides of the marquee.

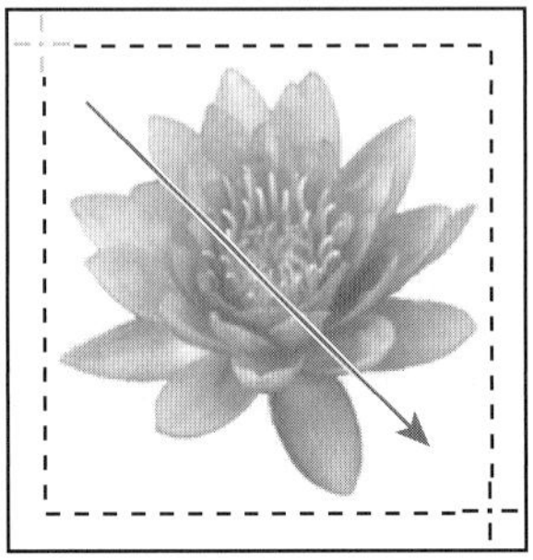

At this point, the water lily and the white background area are selected. You'll subtract the white area from the selection, resulting in only the water lily in the selection.

3 Select the magic wand tool; then in the tool options bar, set the Tolerance to **32**.

Note: *If you left the Tolerance at 70, the magic wand tool would remove some of the light pink and light gray outer petals of the water lily, because those shades would be close enough to the selection color (white) to be included in the range of pixels it removes.*

4 Hold down Alt (Windows) or Option (Mac OS). A minus sign appears with the magic wand pointer.

5 Click anywhere in the selected white area surrounding the water lily. Now all the white pixels are deselected, leaving the water lily perfectly selected.

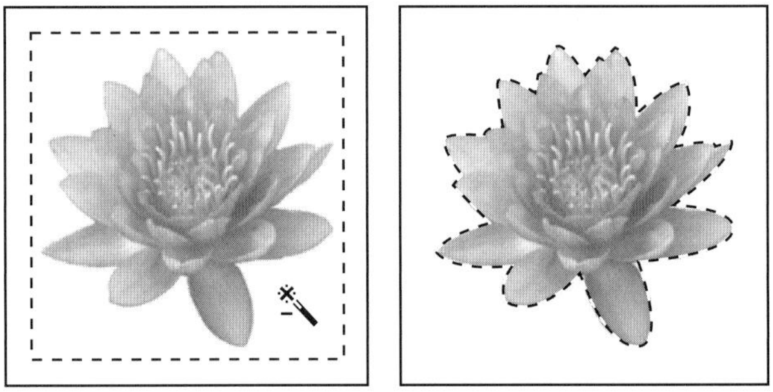

6 Hold down Ctrl (Windows) or Command (Mac OS) and drag the water lily to the lower right side of the book.

7 Choose Select > Deselect, and then save your work.

Cropping an image and erasing within a selection

To complete the artwork, you'll crop the image to a final size and clean up some of the background scraps left behind when you moved selections. In both Photoshop and ImageReady, you can use either the crop tool or the Crop command to crop an image.

In ImageReady, use the Crop command or the crop tool set to Hide when creating animated elements that move from off-screen into the live image area.

1 Select the crop tool (), or press C to switch from the current tool to the crop tool.

2 Move the pointer into the image window, and drag diagonally from the upper left corner to the lower right corner of the completed artwork to create a crop marquee.

After you finish dragging in Photoshop, look on the tool options bar and make sure that the Perspective check box is *not* selected.

3 Adjust the crop marquee, as necessary:

- If you need to reposition the crop marquee, position the pointer anywhere inside the marquee and drag.
- If you want to resize the marquee, drag a handle.

4 When the marquee is positioned where you want it, press Enter (Windows) or Return (Mac OS) to crop the image.

The cropped image may include some scraps of the gray background from which you selected and removed shapes. You'll fix that next.

5 Drag a selection marquee around an area that has some of the unwanted gray background, being careful not to include any of the art work that you want to keep inside the selection.

6 In the toolbox, select the eraser tool (), and then make sure that the foreground and background colors are set to the defaults: black in the foreground and white in the background.

7 Drag the eraser over the gray in the selection area.

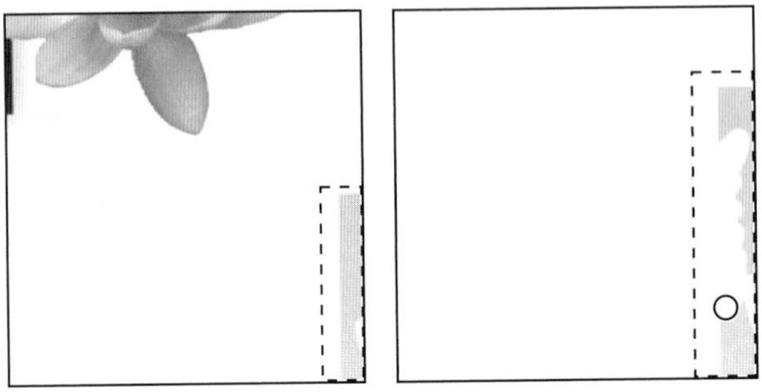

To erase in large strokes, select a larger brush size in the tool options bar. Because all the unselected areas of the image is protected, there is no risk of accidentally erasing parts of the image that are outside the selection.

Notice that if you accidentally go outside the selection, nothing is erased. Only pixels within the selection are replaced with white as you erase; the rest of the image is protected. Next, you'll use a different technique to remove unwanted pixels.

8 Select another area with only unwanted pixels, and then press Delete.

Continue selecting and erasing or deleting until you finish removing all the unwanted scraps of background.

9 Choose File > Save.

The collage is complete.

Review questions

1 Once you've made a selection, what area of the image can be edited?

2 How do you add to and subtract from a selection?

3 How can you move a selection while you're drawing it?

4 When drawing a selection with the lasso tool, how should you finish drawing the selection to ensure that the selection is the shape you want?

5 How does the magic wand tool determine which areas of an image to select? What is tolerance, and how does it affect a selection?

Review answers

1 Only the area within the selection can be edited.

2 To add to a selection, hold down Shift, and then drag or click the active selection tool on the area you want to add to the selection. To subtract from a selection, hold down Alt (Windows) or Option (Mac OS), and then drag or click the active selection tool on the area you want to remove from the selection.

3 Without releasing the mouse button, hold down the spacebar, and drag to reposition the selection.

4 To make sure that the selection is the shape you want, end the selection by dragging across the starting point of the selection. If you start and stop the selection at different points, Photoshop or ImageReady draws a straight line between the start point of the selection and the end point of the selection.

5 The magic wand selects adjacent pixels based on their similarity in color. The Tolerance setting determines how many color tones the magic wand will select. The higher the tolerance setting, the more tones the magic wand selects.

Lesson 5

PROFESS
67mm

5 Layer Basics

Both Adobe Photoshop and Adobe ImageReady let you isolate different parts of an image on layers. Each layer can then be edited as discrete artwork, allowing unlimited flexibility in composing and revising an image.

In this lesson, you'll learn how to do the following:

- Organize artwork on layers.
- Create new layers.
- View and hide layers.
- Select layers.
- Remove artwork from layers.
- Rearrange layers to change the stacking order of artwork in the image.
- Apply blending modes to layers.
- Link layers to work on them simultaneously.
- Apply a gradient to a layer.
- Add text and layer effects to a layer.
- Save a copy of the file with the layers flattened.

This lesson will take about 45 minutes to complete. The lesson is designed to be done in Adobe Photoshop, but information on using similar functionality in Adobe ImageReady is included where appropriate.

If needed, remove the previous lesson folder from your hard drive, and copy the Lesson05 folder onto it. As you work on this lesson, you'll overwrite the start files. If you need to restore the start files, copy them from the *Adobe Photoshop 7.0 Classroom in a Book* CD.

Note: *Windows users need to unlock the lesson files before using them. For more information, see "Copying the Classroom in a Book files" on page 4.*

Getting started

Before beginning this lesson, restore the default application settings for Adobe Photoshop. See "Restoring default preferences" on page 5.

You'll start the lesson by viewing the final lesson file to see what you'll accomplish.

1 Start Adobe Photoshop.

If a notice appears asking whether you want to customize your color settings, click No.

2 Choose File > Open, and open the 05End.psd file from the Lessons/Lesson05 folder.

3 When you have finished viewing the file, either leave it open for reference or close it without saving changes.

About layers

Every Photoshop file contains one or more *layers*. New files are generally created with a *background layer*, which contains a color or an image that shows through the transparent areas of subsequent layers. You can view and manipulate layers with the Layers palette.

All new layers in an image are transparent until you add artwork (pixel values).

Working with layers is analogous to placing portions of a drawing on sheets of acetate: Individual sheets of acetate may be edited, repositioned, and deleted without affecting the other sheets. When the sheets are stacked, the entire drawing is visible.

Viewing information in the Layers palette

Now you'll open the start file and begin the lesson by working with the image as you learn about the Layers palette and layer options.

The Layers palette displays all layers with the layer names and thumbnails of the images on each layer. You can use the Layers palette to hide, view, reposition, delete, rename, and merge layers. The thumbnails are automatically updated as you edit the layers.

1 Choose File > Open, and open the file 05Start.psd from the Lessons/Lesson05 folder on your hard drive.

2 If the Layers palette does not already appear in the work area, choose Window > Layers.

There are three items listed in the Layers palette: first Statue, then Doorway, and finally Background. The Background layer is highlighted, indicating that it is the active layer. There are three icons on the Background layer: a lock icon (🔒) on the right side of the layer listing, an eye icon (👁), and a paintbrush icon (🖌). None of these appear on the other two layers.

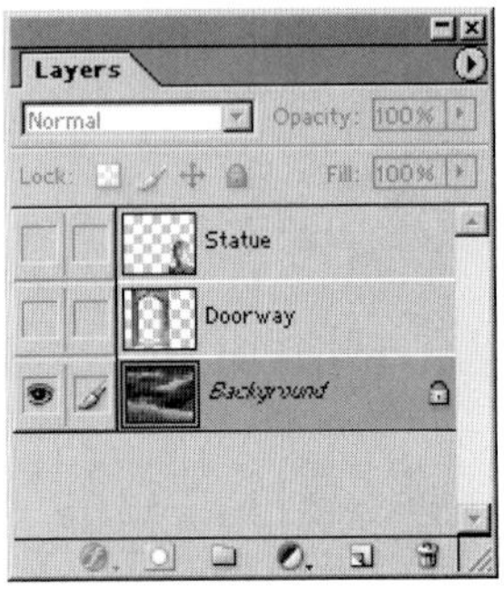

3 Choose File > Open, and open the Door.psd file in the Lesson05 folder.

The Layers palette changes, now displaying the layers for the Door.psd file because it is the active image window. There is only one layer in the Door.psd image: Layer 1.

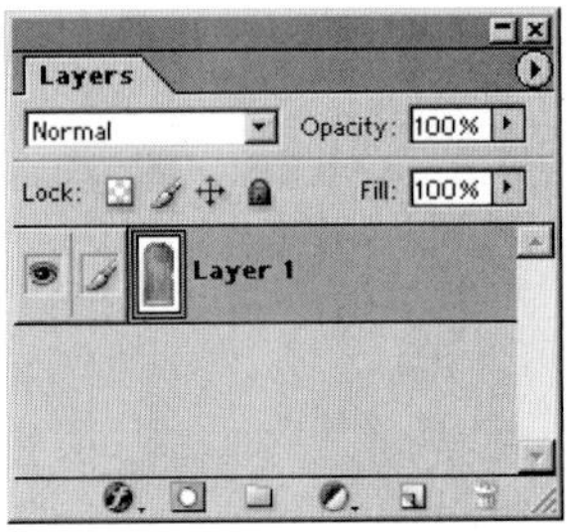

About the background layer

When you create a new image with a white background or a colored background, the bottommost image in the Layers palette is named Background. An image can have only one background. You cannot change the stacking order of a background, its blending mode, or its opacity. However, you can convert a background to a regular layer.

When you create a new image with transparent content, the image does not have a background layer. The bottommost layer is not constrained like the background layer; you can move it anywhere in the Layers palette, and change its opacity and blending mode.

To convert a background into a layer:

1. *Double-click Background in the Layers palette, or choose Layer > New > Layer From Background.*

2. *Set layer options as desired.*

3. *Click OK.*

To convert a layer into a background:

1. *Select a layer in the Layers palette.*

2. *Choose Layer > New > Background From Layer.*

Note: *You cannot create a background by renaming a regular layer Background—you must use the Background From Layer command*

–From Adobe Photoshop 7.0 online Help

Renaming a layer and copying it from one file to another

Creating a new layer can be as simple as dragging an image from one file into another file. Before you begin, make sure that both the 05Start.psd and Door.psd files are open.

First, you will rename Layer 1 with a more descriptive name.

1 In the Layers palette, double-click the name *Layer 1*, and type **Door**.

2 If necessary, drag the Door.psd and 05Start.psd image windows so that you can see at least part of both images. Then select the Door.psd image so that it is the active file.

3 In the toolbox, select the move tool (⊕) and move it anywhere within the Door.psd image window.

4 Drag from the Door.psd file to the 05Start.psd file. As you drag into the 05Start.psd file, the pointer changes, appearing as a hollow arrow with a plus sign inside a small square.

(If you hold down Shift when you drag an image from one file into another, the dragged image automatically centers itself in the target image window.)

When you release the mouse button, the image of the door appears in the garden image of the 05Start.psd file.

5 Close the Door.psd file, and do not save your changes.

In the Layers palette, notice that the door now appears on its own layer, and has the same name it had in the original file, Door.

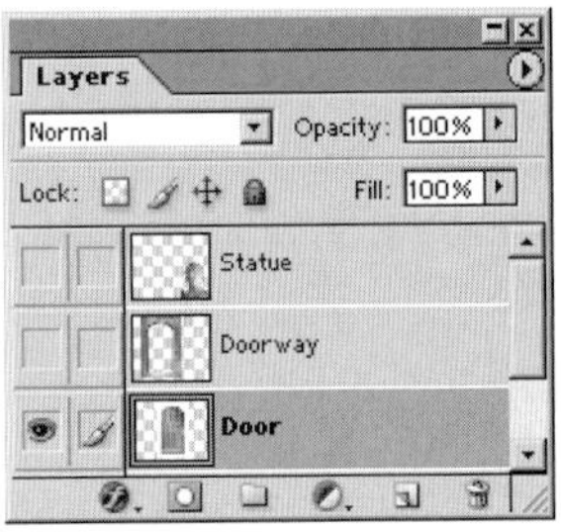

***Note:** If you want to expand the Layers palette, click the minimize/maximize box (Windows) or the resize box (Mac OS) at the top of the palette or drag down from the lower right corner.*

Dragging from the image window of one file into another file moves only the active layer. You can also drag a layer from the Layers palette of one file into the image window of another file.

Viewing individual layers

The Layers palette shows that the file contains three layers in addition to the Door layer, some of which are visible and some of which are hidden. The eye icon (👁) to the far left of a layer name in the palette indicates that that layer is visible. You can hide or show a layer by clicking this icon.

1 Click the eye icon next to the Door layer to hide the door.

2 Click again to redisplay it.

Leave the other layers at their original settings, whether hidden or shown.

Selecting and removing some pixels from a layer

Notice that when you moved the door image onto the garden image in the start file, you also moved the white area surrounding the door. This opaque area blocks out part of the garden image, since the door layer sits on top of the garden background layer.

Now you'll use an eraser tool to remove the white area around the door.

1 Make sure that the Door layer is selected. (To select the layer, click the layer name in the Layers palette.)

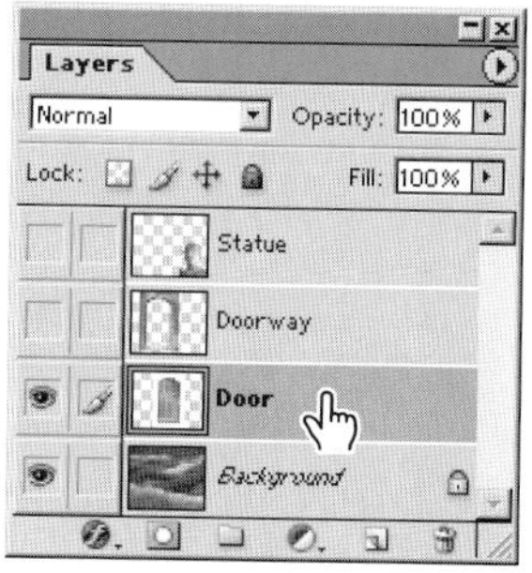

The layer is highlighted, and a paintbrush icon (🖌) appears to the left of the layer name, indicating that the layer is active.

2 To make the opaque areas on this layer more obvious, hide the garden by clicking the eye icon (👁) to the left of the Background layer name.

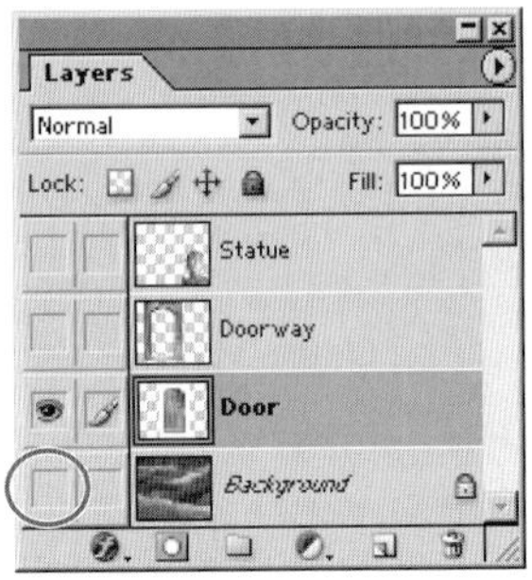

The garden image disappears, and the door appears against a checkerboard backdrop. The checkerboard indicates transparent areas of the active layer.

3 Select the magic eraser tool, hidden under the eraser tool.

You can set the tolerance for the magic eraser tool. If the tolerance is too low, the magic eraser tool leaves some white remaining around the door. If the tolerance setting is too high, the magic eraser tool removes some of the door image.

4 In the tool options bar, enter different values for Tolerance (we used **22**), and then click the white area surrounding the door.

Notice that the checkerboard fills in where the white area had been, indicating that this area is now transparent also.

5 Turn the background back on by clicking the eye icon box next to its name. The garden image now shows through where the white area on the Door layer was removed.

Rearranging layers

The order in which the layers of an image are organized is called the *stacking order.* The stacking order of layers determines how the image is viewed—you can change the order to make certain parts of the image appear in front of or behind other layers.

Now you'll rearrange layers so that the door image moves in front of another image in the file that is currently hidden.

1 Make the Statue and Doorway layers visible by clicking the eye icon boxes next to their layer names.

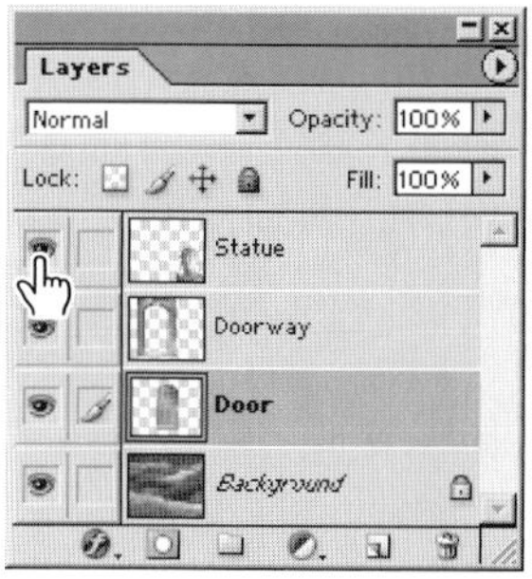

Notice that the door image is partly blocked by the image of the brick doorway.

2 In the Layers palette, drag the Door layer up above the Doorway layer—look for a wider white line between the Doorway layer and the Statue layer—and then release the mouse button.

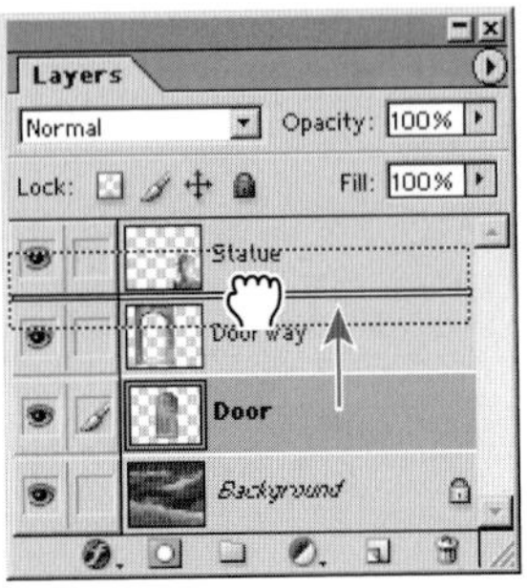

The Door layer moves up one level in the stacking order, and the door image appears in front of the doorway image.

Changing the opacity and mode of a layer

The door image now blocks any images that lie on layers below it. You can reduce the opacity of the door layer, which allows other layers to show through it. You can also apply different *blending modes* to the layer, which affect how the color pixels in the door image blend with pixels in the layers below them. (Currently, the blending mode is Normal.)

1 With the Door layer selected, click the arrow next to the Opacity text box in the Layers palette, and drag the slider to **50%**.

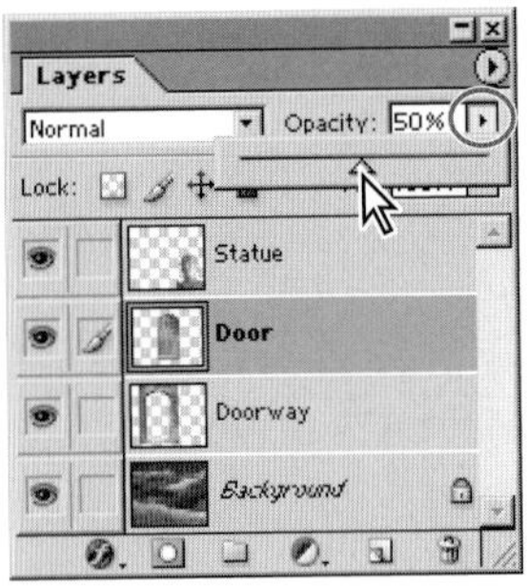

The door becomes partially transparent, and you can see the layers underneath. Notice that the change in opacity affects only the image area of the Door layer. The statue and doorway images remain completely opaque.

2 To the left of the Opacity option in the Layers palette, open the blending modes pop-up menu, and select Luminosity.

3 Readjust the Opacity value, changing it to **90%**.

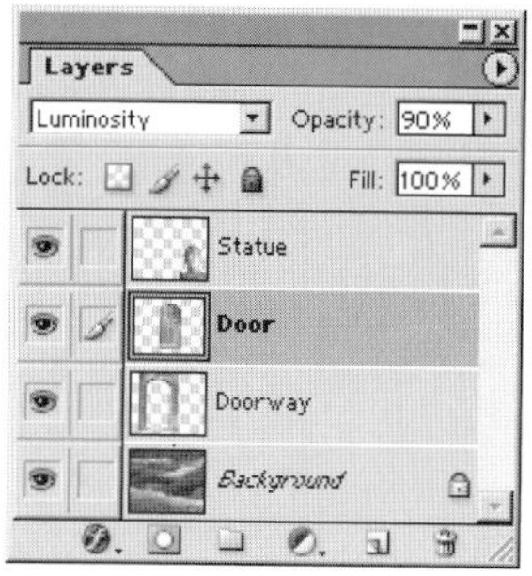

4 Choose File > Save to save your work.

For more information on blending modes, see “Blending an image with the background” on page 220.

Linking layers

An efficient way to work with some layers is to link two or more of them together. By linking layers, you can move and transform them simultaneously, thereby maintaining their alignment with each other.

You’ll now link the Door and Doorway layers, and then move and scale them as a unit.

1 Select the move tool ( ), and drag the door to the left so that the left edge of the door aligns with the right side of the doorway arch.

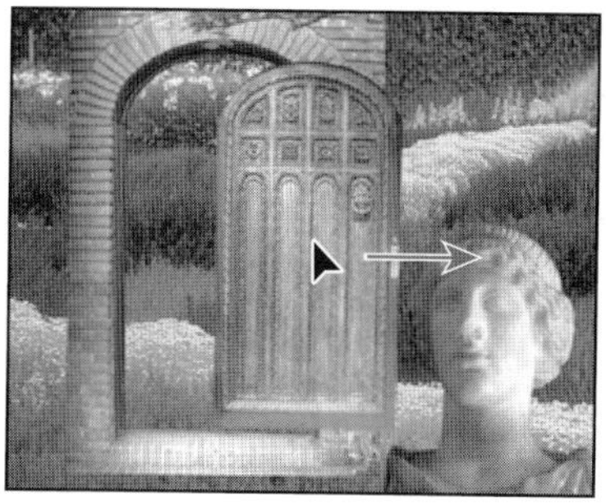

2 With the Door layer active in the Layers palette, click the small box between the Doorway (not *Door*) layer name and the eye icon for the Doorway layer.

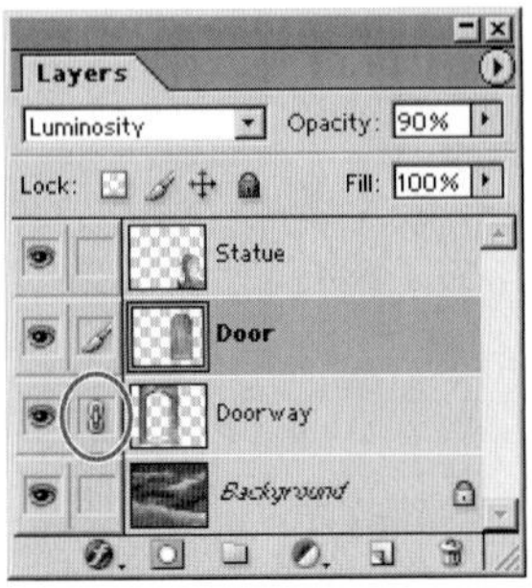

A link icon (🔗) appears in the box, indicating that the Doorway layer is linked to the Door layer. (The active or selected layer does not display a link icon when you create linked layers.)

3 Still using the move tool, drag the doorway to the left side of the image window so that the bricks touch the left margin of the image. The door and doorway images move together.

Now you'll scale the linked layers simultaneously.

4 With the Doorway layer selected in the Layers palette, choose Edit > Free Transform. A transformation bounding box appears around the images in the linked layers.

5 Hold down Shift and drag the one of the corner handles on the right side of the bounding box to scale the door and doorway to a slightly larger size.

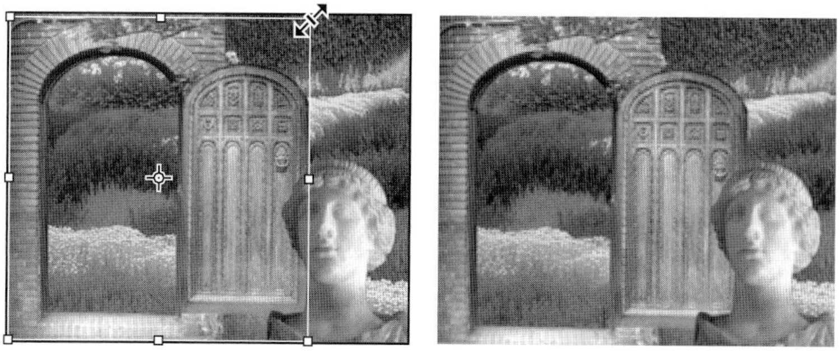

6 If necessary, position the pointer inside the bounding box, and drag to reposition the two images.

7 Press Enter (Windows) or Return (Mac OS) to apply the transformation changes.

8 Choose File > Save.

Adding a gradient to a layer

Next you'll create a new layer with no artwork on it. (Adding empty layers to a file is comparable to adding blank sheets of acetate to a stack of images.) Then you'll add a semi-transparent gradient effect to the new layer, which influences the layers stacked behind it.

In ImageReady, which does not have a gradient tool, you can apply a Gradient/Pattern layer effect from the Layers palette.

1 In the Layers palette, click Background to make it active.

2 Click the New Layer button (▣) at the bottom of the Layers palette. A new layer, named Layer 1, appears between the Background and the Doorway layer.

***Note:** You can also create a new layer by choosing New Layer on the Layers palette menu.*

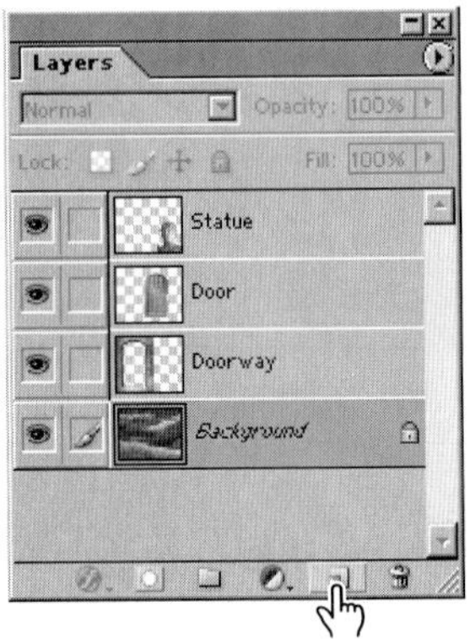

3 Double-click the name Layer 1, and type **Gradient** to rename the layer.

You can now apply a gradient to the new layer. A gradient is a gradual transition between two or more colors. You control the type of transition using the gradient tool.

4 In the toolbox, select the gradient tool (▣).

5 In the tool options bar, make sure that the Linear Gradient button (▣) is selected and then click to expand the gradient picker. Select Foreground to Transparent and then click on the image window to close the gradient picker.

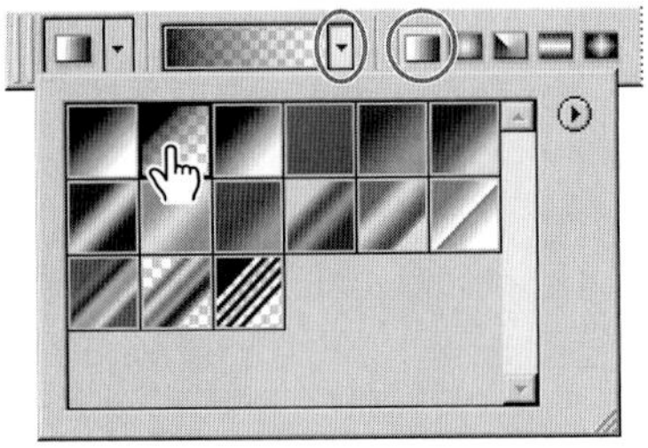

To identify the different types of gradients, let the pointer hover over a thumbnail in the gradient picker until a tooltip appears, showing the name of the gradient. Or, open the palette menu for the gradient picker and select either Small List or Large List.

6 Click the Swatches palette tab to bring it to the front of its palette group, and select any shade of purple that appeals to you.

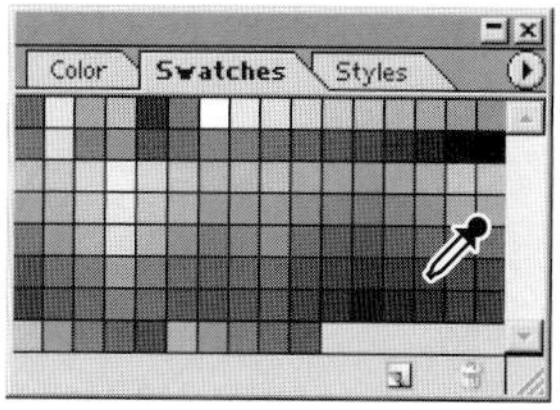

7 With the Gradient layer active in the Layers palette, drag the gradient tool from the right margin of the image to the left margin. (You can hold down Shift as you drag to constrain the gradient horizontally.)

The gradient extends over the width of the layer, starting with purple and gradually blending to transparent, and affects the look of the garden on the layer below it. Because the gradient partially obscures the garden, you'll now lighten the effect by changing the Gradient layer's opacity.

8 In the Layers palette, change the opacity for the Gradient layer to **60%**. The full garden shows through the gradient.

Note: *If you try this procedure in ImageReady, be aware that any Gradient/Pattern effects that you apply in ImageReady do not appear onscreen when you view the file in Photoshop. However, the effects are preserved in the image. An alert icon in Photoshop indicates that the effects are present on the layer. The pattern and gradient effects are not altered in Photoshop unless you rasterize the layer on which the effects are applied.*

Adding text

Now you're ready to create and manipulate some type. You'll create text with the type tool, which places the text on its own type layer. You'll then edit the text and apply a special effect to that layer. (ImageReady also has features for creating and manipulating type, but it uses a palette to display type options, rather than a dialog box.)

1 In the Layers palette, click the Statue layer to make it active.

2 In the toolbox, click the small Default Foreground and Background Color box ( ) near the bottom of the toolbox to set the foreground color to black. This is the color you want for the text.

Note: *If you decide to change a text color later, you can do this by selecting the text with the type tool and using the color swatch in the tool options bar.*

3 In the toolbox, select the type tool (T). Then, in the tool options bar, select the following options for the type tool:

- Select a font from the Font pop-up menu (we used Adobe Garamond).
- Select a font style (we used Regular).
- Enter a point size in the Size text box (we used **60** point).
- Select Crisp from the Anti-Aliasing pop-up menu (aa).
- Select the Center Text alignment option.

4 Click somewhere in the upper left area of the image window.

Notice that the Layers palette now includes a layer named Layer 1 with a "T" icon next to the name, indicating that it is a type layer.

5 Type **Jardin** and then press Enter or Return, and type **2000**.

The text automatically appears on a new layer in the upper left area of the image where you clicked. Now you'll reposition the text in the image.

6 Select the move tool (), and drag the "Jardin 2000" text to center it under the arch of the doorway. The text may be a little difficult to read against the dark shrubbery in the background, but you'll make adjustments for that shortly.

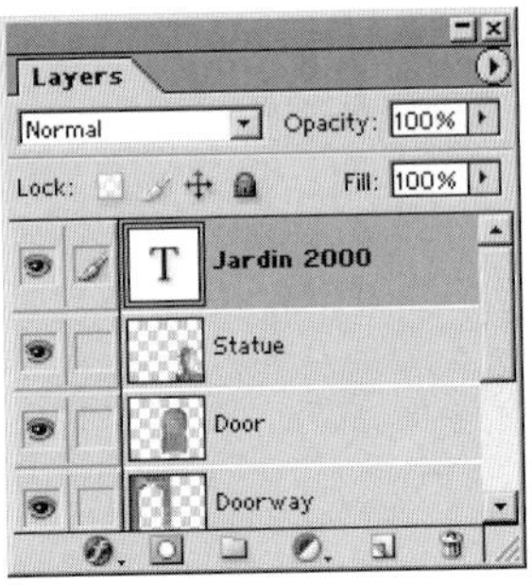

Notice that the layer name changes to Jardin 2000 in the Layers palette.

Applying a layer style

You can enhance a layer by adding a shadow, glow, bevel, emboss, or other special effect from a collection of automated and editable layer styles. These styles are easy to apply and link directly to the layer you specify.

Layer styles are handled differently in Photoshop and ImageReady. In Photoshop, you use the Layer Style dialog box to edit layer styles. In ImageReady, you use the Layer Options/Style palette along with the name of the effect you want to edit.

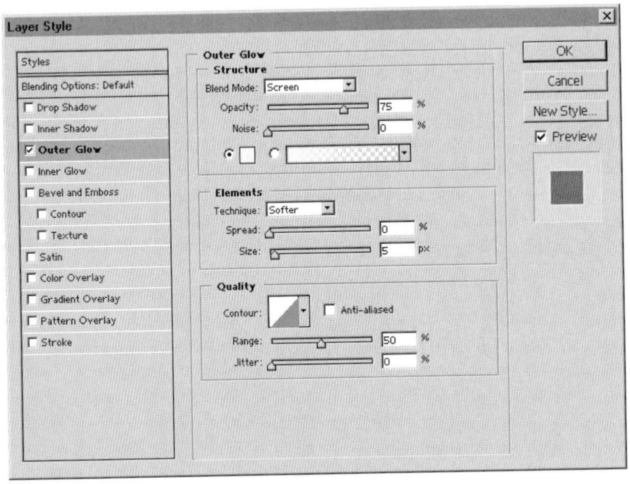

Photoshop Layer Style dialog box

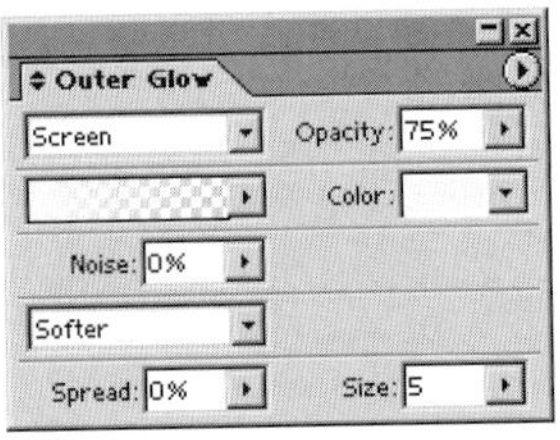

An ImageReady style palette

Individual effects can also be hidden temporarily by clicking the eye icon ( ) in the Layers palette or copied to other layers by dragging the effect onto the destination layer.

Now you'll apply a glowing yellow stroke around the type, and fill the type with a pattern. You'll begin by adding a glow.

1 With the Jardin 2000 type layer still active, choose Layer > Layer Style > Outer Glow. (There may be a slight pause as the Layer Style dialog box opens.)

You can also open the Layer Style dialog box by clicking the Add A Layer Style button ( ) at the bottom of the Layers palette and then choosing a layer style on the pop-up menu.

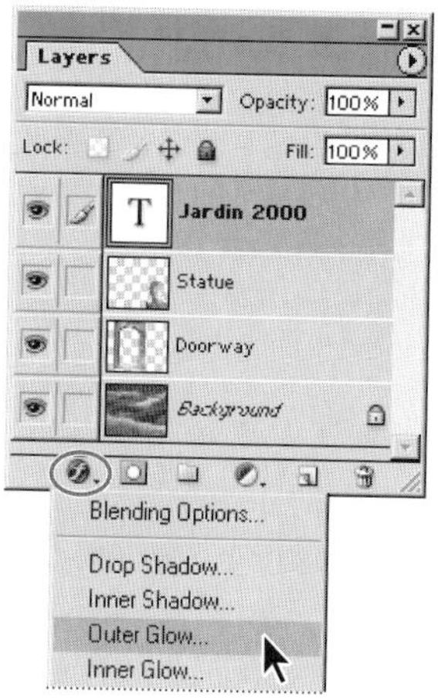

2 In the Layer Style dialog box, select the Preview check box and move the dialog box aside as needed so that you can preview the results in the image window as you change settings.

3 In the Elements area of the dialog box, enter **10** for Spread and **10** for Size in pixels.

4 In the left pane of the Layer Style dialog box, select the Stroke check box, and notice that the right pane of the dialog box still shows the options for the Outer Glow effect. Click the name *Stroke* to change the display so that the Stroke layer style options appear on the right side of the dialog box, and then select the following options:

- In the Structure area, enter **1** for Size to create a 1-pixel-wide stroke.
- Under Fill Type, click the Color swatch to open the color picker. Then choose a yellow color (we used R=**255**, G=**255**, and B=**0**). Close the color picker but leave the Layer Style dialog box open.

5 On the left pane of the dialog box, click the name *Pattern Overlay*. Notice that by clicking the name, you automatically select the Pattern Overlay check box and change the available options on the right side of the dialog box. Select the following options:

- Click the arrow beside the pattern thumbnail to open a pop-up display of available patterns, and select Wood. Click a blank area of the dialog box to close the pop-up.

You can identify the Wood pattern thumbnail by waiting for a tooltip to appear or by choosing Small List or Large List on the palette list for the pattern picker.

- In the Scale option, enter **200**.

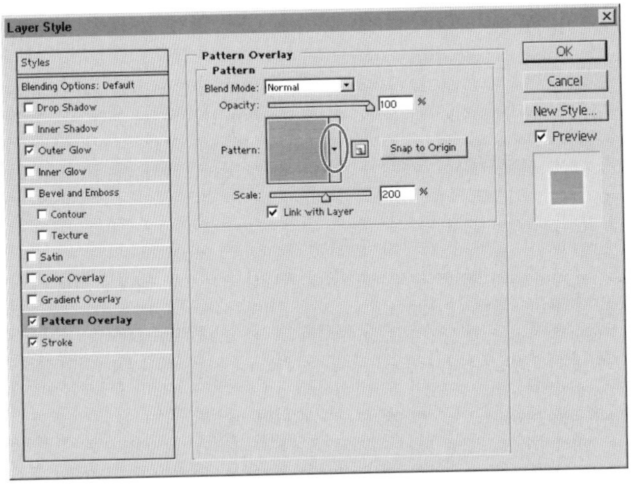

6 Click OK to accept all the settings and close the Layer Style dialog box.

7 If necessary, scroll or resize the Layers palette so that you can see the changes in the palette listings.

Now there are four rows of information nested under the Jardin 2000 text layer. The first of these rows identifies them as Effects. The other three rows are named by the three styles that you applied to the layer: Outer Glow, Pattern Overlay, and Stroke. There is also an icon for layer styles (icon) next to the three style names. This same icon and a small arrow also appear on the right side of the Jardin 2000 layer.

To hide the layer styles listings, click the arrow to collapse the Effects list.

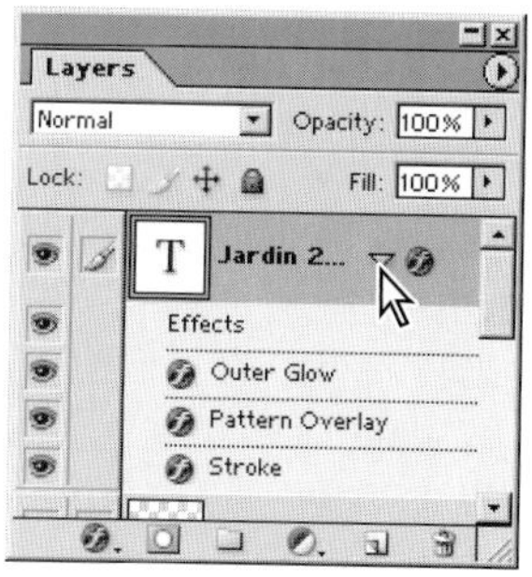

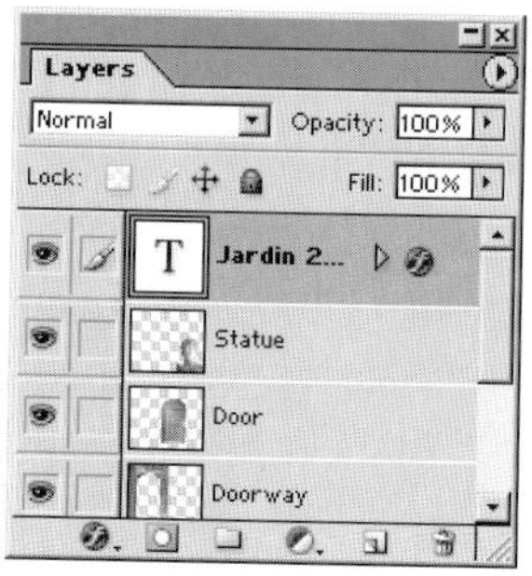

Editing text

Layer effects are automatically applied to changes you make to a layer. You can edit the text and watch how the layer effect tracks the change.

1 In the Layers palette, select the Jardin 2000 layer.

2 In the toolbox, select the type tool (T).

3 In the tool options bar, change the Font Size option from 60 pts to **72** pts.

Although you didn't select the text by dragging the text tool (as you would in a word-processing program), all the text on the layer now appears in 72-point type.

4 Using the type tool, select the last zero in "2000."

5 Type **4** so that the text block now reads "Jardin 2004."

Notice that the text formatting and layer styles remain applied to all the text.

6 On the tool options bar, click the Commit Any Current Edits button (✔) to commit your edits and to switch out of edit mode.

7 Choose File > Save.

Flattening and saving files

When you have edited all the layers in your image, you can make a copy of the file with the layers flattened. Flattening a file's layers merges them into a single background, greatly reducing the file size. However, you shouldn't flatten an image until you are certain you're satisfied with all your design decisions. In most cases, you should retain a copy of the file with its layers intact, in case you need to edit a layer later.

To appreciate what flattening does, notice the two numbers for the file size in the Info bar at the bottom of the application window (Windows) or image window (Mac OS).

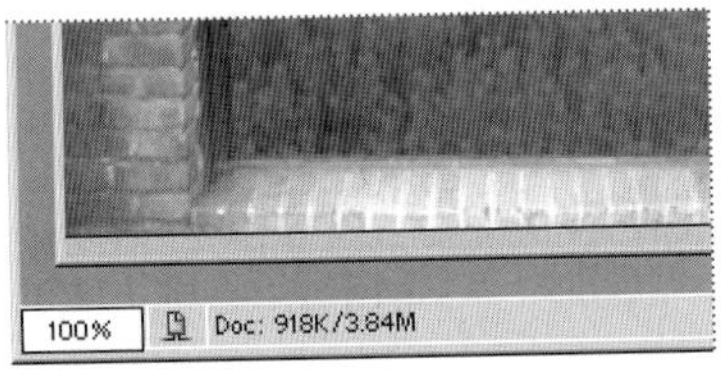

The first number represents what the file size would be if you flattened the image. The second number represents the current file size (without flattening). In our example, the flattened file would be about 900 K but the current file is about 4 MB—approximately four times larger than the flattened version would be, so flattening is well worth doing in this case.

1 If the type tool (T) is currently selected in the toolbox, select any other tool, to be sure that you're no longer in type-editing mode. Choose File > Save, to be sure that all your changes have been saved in the file.

2 Choose Image > Duplicate.

3 In the Duplicate Image dialog box, type **05Flat.psd** to name the file and specify the Lessons/Lesson05 folder. Click Save.

4 Close the 05Start.psd file, leaving only the 05Flat.psd file open.

5 On the Layers palette menu, choose Flatten Image.

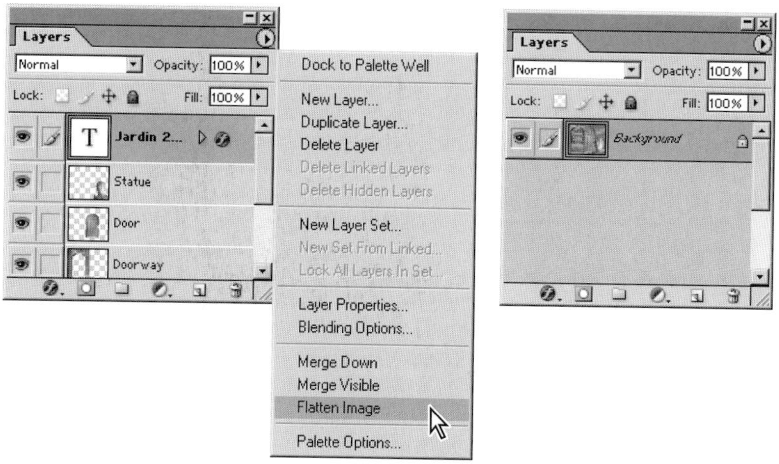

6 Choose File > Save. Even though you selected Save rather than Save As, the Save As dialog box appears.

7 Click Save to accept the default settings and save the flattened file.

Now you have a flattened version of the file while the original file and all its layers remain intact. You can now continue to work in the flattened file and even add more layers above the flattened Background layer.

If you want to flatten only some of the layers in a file, you can click the eye icons to hide the layers you don't want to flatten, and then choose Merge Visible on the Layers palette menu.

Creating a layer set and adding a layer

You can nest layers within the Layers palette. This makes it easier to manage your work and minimizes the clutter when you work on large, complex files.

1 In the Layers palette menu, choose New Layer Set.

2 In the New Layer Set dialog box, type **Conf Info**, and click OK.

In the Layers palette, a Conf Info folder appears above the Background layer.

Adding type layers to a flattened background

You're now going to work on two text layers that will have identical information but in different languages.

1 In the toolbox, select the type tool (T).

2 In the tool options bar, set the following type specifications:

- For Font family, select Adobe Garamond (or another serif font).
- For Font Style, select Italic.
- For Font Size, enter **24** pts.
- Click the color swatch to open the color picker and select the same yellow color you used for Outer Glow earlier in this lesson (R=**255**, B=**255**, G=**0**); then click OK to close the color picker.
- Make sure that the Crisp option and the Center Text icon (≡) are selected.

3 Make sure that the Conf Info layer set is selected in the Layers palette. Then click the type tool (T) in the upper right area of the image window and type the following: **The Frinds of the Flowers**. Then press Enter or Return, and type **Montreal**. (The misspelling "Frinds" is deliberate, so be sure you type it exactly as shown here.)

In the Layers palette, a new type layer appears, nested under the Conf Info layer set.

4 Select the move tool (▶✥) and drag the text so that it is nicely centered between the brick archway and the upper right side of the image.

Notice that the name of the layer in the Layers palette is now "The Frinds of the Flowers."

5 Select the "The Frinds..." layer in the Layers palette and drag it to the New Layer button at the bottom of the palette. When you release the mouse button, a duplicate of the text layer appears, also nested in the Conf Info layer set.

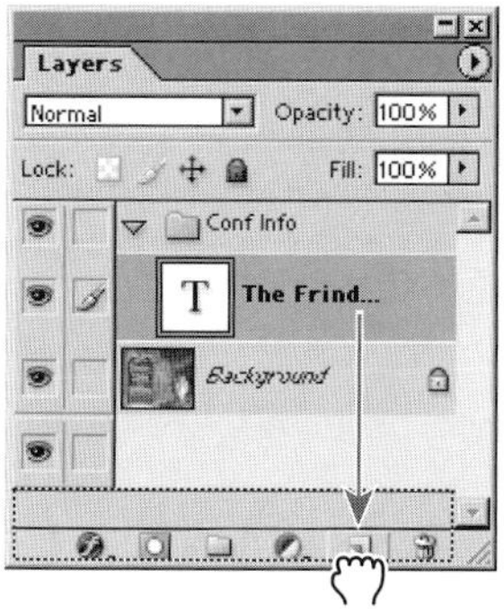

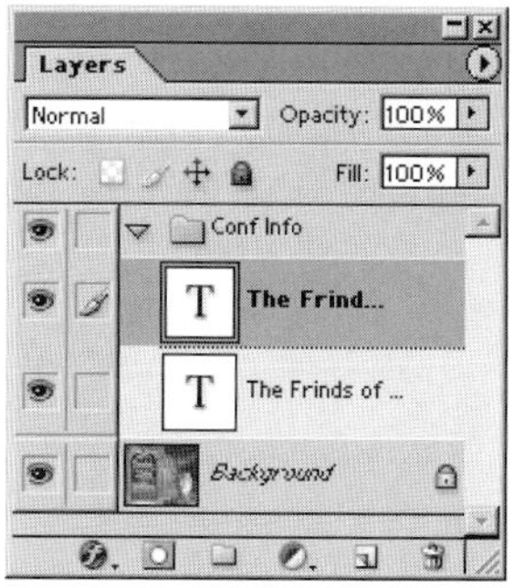

If you decide later that you want to reposition the two text layers, you can select the Conf Info layer set in the Layers palette, and then use the move tool to drag both layers, as if they were linked.

You now have an identically formatted and positioned text layer that you can simply edit to create alternative text about the conference information.

Creating alternate text and designating dictionaries

Photoshop 7.0 now includes the power of a spelling checker that can selectively reference dictionaries for various languages. You can designate entire text layers or individual words to be checked in different dictionaries. When you run the spelling checker, Photoshop automatically compares each word to the appropriate dictionary.

1 In the Layers palette, click the eye icon (👁) for the unselected copy of "The Frinds..." text layer to hide that layer. Leave the other copy selected.

2 Drag the type tool to select the words *The Frinds of the Flowers,* and type **Les Amis des Fleurs** to overwrite the upper line of the original text.

If necessary, press Enter or Return to keep the word *Montreal* on a separate line.

3 Choose Window > Character to open the Character palette.

4 Make sure that the Les Amis des Fleurs layer is selected in the Layers palette. Then, on the dictionary pop-up menu in the lower left corner of the Character palette, select French.

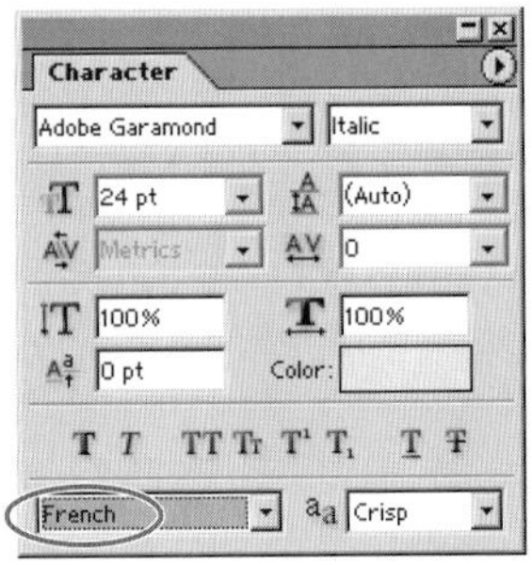

Using the multilingual spelling checker

Now that you've designated the dictionaries that Photoshop will use for different text within your file, you're ready to review the text for spelling errors.

1 In the Layers palette, click the eye icon (👁) for the The Frinds of the Flowers layer without selecting it, so that both text layers appear in the image window. Since these are right on top of each other, you won't be able to read the text easily, but that is OK for now.

2 Choose Edit > Check Spelling. The Check Spelling dialog box appears, indicating that the word Montreal is misspelled in French because it lacks an accent over the letter e.

3 Click the Change button to accept the suggested replacement, *Montréal.*

The text in the image changes, and the display in the dialog box also changes, now indicating that the word *Frinds* is not in the English: USA dictionary. Notice that the Change To option is (probably) *Finds*—not the word you want.

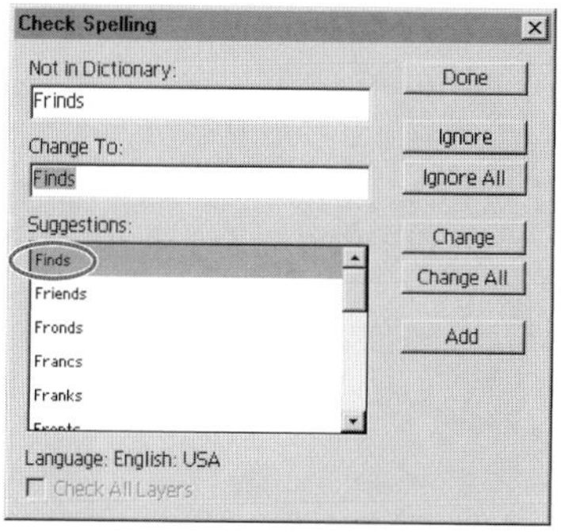

4 In the Suggestions list, click the word *Friends* to select it in the Change To option, or type **Friends** to enter the word manually. Then click Change.

5 If a message appears indicating that the spell check is complete, click OK.

6 Alternately click the eye icons on and off for the Les Amis des Fleurs and The Friends of the Flowers text layers to see the two versions of the text.

7 Choose File > Save to save the image with one flattened layer and two unflattened text layers.

Notice the change in file size in the Info bar. Although your file size has grown slightly, it is still not nearly as large as the completely unflattened project would be.

Your image for the garden event is now complete.

Editing a quick mask

Next, you will refine the selection of the egret by adding to or erasing parts of the masked area. You'll use the brush tool to make changes to your quick mask. The advantage of editing your selection as a mask is that you can use almost any tool or filter to modify the mask. (You can even use selection tools.) In Quick Mask mode, you do all of your editing in the image window.

In Quick Mask mode, Photoshop automatically defaults to Grayscale mode. The foreground color defaults to black, and the background color defaults to white. When using a painting or editing tool in Quick Mask mode, keep these principles in mind:

- Painting with white erases the mask (the red overlay) and increases the selected area.
- Painting with black adds to the mask (the red overlay) and decreases the selected area.

Adding to a selection by erasing masked areas

You'll begin by painting with white to increase the selected area within the egret. This erases some of the mask.

1 To make the foreground color white, select the Switch Foreground and Background Colors icon (↰) above the foreground and background color-selection boxes.

2 Select the zoom tool(🔍) and magnify your view of the image, if needed.

Zoom tool shortcuts

Many times when you are editing an image, you'll need to zoom in to work on a detail and then need to zoom out again to see the changes in context. You can use various keyboard shortcuts that make it easier than constantly switching between editing tools and the zoom tool.

Switching to the zoom tool

You can select the zoom tool in these ways:

- *Click the zoom tool in the toolbox to switch from the currently selected tool.*
- *Hold down Ctrl+spacebar (Windows) or Command+spacebar (Mac OS) to temporarily select the zoom tool from the keyboard. When you finish zooming, release the keys to go back to the tool you were using.*

Zooming in

You can use the zoom tool to zoom in (magnify the image view) in these ways:

- *Click the area you want to magnify. Each click magnifies the image by the next preset increment.*
- *Drag around the part of the image you want to magnify, creating a zoom marquee. When you release the mouse, the image portion within that marquee fills the image window.*

Zooming out

You can use the zoom tool to zoom out (shrink the image view) in the following ways:

- *In the toolbox, double-click the zoom tool to return the image to 100% view.*
- *Hold down Alt (Windows) or Option (Mac OS) and click the area of the image you want to reduce. Each Alt/Option-click reduces the image by the next preset increment.*

3 Select the brush tool (🖌).

4 In the tool options bar, make sure that the mode is Normal. Then click the arrow to display the Brushes pop-up palette, and select a medium-sized brush, such as one with a diameter of 13 pixels.

Note: *You'll switch brushes several times as you do this lesson. For convenience, you can choose Window > Brushes to open the Brushes palette as a separate window (or drag its tab from the palette well) so that your brush choices are readily available as you work. Or, you can just click the Brushes tab in the palette well to open it temporarily.*

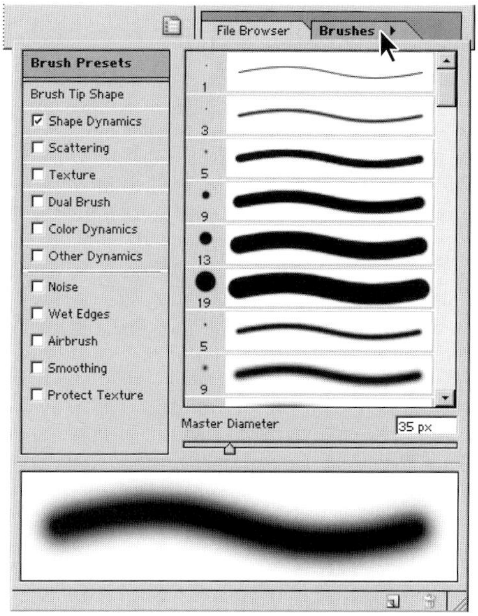

5 Using the brush tool, begin painting over the red areas within the egret's body. As you paint with white, the red areas are erased.

Don't worry if you paint outside the outline of the egret's body. You'll have a chance to make adjustments later by masking areas of the image as needed.

Unedited mask *Painting with white* *Result*

6 Continue painting with white to erase all of the mask (red) in the egret, including its beak and legs. As you work, you can easily switch back and forth between Quick Mask mode and Standard mode to see how painting in the mask alters the selected area.

Notice that the selection border has increased, selecting more of the egret's body.

Standard mode *Edited mask in Standard mode* *Quick mask selection*

For an illustration of the selection in Standard and Quick Mask modes, see figure 6-1 in the color section.

If any areas within the body of the egret still appear to be selected, it means that you haven't erased all of the mask.

Selection in Standard mode

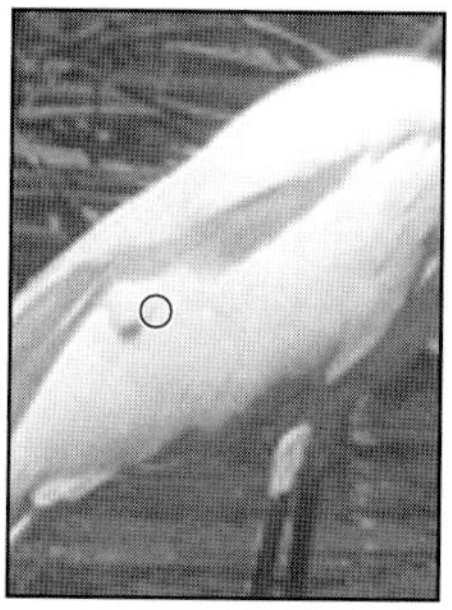

Erasing in Quick Mask mode

7 Once you've erased all of the red areas within the egret, click the Standard mode icon (◻) again to view your quick mask as a selection. Don't worry if the selection extends a bit beyond the egret. You'll learn how to fix that later.

8 If necessary, zoom out so that you can see the entire image.

9 Choose File > Save to save your work.

Subtracting from a selection by adding masked areas

You may have erased the mask beyond the edges of the egret. This means that part of the background is included in the selection. Now you'll return to Quick Mask mode and restore the mask to those edge areas by painting with black.

1 Click the Quick Mask Mode button ( ) to return to Quick Mask mode.

2 To make the foreground color black, select the Switch Foreground and Background Colors icon ( ) above the foreground and background color-selection boxes. Make sure that the black color box now appears on top. Remember that in the image window, painting with black will add to the red overlay.

3 Choose a brush from the Brush pop-up palette. Select a small brush from the first row of brushes, because you'll be refining the edges of the selection.

4 Now paint with black to restore the mask (the red overlay) to any of the background area that is still unprotected. Continue working until only the area inside the egret remains unmasked and you are completely satisfied with your mask selection.

Remember that you can zoom in and out as you work. You can also switch back and forth between Standard mode and Quick Mask mode.

Note: *In Quick Mask mode, you can also use the eraser tool to remove any excess selection.*

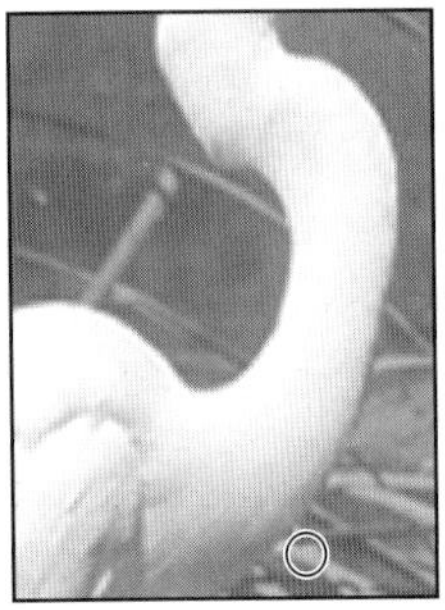

Painting with black to restore mask

For a color illustration of painting in Quick Mask mode, see figure 6-2 in the color section.

5 In the toolbox, switch to Standard mode to view your final egret selection.

6 Double-click the hand tool ( ) to make the egret image fit in the window.

Saving a selection as a mask

Now you'll save the egret selection as an alpha channel mask. Your time-consuming work won't be lost, and you can use the selection again later.

Quick masks are temporary. They disappear when you deselect. However, any selection can be saved as a mask in an alpha channel. Think of alpha channels as storage areas for information. When you save a selection as a mask, a new alpha channel is created in the Channels palette. (An image can contain up to 24 channels, including all color and alpha channels.) You can use these masks again in the same image or in a different image.

Note: *If you save and close your file while in Quick Mask mode, the quick mask will show in its own channel the next time you open your file. However, if you save and close your file while in Standard mode, the quick mask will be gone the next time you open your file.*

1 Choose Window > Channels to open the Channels palette in the Layers palette group.

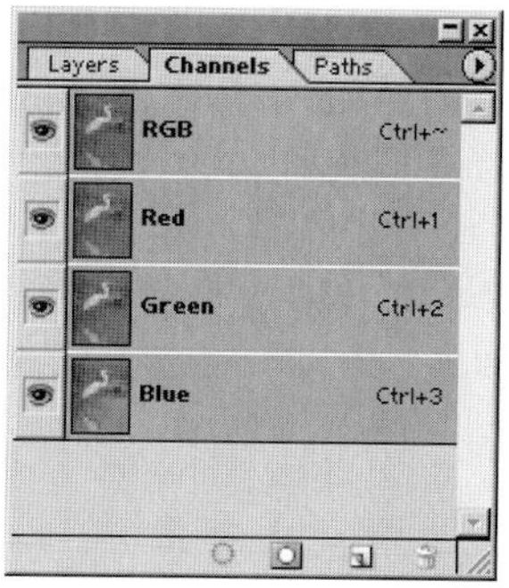

In the Channels palette, the default color-information channels are listed—a full-color preview channel for the RGB image and separate channels for red, green, and blue.

2 Click the eye icon( ) for the Red channel to hide just the red channel and notice the results in the image window. Using the eye icons, experiment with the visibility to view the various channels individually. (To show or hide multiple channels, drag up or down the eye-icon column.)

3 When you finish experimenting with the channel views, click to set an eye icon for the RGB channel to redisplay the composite channel view.

4 With the (Standard Mode) egret selection still active in the image window, click the Save Selection as Channel button (![icon]) at the bottom of the Channels palette.

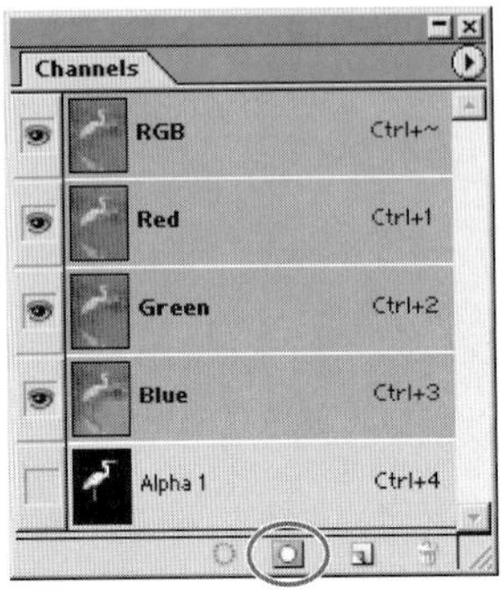

A new channel, Alpha 1, appears in the Channels palette. All new channels have the same dimensions and number of pixels as the original image.

Using alpha channels

In addition to the temporary masks of Quick Mask mode, you can create more permanent masks by storing and editing selections in alpha channels. This allows you to use the masks again in the same image or in a different image.

You can create an alpha channel in Photoshop and then add a mask to it. You can also save an existing selection in a Photoshop or ImageReady image as an alpha channel that will appear in the Channels palette.

An alpha channel has these properties:

- *Each image (except 16-bit images) can contain up to 24 channels, including all color and alpha channels.*
- *All channels are 8-bit grayscale images, capable of displaying 256 levels of gray.*
- *You can specify a name, color, mask option, and opacity for each channel. (The opacity affects the preview of the channel, not the image.)*
- *All new channels have the same dimensions and number of pixels as the original image.*
- *You can edit the mask in an alpha channel using the painting tools, editing tools, and filters.*
- *You can convert alpha channels to spot color channels.*

–From Adobe Photoshop 7.0 online Help

5 Double-click the Alpha 1 channel and type **Egret** to rename it.

If you display all of the color channels plus the new alpha mask channel, the image window looks much as it did in Quick Mask mode (with the rubylith appearing where the selection is masked).

6 Choose Select > Deselect to deselect everything.

Alpha channels can be added and deleted, and, like quick masks, can be edited using the painting and editing tools.

To avoid confusing channels and layers, think of channels as containing an image's color and selection information; think of layers as containing painting and effects.

Editing a mask

Now you'll touch up your selection of the egret by editing the mask channel. It's easy to miss tiny areas when making a selection. You may not even see these imperfections until you view the saved selection as a channel mask.

You can use most painting and editing tools to edit a channel mask, just as you did when editing in Quick Mask mode. This time you'll display and edit the mask as a grayscale image.

1 With the Egret channel selected, click any eye icon (👁) appearing next to the other channels to hide all channels except the Egret channel (if necessary).

When only the Egret channel has an eye icon, the image window displays a black-and-white mask of the egret selection. (If you left all of the channels selected, the colored egret image would appear with a red overlay.)

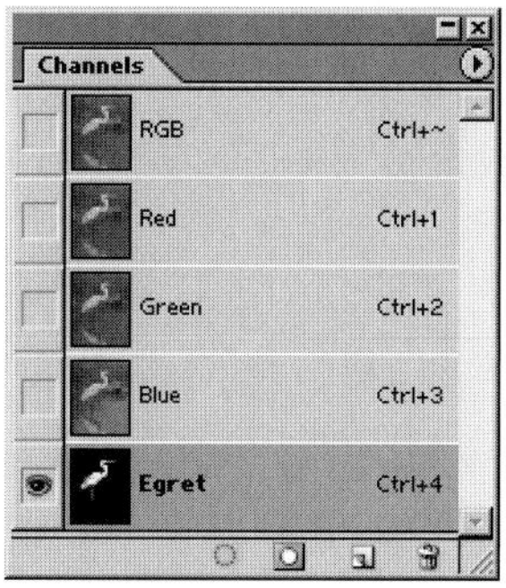

Look for any black or gray flecks within the body of the egret. You'll erase them by painting with white to increase the selected area. Remember these guidelines on editing a channel with a painting or editing tool:

- Painting with white erases the mask and increases the selected area.
- Painting with black adds to the mask and decreases the selected area.
- Painting with gray values adds to or subtracts from the mask in varying opacity, in proportion to the level of gray used to paint. For example, if you paint with a medium gray value, when you use the mask as a selection the pixels will be 50% selected. If you paint with a dark gray and then use the mask as a selection, the pixels will be less than 50% selected (depending on the gray value you choose). And, if you paint with a light gray and then use the mask as a selection, the pixels will be more than 50% selected.

2 Make sure that the Egret channel is the active channel by clicking on the channel in the Channels palette. A selected channel is highlighted in the Channels palette.

3 Now make sure that white is the foreground color. (If necessary, select the Switch Foreground And Background Colors icon (↰) in the toolbox.) Then select a small brush in the Brushes palette, and paint out any black or gray flecks.

Selection in channel

Painting out black or gray

4 If any white specks appear in the black area of the channel, make black the foreground color and paint those out as well. Remember that when you paint with black, you increase the masked area and decrease the selection.

5 Choose File > Save.

Loading a mask as a selection and applying an adjustment

Now you'll load the Egret channel mask as a selection. The channel mask remains stored in the Channels palette even after you've loaded it as a selection. This means that you can reuse the mask whenever you want.

1 In the Channels palette, click the RGB preview channel to display the entire image, and then click the eye icon (👁) for the Egret channel to hide it (if necessary).

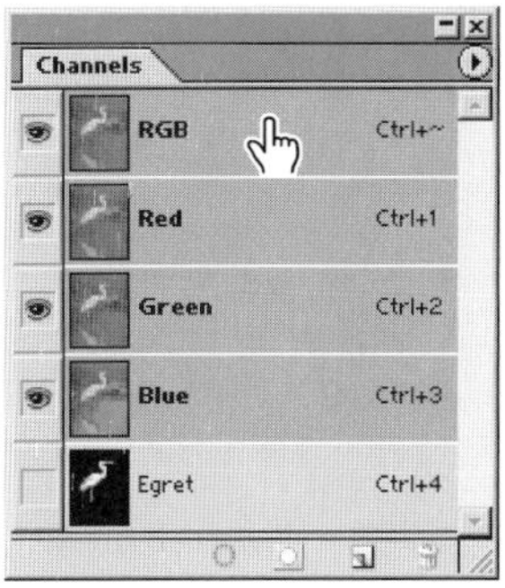

Loading a selection into an image using shortcuts

You can reuse a previously saved selection by loading it into an image.

To load a saved selection using shortcuts, do one of the following in the Channels palette:

- *Select the alpha channel, click the Load Selection button at the bottom of the palette, and then click the composite color channel near the top of the palette.*
- *Drag the channel containing the selection you want to load onto the Load Selection button.*
- *Ctrl-click (Windows) or Command-click (Mac OS) the channel containing the selection you want to load.*
- *To add the mask to an existing selection, press Ctrl+Shift (Windows) or Command+Shift (Mac OS), and click the channel.*
- *To subtract the mask from an existing selection, press Ctrl+Alt (Windows) or Command+Option (Mac OS), and click the channel.*
- *To load the intersection of the saved selection and an existing selection, press Ctrl+Alt+Shift (Windows) or Command+Option+Shift (Mac OS), and select the channel.*

–From Adobe Photoshop 7.0 online Help

2 Choose Select > Load Selection. Click OK.

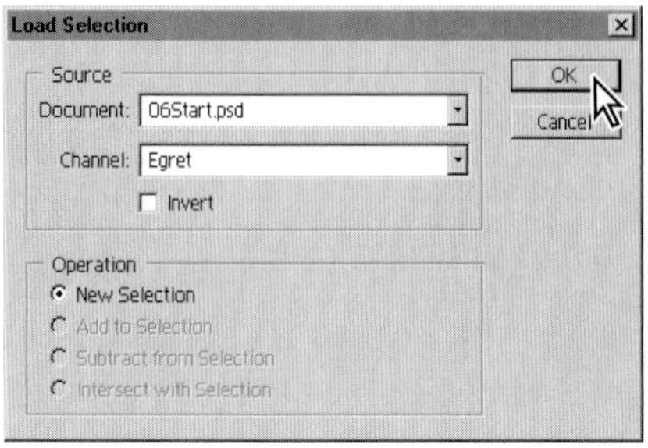

The egret selection appears in the image window.

Now that you've corrected any flaws in the selection by painting in the channel, you'll adjust the tonal balance of the egret.

3 Choose Image > Adjustments > Auto Levels. This automatically adjusts the tonal balance of the colors within the selection.

Auto Levels defines the lightest and darkest pixels in each channel as white and black, and then redistributes the intermediate pixel values proportionately.

4 Choose Edit > Undo to compare the adjustment you just made. Then choose Edit > Redo to reapply the adjustment.

5 Choose Select > Deselect.

6 Choose File > Save.

Extracting an image

Now you'll work with another masking and selection tool, the Extract command, to make some difficult selections—some marsh grasses and a foxtail.

The Extract command provides a sophisticated way to isolate a foreground object from its background. Even objects with wispy, intricate, or undefinable edges can be clipped from their backgrounds with a minimum of manual work.

You'll start with an image that consists of only one layer. You must be working in a layer to use the Extract command. If your original image has no layers (that is, has only a Background), you can duplicate the image to a new layer.

For an illustration of extracting, see figure 6-3 in the color section.

Extracting an object from its background

You'll use the Extract command on a foxtail image set against a dark background.

1 Choose File > Open, and open the file Foxtail.psd from the Lessons/Lesson06 folder.

The Foxtail grass image has the same resolution as the Egret image, 72 pixels per inch (ppi). To avoid unexpected results when combining elements from other files, you must either use files with the same image resolution or compensate for differing resolutions.

For example, if your original image is 72 ppi and you add an element from a 144-ppi image, the additional element will appear twice as large because it contains twice the number of pixels.

For complete information on differing resolutions, see "About image size and resolution" in Adobe Photoshop7.0 online Help.

2 Choose Filter > Extract.

The Extract dialog box appears with the edge highlighter tool ( ) selected in the upper left area of the dialog box.

To extract an object, you use the Extract dialog box to highlight the edges of the object. Then you define the object's interior and preview the extraction. You can refine and preview the extraction as many times as you wish. Applying the extraction erases the background area to transparency, leaving just the extracted object.

If needed, you can resize the dialog box by dragging its bottom right corner. You specify which part of the image to extract by using the tools and previews in this dialog box.

Now you'll choose a brush size for the edge highlighter tool. You'll start with a fairly large brush.

3 If necessary, enter **20** in the Brush Size text box.

It's easiest to start with a large brush to highlight the general selection, and then switch to a finer brush to fine-tune the selection.

4 Using the edge highlighter tool, drag over the fuzzy ends and tip of the foxtail until you've completely outlined, but not filled, the foxtail. Draw the highlight so that it slightly overlaps both the foreground and background regions around the edge.

It's OK if the highlight overlaps the edge. The Extract command makes its selection by finding the difference in contrast between pixels. The foxtail has a well-defined interior, so make sure that the highlight forms a complete outline. You do not need to highlight areas where the object touches the image boundaries.

Now you'll highlight the fine stem.

5 Decrease the Brush Size to **5**.

6 If desired, select the zoom tool ( ), or press spacebar+Ctrl (Windows) or spacebar+Command (Mac OS) and click to zoom in on the stem. You can also use the hand tool ( ) to reposition the image preview.

7 Using the edge highlighter tool, drag over the stem to select it.

If you make a mistake and highlight more than desired, select the eraser tool ( ) in the dialog box and drag over the highlight in the preview.

8 Select the fill tool ( ) in the Extract dialog box. Then, click inside the object to fill its interior. You must define the object's interior before you can preview the extraction.

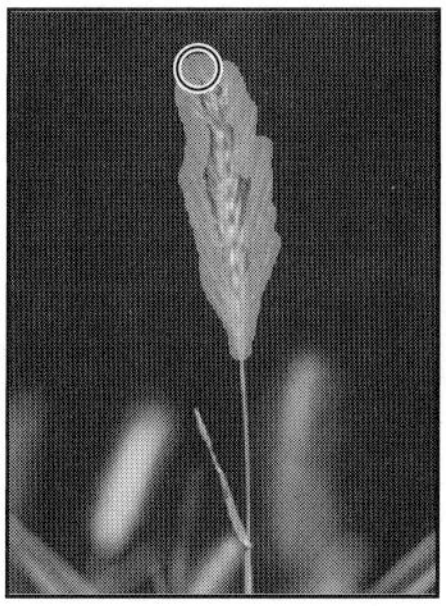

Highlighting edges of foxtail tip

Highlighting stem and leaves; then filling

The default Fill color (bright blue) contrasts well with the highlight color (green). You can change either color if you need more contrast with the image colors, using the Highlight and Fill menus in the Extract dialog box.

9 Click the Preview button to view the extraction.

You can control the preview using one of these techniques:

• To magnify the preview, select the zoom tool (🔍) in the Extract dialog box, and click in the preview. To zoom out, hold down Alt (Windows) or Option (Mac OS), and click with the zoom tool in the preview.

• To view a different part of the preview, select the hand tool (✋) in the Extract dialog box and drag the image in the preview.

To toggle quickly between the edge highlighter and eraser tools when one of the tools is selected, press B (edge highlighter) or E (eraser).

10 To refine your selection, edit the extraction boundaries using these techniques:

• Switch between the Original and Extracted views using the Show menu in the Extract dialog box.

• Click a filled area with the fill tool to remove the fill.

• Select the eraser tool (🧽) in the Extract dialog box, and drag to remove any undesired highlighting.

• Select the Show Highlight and Show Fill options in the Extract dialog box to view the highlight and fill colors; deselect the options to hide them.

• Zoom in on your selection using the zoom tool in the Extract dialog box. You can then use a smaller brush size as you edit, switching between the edge highlighter tool and the eraser tool as needed for more precise work.

• Switch to a smaller brush by entering a different size in the Brush Size text box and continue to refine the selection's border using the edge highlighter or to erase using the eraser tool.

11 When you are satisfied with your selection, click OK to apply the extraction.

Adding the extracted image as a layer

Now you'll add the extracted image to the Egret image.

1 With the image window of the Foxtail image active, use the move tool (✥) to drag the image to the right side of the Egret image. The foxtail is added as a new layer to the Egret image.

2 Close the Foxtail.psd image window without saving your changes. The 06Start.psd is now the active file, and the new layer with the foxtail is selected.

3 Choose Edit > Transform > Scale. Drag the resize handles, holding down Shift to constrain the proportions, until the foxtail is about two-thirds the original image height. Press Enter (Windows) or Return (Mac OS) to apply the scaling.

Moving foxtail copy *Scaling foxtail* *Result*

4 In the Layers palette with the Foxtail layer (Layer 1) selected, decrease its opacity to **70%**.

5 Choose File > Save.

6 Save and close the Foxtail.psd image.

Extracting by forcing the foreground

The Force Foreground option lets you make intricate selections when an object lacks a clear interior.

For an illustration of extracting the weeds image, see figure 6-4 in the color section.

1 Choose File > Open, and open the file Weeds.psd image from the Lessons/Lesson06 folder on your hard drive.

2 Choose Filter > Extract.

3 Under the Extraction area of the dialog box, select the Force Foreground check box.

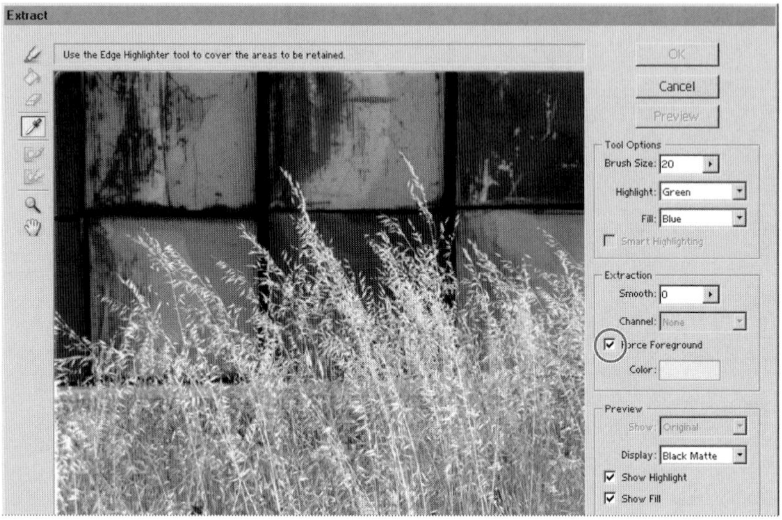

You'll start by selecting the color on which to base your selection. The Force Foreground technique works best with objects that are monochromatic or fairly uniform in color.

4 Select the eyedropper tool (🖉) in the Extract dialog box, and then click a light area of the weeds to sample the color to be treated as the foreground.

5 Select the edge highlighter tool (🖍) in the Extract dialog box.

6 For Brush Size, use the slider or enter a value to select a fairly large brush (about 20 or 30).

7 Drag to begin highlighting the wispy ends of the weeds where they overlap the dark background.

8 When you've enclosed the weed tips, drag to highlight the top third of the weeds fully. The highlight should be solid.

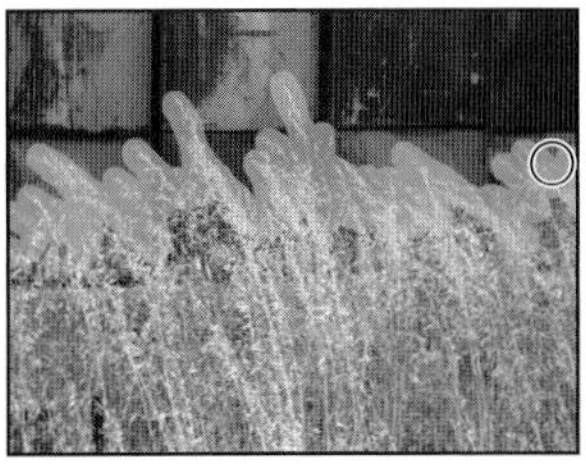

Highlighting weed edges

Selecting top third of weeds

9 Choose Black Matte from the Display menu in the Extract dialog box.

A black matte provides good contrast for a light-colored selection. For a dark selection, try the Gray or White Matte option. None previews a selection against a transparent background.

10 Click the Preview button to preview the extracted object.

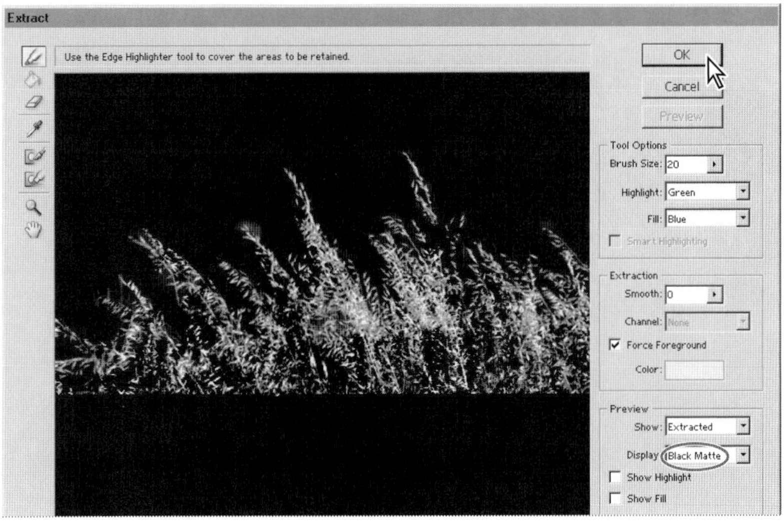

11 To view and refine the extraction, use one of the following techniques:

- Use the Show menu to switch between previews of the original and extracted images.
- Select the Show Highlight option to display the object's extraction boundaries.

12 When you are satisfied with the selection, click OK to apply the final extraction. All pixels on the layer outside the extracted object are erased to transparency.

Note: *An alternate method for making intricate selections is to select areas by color. To do so, choose Select > Color Range. Then use the eyedropper tools from the Color Range dialog box to sample the colors for your selection. You can sample from your image window or from the preview window.*

Adding the forced-foreground extraction as another layer

Once you've extracted an image, you can also use the background eraser and history brush tools to clean up any stray edges in the image.

Now you'll add the extracted weeds to the Egret image.

1 With the Weeds.psd file active, use the move tool (▸✥) to drag the extracted selection to the Egret image. Position the weeds so that they fill the bottom third of the Egret image.

The selection is added to the Egret image as a new layer.

2 In the Layers palette, decrease the opacity of the new layer by entering a value of **70%**.

Weed image copy added to egret image

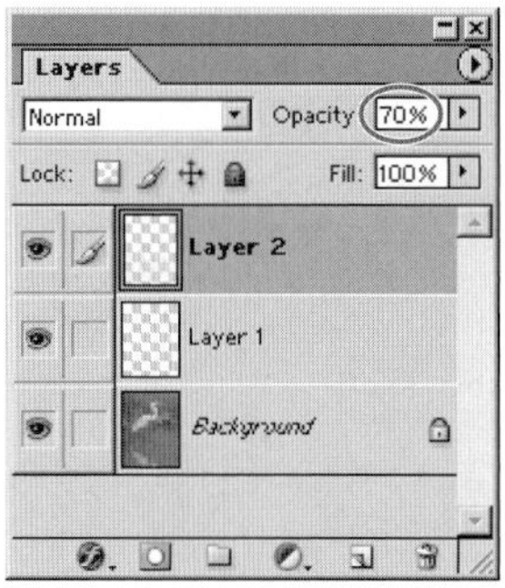

New layer opacity set to 70%

3 Choose File > Save.

4 Save and close the Weeds.psd file.

Applying a filter effect to a masked selection

To complete the composite of the marsh grasses and Egret image, you'll isolate the egret as you apply a filter effect to the image background.

1 In the Layers palette, select the Background.

2 In the Channels palette, drag the Egret channel to the Load Channel As Selection button (◌) at the bottom of the palette. This loads the channel onto the image.

Next, you'll invert the selection so that the egret is protected and you can work on the background.

3 Choose Select > Inverse.

The previous selection (the egret) is protected, and the background is selected. You can now apply changes to the background without worrying about the egret.

4 Click the Layers palette tab and make sure that the background layer is selected. Then choose Filter > Artistic > Colored Pencil. Experiment with the sliders to evaluate the changes before you apply the filter.

Preview different areas of the background by dragging the image in the preview window of the Colored Pencil filter dialog box. This preview option is available with all filters.

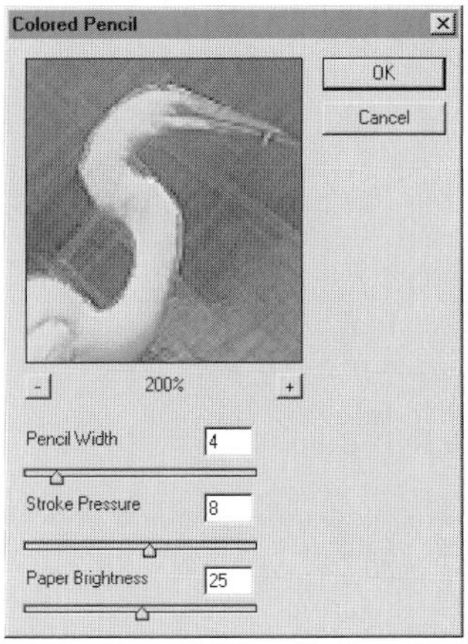

Filter preview

Filter applied

5 Click OK when you're satisfied with the Colored Pencil settings. The filter is applied to the background selection.

You can experiment with other filter effects for the background. Choose Edit > Undo to undo your last performed operation.

6 Choose Select > Deselect to deselect everything.

Before you save your file, you'll flatten your image to reduce the file size. Make sure that you are satisfied with the image before you go on to the next step, because you won't be able to make corrections to the separate layers after the image is flattened.

7 Choose Layer > Flatten Image.

8 Choose File > Save.

Creating a gradient mask

In addition to using black to indicate what's hidden and white to indicate what's selected, you can paint with shades of gray to indicate partial transparency. For example, if you paint in a channel with a shade of gray that is at least halfway between white and black, the underlying image becomes partially (50% or more) visible.

You'll experiment by adding a gradient (which makes a transition from black to gray to white) to a channel and then filling the selection with a color to see how the transparency levels of the black, gray, and white in the gradient affect the image.

1 In the Channels palette, create a new channel by clicking the New Channel button () at the bottom of the palette.

The new channel, labeled Alpha 1, appears at the bottom of the Channels palette, and the other channels are hidden in the image window.

2 Double-click the Alpha 1 channel and type **Gradient** to rename it.

3 Select the gradient tool ().

4 In the tool options bar, click the arrow to display the Gradients picker and select the Black, White gradient.

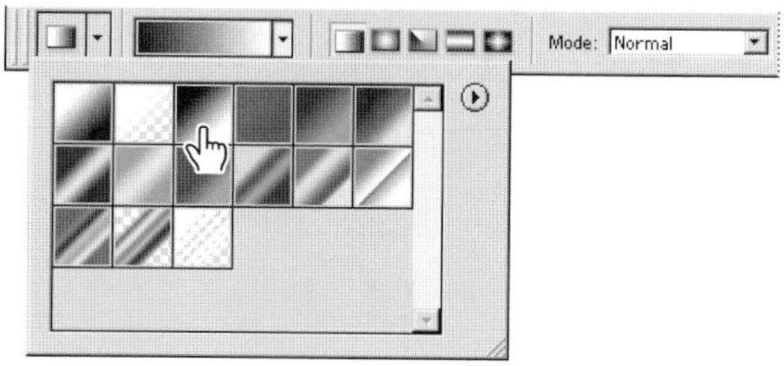

5 Hold down Shift to keep the gradient vertical, and drag the gradient tool from the top of the image window to the bottom of the window.

The gradient is applied to the channel.

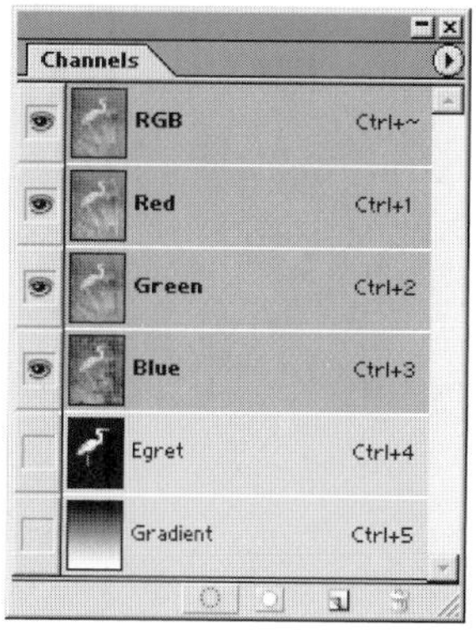

Applying effects using a gradient mask

Now you'll load the gradient as a selection and fill the selection with a color.

When you load a gradient as a selection and then fill the selection with a color, the opacity of the fill color varies over the length of the gradient. Where the gradient is black, no fill color is present; where the gradient is gray, the fill color is partially visible; and where the gradient is white, the fill color is completely visible.

1 In the Channels palette, click the RGB channel to display the full-color preview.

Next, you'll load the Gradient channel as a selection.

2 Without deselecting the RGB channel, drag the Gradient channel to the Load Channel As Selection button (◌) at the bottom of the palette to load the gradient as a selection.

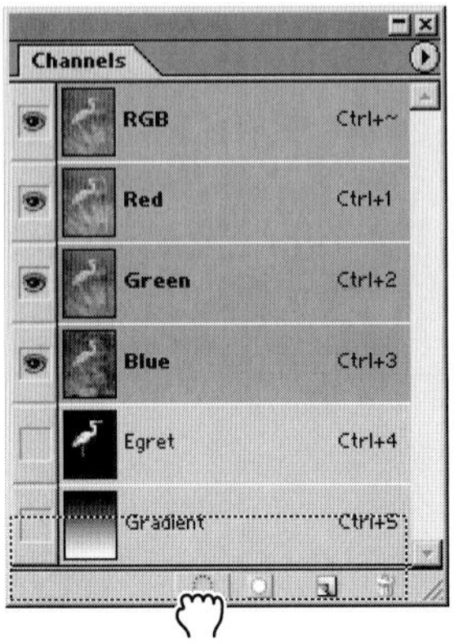

A selection border appears in the window. Although the selection border appears over only about half the image, it is correct.

3 Make sure that the foreground and background colors are set to their defauls (black and white, respectively). If necessary, click the Default Foreground and Background Colors icon (■) at the lower-left corner of the color-selection boxes.

4 Press Delete to fill the gradient selection with the current background color (white).

5 Choose Select > Deselect to deselect everything.

6 Choose File > Save.

You have completed this lesson. Although it takes some practice to become comfortable using channels, you've learned all the fundamental concepts and skills you need to get started using masks and channels.

Review questions

1 What is the benefit of using a quick mask?

2 What happens to a quick mask when you deselect it?

3 When you save a selection as a mask, where is the mask stored?

4 How can you edit a mask in a channel once you've saved it?

5 How do channels differ from layers?

6 How do you use the Extract command to isolate an object with intricate borders from an image?

Review answers

1 Quick masks are helpful for creating quick, one-time selections. In addition, using a quick mask is an easy way to edit a selection using the painting tools.

2 The quick mask disappears when you deselect it.

3 Masks are saved in channels, which can be thought of as storage areas in an image.

4 You can paint directly on a mask in a channel using black, white, and shades of gray.

5 Channels are used as storage areas for saved selections. Unless you explicitly display a channel, it does not appear in the image or print. Layers can be used to isolate various parts of an image so that they can be edited as discrete objects with the painting or editing tools or other effects.

6 You use the Extract command to extract an object and the Extract dialog box to highlight the edges of the object. Then you define the object's interior and preview the extraction. Applying the extraction erases the background to transparency, leaving just the extracted object. You can also use the Force Foreground option to extract a monochromatic or uniform-colored object based on its predominant color.

Lesson 7

67mm

7 Retouching and Repairing

New features in Adobe Photoshop 7.0 and ImageReady 7.0 build on the success of the clone tool to make retouching photographs even easier and more intuitive. Thanks to the underlying technology supporting these new features, even touchups of the human face appear so lifelike and natural that it is difficult to detect that the photograph has been altered.

In this lesson, you'll learn how to do the following:

- Use the clone stamp tool to eliminate an unwanted part of an image.
- Use the pattern stamp tool and pattern maker to replace part of an image.
- Use the healing brush and patch tool to blend in corrections.
- Make corrections on a duplicate layer and adjust it for a natural look.
- Backtrack within your work session using the History palette.
- Use the history brush to partially restore an image to a previous state.
- Use snapshots to preserve earlier states of your work and to compare alternate treatments of the image.

This lesson will take about 45 minutes to complete. The lesson is designed to be done in Adobe Photoshop. Several of the tools and features used in these procedures are not available in ImageReady, including the healing brush tool, patch tool, pattern stamp tool, and Pattern Maker.

If needed, remove the previous lesson folder from your hard drive, and copy the Lesson07 folder onto it. As you work on this lesson, you'll overwrite the start files. If you need to restore the start files, copy them from the *Adobe Photoshop 7.0 Classroom in a Book* CD.

Note: *Windows users need to unlock the lesson files before using them. For more information, see "Copying the Classroom in a Book files" on page 4.*

Getting started

Before beginning this lesson, restore the default application settings for Adobe Photoshop. See "Restoring default preferences" on page 5.

Unlike most other lessons in this book, you'll work on three separate image files in this lesson. Each of these employs the different retouching tools in unique ways, so you'll witness the strengths and special uses of the various tools.

You'll start by using the File Browser to preview the three finished images that you'll retouch in this lesson and to open your first start file.

1 Start Adobe Photoshop.

If a notice appears asking whether you want to customize your color settings, click No.

2 Choose File > Browse, or drag the File Browser tab from the palette well on the tool options bar to the center of your work area.

Or, after you select the File Browser tab in the palette well, you can click the arrow on the tab to open the File Browser palette menu, and then choose Show In Separate Window.

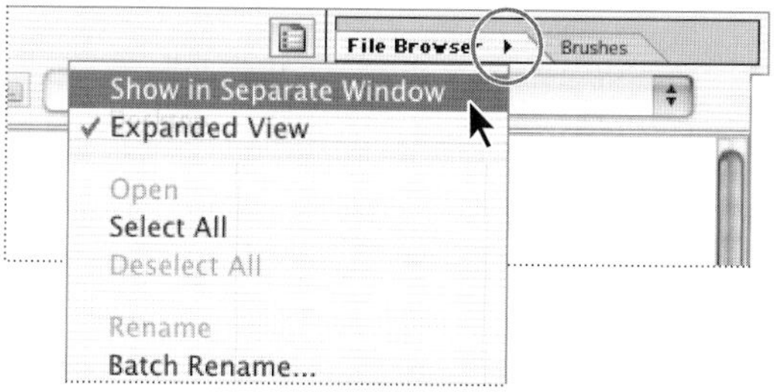

3 In the upper left pane of the File Browser, locate and select the Lessons/Lesson07 folder.

4 In the right pane, select the thumbnail for the 07A_End.psd file. If necessary, resize the middle pane on the left side of the File Browser (by dragging its upper, lower, and right edges) to see an enlarged thumbnail of the image.

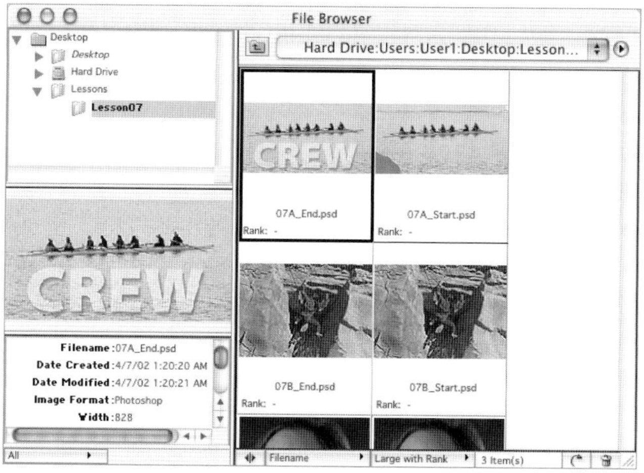

The image includes a photograph ofa women's crew team and some text in the foreground.

5 Select the other thumbnails in the Lesson07 folder to see the "before" and "after" states of the three images you'll work on in this lesson:

• In the first project, you'll repair a torn-off corner of the scanned image and then remove some distracting areas where a boat and its wake appear behind the rowers.

• In the second project, you'll clean up the stone wall beside the climber to remove some graffiti and bullet holes from the surface of the rock.

• In the third project, you'll retouch the portrait to remove some of the fine lines from the man's forehead and around his eyes.

6 When you have finished previewing the files, double-click the thumbnail for the 07A_Start.psd to open the file. If necessary, zoom in to 100% and resize the image window so that you can see the entire image.

7 On the File Browser palette menu, choose Dock to Palette Well, or click the File Browser close button to close it.

Repairing areas with the clone stamp tool

The clone stamp tool uses pixels from one area of an image to replace the pixels in another part of the image. Using this tool, you can not only remove unwanted objects from your images, but you can also fill in missing areas in photographs you scan from damaged originals.

You'll start by filling in the torn corner of the photograph with cloned water from another area of the picture.

1 Select the clone stamp tool ( ).

2 In the tool options bar, open the Brush pop-up palette and select a medium-sized brush with a soft edge, such as Soft Round 21. Then, make sure that the Aligned option is selected.

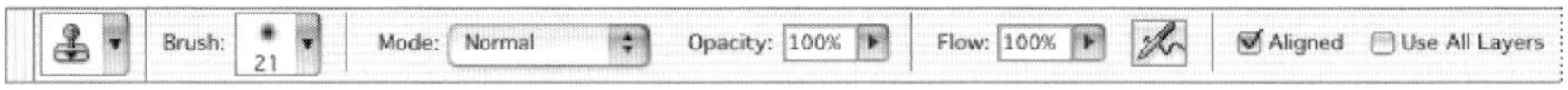

3 Move the clone stamp tool pointer to the center of the image so that it is at the same horizontal level as the top edge of the torn corner. Then, hold down Alt (Windows) or Option (Mac OS) so that the pointer appears as target cross hairs, and click to start the sample or copy at that part of the image.

4 Starting at the top edge of the torn corner of the photograph, drag the clone stamp tool over the missing area of the image.

Notice the cross hairs to the right of the clone stamp tool and how they follow the brush as you paint. The crosshairs indicate the area of the image that the clone stamp tool is using to paint.

5 When you finish cloning a small area of the missing corner, release the mouse button. Move the pointer to another area of the missing corner, and start dragging again.

Notice that the crosshairs reappear at the original sampling position. This happens because you selected the Aligned option, which resets the crosshairs at that position regardless of the position of the brush.

Note: *When the Aligned option is not selected and you make multiple brush strokes, the crosshairs and the brush maintain the same spatial relationship (distance and direction) that they had when you started your first brush stroke, regardless of the location of the original sample site.*

6 Continue cloning the water until the entire missing corner of the image is filled in with water.

If necessary to help make the surface of the water appear to blend in naturally with the rest of the image, you can adjust your cloning by resetting the sample area (as you did in Step 3) and recloning. Or, you can try deselecting the Aligned option and cloning again.

7 When you are satisfied with the appearance of the water, choose File > Save.

Using the pattern stamp tool

The next task to be done is to remove the boat and its wake from the upper area of the image. You could do this with the clone stamp tool, but instead you'll use another technique. Since the entire area has a similar pattern, you can use the new Pattern Maker feature in Photoshop 7.0 to create a realistic pattern that you can use to paint out the wake and boat.

Creating a pattern

You'll begin by defining a new pattern for your project.

1 In the toolbox, select the rectangular marquee tool (⬚). Then, drag to select an area of the water between the right end of the rowing shell and the wake. Make sure that your selection includes only water and that it does not include any of the wake behind the passing motor boat.

2 Choose Filter > Pattern Maker.

3 Under Tile Generation in the Pattern Maker dialog box, click the Use Image Size button.

4 Click Generate. The Pattern Maker image area fills with your water pattern.

You can click Generate again to create variations on the pattern. Then, you can use the arrow buttons at the bottom of the right side of the dialog box to review the different patterns and select the one you want to use. However, for the water image, these will probably be quite similar.

5 Under Tile History in the lower right area of the dialog box, click the Saves Preset Pattern button ( ).

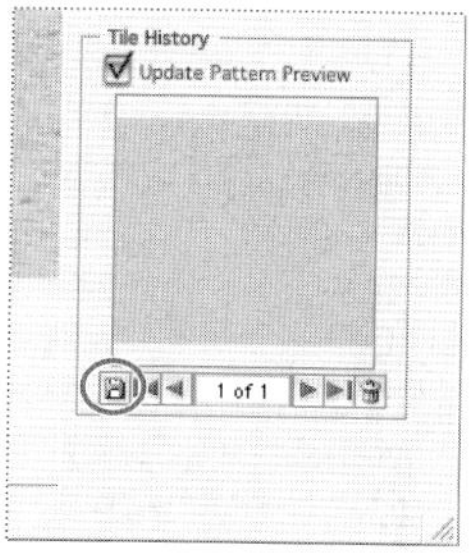

6 In the Pattern Name dialog box, type **Water**, and click OK to return to the Pattern Maker dialog box.

7 In the Pattern Maker dialog box, click Cancel to close the dialog box without replacing the image with the Water pattern.

If you clicked OK instead of Cancel, the Pattern Maker dialog box would replace the entire image with the new pattern you've just created and saved. Replacing the image is not what you want to do, so Cancel is the right button to click.

Note: *If you accidentally filled the image with water, choose Edit > Undo. Because you already saved your Water pattern, it is not lost and there is no need to redo this procedure. Furthermore, this pattern is now a permanent part of your Pattern set until you actively delete it, so you can apply the Water pattern to other Photoshop images, even in later work sessions.*

Applying a pattern

Now you're ready to use your pattern to take out the boat and wake.

1 Choose Select > Deselect.

2 In the toolbox, select the pattern stamp tool (), hidden under the clone stamp tool ().

3 In the tool options bar, change the Brush selection to a brush about 13 pixels in diameter. Leave the Mode set to Normal, Opacity at 100%, Flow at 100%, and the Aligned checked box selected.

4 Click the arrow for the Pattern option to open the pattern picker. Then select the Water pattern you created earlier, and click outside the palette to close it. The Water thumbnail now appears in the Pattern option on the tool options bar.

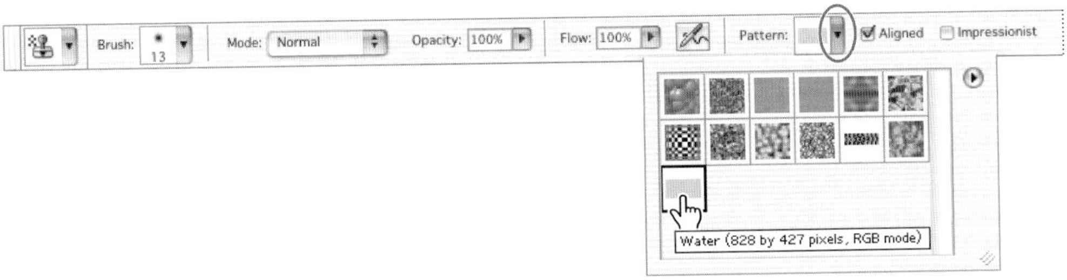

To identify a pattern, let the pointer hover over the thumbnail in the pattern picker for a few seconds until a tooltip appears, showing the pattern name and information about its dimensions and mode. Or, click the arrow button in the upper right area of the pattern picker to open the palette menu, and select one of the other display options that include the names: Text Only, Small List, or Large List.

5 In the image window, drag the pattern stamp tool brush over the wake and boat to replace them with the Water pattern. Continue painting with the pattern stamp tool until you are satisfied with the results.

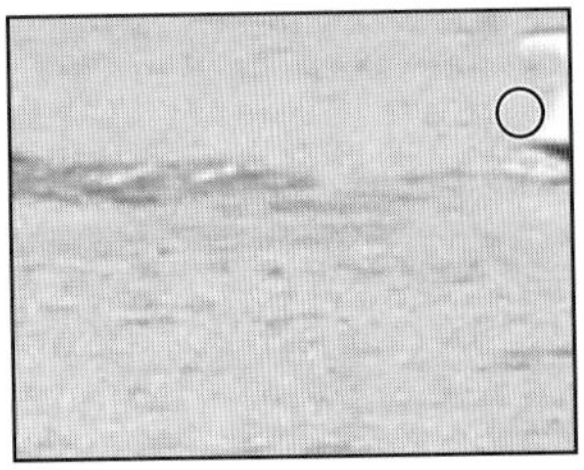

You'll add just one final touch to this retouching project, and then you'll be finished working on this image.

6 In the Layers palette, click to place an eye icon (👁) in the CREW layer, so that the text is visible in the image window.

7 Choose File > Save, and then close the 07A_Start.psd file.

Using the healing brush and patch tools

The new healing brush and patch features in Photoshop 7.0 go one step beyond the capabilities of the clone stamp and pattern stamp tools. Using their ability to simultaneously apply and blend pixels from area to area, they open the door to natural-looking touchups in areas that are not uniform in color or texture.

In this project, you'll touch up the stone wall, removing some graffiti and bullet holes marring its surface. Because the rock has variations in its colors, textures, and lighting, it would be challenging to successfully use the clone stamp tool to touch up the damaged areas. Fortunately, the healing brush and patch tools make this process easy.

If you want to review the "before" and "after" versions of this image, use the File Browser, as described in "Getting started" on page 194.

Using the healing brush to remove flaws

Your first goal for this image is to remove the initials marring the natural beauty of the rock wall.

1 Choose File > Open, and open the 07B_Start.psd file, or use the File Browser and double-click the thumbnail to open the file.

2 Select the zoom tool (🔍) and click the initials "DJ" that have been scratched into the lower left area of the rock, so that you see that area of the image at about 200%.

3 In the toolbox, select the healing brush tool ().

4 In the tool options bar, click the Brush option arrow to open the pop-up palette of controls, and drag the slider or type to enter a Diameter value of **10 px**. Then, close the pop-up palette and make sure that the other settings in the tool options bar are set to the default values: Normal in the Mode option, Sampled in the Source option, and the Aligned check box deselected.

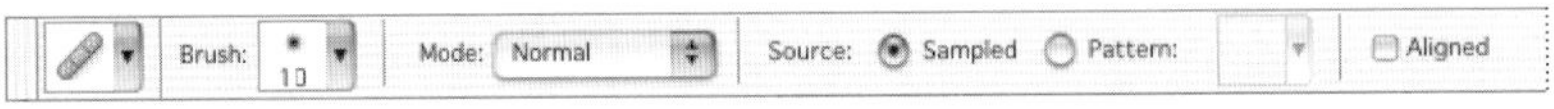

5 Hold down Alt (Windows) or Option (Mac OS) and click a short distance above the scratched-in graffiti in the image to sample that part of the rock. Release the Alt/Option key.

6 Starting above the graffiti "D," paint straight down over the top part of the letter, using a short stroke.

Notice that as you paint, the area the brush covers temporarily looks as if it isn't making a good color match with the underlying image. However, when you release the mouse button, the brush stroke blends in nicely with the rest of the rock surface.

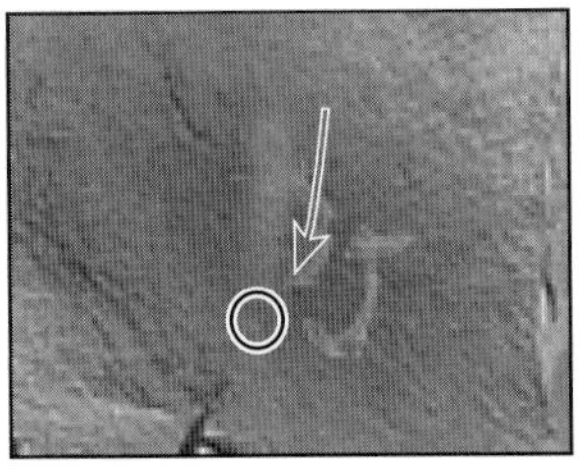

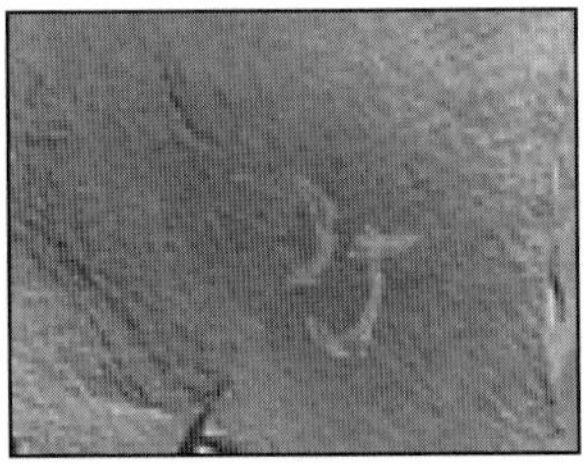

7 Continue using short strokes to paint over the graffiti, starting at the top and moving down until you can no longer detect the graffiti letters.

When you finish removing the graffiti, look closely at the surface of the rock, and notice that even the subtle striations in the rock appear to be fully restored and natural in the image.

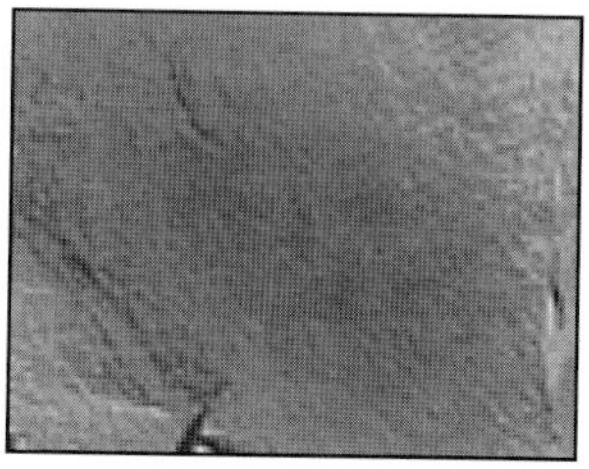

8 Zoom out to 100%, and choose File > Save.

About snapshots and History palette states

When you do retouching work, it can be easy to over-edit images until they no longer look realistic. One of the safeguards you can take to save intermediate stages of your work is to take Photoshop snapshots of the image at various points in your progress.

The History palette automatically records the steps you take when you work on a Photoshop file. You can use the History palette states like a multiple Undo command to restore the image to previous stages in your work. For example, to undo the most recent six steps, simply click the sixth step above the current state in the History palette. To return to the latest state, scroll back down the History palette and select the state in the lowest position on the list.

The number of steps saved in the History palette is determined by a Preferences setting. The default specifies that only the 20 most recent steps are recorded. As you perform additional steps, the earliest states are lost as the latest ones are added to the History palette.

When you select an earlier step in the History palette, the image window reverts to the condition it had at that phase. All the subsequent steps are still listed below it in the palette. However, if you select an earlier state in your work and then make a new change, all the states that appeared after the selected state are lost, replaced by the new state.

Note: *The following technique is not recommended when you work with large or complex images, such as ones with many layers, because this can slow down performance. Saving many previous states and snapshots is RAM-intensive. If you work frequently with complicated images that require maximum RAM, you should consider reducing the number of history states saved by changing that setting in your Photoshop Preferences.*

Snapshots give you an opportunity to try out different techniques and then choose among them. Typically, you might take a snapshot at a stage of the work that you are confident that you want to keep, at least as a base point. Then, you could try out various techniques until you reached a possible completed phase. If you take another snapshot at that phase, it will be saved for the duration of the current work session on that file. Then, you can revert to the first snapshot and try out different techniques and ideas for finishing the image. When that is finalized, you could take a third snapshot, revert to the first snapshot, and try again.

When you finish experimenting, you could scroll to the top of the History palette to where the snapshots are listed. Then, you can select each of the final snapshots in turn and compare the results.

Once you identify the one you like best, you could select it, save your file, and close it. At that time, your snapshots and History palette steps would be permanently lost.

4 In the Layers palette, change the Opacity value of the Retouch layer to **65%**. Now hints of the heaviest skin creases appear in the image, giving the enhanced image a convincing realism.

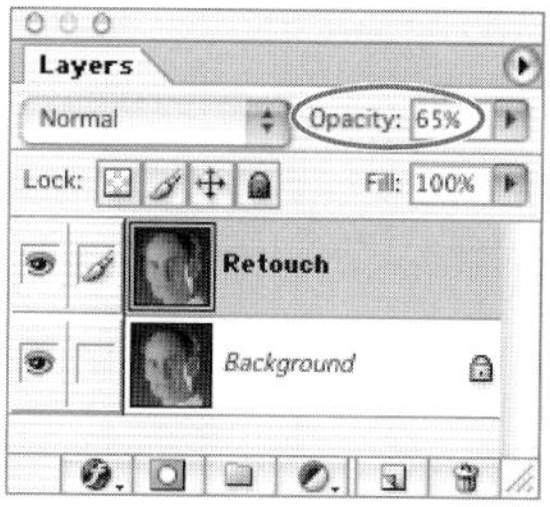

5 Click the eye icon (👁) for the Retouch layer off and on to see the difference between the original image and the corrected one.

6 When you are satisfied with your results, open the Layers palette menu and choose Flatten Image.

Flattening the image reduces the file size, making the file more efficient. However, after you flatten the image, you cannot separate the two layers again.

7 Choose File > Save.

Now the image has just one layer, combining the unaltered original background and the partly transparent retouched layer.

Congratulations, you've finished your work on this lesson. Close any open files.

Review questions

1 Describe the similarities and differences of the clone stamp tool, the pattern stamp tool, the healing brush tool, the patch tool, and the history brush tool.

2 What is a snapshot and how is it useful?

3 What difference does it make if you select or don't select the Aligned option for a retouching tool?

4 Can you use patterns and snapshots in later work sessions or other image files?

Review answers

1 The retouching tools have the following similarities and differences:

- Clone stamp tool: As you paint, the tool duplicates the pixels from another area of the image. You set the sample area by holding down Alt (Windows) or Option (Mac OS) and clicking the clone stamp tool.

- Pattern stamp tool (Photoshop only): As you paint, the tool lays down pixels based on a pattern that you designate. You can create this pattern from an area of the current image, from another image file, or from the default set provided with Adobe Photoshop 7.0.

- Healing brush tool (Photoshop only): This tool works like the clone stamp tool except that Photoshop calculates a blending of the sample pixels and the painting area, so that the restoration is especially subtle yet effective.

- Patch tool (Photoshop only): This tool works like the healing brush tool except that instead of using brush strokes to paint from a designated area, you drag a marquee around the area and then drag the marquee over another area to mend the flawed area.

- History brush tool: This tool works like the clone stamp tool except that it paints pixels from a designated previous state or snapshot that you select in the History palette.

2 A snapshot is a temporary record of a specific stage in your work session. The History palette saves only a limited number of steps. After that, each new step you perform removes the earliest step from the History palette. However, if you take a snapshot of your work at any available step and then continue working, you can revert to that phase later by selecting the snapshot in the History palette, regardless of how many steps you've done in the meantime. You can save multiple snapshots, as needed.

3 The Aligned option governs the relationship between the sample site and the brush. The difference between selecting or not selecting the Aligned option is significant only if you use multiple strokes as you retouch—that is, if you change the position of the pointer between brush strokes.

• If Aligned is selected, then the sampling crosshairs go back to the original sample site each time you start a new brush stroke.

• If Aligned is not selected, then the sampling crosshairs maintain the same relative position to the brush as when you started the first brush stroke, so that an imaginary line between the brush and the crosshairs would always have the same length and direction.

4 The patterns you create and save in the Photoshop Pattern Maker dialog box are saved with the application. Even if you close the current file, switch to another project, quit Photoshop, or reset your Photoshop preferences, that pattern will still be available in the pattern picker. (However, you can actively remove patterns, which deletes the pattern permanently.) Snapshots are deleted when you close the image file and cannot be recovered in later work sessions on that file. Snapshots are available only in the image file in which you created them.

Lesson 8

Notice that the strokes you make with the history brush tool remove the strokes that you made with the art history brush tool and uncover the original dark lines of the image.

8 When you are satisfied with the look of the tree, click the arrow beside the Tree layer set in the Layers palette to collapse the list, and then choose File > Save.

Getting the most from the brush tool

The Brushes palette includes a variety of preset brush tips with different sizes, shapes, and densities. The Brushes palette and tool options bar for the brush tool also include a complex variety of settings that you can use with your selected brush. This flexibility gives you a powerful set of combinations that challenges you to use brushes in imaginative new ways.

One of the useful properties of brushes is that you can select different blending modes and opacity settings as you paint on a single layer. These settings are independent of each other and of any blending modes or opacity settings that you apply to the entire layer.

For color illustrations of brush blending modes, see figure 8-2 of the color section.

Another enhancement in Photoshop 7.0 is that you can do more with the custom brush shapes that you create and save. You can now assign different sizes and other properties to your custom brushes and even change them on the fly like any other brush.

Painting with a specialty brush

Among the preset brushes are several that paint in preshaped units, so that a single stroke paints a series of stars, leaves, or blades of grass. You'll use one of the grass-shaped brushes to create a hillside for your image landscape.

1 In the Layers palette, select the Tree layer set and click the New Layer button ( ). Double-click Layer 1, and type **Grass** to rename the layer.

2 In the toolbox, select the brush tool ( ), and then scroll down the Brushes palette and select the Dune Grass brush shape.

To reduce the amount of scrolling needed in the Brushes palette, open the Brushes palette menu and choose Small Thumbnail (the display shown in the illustration below step 3). You can confirm your brush choice by letting the pointer hover over the thumbnail until a pop-up appears, identifying the brush by name. If you prefer to see the brush descriptions as you scroll, you can still reduce your scrolling by choosing Small List on the Brushes palette menu.

3 Above the sample displayed at the bottom of the Brushes palette, drag the Master Diameter slider or type to change the value to **60 pixels**.

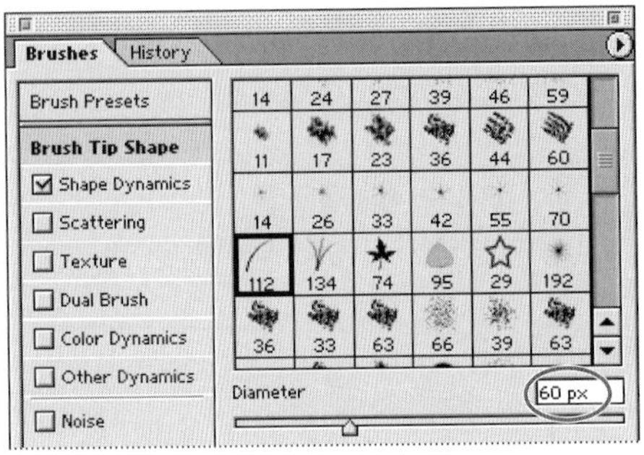

4 In the Color palette, select a pale yellow color, such as R=**230**, G=**235**, B=**171**.

5 If necessary, adjust the size and magnification of the image window so that you can see the entire image. Then drag the brush tool in a gently waving line from the center of the left side of the image to the lower right corner. (Refer to the 08End.psd file as a guide.)

6 Continue dragging the brush tool across the lower left area of the image to fill in the hillside of grass. Do not try to fill the area with solid color, but leave a little bit of the sky showing through so that you can still see most of the individual blades of grass.

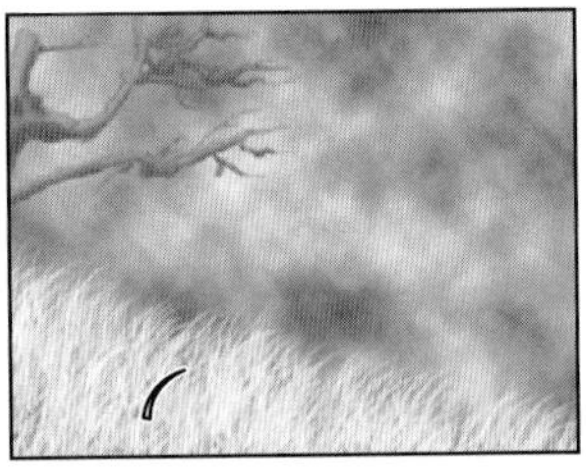

7 In the Color palette, select a light olive-green color, such as R=**186**, G=**196**, B=**93**.

8 In the tool options bar, select Multiply in the Mode pop-up menu, and change the Opacity value to **50%**.

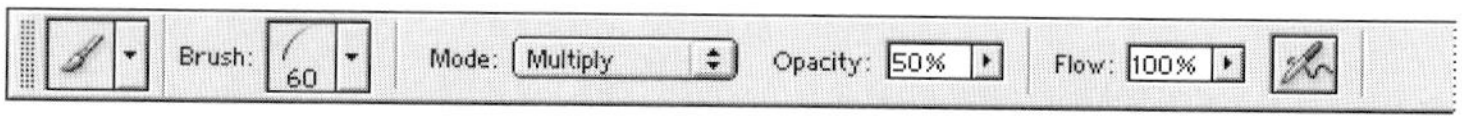

9 Resume painting over the same area of your image, building up color until you are satisfied with the results. If you make a mistake or want to start over, select a previous state in the History palette, and start again from that state.

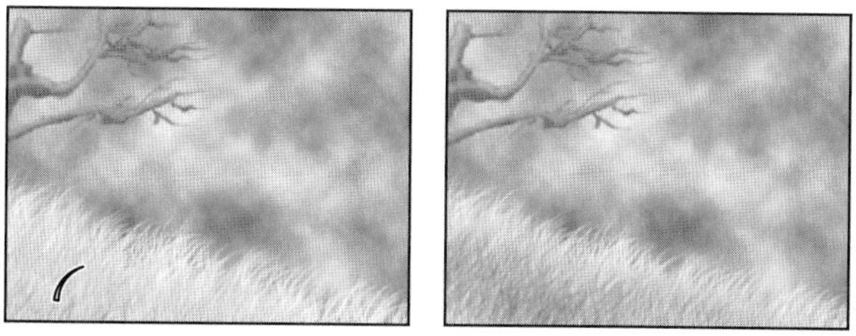

Notice that when you first start painting the olive color, the results are relatively faint. As you continue to drag the brush over the same areas, the color you add multiplies itself by the underlying pixel colors, producing increasingly darker shades of green. This process effectively demonstrates the way the Multiply blending mode works.

10 Choose File > Save.

Creating new color swatches for the umbrella image

Now you'll use traditional painting techniques and brushes to complete more painting layers that have been started for you, and which together become an umbrella.

1 In the Layers palette, click the eye-icon box for the Umbrella layer set to make those layers visible in the image window. Then click the arrow to expand the layer set, so that five layers appear within that set, only some of which are visible.

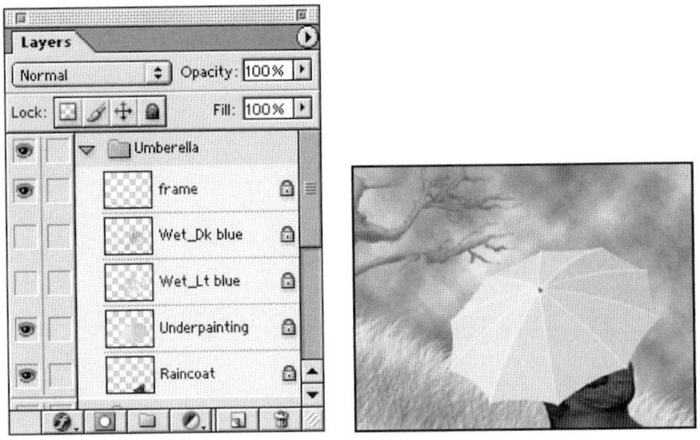

2 Click to set an eye icon (👁) for the Wet_Lt blue layer. A series of brush strokes have been laid down for you, so that the color and shape are developing definition.

3 Click to set an eye icon for the Wet_Dk blue layer.

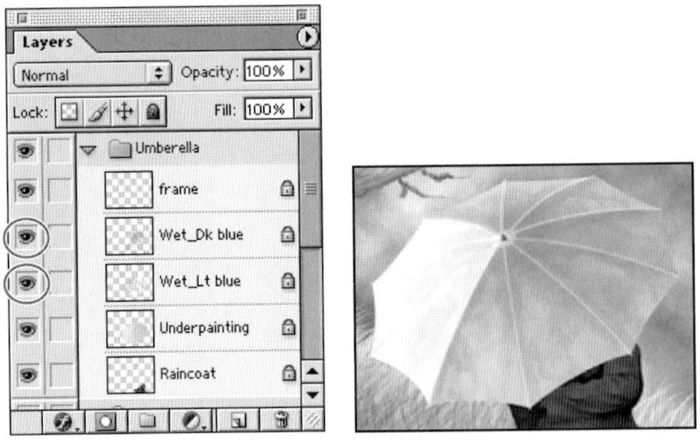

Seven of the ten segments of the umbrella have been painted with additional color, but the three segments on the left side of the umbrella have not. Before you begin painting, you'll define two new color swatches that you'll use for this task.

4 Drag the Swatches palette tab out of the Color palette group so that it becomes a stand-alone palette. Move the Swatches palette so that it is near the Color palette and you can see both palettes completely.

5 In the Color palette, select a medium blue color, such as R=**150**, G=**193**, B=**219**.

6 Move the pointer into the blank (gray) area to the right or below the last swatch in the bottom row of the Swatches palette. When the pointer appears as a paint bucket icon (), click to add the medium blue color to the collection of swatches.

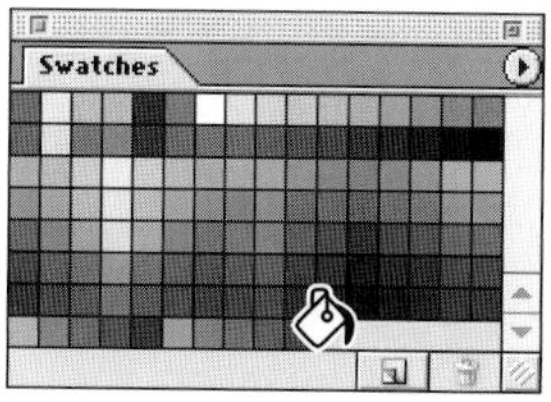

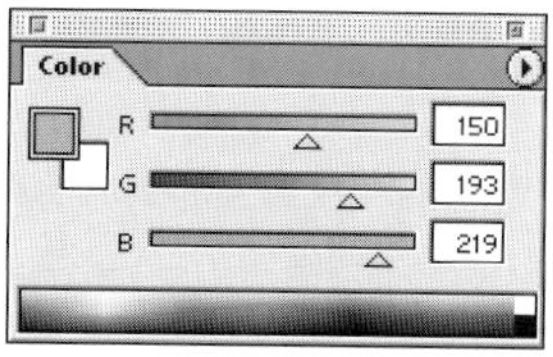

7 In the Color Swatch Name dialog box, click OK to accept the default name.

8 Define a darker blue color in the Colors palette, such as R=**132**, G=**143**, B=**199**, and add that color to the Swatches palette, using the technique you just learned.

Adding brush libraries to the Brushes palette

The brushes available to you go beyond the default set. You'll add a new brush library to the brush presets in the Brushes palette, and select settings for one of those brushes.

1 On the Brushes palette menu, choose Large List. Now both the thumbnail of the tip and the name appears for each brush shape.

2 Again on the Brushes palette menu, choose Wet Media Brushes.

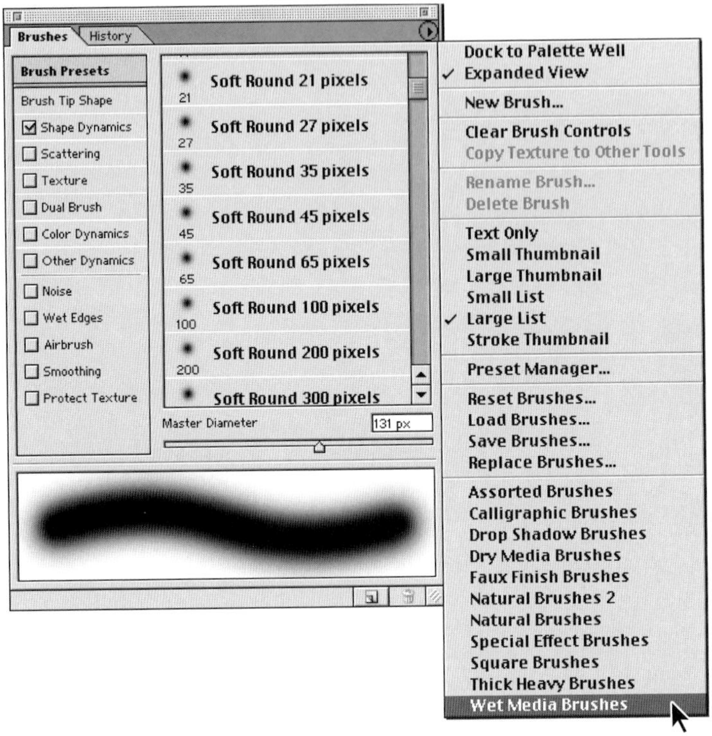

3 A small dialog box appears; select Append to add the Wet Media Brushes library to the set currently listed in the Brushes palette.

Note: *If you accidentally click OK instead of Append, Photoshop replaces the existing brush set with the Wet Media Brushes set. To restore the original brush set, choose Reset Brushes on the Brushes palette menu, and then repeat step 1 to append the Wet Media Brushes to the default brush library.*

4 Scroll to the bottom of the list in the Brushes palette, and select the Watercolor Light Opacity brush. Then, just below the list, use the Master Diameter slider or type to set the value at **25 pixels**.

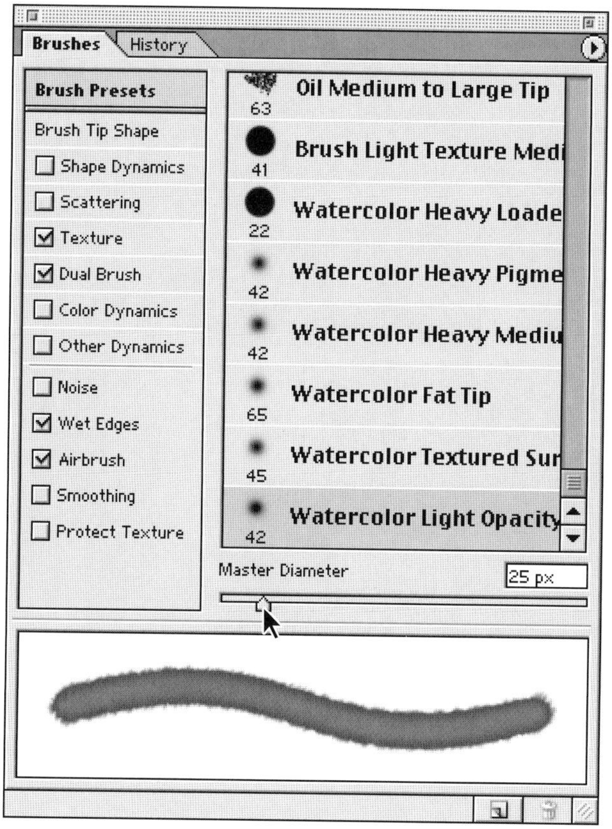

5 In the tool options bar, select Normal on the Mode pop-up menu and change the Opacity value to **15%**.

6 In the Swatches palette, select the medium blue swatch you created in the previous topic.

Creating form and dimension with wet media brushes

Before you begin painting, you'll load one of the alpha channels that has been prepared for you. You'll use three different prepared alpha channels to restrict your painting to each of the three segments you're going to paint, so you don't have to worry about getting paint in other areas of the image or painting out the ribs of the umbrella.

1 In the Layers palette, select the Wet_Dk blue layer.

2 Choose Select > Load Selection.

3 In the Load Selection dialog box, select Alpha 1 from the Channel pop-up menu, and then click OK.

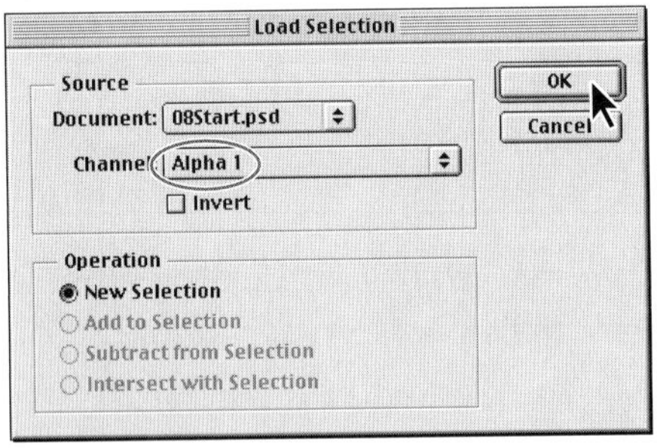

In the image window, a selection border appears around the lower of the three umbrella panels that you'll paint.

If you find the selection border distracting, you can hide it by pressing Ctrl+H (Windows) or Command+H (Mac OS). Even though the marquee is not visible, your painting is still restricted to the area within it. To make the selection border visible again, use the same keyboard shortcut.

4 Starting near the center of the umbrella, paint with short, downward strokes to build up a subtle shading, concentrating on the areas next to the umbrella spokes.

As you work, you can experiment with different brush sizes and opacity settings to create varied texture and shadows.

5 In the Swatches palette, select the darker blue swatch that you created earlier, and continue to paint until that section of the umbrella coordinates nicely with the panels of the umbrella that are already painted.

6 Choose Select > Deselect. Then choose Select >Load Selection and select the Alpha 2 Channel in the pop-up menu. Repeat steps 4 and 5 to shade in the second of the three umbrella sections.

7 Repeat step 6, but this time select the Alpha 3 Channel and paint the third umbrella section.

8 When you finish painting, click the arrow to collapse the Umbrella layer set in the Layers palette, drag the Swatches palette back into the Color palette layer group, and then choose File > Save.

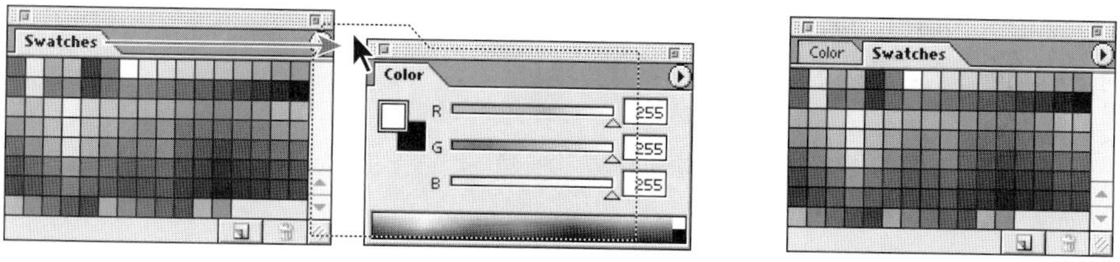

Saving a customized preset brush

Now you'll create and save a brush based on an existing preset, and use it in your painting.

1 In the Layers palette, select the Umbrella layer set, if necessary, and then click the New Layer button (▣) at the bottom of the palette. Double-click the new layer and type **Leaves** to name the layer.

2 With the brush tool selected in the toolbox, scroll through the Brushes palette and select the Scattered Maple Leaves brush.

3 On the left side of the Brushes palette, click the words *Shape Dynamics* to display the Shape Dynamics options on the right side of the palette. Enter the following settings, noticing how the stroke sample at the bottom of the palette changes each time you change a setting:

- In the Control pop-up menu near the top of the palette, select Fade, and then type **50** as the Fade value.
- In Roundness Jitter, drag the slider or type to set the value at **40%**.

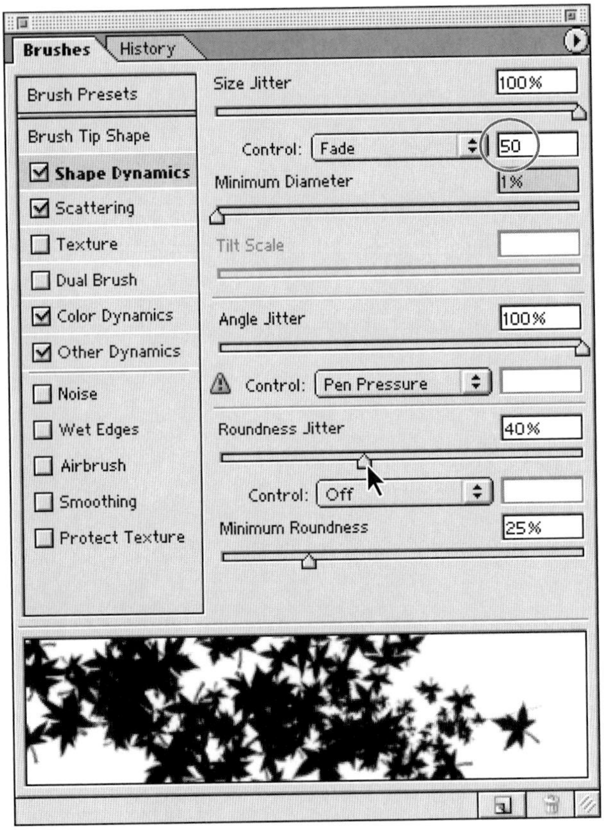

4 Again on the left side of the Brushes palette, click the word *Scattering* and drag the sliders or type on the right side of the palette to change the following settings:

- For Scatter, set the value at **265%**.
- For Count, set the value at **1**.

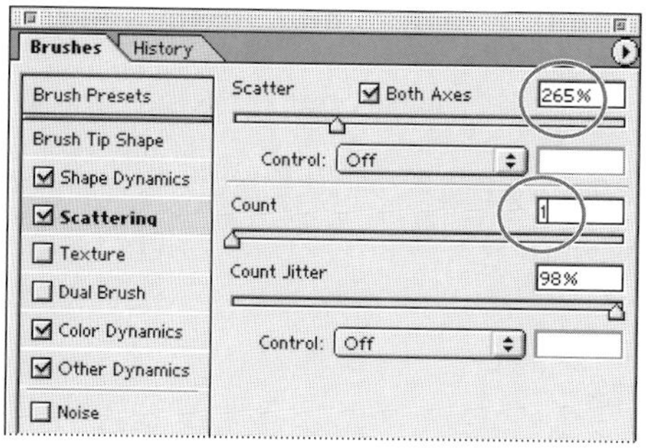

5 In the upper left corner of the Brushes palette, click the Brush Presets to display the list of brushes again. Then drag the Master Diameter slider or type **65 pixels**.

6 At the bottom of the Brushes palette, click the New Brush button (), and then type **Leaves 65** as the brush name and click OK.

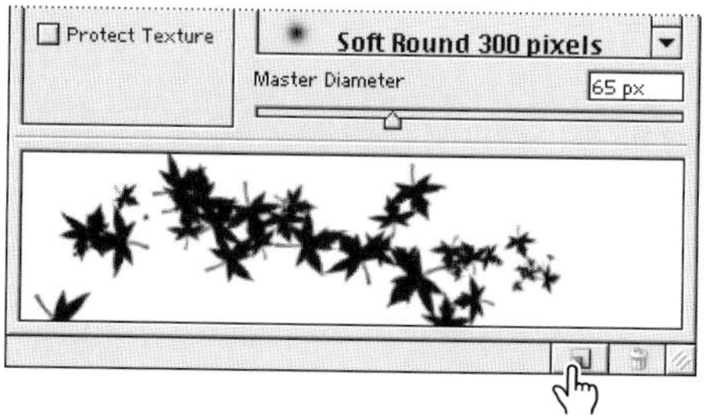

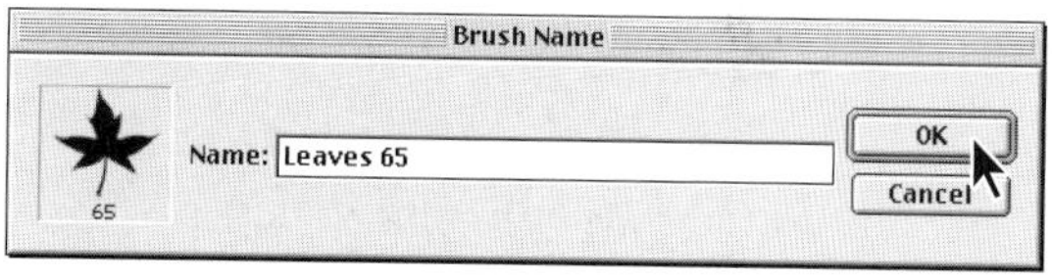

The new brush appears at the bottom of the list of brushes in the palette.

Painting from the image onto a created border

In the final artwork, a white border surrounds the painting, and leaves appear to fly outside the edges of the picture and onto the border area. To create that effect, your first step is to create the border.

1 In the toolbox, make sure that the background color is white. Then choose Image > Canvas Size.

2 In the Canvas Size dialog box, type **580** as the Width and select pixels from the units pop-up menu. Then type **440** as the Height and set those units also to pixels, and click OK.

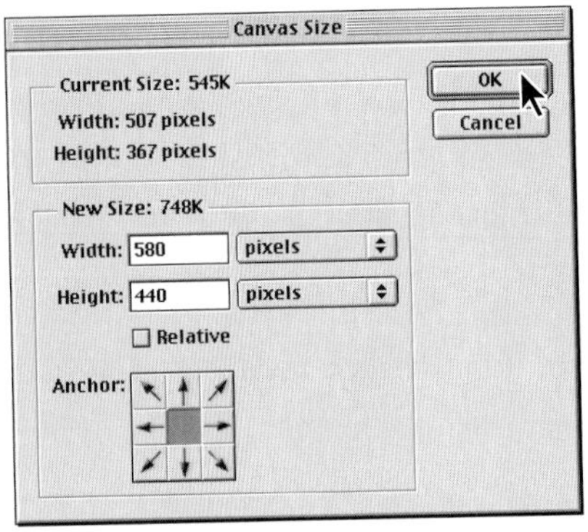

3 On the Color palette, select a dark, warm yellow, such as R=**185**, G=**141**, B=**59**. This will be the base color for the autumn leaves you'll add.

You're now ready to start painting your leaves. Make sure that your Leaves 65 brush is still selected in the Brushes palette and that the tool options bar shows Normal as the Mode option and Opacity at 100%.

4 Drag the Leaves 65 brush in a gentle arc from the tips of the tree branches to the right, letting the stroke wander into the top border and onto the border on the right side. Refer to the 08End.psd file as a guide.

5 If you are not satisfied with the result, choose Edit > Undo, and try again.

Because brush Scatter settings are designed to create random patterns, each brush stroke produces slightly different results. It may take several tries before you get a pattern that you like. Remember that you can use either the Undo command or the History palette to backtrack through these attempts.

To save some results of the painting as potential candidates, use the History palette to take a snapshot of the image and then revert to an earlier state. Try painting again from that state to see if you can improve on your results. By taking snapshots of a series of attempts, you can compare them and select the one you like best as the basis for the remaining work in this lesson.

6 When you get the results you want, choose File > Save.

Creating a custom brush

Now that you've tried out the maple-leaf and dune-grass brush shapes, you may be wondering about other similar brushes you could use in your work. With Photoshop 7.0, you can create and save brushes in any shape you choose, even using other photographs as the basis of your custom brush shapes. You can then set options for the brush.

1 Choose File > Open, and open the Flower.jpg file in the Lessons/Lesson 08 folder.

2 Choose Edit > Define Brush. In the Brush Name dialog box, type Flower, and click OK. The Flower brush appears in the Brushes palette and is selected.

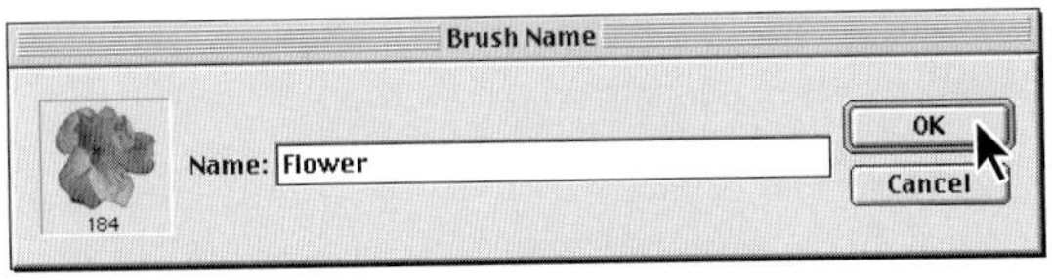

3 Close the Flowers.jpg image file.

4 In the Brushes palette, click Brush Tip Shape near the top of the left side of the palette. Then on the right side, drag the sliders or type to set the Diameter value at **25** and the Spacing at **80%**.

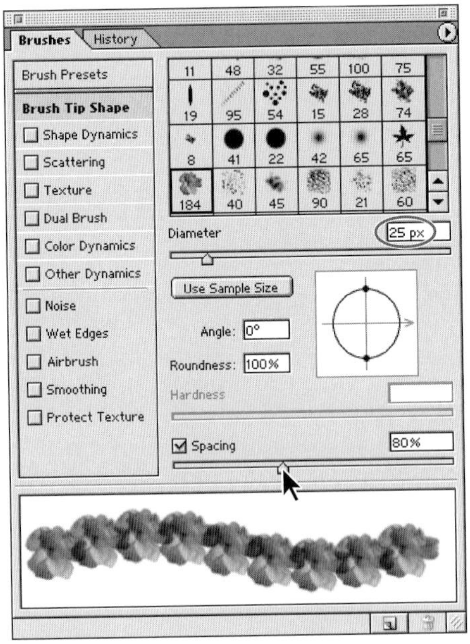

5 On the left side of the palette, click Shape Dynamics. Then, on the right side, set the following options:

- In the Control pop-up menu, select Off.
- For Roundness Jitter, drag the slider or type **44%**.
- For Minimum Roundness, drag the slider or type **39%**.

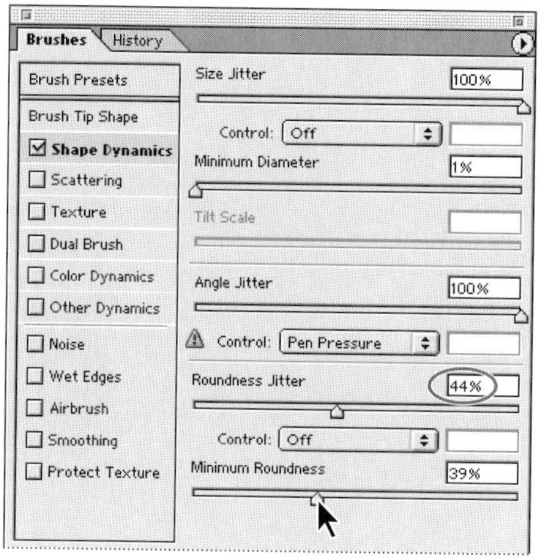

6 Once more on the left side of the palette, click Scattering, and use the slider or type to set the Scatter value at **500%** and the Count at **1**.

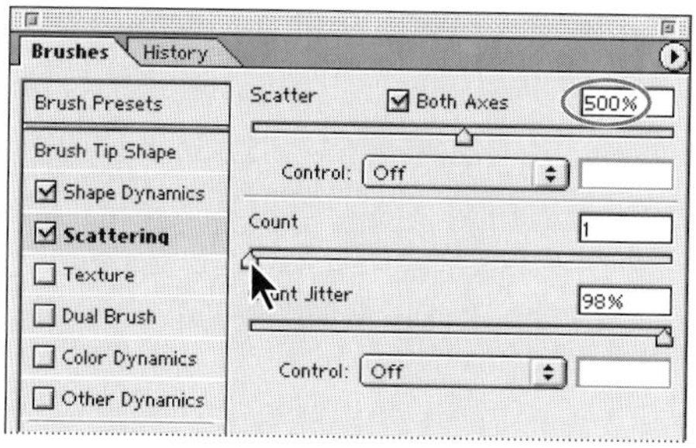

7 Finally, click Color Dynamics on the left side of the palette and change the Hue Jitter to **15%**.

Your brush is now ready for show business.

Painting with a custom brush

You're going to use your custom flower brush to paint a design on the fabric of the umbrella. To prevent yourself from accidentally painting the other parts of the image, you'll use another alpha channel, in the same way that you used alpha channels when you painted the shadings into the umbrella earlier in this lesson.

1 In the Layers palette, click the Umbrella layer set to make it active, and then click the arrow to expand it so that you can see the five layers nested in that set.

2 Click the New Layer button () at the bottom of the Layers palette. Double-click the new layer, which appears at the top of the Umbrella layer set layers, and type **Flowers** to name the layer.

3 Drag the Flowers layer down in the Layers palette so that it is between the Frame layer and the Wet_Dk blue layer.

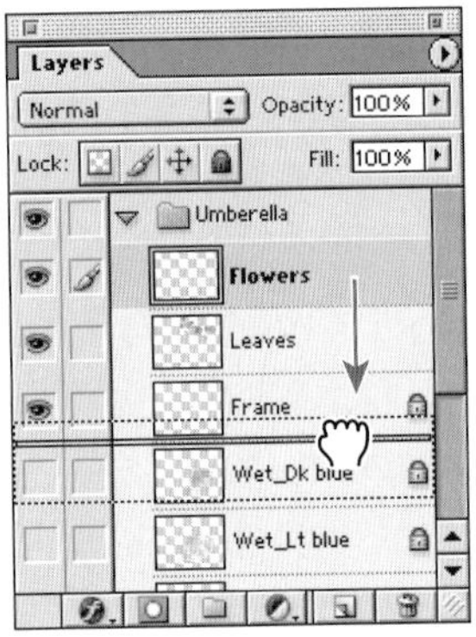

4 Choose Select > Load Selection, and then select the Alpha 4 option from the pop-up menu in the Load Selection dialog box, and click OK.

This alpha channel selects the entire umbrella shape. Remember that you can hide the selection marquee using Ctrl+H (Windows) or Command+H (Mac OS) if you prefer not to be distracted by the movement in the marquee.

5 Make sure that the brush tool is still selected in the toolbox and that the Flower brush is still selected in the Brushes palette.

6 In the Color palette or Swatches palette, select a bright red color.

7 Using a series of short brush strokes, paint flowers onto the surface of the umbrella, creating a random pattern of fairly uniform density. Continue painting until you are satisfied with the result.

8 In the Layers palette, keep the Flowers layer selected and select Multiply from the blending mode pop-up menu. Then set the Opacity value for the layer to **70%**.

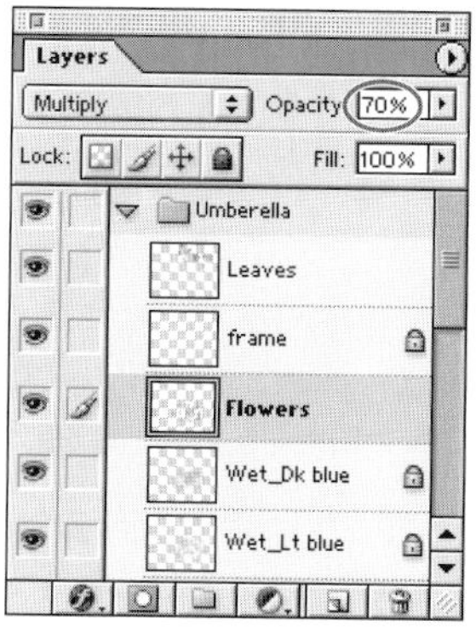

9 Choose File > Save.

Using the Pattern Maker to create a picture frame

In previous versions of Photoshop you could generate tiled patterns, but the new Pattern Maker in Photoshop 7.0 marks a significant improvement in this functionality. Using this new feature, you can generate multiple, seamless patterns that you can use anywhere in your images.

Defining a new pattern

You'll use a prepared texture file as the basis of your custom pattern.

1 Choose File > Open, and open the Texture.jpg in your Lessons/Lesson08 folder.

2 In the toolbar, make sure that the background color is white, and then choose Image > Canvas Size.

3 In the Canvas Size dialog box, change the units to pixels, and set Width at **780** and Height at **580**. Then click OK.

4 Choose Filter > Pattern Maker.

5 In the Pattern Maker dialog box, use the rectangular marquee tool (⬚) in the upper left corner of the dialog box to select a large area of the textured image. Be careful not to include any of the white background in your selection.

If you want to change your selection, hold down Alt (Windows) or Option (Mac) and click the Reset button in the upper right corner of the Pattern Maker dialog box (which appears as the Cancel button when you release Alt/Option); then make a new selection.

6 Click the Generate button.

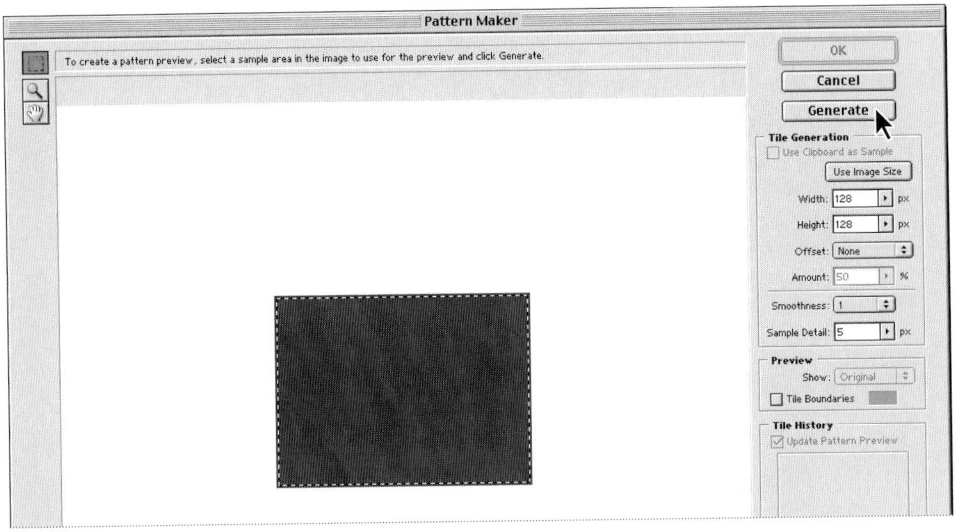

Notice the dimension information listed in the dialog box. The default tile size is 128x128 pixels, so that is the size of the pattern generated.

7 Under Preview (on the right side of the dialog box), select the Tile Boundaries check box.

A grid appears over your pattern, displaying the boundaries of the individual pattern tiles, each 128x128 pixels. Click the Tile Boundaries check box again to deselect it and hide the grid.

8 Under Tile Generation (on the right side of the dialog box), click the Use Image Size button so that the tile size matches the image size. Notice that the dimensions in the Width and Height displays are now the same as the dimensions of the image.

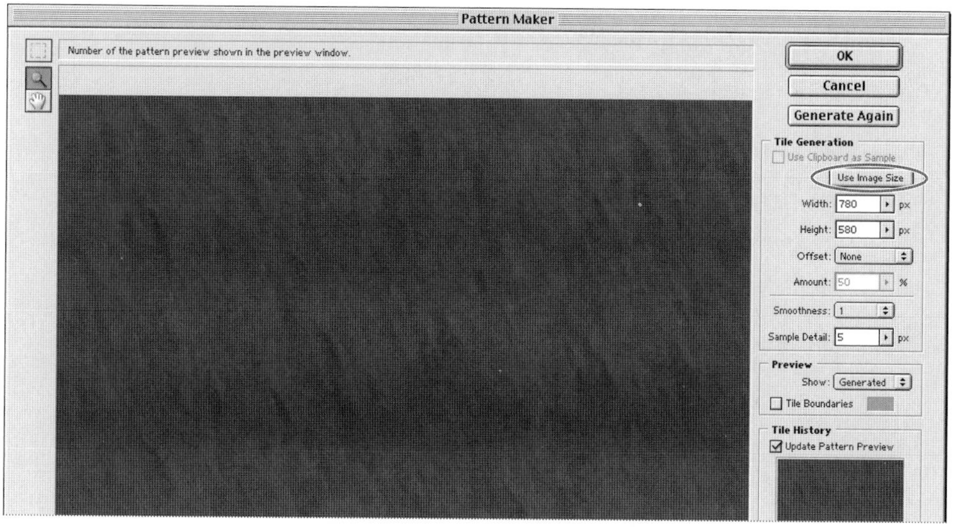

9 Click the Generate Again button a few times to generate variations of your pattern. Then use the Previous and Next buttons at the bottom of the Tile History area of the dialog box to cycle through the patterns you've created. Select one of the patterns to use, and click OK.

In the image window, a new, seamless pattern fills the entire canvas.

10 Choose File > Save As, and name the file **Matte.psd**, saving it in your Lessons/Lesson08 folder.

Patterns can be saved and used repeatedly in any number of projects. Because you'll use this pattern just once, you won't bother to save it as a permanent pattern.

Composing the patterned image with your painting

This is it—the final phase of your work. Because you're going to flatten the painting image as part of the process, you'll create a duplicate of the original as a safeguard, in case you ever need to go back and edit it. You'll add one last touch to give the textured picture frame a dimensional appearance.

1 Click the image window for your umbrella painting to make it active.

2 Choose Image > Duplicate to create a duplicate image file, and name the duplicate **Autumn_flat.psd**. Click OK.

3 In the Layers palette menu, choose Flatten Image to combine all the layers in the Autumn_flat file.

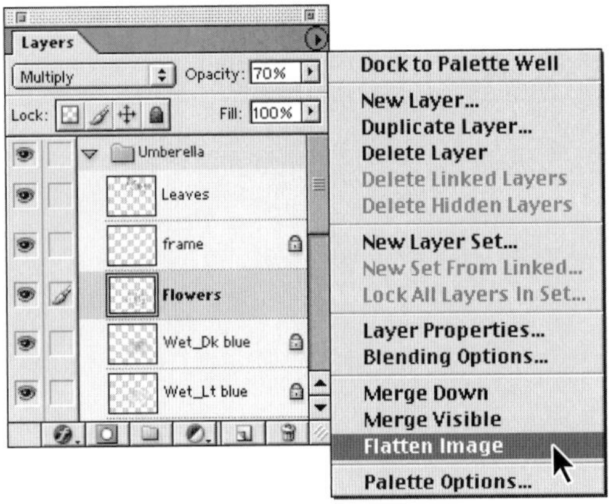

4 In the toolbox, select the move tool (►✥).

5 Hold down Shift and drag the painting from the Autumn_flat.psd image window into the Matte.jpg image window. The flattened painting appears as Layer 1 in the Matte.jpg Layers palette.

Holding down the Shift key as you drag in the painting image automatically centers it in the Matte.jpg image, so that the textured picture frame is equally sized around the painting.

6 With Layer 1 selected in the Layers palette, click the Add A Layer Style button () at the bottom of the palette to open the pop-up menu, and choose Inner Shadow.

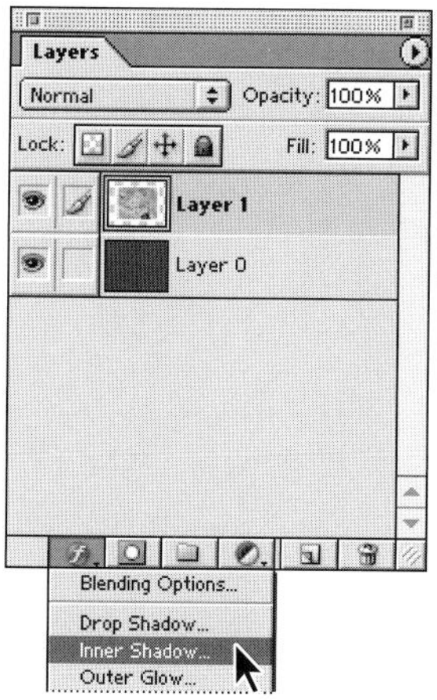

7 In the Layer Style dialog box, set the Inner Shadow options, with the Opacity value at **85%**, the Distance at **6**, and the Size at **7**. Leave the other settings unchanged, and click OK.

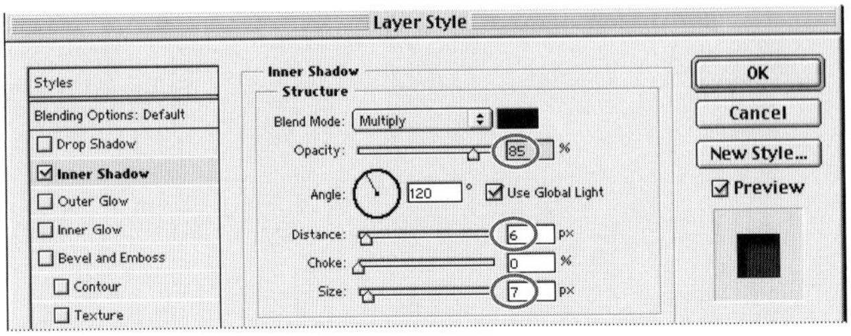

Congratulations, you've finished your painting. You can save your file or print it on a color printer as a souvenir.

This lesson represents just the tip of the metaphorical iceberg in terms of the potential of the painting tools. For more information, see the painting topics in Adobe Photoshop 7.0 online Help.

Review questions

1 What is a blending mode, and what are the three types of color that are helpful for visualizing a blending mode's effect?

2 What do the History palette, eraser tool, and history brush tools have in common?

3 What is the difference between the art history brush tool and the history brush tool?

4 Describe two techniques for protecting transparent areas.

5 How can you add to your brush collection?

Review answers

1 A blending mode controls how pixels in an image are affected by the tools or other layers. It's helpful to think in terms of the following colors when visualizing a blending mode's effect:

- The *base color* is the original color in the image.
- The *blend color* is the color being applied with the painting or editing tool.
- The *result color* is the color resulting from the blend.

2 The History palette, eraser tool, and history brush tools can all restore your image to an earlier state so that you can undo an operation or correct a mistake.

3 The art history brush tool paints with a stylized stroke based on a selected state or snapshot. The stylized stroke of the art history brush tool simulates the look of different paint styles. The history brush tool paints a copy of the selected state or snapshot into the current image window. You can use the history brush tool to remove the strokes made with the art history brush tool.

4 One method of preserving areas of transparency on a layer that you are painting is to use the Lock Transparent Pixels option—one of four Lock options on the Layers palette. A second method is to create a new layer above the layer with the transparent pixels you want to protect and then to group the new layer with the layer below it. With the layers grouped, you can paint freely on the new layer because the paint applies only to areas with colored pixels in the underlying layer.

5 Two ways of adding to the default set of available brushes are to load additional brush libraries and to create new custom brush shapes. Adobe Photoshop 7.0 includes a number of brush libraries that are available but not loaded by default, keeping the number of brushes on the Brushes palette down to a manageable number. You can switch from one library of brushes to another, or you can open more libraries and append them to the current set. You can define custom libraries that include the brushes you use most often, just as you can define custom brush shapes to suit your work needs. For more information, see "Managing libraries with the Preset Manager" in Photoshop 7.0 online Help.

Lesson 9

9 Basic Pen Tool Techniques

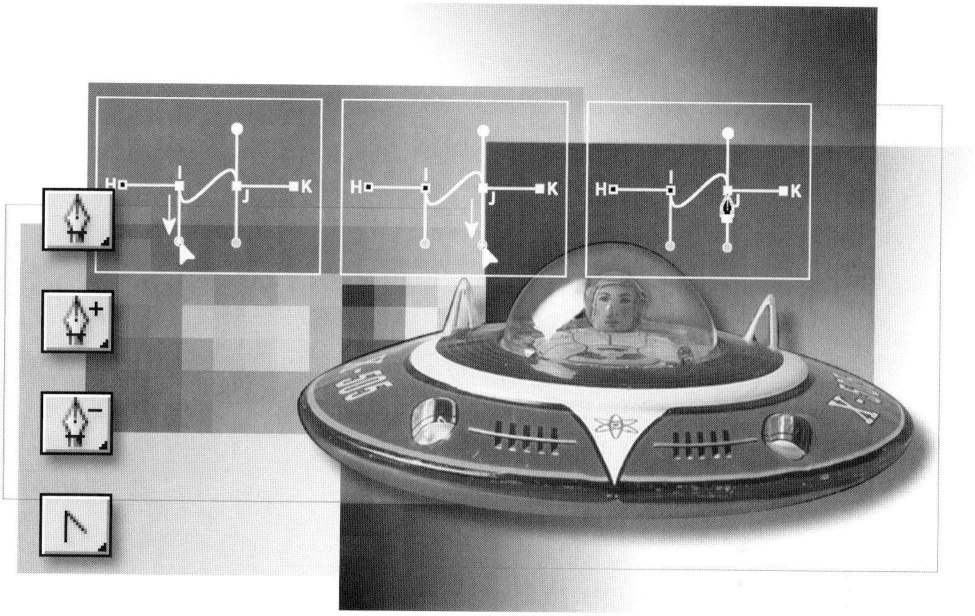

The pen tool draws precise straight or curved lines called paths. You can use the pen tool as a drawing tool or as a selection tool. When used as a selection tool, the pen tool always draws smooth, anti-aliased outlines. These paths are an excellent alternative to using the standard selection tools for creating intricate selections.

In this lesson, you'll learn how to do the following:

- Practice drawing straight and curved paths using the pen tool.
- Save paths.
- Fill and stroke paths.
- Edit paths using the path-editing tools.
- Convert a path to a selection.
- Convert a selection to a path.

This lesson will take about 50 minutes to complete. The lesson is designed to be done in Adobe Photoshop. Adobe ImageReady does not have a pen tool and does not support paths.

If needed, remove the previous lesson folder from your hard drive, and copy the Lesson09 folder onto it. As you work on this lesson, you'll overwrite the start files. If you need to restore the start files, copy them from the *Adobe Photoshop 7.0 Classroom in a Book* CD.

Note: *Windows users need to unlock the lesson files before using them. For more information, see "Copying the Classroom in a Book files" on page 4.*

Getting started

You'll start the lesson by viewing a copy of the finished image that you'll create. Then, you'll open a series of template files that guide you through the process of creating straight paths, curved paths, and paths that are a combination of both. In addition, you'll learn how to add points to a path, how to subtract points from a path, and how to convert a straight line to a curve and vice versa. After you've practiced drawing and editing paths using the templates, you'll open an image of a toy space ship and get more practice making selections using the pen tool.

Before beginning this lesson, restore the default application settings for Adobe Photoshop. See "Restoring default preferences" on page 5.

1 Start Adobe Photoshop.

If a notice appears asking whether you want to customize your color settings, click No.

2 Choose File > Open, and open the file 09End.psd from the Lessons/Lesson09 folder on your hard drive. The End file represents the finished state of the flying saucer image, which you'll begin working on at "Using paths with artwork" on page 280, after you finish practicing on the drawing templates.

3 When you have finished viewing the file, either leave it open for reference or close it without saving changes.

Now you'll open the first template for drawing straight paths and start practicing pen tool techniques.

4 Choose File > Open and open the file Straight.psd from the Lessons/Lesson09 folder.

5 If desired, select the zoom tool (), and drag over the image to magnify the view.

About paths and the pen tool

The pen tool draws straight and curved lines called *paths*. A path is any contour or shape you draw using the pen, magnetic pen, or freeform pen tool. Of these tools, the pen tool draws paths with the greatest precision; the magnetic pen and freeform pen tools draw paths as if you were drawing with a pencil on paper.

Press P on the keyboard to select the pen tool. Pressing Shift+P repeatedly toggles between the pen and freeform pen tools. (In this lesson, you'll stay with the regular pen tool.)

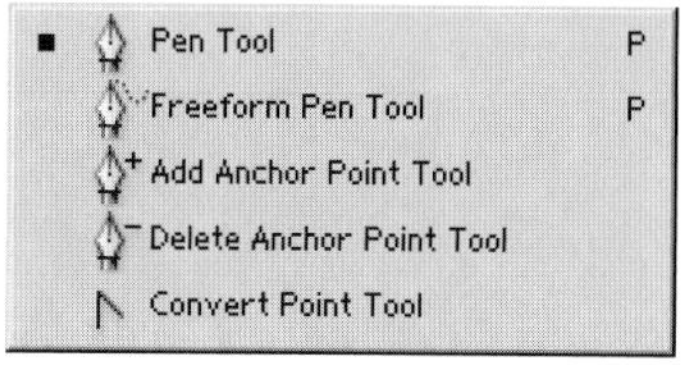

Paths can be open or closed. Open paths have two distinct endpoints. Closed paths are continuous; for example, a circle is a closed path. The type of path you draw affects how it can be selected and adjusted.

Paths that have not been filled or stroked do not print when you print your artwork. (This is because paths are vector objects that contain no pixels, unlike the bitmap shapes drawn by the pencil and other painting tools.)

Before you start drawing, you'll configure the pen tool options and your work area in preparation for the procedures in this lesson.

1 In the toolbox, select the pen tool (✎).

2 In the tool options bar, select or verify the following option settings:

- Select the Paths (▣) option.
- Click the arrow for Geometry Options and make sure that the Rubber Band check box is *not* selected in the Path Options pop-up palette.
- Make sure that the Auto Add/Delete option is selected.
- Select the Add To Path Area option (▣).

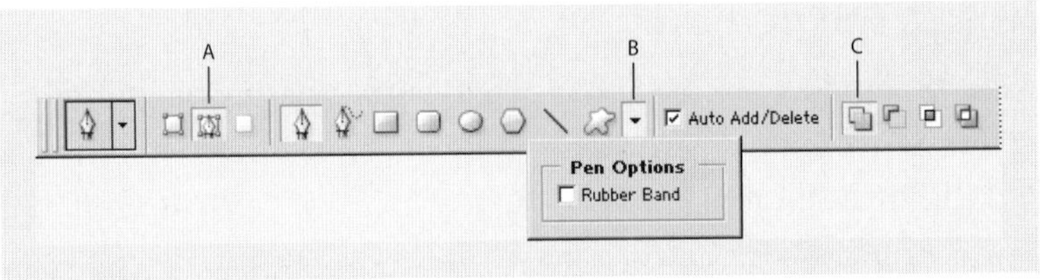

***A.** Paths option* ***B.** Geometry Options menu* ***C.** Add to Path Area option*

3 Click the Paths palette tab to bring the palette to the front of the Layers palette group.

The Paths palette displays thumbnail previews of the paths you draw. Currently, the palette is empty because you haven't started drawing.

Drawing straight paths

Straight paths are created by clicking the mouse button. The first time you click, you set a starting point for a path. Each time thereafter that you click, a straight line is drawn between the previous point and the current point.

1 Using the pen tool, position the pointer on point A in the template and click the pen tool. Then click point B to create a straight-line path.

As you draw paths, a temporary storage area named Work Path appears in the Paths palette to keep track of the paths you draw.

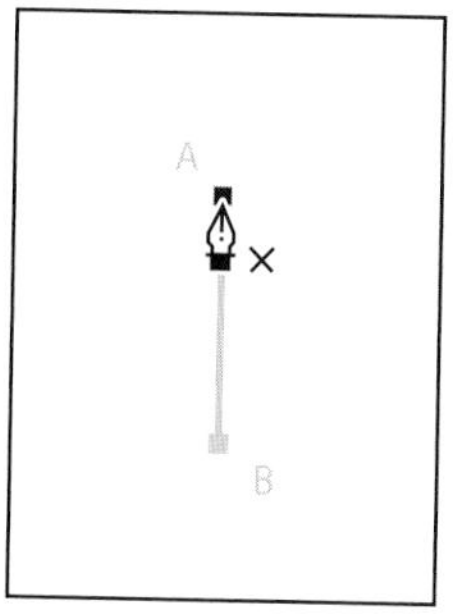

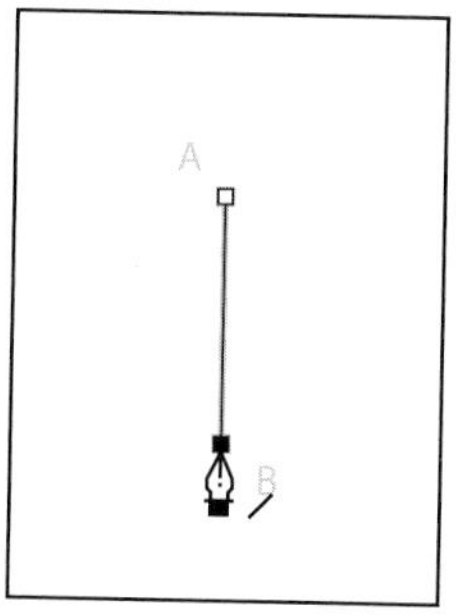

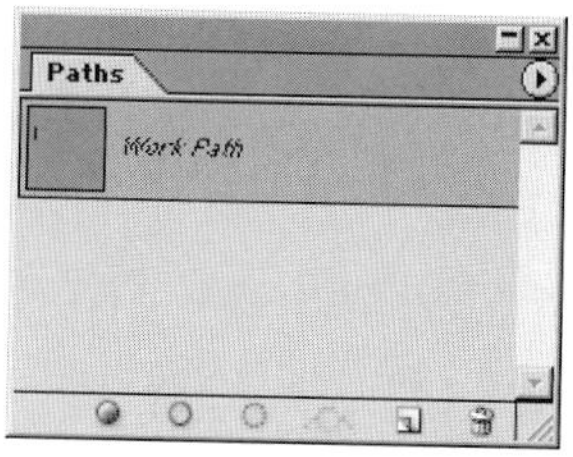

2 End the path in the image by clicking the pen tool (✒) in the toolbox.

The points that connect paths are called *anchor points*. You can drag individual anchor points to edit segments of a path, or you can select all the anchor points to select the entire path.

3 In the Paths palette, double-click the Work Path to open the Save Path dialog box. For Name, type **Straight lines**, and click OK to rename and save the path.

The path remains selected in the Paths palette.

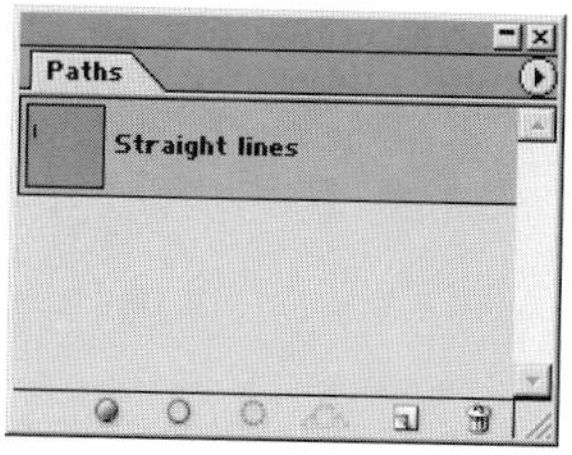

Saving a work path is a good habit to acquire and a necessity if you use multiple discrete paths in the same image file. If you deselected an existing Work Path in the Paths palette and then started drawing again, a new work path would replace the original one, which would be lost.

However, if you deselect a Work Path in the Paths palette, the Work Path and your drawing on it remain there while you perform other non-drawing tasks. You can also reselect the Work Path and continue to add to your drawing.

About anchor points, direction lines, direction points, and components

A path consists of one or more straight or curved segments. Anchor points mark the endpoints of the path segments. On curved segments, each selected anchor point displays one or two direction lines, ending in direction points. The positions of direction lines and points determine the size and shape of a curved segment. Moving these elements reshapes the curves in a path.

A path can be closed, with no beginning or end (for example, a circle), or open, with distinct endpoints (for example, a wavy line).

Smooth curves are connected by anchor points called smooth points. Sharply curved paths are connected by corner points.

When you move a direction line on a smooth point, the curved segments on both sides of the point adjust simultaneously. In comparison, when you move a direction line on a corner point, only the curve on the same side of the point as the direction line is adjusted.

A path does not have to be all one connected series of segments. It can contain more than one distinct and separate path component. Each shape in a shape layer is a path component, as described by the layer's clipping path.

–From Adobe Photoshop 7.0 online Help

Moving and adjusting paths

You use the direct selection tool to select and adjust an anchor point, a path segment, or an entire path.

1 Select the direct selection tool (↖) hidden under the path selection tool (↖) in the toolbox.

To select the direct selection tool by using a keyboard shortcut, press A. Also, when the pen tool is active you can temporarily switch to the direct selection tool by holding down Ctrl (Windows) or Command (Mac OS).

2 Click the A-B path in the window to select it, and then move the path by dragging anywhere on the path using the direct selection tool.

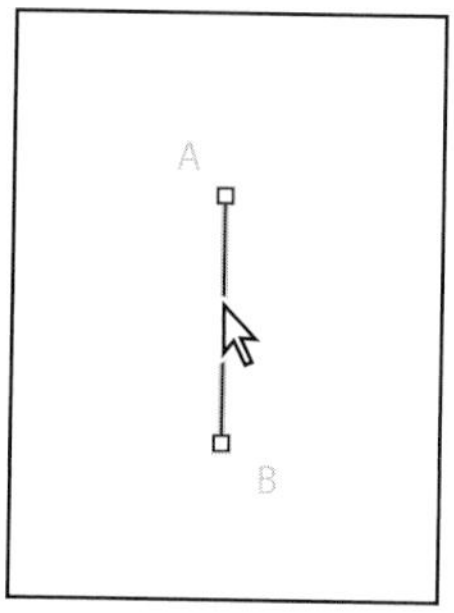

Selecting a path

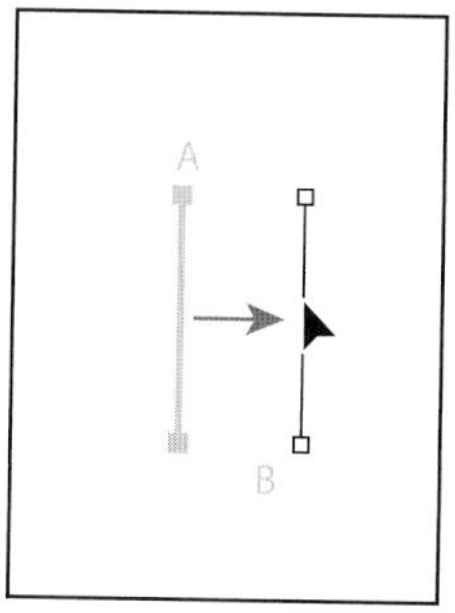

Moving a path

3 To adjust the slope or length of the path, drag one of the anchor points with the direct selection tool.

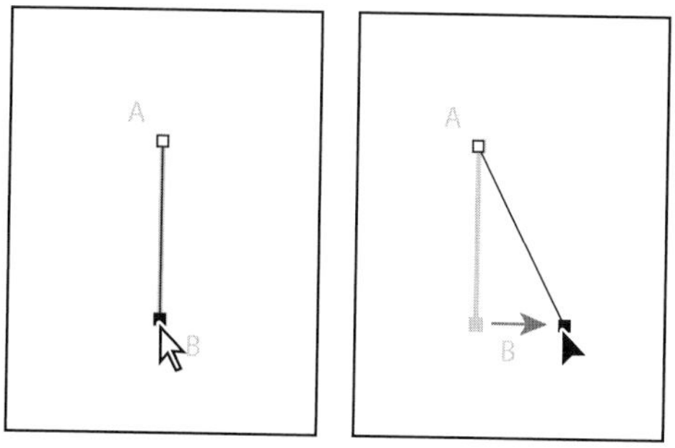

Adjusting the path angle

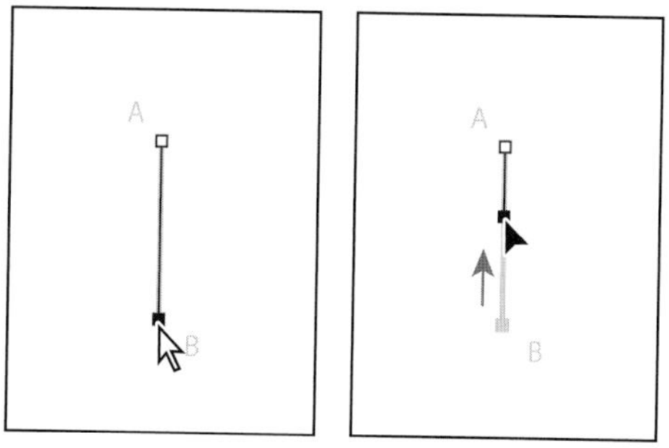

Adjusting the path length

4 Select the pen tool (✒).

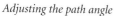

5 To begin the next path, hold the pointer over point C so that an *x* appears in the pen tool pointer to indicate that clicking will start a new path; then click point C.

6 Click point D to draw a path between the two points.

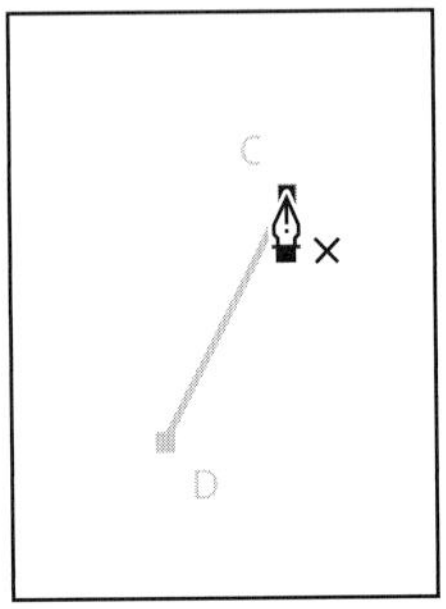

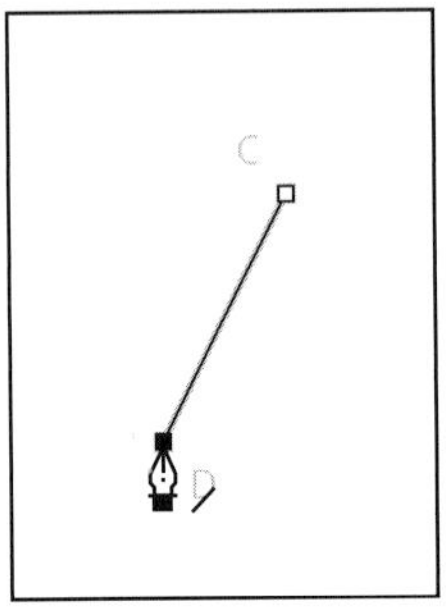

7 End the path using either of the following methods:

- Click the pen tool in the toolbox.
- Hold down Ctrl (Windows) or Command (Mac OS) to temporarily switch to the direct selection tool, and then click away from the path.

Drawing straight paths with multiple segments

So far, you've worked with two-point paths. You can draw complex straight-segment paths with the pen tool simply by continuing to add points. These segments and anchor points can be moved later, either individually or as a group.

1 Using the pen tool (), click point E to begin the next path. Then hold down Shift and click points F, G, H, and I. Holding down Shift as you click restricts the positions along 45° angles.

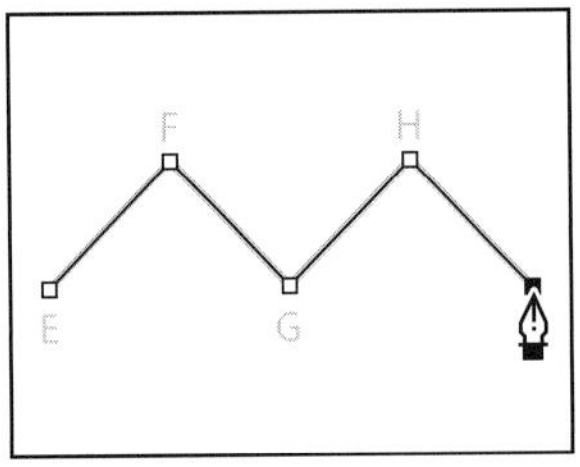

***Note:** If you make a mistake while you're drawing, choose Edit > Undo to undo the last-placed anchor point. Then try again.*

2 End the path using one of the methods you've learned.

When a path contains more than one segment, you can drag individual anchor points to adjust individual segments of the path. You can also select all of the anchor points in a path to edit the entire path.

3 Select the direct selection tool (↖).

4 Click a segment of the zigzag path and drag to move the whole segment. As you drag, both the anchor points for that segment move and the connecting segments adjust accordingly. The length and slope of the selected segment and the positions of the other anchor points do not change.

5 Select one of the individual anchor points on the path and drag it to a new position. Notice how this changes the adjacent segment or segments of the path.

6 Alt-click (Windows) or Option-click (Mac OS) to select the entire path. When an entire path is selected, all the anchor points are solid.

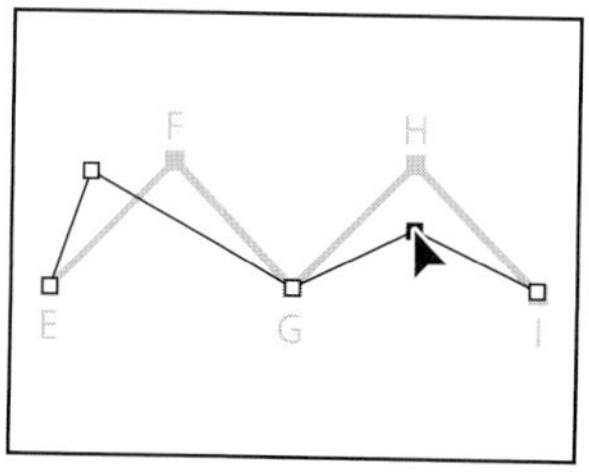

Dragging individual points

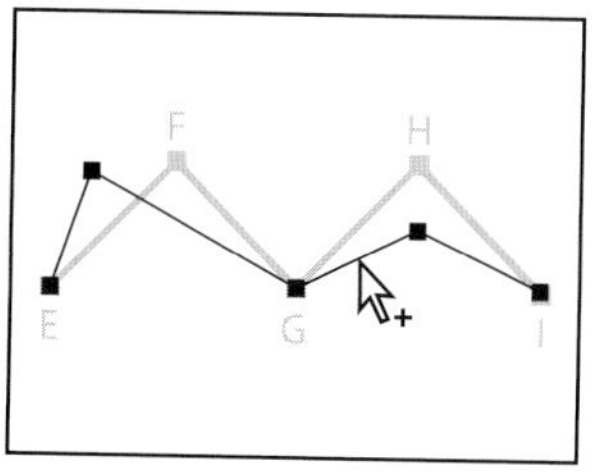

Alt/Option-clicking to select entire path

7 Drag the path to move the entire path without changing its shape.

Creating closed paths

Next you'll draw a closed path. Creating a closed path differs from creating an open path in the way that you end the path.

1 Select the pen tool (✒).

2 Click point J to begin the path; then click point K and point L.

3 To close the path, position the pointer over the starting point (point J), and click.

When you position the pointer over the starting point of a path (J), a small circle appears with the pen tool to indicate that the path will be closed when you click.

Closing a path automatically ends the path. After the path closes, the pen tool pointer again appears with a small x, indicating that your next click would start a new path.

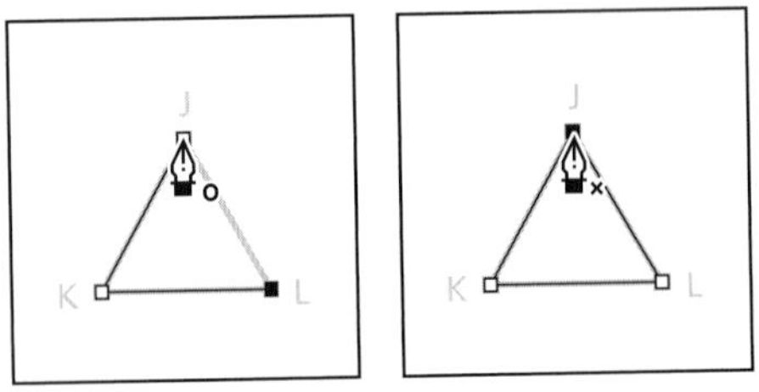

4 For more practice, draw another closed path, using the star-shape template.

5 Examine the thumbnail in the Paths palette.

At this point, all of the paths you've drawn appear in the Straight Lines work path in the Paths palette. Each individual path on the Straight Lines path is called a *subpath*.

Painting paths

Paths and anchor points are non-printing elements of the image. Because the black lines you see on screen as you draw with the pen tool are paths—not strokes—they do not represent any pixels in the image. When you deselect a path, the anchor points and path are hidden.

You can make a path visible in your printed image by painting the stroke, which adds pixels to the image. *Stroking* paints color along the path. *Filling* paints the interior of a closed path by filling it with color, an image, or a pattern. To stroke or fill a path, you must first select it.

1 Click the Swatches palette tab to bring the palette forward. Click any swatch (except white) to select a foreground color to use to paint the path.

2 Select the direct selection tool (↖) and click to select the zigzag line in the image window.

4 Now select and drag the path upward.

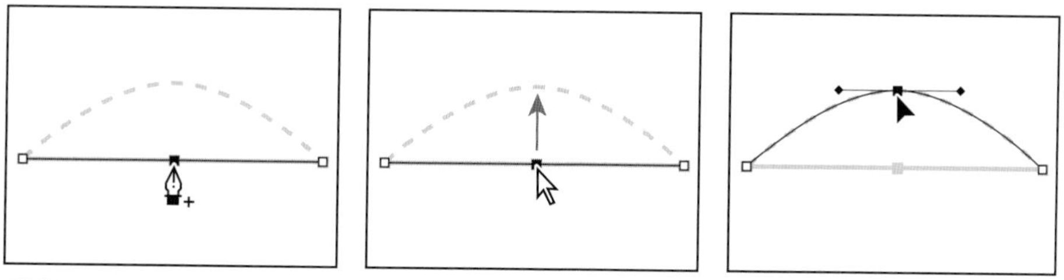

Clicking with the add-anchor-point tool *Dragging the anchor point* *Result*

Next you'll subtract an anchor point from a path.

5 Select the direct selection tool (↖) and select the second path.

Note: *You must select a path before you can delete points from it. However, you can select the path and the anchor points without first selecting a tool. If a path is selected, just move the pen tool over a segment to change it to the add-anchor-point tool. Move the pen tool over an end point to change the tool to the delete-anchor-point tool.*

6 Select the delete-anchor-point tool (✒−) hidden under the add-anchor-point tool (✒+), position the pointer on the red dot over the center anchor point, and then click to remove the anchor point.

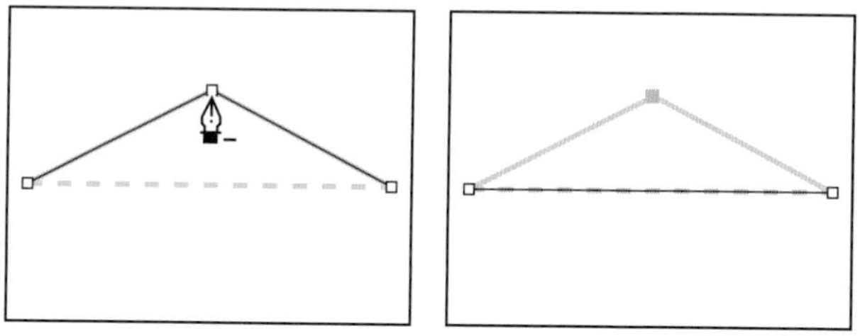

Clicking with the delete-anchor-point tool *Result*

Converting points

Sometimes you may want to change a curve to a corner point or vice versa. Using the convert point tool, you can easily make the adjustment.

Using the convert point tool is very much like drawing with the pen tool. To convert a curve to a corner point, you click the anchor point, and to convert a corner to a curve, you drag from the anchor point.

1 In the Paths palette, select the Convert Directions path.

The shaped path has both corner points and curves. You'll start by converting the corner points to curves, and then you'll convert the curves to corner points.

2 Using the direct selection tool (), select the outer subpath.

3 Select the convert point tool (), hidden under the delete-anchor-point tool ().

4 Position the pointer on a point of the outer path; then click and drag clockwise to convert the point from a corner point to a curve.

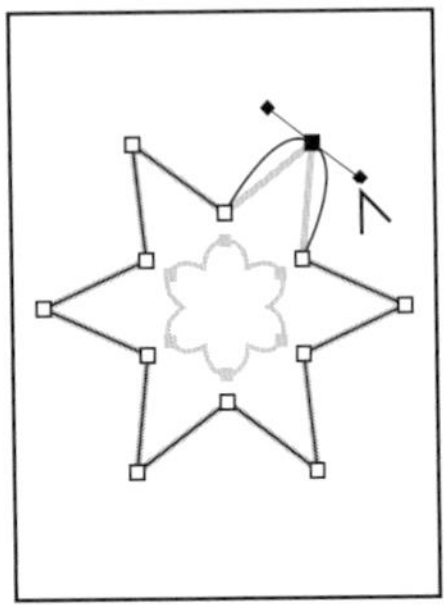

5 Convert the rest of the corner points to smooth points to complete the outer path.

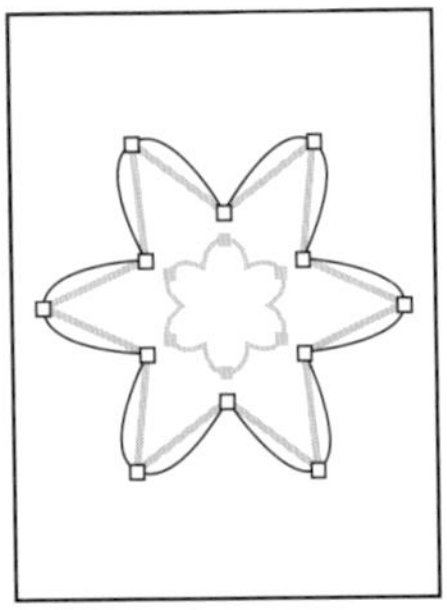

6 Using the convert point tool (↖), click the inner subpath to select it and then click the anchor point at the tips of each curve to convert the curves to corner points.

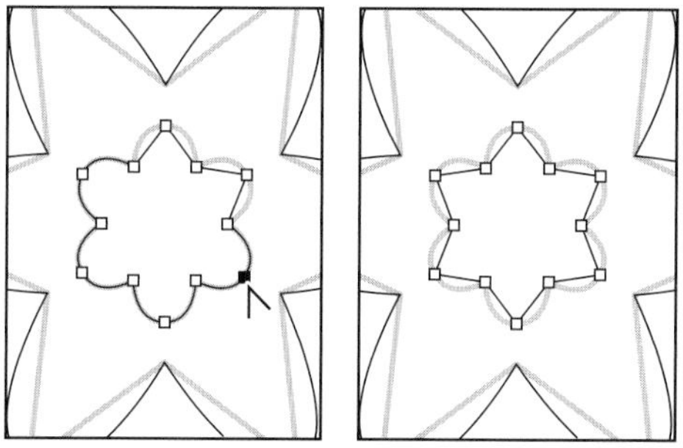

You can also use the convert point tool to adjust only one side of a curved segment. You'll try this on the outer path.

7 Click the outer path with the direct selection tool (↖); then click a curved segment so that direction lines and direction points emanate from the anchor point.

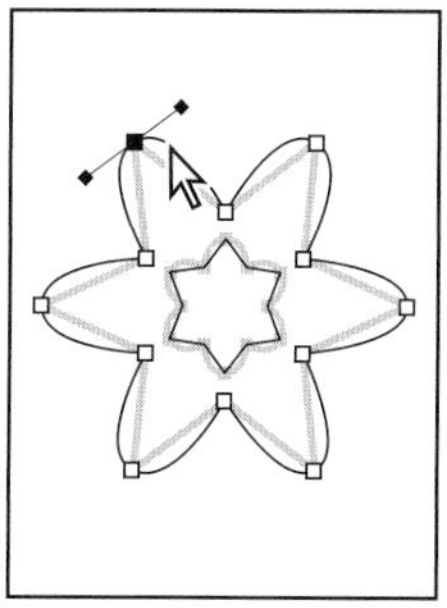

8 Select the convert point tool (↖) again, and drag one of the direction points to change the shape of only one side of the curve.

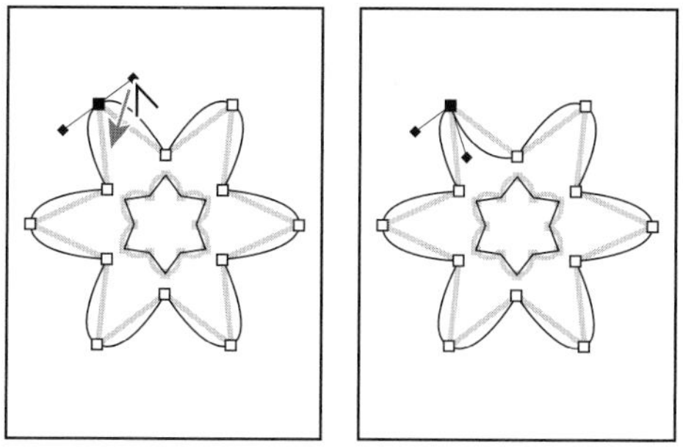

9 Choose File > Close, and don't save changes.

Using paths with artwork

Now that you've had some practice using the templates, you'll use the pen tool to make selections in the fanciful image of a flying saucer traveling through outer space. The saucer has long, smooth, curved edges that would be difficult to select using other methods.

You'll draw a path around the image and create two paths inside the image. After you've drawn the paths, you'll convert them to selections. Then you'll subtract one selection from the other so that only the saucer is selected and none of the starry sky. Finally, you'll make a new layer from the saucer image and change the image that appears behind it.

***Note:** If you want to review the final results of this project, choose File > Open and select the 09End.psd file in your Lessons/Lesson09 folder.*

When drawing a freehand path using the pen tool, use as few points as possible to create the shape you want. The fewer points you use, the smoother the curves are and the more efficient your file is.

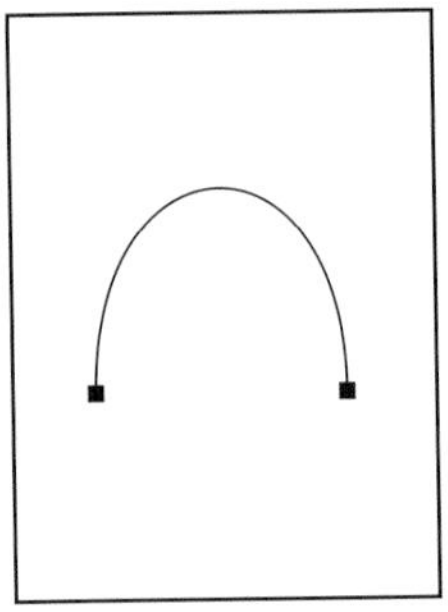

Correct number of points

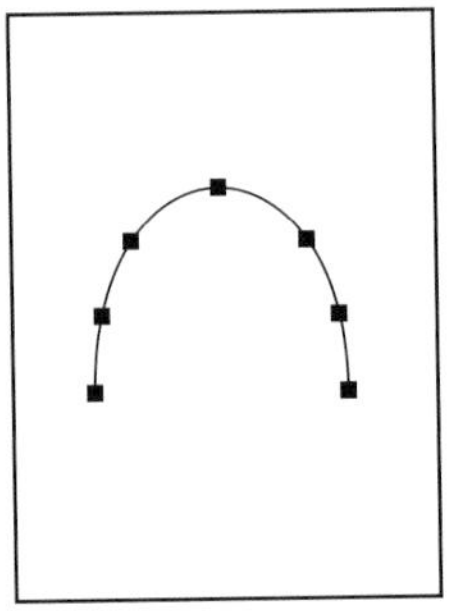

Too many points

Essentially, in this procedure you're going to use the pen tool to connect the dots from point A to point N and then back to point A, practicing what you learned earlier in this lesson about how to set different kinds of points.

- You'll set some straight segments (by simply clicking the points) at points C, F, J, and M.
- You'll set smooth curve points (by dragging to the red dots) for points A, D, E, G, H, I, K, and L.

• You'll set a corner point for a transition from a curved to a straight segment (at point B) by first creating a smooth curve point—again, by dragging to the red dots—and then removing one of the directional lines by Alt+clicking (Windows) or Option+clicking (Mac OS) the point itself.

• You'll set a corner point for a transition from a straight to a curved segment (by first clicking without dragging to create a corner point and then holding down Alt or Option and clicking the point) for point N.

If you're ready to challenge yourself, you can try to do this task using just the instructions above. Or, follow the steps below first, to make sure that you make all the right moves.

Drawing the outline of a shape

Use the following steps to create a path, outlining the shape of the space ship.

1 Choose File > Open, and open the file Saucer.psd from the Lessons/Lesson09 folder.

2 Select the pen tool (), hidden under the convert point tool ().

If necessary, zoom in so that you can easily see the lettered points and red dots on the shape template that has been created for you.

3 Position the pointer on point A, and drag to the red dot to set the first anchor point and the direction of the first curve. Then do the same thing at point B.

At the corner of the cockpit (point B), you'll need to make the point a corner point, to create a sharp transition between the curved segment and the straight one.

4 Alt-click (Windows) or Option-click (Mac OS) point B to convert the smooth point into a corner point by removing one of the direction lines.

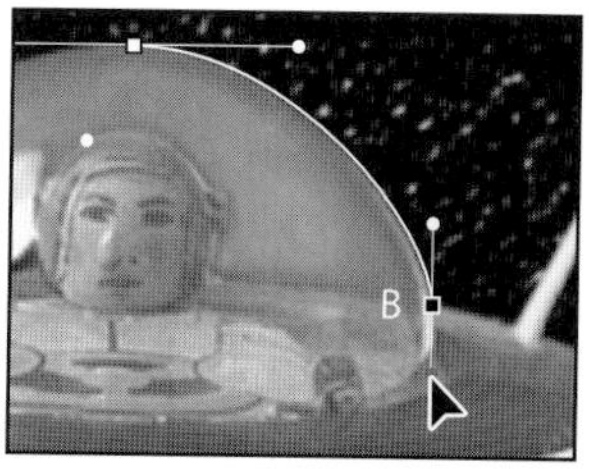

Setting a smooth point at B

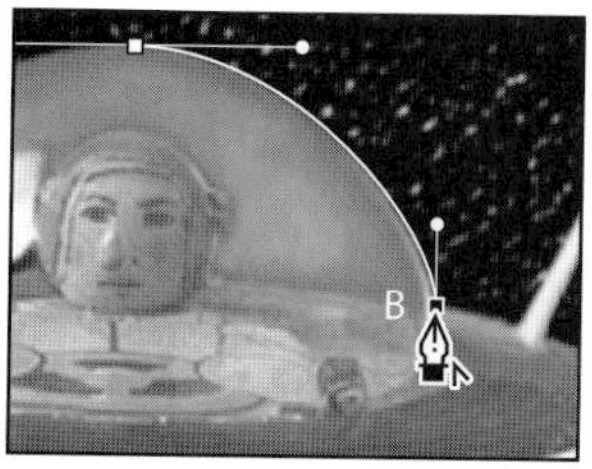

Converting the smooth point to a corner point

5 Click point C to set a straight segment (don't drag).

If you make a mistake while you're drawing, choose Edit > Undo to undo the step. Then resume drawing.

6 Drag up from point D to the red dot. Then drag down from point E to its red dot.

7 Click point F.

8 Set curve points at G, H, and I by dragging from the points to their respective red dots.

9 Click point J.

10 Set curve points at K and L by dragging from each one to its respective red dot.

11 Click point M and then point N.

12 Hold down Alt (Windows) or Option (Mac OS) and drag from point N to the red dot, to add one direction line to the anchor point at N.

13 Move the pointer over point A so that a small circle appears in the pointer icon, and click to close the path. (The small circle may be difficult to see because the image is dark and the circle is faint.)

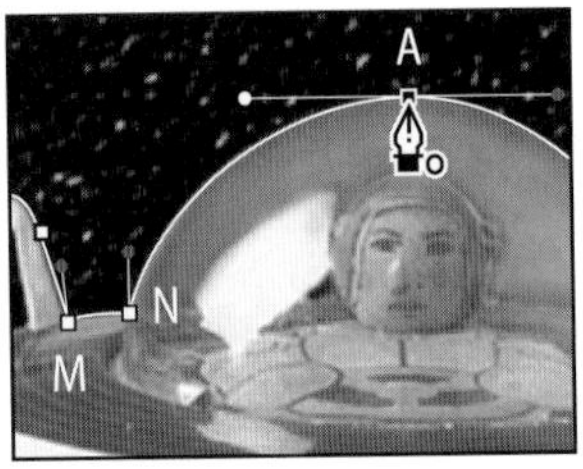

14 In the Paths palette, double-click the Work Path, type **Saucer** in the Name text box, and click OK to save it.

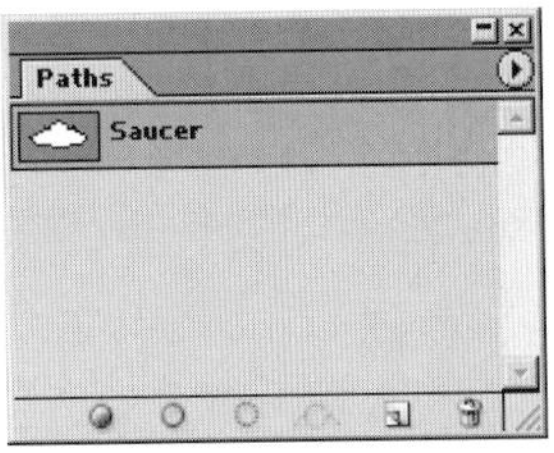

15 Choose File > Save to save your work.

Converting selections to paths

Now you'll create a second path using a different method. First you'll use a selection tool to select a similarly colored area, and then you'll convert the selection to a path. (You can convert any selection made with a selection tool into a path.)

1 Click the Layers palette tab to display the palette, and then drag the Template layer to the Trash button at the bottom of the palette. You no longer need this layer.

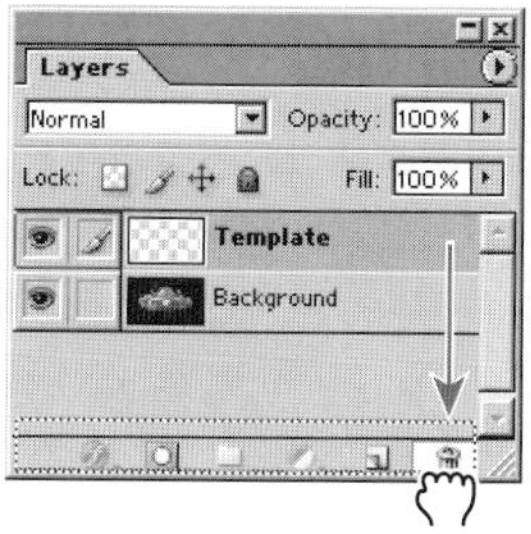

2 Select the magic wand tool ().

3 In the Magic Wand tool options bar, make sure that the Tolerance value is **32**.

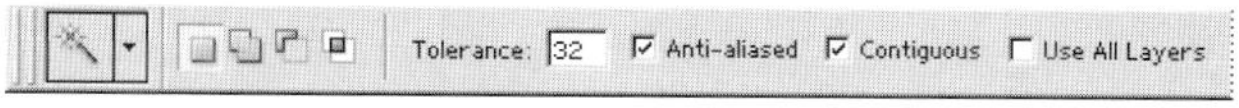

4 Carefully click the black area inside one of the saucer's vertical fins.

5 Shift+click inside the other fin to add that black area to the selection.

6 Click the Paths palette tab to bring the Paths palette to the front. Then click the Make Work Path From Selection button ( ) at the bottom of the palette.

The selections are converted to paths, and a new Work Path is created.

Note: *If desired, adjust the points on the path, using the tools and techniques you've learned.*

7 Double-click the Work Path, and name it **Fins**; then click OK to save the path.

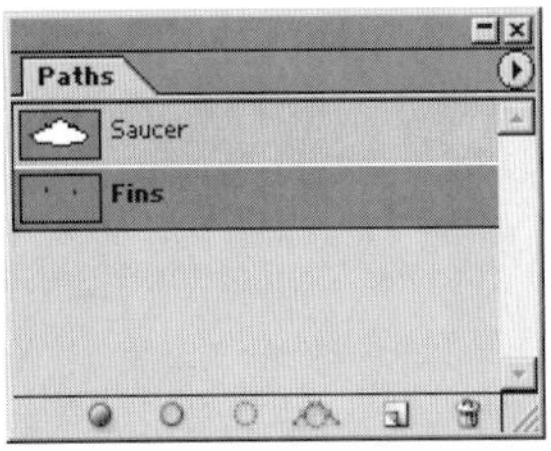

8 Choose File > Save to save your work.

Converting paths to selections

Just as you can convert selection borders to paths, you can convert paths to selections. With their smooth outlines, paths let you make precise selections. Now that you've drawn paths for the space ship and its fins, you'll convert those paths to a selection and apply a filter to the selection.

1 In the Paths palette, click the Saucer path to make it active.

2 Convert the Saucer path to a selection using either of the following methods:

• On the Paths palette menu, choose Make Selection, and then click OK to close the dialog box that appears.

• Drag the Saucer path to the Load Path As Selection button ( ) at the bottom of the Paths palette.

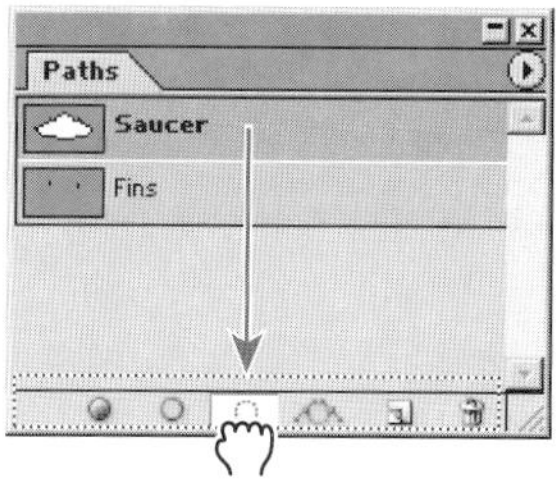

Next, you'll subtract theFins selection from the Saucer selection so that you can see the background change through the vacant areas in the fins.

3 In the Paths palette, click the Fins path; then on the Paths palette menu, choose Make Selection.

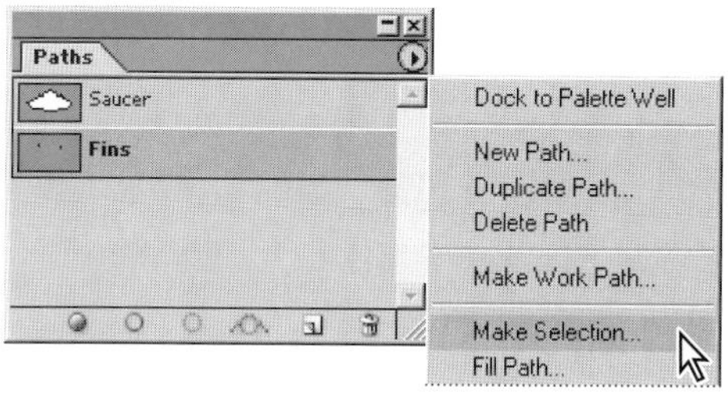

4 In the Operation area of the Make Selection dialog box, select Subtract from Selection, and click OK.

The Fins path is simultaneously converted to a selection and subtracted from the Saucer selection.

Leave the paths selected because you're going to use the selection in the next procedure.

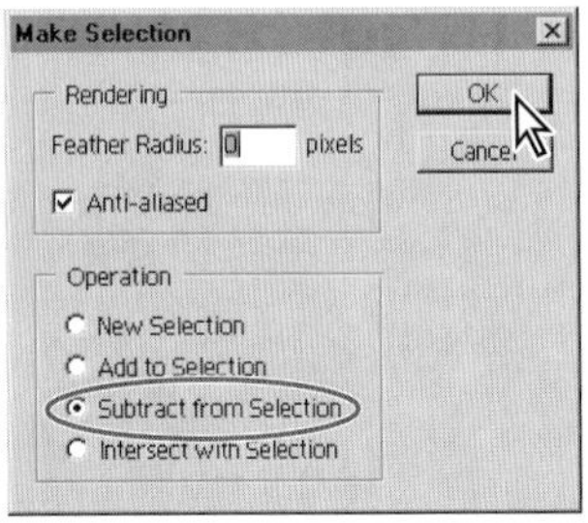

Subtracting the Fins selection from the Saucer selection

Result

Adding layers to complete the effect

Now, just for fun, you'll see how creating the selection with the pen tool can help you achieve interesting effects in an image. Because you've now isolated the space ship, you can create an exact duplicate of the selection on a new layer. Then, when you add a new object to a layer between the original layer and the duplicate saucer layer, that new object appears to be between the saucer and the starry sky background.

1 In the Layers palette, make sure that the background layer is selected, so that you see the selection outline in the image window. If you deselected it, you need to repeat the previous procedure ("Converting paths to selections" on page 285).

2 Choose Layer > New > Layer Via Copy.

A new layer appears in the Layers palette, named Layer 1. The Layer 1 thumbnail shows that the layer contains only the image of the flying saucer, not the sky areas of the original layer.

3 In the Layers palette, double-click Layer 1 and type **Saucer** to rename the layer.

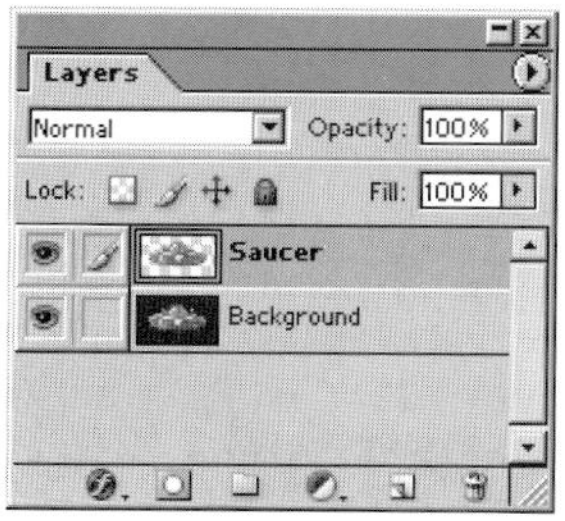

4 Choose File > Open, select the Planet.psd file in your Lesson09 folder, and click Open.

This is a Photoshop image of a planet with a transparent area already defined around the image.

5 If necessary, move the image windows so that you can see at least part of both the Saucer.psd window and the Planet.psd window.

6 In the toolbox, select the move tool (), and drag from the Planet.psd image window into the Saucer.psd image window.

7 Close the Planet.psd image, leaving the Saucer.psd file open and active.

The planet appears to be in front of the space ship. You'll correct that now so that the saucer is flying away from the planet.

8 In the Layers palette, drag the Planet layer between the Saucer layer and the Background layer.

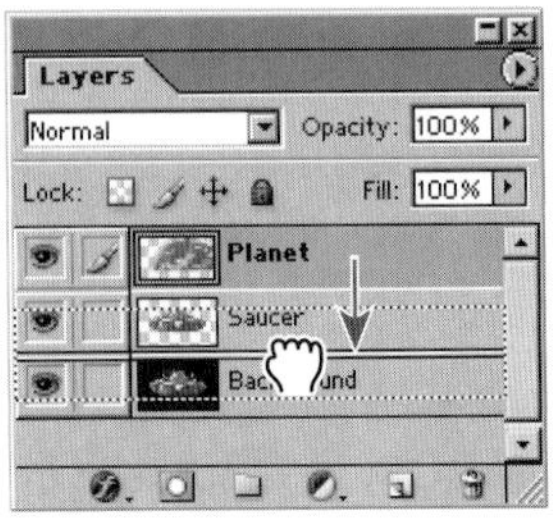

9 Still using the move tool, drag the planet image to change its position in the Saucer.psd window until you are satisfied with the appearance of your composition.

10 Choose File > Save.

You've completed the Basic Pen Tool lesson. Try drawing paths around different objects in your artwork to practice using the pen tool. With practice, you'll find that the pen tool can be invaluable for creating intricate outlines and selections.

Review questions

1 How do you modify individual segments of a path?

2 How do you select an entire path?

3 How do you add points to a path?

4 How do you delete points from a path?

5 When you drag with the pen tool to create a curved path, how does the direction in which you drag affect the curve?

6 How can the pen tool be useful as a selection tool?

Review answers

1 To modify individual segments of paths, you drag the anchor points on the path using the direct selection tool. You can also edit the shape of curved segments by dragging the direction points at the ends of the direction lines that extend from the anchor point of the curve.

2 To select an entire path, hold down Alt (Windows) or Option (Mac OS), and click the path using the direct selection tool. When an entire path is selected, all the anchor points are solid.

3 To add points to a path, you select the add-anchor-point tool hidden under the pen tool and then click the path where you want to add an anchor point.

4 To delete points from a path, you select the delete-anchor-point tool hidden under the pen tool and then click the anchor point you want to remove from the path.

5 The direction you drag with the pen tool defines the direction of the curve that follows.

6 If you need to create an intricate selection, it can be easier to draw the path with the pen tool and then convert the path to a selection.

Lesson 10

10 Vector Masks, Paths, and Shapes

You can make simple illustrations using vector paths in Adobe Photoshop or Adobe ImageReady. Working with vectors allows you to create shapes, which can be filled or stroked, and use vector masks to control what is shown in an image. This lesson will introduce you to advanced uses of vector shapes and vector masks.

In this lesson, you'll learn how to do the following:

- Differentiate between bitmap and vector graphics.
- Draw and edit layer shapes and layer paths.
- Describe and use the thumbnails and link icon for a shape layer.
- Create complex layer shapes by combining or subtracting different shapes.
- Combine vector paths to create a shape.
- Use edit mode to add and edit a text layer.
- Use a text layer to create a work path.
- Use a work path to create a vector mask.
- Load and apply custom layer shapes.

This lesson will take about 60 minutes to complete. The lesson is designed to be done in Adobe Photoshop, but information on using similar functionality in Adobe ImageReady is included where appropriate.

If needed, remove the previous lesson folder from your hard drive, and copy the Lesson10 folder onto it from the *Adobe Photoshop 7.0 Classroom in a Book* CD.

Note: *Windows users need to unlock the lesson files before using them. For more information, see "Copying the Classroom in a Book files" on page 4.*

About bitmap images and vector graphics

Before working with vector shapes and vector paths, it's important that you understand the basic differences between the two main categories of computer graphics: *bitmap images* and *vector graphics*. You can use Photoshop or ImageReady to work with either type of graphics; moreover, in Photoshop you can combine both bitmap and vector data in an individual Photoshop image file.

Bitmap images, technically called *raster images*, are based on a grid of colors known as pixels. Each pixel is assigned a specific location and color value. In working with bitmap images, you edit groups of pixels rather than objects or shapes. Because bitmap graphics can represent subtle gradations of shade and color, they are appropriate for continuous-tone images such as photographs or artwork created in painting programs. A disadvantage of bitmap graphics is that they contain a fixed number of pixels. As a result, they can lose detail and appear jagged when scaled up on-screen or if they are printed at a lower resolution than that for which they were created.

Vector graphics are made up of lines and curves defined by mathematical objects called *vectors*. These graphics retain their crispness whether they are moved, resized, or have their color changed. Vector graphics are appropriate for illustrations, type, and graphics such as logos that may be scaled to different sizes.

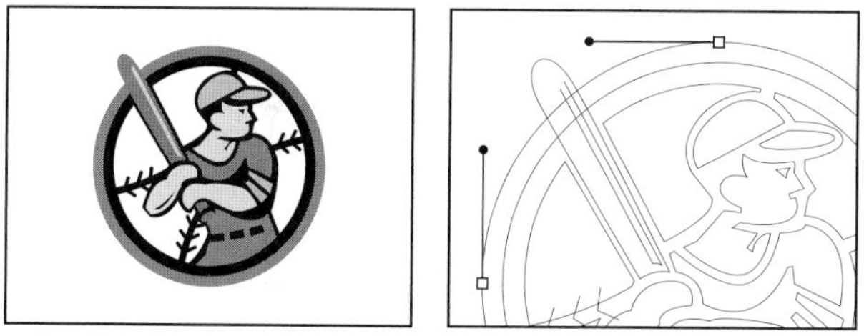

Logo drawn as vector art

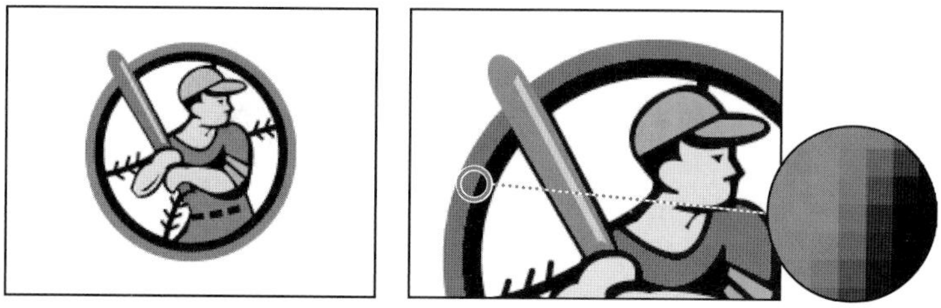

Logo rasterized as bitmap art

Getting started

In the previous lesson, you learned how to use the pen tool to create simple shapes and paths. In this lesson, you'll learn advanced uses of paths and vector masks to create a poster for a fictitious golf tournament. You'll learn how to add text to an image by incorporating the tournament information.

Before beginning this lesson, restore the default application settings for Adobe Photoshop. See "Restoring default preferences" on page 5.

You'll start the lesson by viewing the final image, which is an example of a poster for an early autumn golf tournament.

1 Start Adobe Photoshop.

If a notice appears asking whether you want to customize your color settings, click No.

2 Choose File > Open, and open the file 10End.psd in the Lessons/Lesson10 folder.

If a notice appears asking whether you want to update the text layers for vector-based output, click Update.

Note: *The "update text layers" notice might occur when transferring files between computers, especially between Windows and Mac OS.*

3 When you have finished viewing the 10End.psd file, leave it open for reference.

Now you'll start the lesson by creating a new document for the poster.

Creating the poster background

Many posters are designed to be scalable, either up or down, while retaining a crispness to their appearance. You'll create shapes with paths and use masks to control what appears in the poster.

Adding a colored shape to the background

You'll begin by creating the backdrop for a poster image.

1 Choose File > Open and select the 10Start.psd file in your Lessons/Lesson10 folder.

Some work on the file has been done for you; the image already contains a background layer with a green gradient fill and a series of horizontal and vertical guides. The guides are locked in position. (If you do not see the guides, choose View > Show > and make sure that the Guides command is checked, or choose it now.)

2 Choose View > Rulers to display a horizontal and a vertical ruler.

3 Using the tab for the Paths palette, drag the palette out of the Layers palette group. Since you'll be using these two palettes frequently, it's convenient to have them separated.

4 In the Color palette, set the foreground RGB color to a deep blue color by typing **0** as the R value, **80** as the G value, and **126** as the B value.

5 On the toolbox, select the rectangle tool ( ). Then, in the tool options bar, make sure that the Shape Layers option is selected.

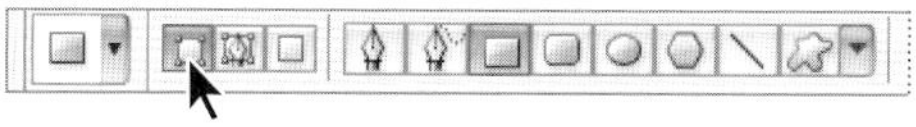

6 Drag a rectangle from the intersection of the top and leftmost guides to the third horizontal guide (about three-fourths of the way down the image, slightly below the 5-inch mark on the ruler) and the right margin of the page.

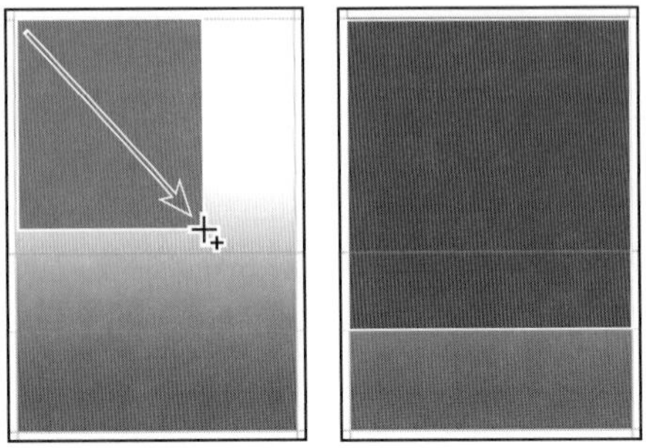

You've created a rectangle with a deep blue fill. (If you don't get that result, make sure that you've selected the rectangle tool, which is below the type tool on the toolbox, and not the rectangular marquee tool. Also make sure that the Shape Layers option is selected in the toolbar.)

7 In the toolbox, select the direct selection tool (), hidden under the path selection tool (), and click anywhere on the path (edge) of the blue rectangle to select the path, so that selection handles appear in the four corners.

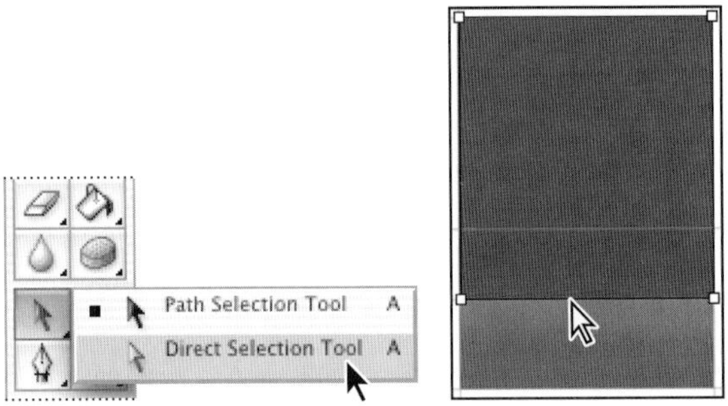

8 Select the lower left handle of the blue shape, being careful to select just the handle and not a path segment.

9 Shift+drag the handle upwards to the next horizontal guide (at about the four-inch mark on the ruler) and release the mouse button when the handle snaps into place against the guide.

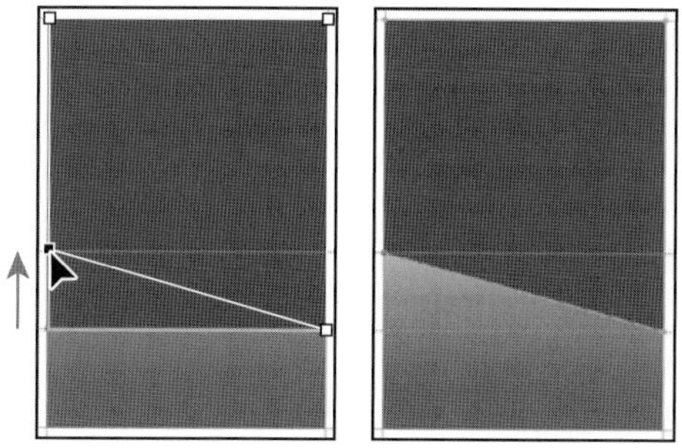

Now the lower edge of the blue shape slopes down from left to right.

10 Choose View > Show > Guides to hide the guides, because you are finished using them for this lesson. You'll be using the rulers again, so do not hide them yet.

11 Click anywhere inside or outside the blue rectangle in the image window to deselect the path and hide its handles.

Notice that the border between the blue shape and the green background has a grainy quality. What you see is actually the path itself, which is a non-printing item. This is a visual clue that the Shape 1 layer is still selected.

About shape layers

A shape layer has two components: a fill and a shape. The fill properties determine the color (or colors), pattern, and transparency of the layer. The shape is a layer mask that defines the areas in which the fill can be seen and those areas in which the fill is hidden.

In the blue layer you've just created, the fill is your dark blue color. The color is visible in the upper part of the image, within the shape you drew, and is blocked in the lower part of the image so that the gradient green can be seen behind it.

In the Layers palette for your poster file, you'll see a new layer, named Shape 1, above the Background layer. There are three items represented along with the layer name: two thumbnail images and an icon between them.

The left thumbnail shows that the entire layer is filled with the deep blue foreground color. The small slider underneath the thumbnail is not functional but symbolizes that the layer is editable.

The thumbnail on the right shows the vector mask for the layer. In this thumbnail, white indicates the area where the image is exposed, and black indicates the areas where the image is blocked.

The icon between the two thumbnails indicates that the layer and the vector mask are linked.

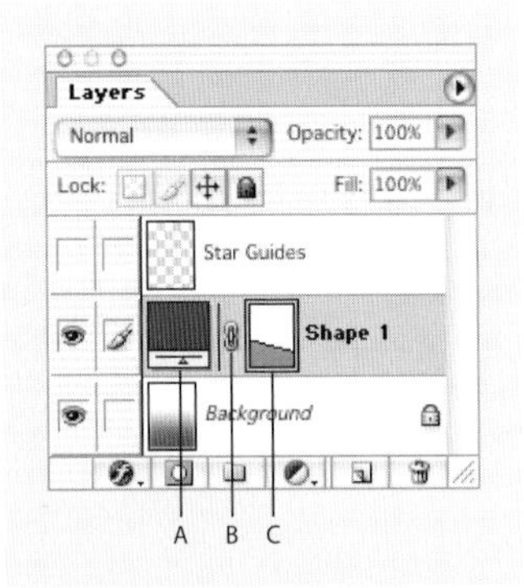

A. *Fill thumbnail* ***B.*** *Layer-mask link icon* ***C.*** *Vector-mask thumbnail*

Subtracting more shapes from a shape layer

After you create a shape layer (vector graphic), you can set options to subtract new shapes from the vector graphic. You can also use the path selection tool and the direct selection tool to move, resize, and edit shapes. You'll add some stars to your "sky" (the blue rectangle you just created) by subtracting star shapes from the blue shape. To help you position the stars, you'll refer to the Star Guides layer, which has been created for you. Currently, that layer is hidden.

1 In the Layers palette, click the box to the far left of the Star Guides layer to display the eye icon ( ) for that layer (but leave the Shape 1 layer selected). The Star Guides layer is now visible in the image window.

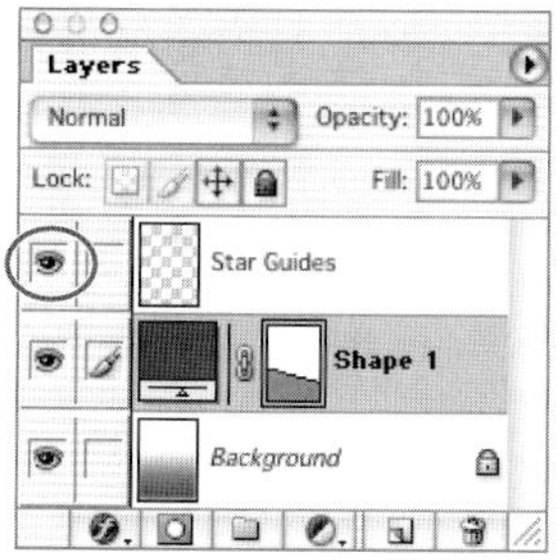

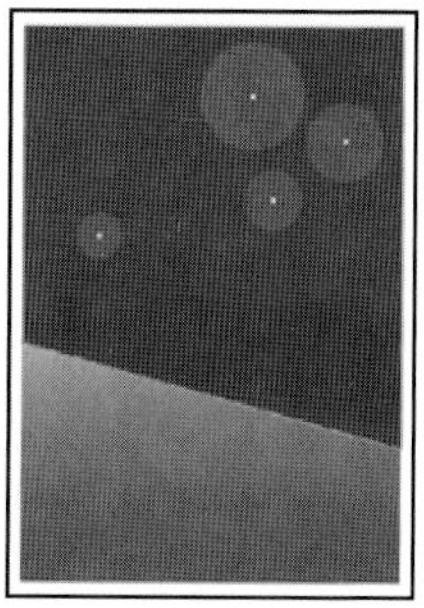

2 In the Paths palette, make sure that the Shape 1 Vector Mask is selected.

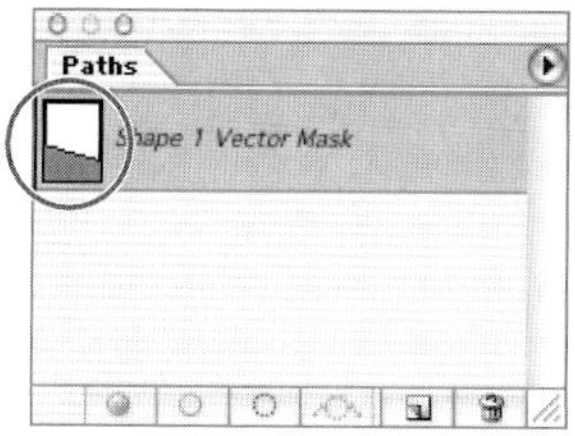

3 In the toolbox, select the polygon tool ( ), hidden under the rectangle tool ( ).

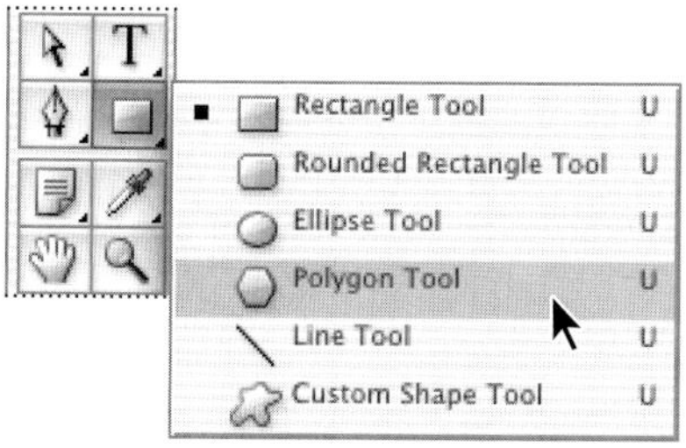

4 In the tool options bar, select the following:

• In Sides, type **9** and press Enter.

• Click the Geometry Options arrow (immediately to the left of the Sides option) to open the Polygon Options. Select the Star check box, and type **70%** in the Indent Sides By option. Then click anywhere outside the Polygon Options to close it.

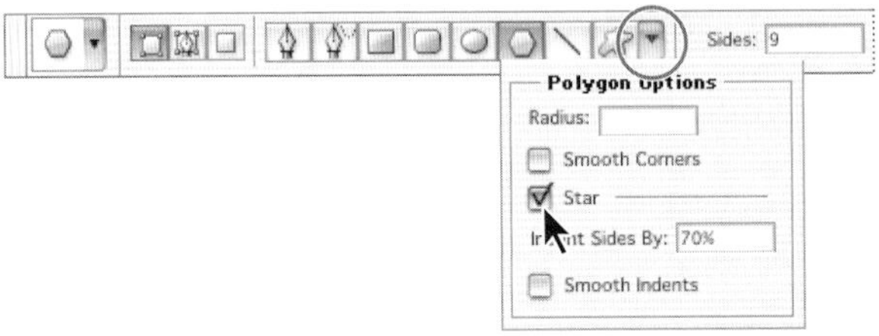

• Select the Subtract From Shape Area option ( ) or press either hyphen or minus to select it with a keyboard shortcut. The polygon tool pointer now appears as crosshairs with a small minus sign (+-).

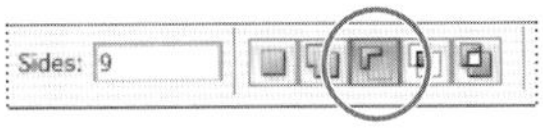

5 Move the polygon tool crosshairs over the center of one of the white dots and drag outward until the tips of the star rays reach the edge of the faint circle around the dot.

Note: *As you drag, you can rotate the star by dragging the pointer to the side.*

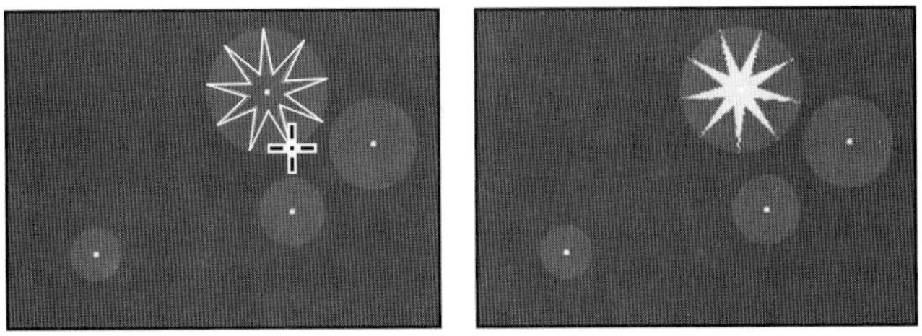

When you release the mouse, the star shape appears to fill with white. However, this is not a fill; the star is a cutout from the blue shape, and the white you see is the background layer underneath it. If the background layer were another image, pattern, or color, that's what you would see inside the star shape.

6 Repeat step 5 for the other three white dots to create a total of four stars.

Notice that all the stars have grainy outlines, reminding you that the shapes are selected. Another indication that the shapes are selected is that the Shape 1 vector mask thumbnail is highlighted (outlined in white) in the Layers palette.

7 In the Layers palette, click the eye icon for the Star Guides layer to hide it.

Notice how the thumbnails have changed in the palettes. In the Layers palette, the left thumbnail is as it was, but the vector mask thumbnails in both the Layers palette and Path palette show the slant of the blue shape with the star-shaped cutouts.

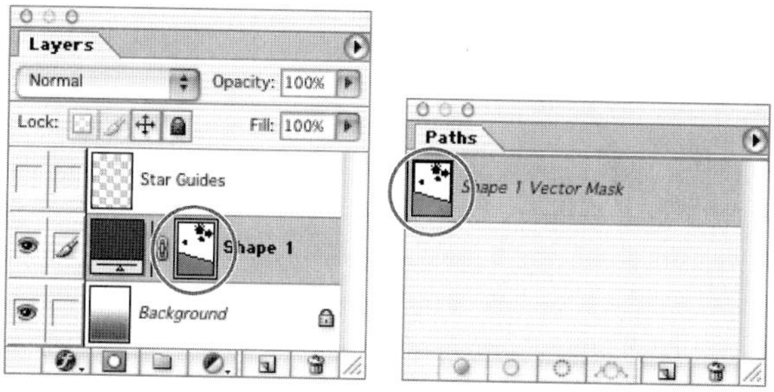

Deselecting paths

Deselecting paths is sometimes necessary to see the appropriate tool options bar when you select a vector tool. Deselecting paths can also help you view certain effects that might be obscured if a path is highlighted. Before proceeding to the next section of this lesson, you'll make sure that all paths are deselected.

1 Select the path selection tool (), which is currently hidden under the direct selection tool ().

2 In the tool options bar, click the Dismiss Target Path button (✔).

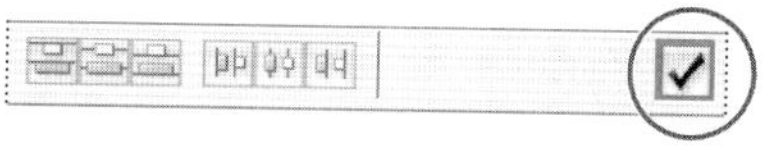

Note: An alternate way to deselect paths is to click in the blank area below the paths in the Paths palette.

Your paths are now deselected and the grainy path lines have disappeared, leaving a sharp edge between the blue and green areas. Also, the Shape 1 Vector Mask is no longer highlighted in the Paths palette.

Drawing paths

Next, you'll add more elements to your poster, but you'll work with these elements on different layers. Throughout this lesson, you'll create new layers so you can draw, edit, paste, and reposition elements on one layer without disturbing other layers.

Before you begin, make sure that the Shape 1 layer is still selected in the Layers palette.

1 In the Layers palette, click the New Layer button () at the bottom of the palette to create a new layer.

A new layer, named Layer 1, appears above the Shape 1 layer in the Layers palette and is automatically selected.

2 Select the ellipse tool (), which is currently hidden under the polygon tool ().

3 In the tool options bar, select the Paths option ().

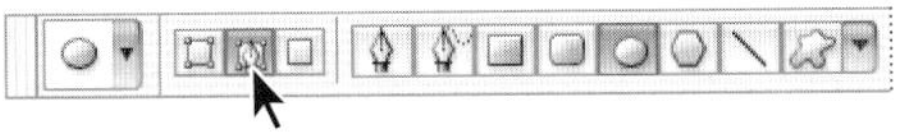

4 Start dragging the ellipse tool in the upper left area of the poster and then hold down Shift as you continue dragging. Release the mouse button when the circle is close to the bottom edge of the blue shape.

5 In the tool options bar, select the Exclude Overlapping Path Areas option ().

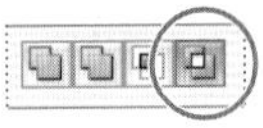

6 Hold down Shift and draw a second circle within the first.

7 Compare the sizes and positions of your circles to the 10End.psd image and make any necessary changes:

- To move a circle, select it with the path selection tool ( ) and then drag it to another location. (If necessary, choose View > Snap To > Guides to deselect this command so that you can move the circles exactly where you want them.)
- To resize a circle, select it with the path selection tool and choose Edit > Free Transform Path; then hold down Shift and drag a corner handle to resize the circle without distorting its shape. When you finish, press Enter to apply the transformation.

Note: *In the Paths palette, only the new Work Path appears at this time. The Shape 1 Vector Mask that you created earlier (the blue shape with star cutouts) is associated with the Shape 1 layer. Since you are not working on the Shape 1 layer now, that vector mask does not appear in the Paths palette.*

Understanding work paths

When you draw a shape in Photoshop, the shape is actually a vector mask that defines the areas in which the foreground color appears. That's why you see two thumbnails in the Layers palette for each shape layer: one for the layer color and a second one for the shape itself (as defined by the layer mask).

A work path is sort of a shape-for-hire: It stands at the ready, independent of any but available to serve as the basis of a vector mask on a layer. You can use the work path repeatedly to apply it to several different layers.

This concept differs from the approach used by many popular vector-graphics applications, such as Adobe Illustrator, so if you are used to working in that kind of program, this may take some getting used to. It may help you understand this if you bear in mind that the underlying metaphor behind Photoshop is traditional photography, where the admission of light into a camera lens determines the shapes, colors, and transparencies of the negative, and then darkroom exposure determines what areas of the photographic paper develop into areas of color or darkness and light.

The Paths palette displays only two types of paths. The first type includes any vector paths associated with the currently selected Layer. The other type is the Work Path—if one exists—because it is available to be applied to any layer.

Because a vector path is automatically linked to a layer when you create it, transforming either the layer or the vector path (such as by resizing or distortion), causes both the layer and the vector path to change. Unlike a vector path, a work path is not tied to any specific layer, so it appears in the Paths palette regardless of which layer is currently selected.

In the Paths palette, the thumbnail shows the two subpaths with a white area between them.

***Note:** This may be difficult to see if the palette icons are small. To enlarge them, choose Palette Options on the Paths palette menu and select a larger Thumbnail Size option.)*

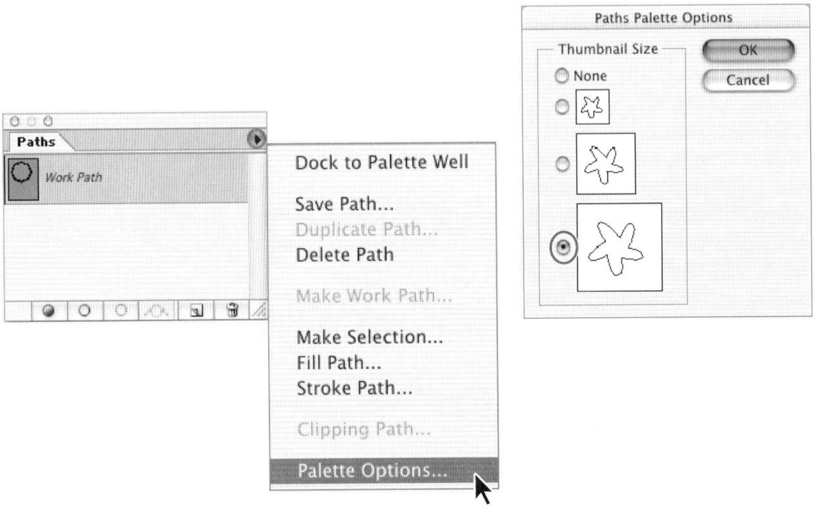

Combining paths into a filled shape

Your next task is to define the two circles as a single element, so that you can add a colored fill.

1 Using the path selection tool (➤), select one of your circles, and then hold down Shift and select the second circle. Both paths are now selected.

2 In the tool options bar, click the Combine button.

The Combine button is now dimmed because the two paths are now treated as one shape.

3 In the toolbar, click the Default Foreground And Background Colors button ( ), which is to the lower left of the two larger color swatches and changes them back to black and white.

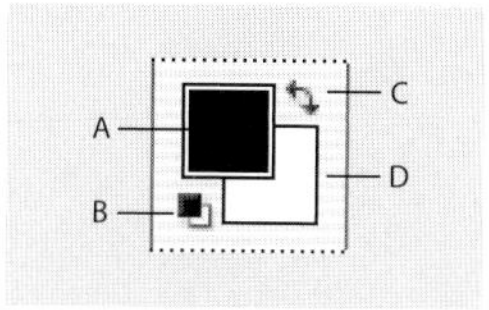

A. Foreground Color button
B. Default Foreground and Background Colors button
C. Switch Foreground and Background Colors button
D. Background Color button

4 In the same area of the toolbar, click the Switch Foreground And Background Colors button ( ), so that the foreground is white and the background black.

5 In the Paths palette, drag the work path to the Fill Path With Foreground Color button ( ) at the bottom left of the palette.

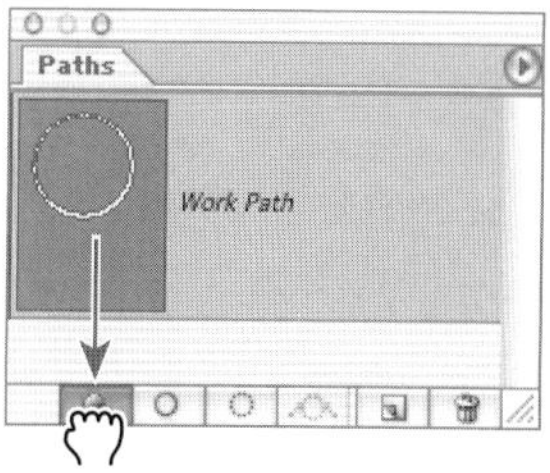

6 In the Layers palette, change the Opacity to **40%**, either by typing or by clicking the Opacity arrow to open the pop-up slider and dragging it.

You can try different Opacity values and compare the results they produce.

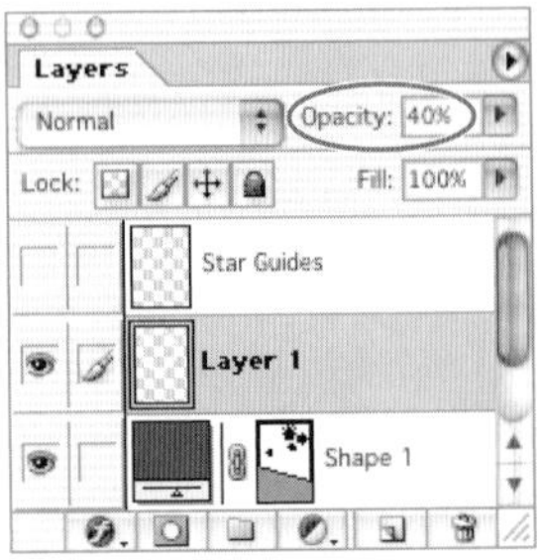

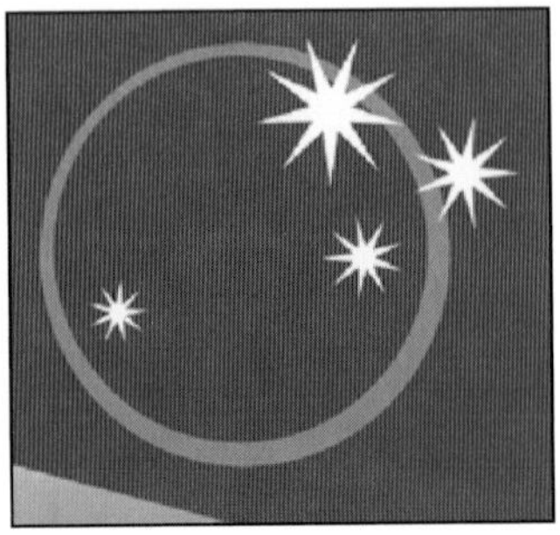

7 If the circle shape is still selected, click the Dismiss Target Path button (✔) in the tool options bar, and then choose File > Save.

Unlike the star-shaped cutouts on the Shape 1 layer, the area between the two circles on Layer 1 now has a white fill. Otherwise, you could not change the opacity of the white area. For example, if you experimented with reducing the layer opacity for the Shape 1 layer, the blue shape would become more transparent, but the stars would remain solid white because that is the color on the layer behind that area of Layer 1.

Working with type

In Adobe Photoshop, you create and edit type directly on-screen (rather than in a dialog box) and quickly change the font, style, size, and color of the type. You can apply changes to individual characters and set formatting options for entire paragraphs. In this part of the lesson, you'll learn about working with type by adding text to your logo.

When you click in an image with the type tool (T) to set an insertion point, you put the type tool in *edit mode*. You can then enter and edit characters on the currently targeted layer; however, you must also commit your editing in the layer or reject them before you can perform other operations, which you can do in several ways.

If you select another tool in the toolbox, this automatically commits your text changes. Or, on the tool options bar, you can click the Commit Any Current Edits button (✔) to accept the text edits or click the Cancel Any Current Edits button (⊘) to reject them. Any of these actions takes the type tool out of edit mode.

Adding type to the image in edit mode

Your first editing task is to enter formatted text into the image.

1 Select the type tool (T), and then choose Window > Character to open the Character palette group.

2 In the Character palette, select the following options:

• For the font family, select a sans serif font (such as Myriad, one of the fonts you can install on your computer from the *Adobe Photoshop 7.0 Classroom in a Book* CD; see "Installing the Classroom in a Book fonts" on page 3).

• For the font style, select Roman (sometimes called Plain or Regular, depending on the font family you use).

• For the font size (T), type **38** pt.

• For the leading (A), type **28** pt.

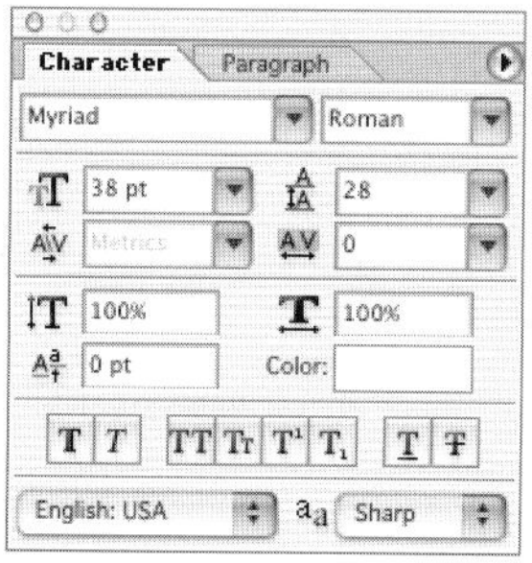

3 In the Character palette group, click the Paragraph palette tab, and then select the Center Text alignment option.

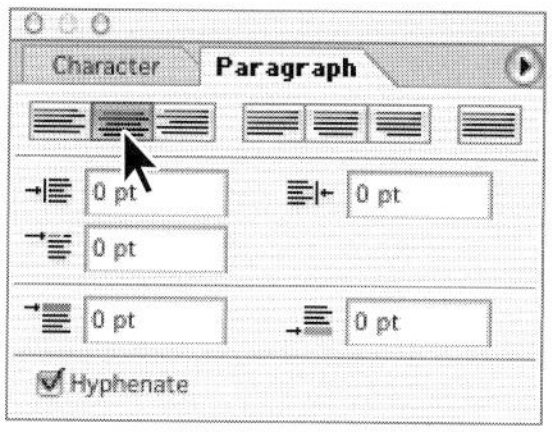

Notice that most of these character and paragraph options are also available in the tool options bar. Of the selections you've made so far, only the Leading option is not there.

4 In the toolbar, make sure that the foreground color is white.

Try the following keyboard shortcuts for setting black and white colors: First, press D. This is the same as clicking the Default Foreground And Background Colors button on the toolbox, which sets the foreground to black and the background to white. Then, press X. This is the same as clicking the Switch Foreground And Background Colors button in the toolbox, which reverses the colors, making the foreground white and the background black.

5 Click the type tool just below the "horizon" (where the blue rectangle meets the gradient green background) and slightly to the left of center. Then type the following three lines, pressing the Return key so that the lines break as shown:

the full

moon

pro-am

6 Double-click the word *moon* to select it, and then using either the tool options bar or the Character palette, change the font size to **48**.

Note: *If you need to adjust the placement of the text, select the move tool (▸✥) and drag the text. Then reselect the type tool.*

7 Choose File > Save.

Stylizing and warping text

In keeping with the spirit of the tournament, you'll distort the text so that it suggests a full moon. After you warp the text, you can continue to edit it with the type tool, as needed. Before you begin, make sure that the "the full moon pro-am" text layer is still targeted.

1 With the type tool (T) selected in the toolbox, click the Create Warped Text button ( ) on the tool options bar to open the Warp Text dialog box.

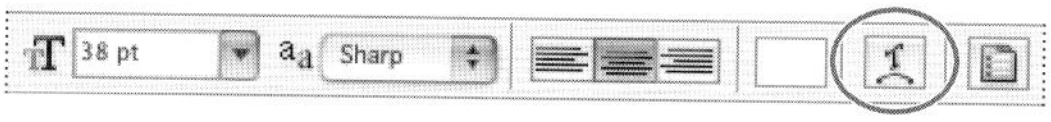

2 In the Style pop-up menu, select Inflate and then click OK to close the dialog box, leaving the other settings at the default values.

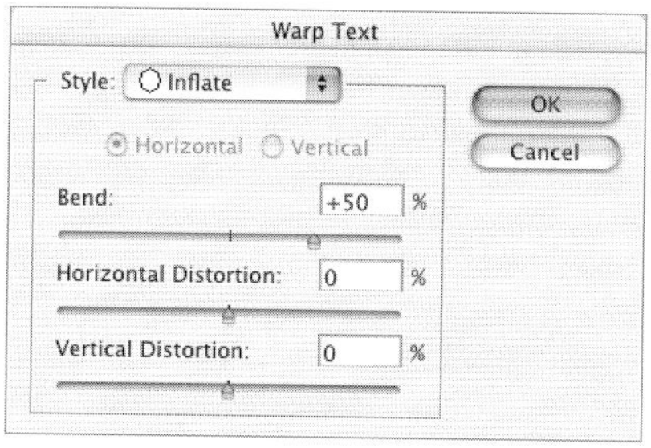

3 Drag the type tool to select the words *full* and *moon*.

4 In the Character palette or the tool options bar, select Bold as the font style.

5 Double-click the word *full* to select it (but not the word *moon*).

6 In the Color palette, select a bright yellow color by entering the following values: R=**239**, G=**233**, B=**7**.

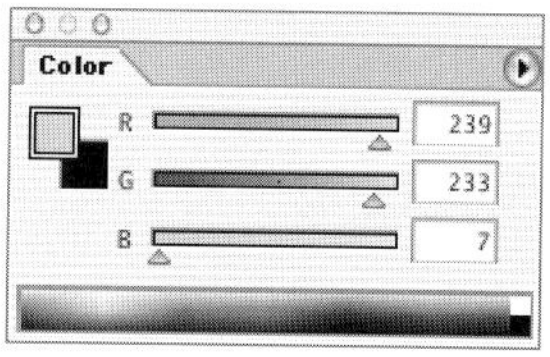

7 In the tool options bar, click the Commit Any Current Edits button (✔) to deselect the text so that you can see the results.

8 Choose File > Save.

When you select the Commit Any Current Edits button, you deselect the text. However, that doesn't mean the text has to be absolutely final. You can still reselect it later with the type tool and make additional edits.

Adding a new text layer

You'll get a little more practice using text by adding another word to your poster.

1 In the Layers palette, select Layer 1.

2 With the type tool (T) selected, click the Default Foreground And Background Colors button to set them to black and white, respectively. (Or, press T and then D to do this.)

3 In the Character palette, select the same sans serif font that you used to type *the full moon pro-am*, select Roman as the font style, **36** as the font size, and **28** as the leading.

4 Click anywhere in the upper area of the poster (so that it is clearly separated from the area of the warped "full moon" text) and type **invitational**.

The word appears in black text in the image window. In the Layers palette, a new, active layer, named Layer 2, is above Layer 1.

5 Select the move tool (▸✥) and drag the word *invitational* to center it in the lower part of the image window, just below the "the full moon pro-am" text block.

Notice that the layer name changes from "Layer 2" to "invitational" in the Layers palette.

6 Close the Character palette group.

7 Choose File > Save.

Creating work paths from text

Currently, the word *invitational* appears on a type layer, not as a work path. That's about to change. After you use the type layer to create a work path, you can save the work path and manipulate it like any other path. Because it is a vector path instead of rasterized, the characters maintain their sharp edges.

Before you begin, compare the position of the word *invitational* in the 10End.psd sample file to your file and make sure that it is sized, spelled, and positioned exactly the way you want it to be. After you create the work paths, you won't be able to change the position easily and may have to start the process over if you aren't satisfied with the results.

1 In the Layers palette, make sure that the "invitational" type layer is selected, and then choose Layer > Type > Create Work Path.

On the Paths palette, notice that a new Work Path listing appears, including a thumbnail of the "invitational" text.

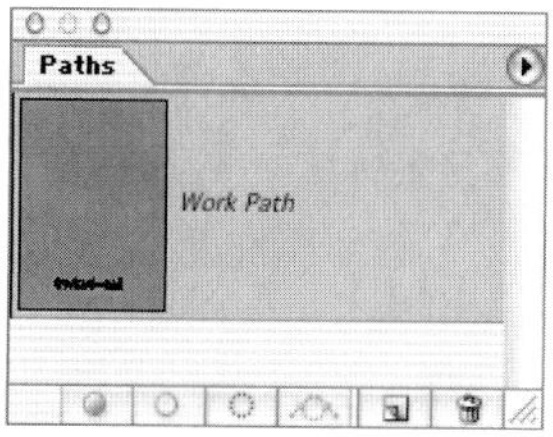

2 In the Layers palette, select the "invitational" text layer and drag it to the Delete Layer button (🗑) at the bottom of the palette, and then choose File > Save.

Now, only the grainy outlines of the work path remain to represent the word *invitational*.

Creating work paths from a type layer leaves the original type layer intact and fully editable as text—that is, you can still use the type tool to select and alter it. However, you are going to use just the work paths to manipulate the shape of the text. You don't want to keep the "invitational" text layer because it would appear in the poster and visually compete with what you're going to create from the work path.

Altering the appearance of the work paths

You can now start working with the new work path as vector shapes. You'll use the direct selection tool, which can be used to edit any path.

1 Zoom in to 200 or 300% so that you can easily see the details in the letter L of the word *invitational* and at least an inch of the blue shape directly above it.

2 In the toolbox, select the direct selection tool (), hidden under the path selection tool ().

3 In the image window, click the "L" part of the work path.

4 Select the two path points at the top of the L subpath by clicking one of the points and then Shift-clicking the other. (The points appear solid when selected and hollow when not selected.)

5 Start dragging the two points upward and then hold down Shift to constrain the movement, stopping when the L extends to about the level of the lower edge of the shape you created from two circles. The L is now about five or six times as tall as it was originally.

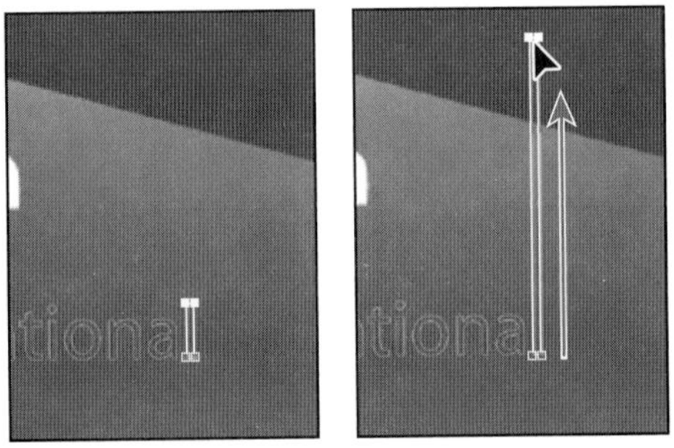

6 Click outside the work path to deselect it, and then zoom out again so that you can see the entire poster.

To quickly switch to 100% view, double-click the zoom tool icon ( ) in the toolbox. To switch to Fit on Screen view, double-click the hand tool icon ( ).

7 Choose File > Save.

Adding a gradient layer

Right now, your "invitational" element is merely a work path, not something that would show up in print. To start the process of making it appear in the poster, you'll create a gradient layer that you can combine with the work path in the procedure following this one.

1 In the Layers palette, click the New Layer button ( ) to create a new Layer 2.

2 In the toolbox, select the gradient tool ( ).

3 Set the foreground to white and the background to black, by pressing D to set the default colors (black and white) and then pressing X to reverse them (white and black).

4 In the tool options bar, click the pop-up arrow to open the gradient picker.

5 Select the second gradient option in the top row (Foreground to Transparent), and then press Enter.

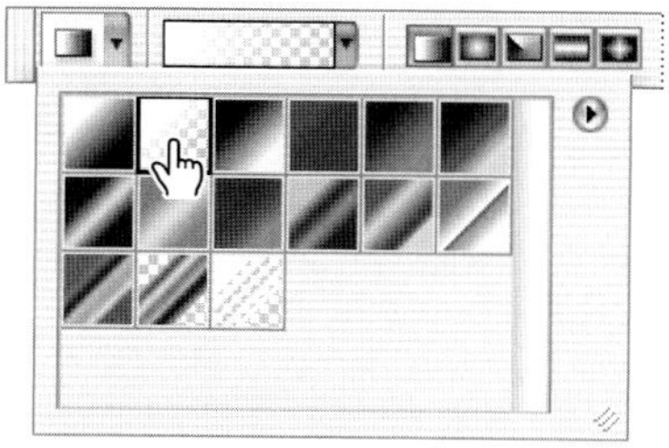

6 Shift-drag the gradient tool from left to right across the image.

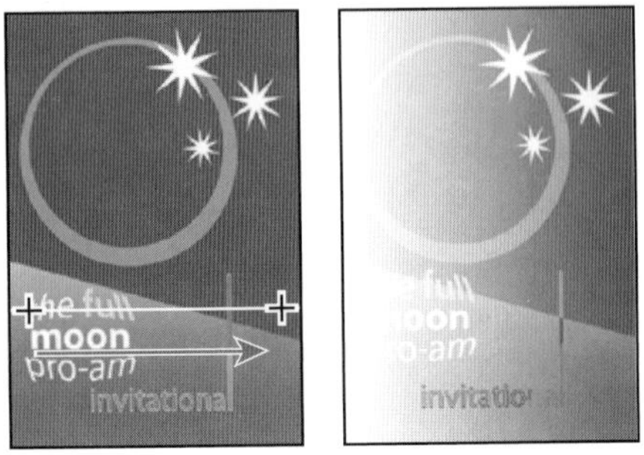

The gradient covers the entire image, with the underlying layers showing through the transparent areas.

Applying a work path to a layer as a vector mask

Your "invitational" work path is not yet applied to any layer. Now, you'll use it to create a vector mask for the gradient layer, limiting the visible area of the gradient fill to the insides of the letter shapes.

1 In the Paths palette, make sure that the Work Path is selected.

2 Choose Layer > Add Vector Mask > Current Path.

The work path becomes the basis of a new layer mask, shown in the thumbnails on Layer 2 in the Layers palette and in the Paths palette, where the mask is identified as "Layer 2 Vector Mask." This mask now hides the gradient in all areas of the image except the area inside the letter shapes of the word *invitational.*

3 Select the path selection tool (), hidden under the direct selection tool (), and then click the Dismiss Target Path button () in the tool options bar to deselect all paths.

Note: You can also click the blank area below the paths in the Paths palette to deselect all paths.

4 In the Layers palette, click the link icon () in Layer 2 to unlink the path from the gradient layer.

5 Select the move tool (), and drag left or right in the image to adjust the placement of the gradient behind the vector mask. When you are satisfied with the appearance of the gradient, choose File > Save.

Creating a flag image and more text

In this section, you'll create a light red triangular shape for a flag in one layer and text in a separate layer. Before you begin, make sure that Layer 1 is selected in the Layers palette.

1 In the Layers palette, select Layer 2, and then click the New Layer button () to create another layer, Layer 3.

2 Select the polygon tool (), hidden under the ellipse tool ().

3 In the tool options bar, do the following:

- Select Fill Pixels (□)—the third of three buttons near the left end of the bar.
- Click the Geometry Options arrow (to the left of the Sides option) to open the Polygon Options pop-up palette. Deselect the Star check box, and press Enter to close the pop-up.
- In the Sides option, type **3**.

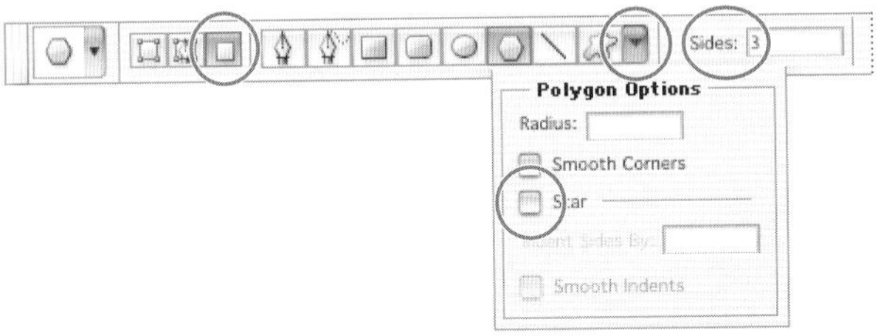

Note: The Fill Pixels option converts vector graphics into rasterized images. This helps reduce the file size and speeds up processing. The flag image is a good opportunity for using this option.

4 In the Color palette, set the foreground to a salmon color, using R= **244**, G=**128**, and B=**118**.

5 Hold down Shift and drag the polygon tool to draw a triangle. Make the triangle large enough to just fit between the word *invitational* and the right edge of the image, and so that the left side of the triangle is parallel to the L.

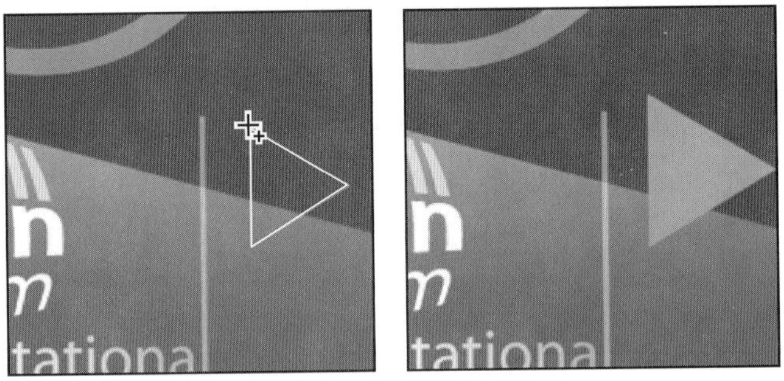

You can rotate as you drag to change the orientation of the triangle. .

6 Select the type tool (T) and select the following options in the tool options bar:

• For font family, select the same sans serif font that you used for the word *invitational.*

• For font style, select Bold.

• For font size, select **30** pt.

• Click the text color swatch and select white. Or, you can use the Color palette or the Foreground Color box on the toolbox to select white.

7 Type **oct 2nd** anywhere in the image. This automatically creates a new type layer (Layer 4), which appears immediately above the flag layer (Layer 3).

8 Select the move tool (▶✥) and drag the "oct 2nd" text over the triangular flag shape.

When you select the move tool, Layer 4 is renamed "oct 2nd" in the Layers palette. The text does not fit within the flag area, but you'll fix that next.

9 With the "oct 2nd" layer selected in the Layers palette, choose Edit > Free Transform. Handles now appear around the text element.

10 Drag the center-left and center-right handles as needed to compress the text bounding box so that all the text fits within the triangle. Then press Enter.

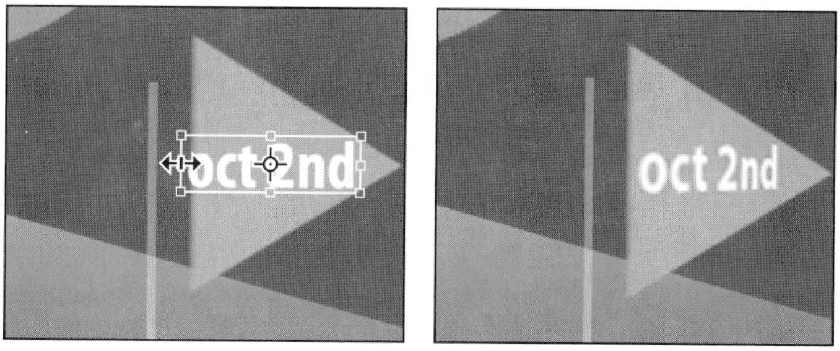

Leave the "oct 2nd" layer selected in the Layers palette for the next task.

Merging and distorting layer combinations

By merging layers, layer paths, vector masks, linked layers, or adjustment layers, you can combine several layers into one and keep your file size manageable. Typically, you want to be sure that you've finalized the characteristics and position of the layer contents before you merge the layers, so make sure that you're satisfied with the appearance of the flag and the date text before starting this procedure.

1 With the "oct 2nd" layer selected, open the Layers palette menu and choose Merge Down.

The "oct 2nd" layer and polygon shape layer are now merged into a single layer, Layer 3. From now on, you can no longer use the type tool to edit the "oct 2nd" graphic.

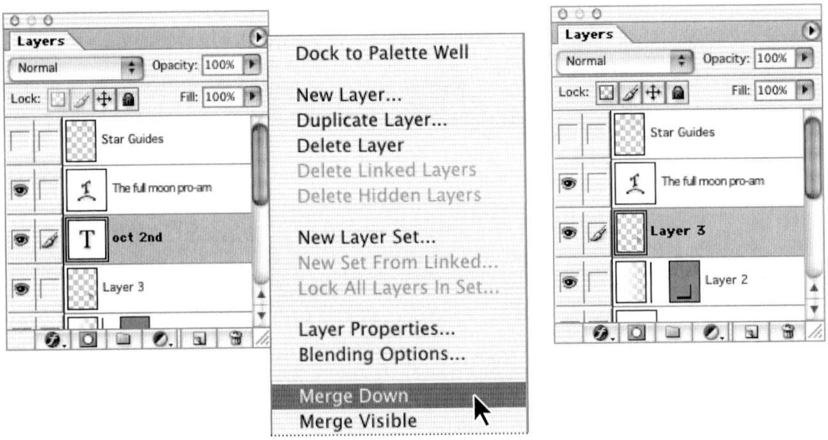

2 With Layer 3 selected, choose Edit > Transform > Distort. To create the illusion of foreshortening, drag the center right handle to the left until the flag is about 1 inch wide.

3 Drag the upper right handle slightly down and the lower right handle slightly up to further enhance the effect of a perspective view.

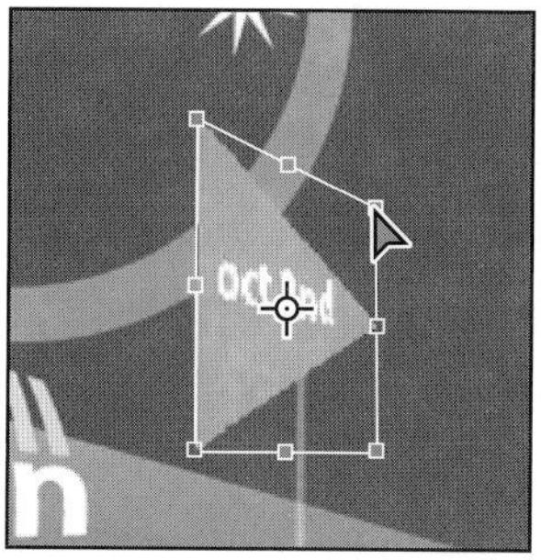

4 Press Enter (Windows) or Return (Mac OS) to apply the transformation.

5 Select the move tool (), and drag the flag shape into position near the top of the stretched letter L in "invitational."

6 Choose File > Save.

Working with defined custom shapes

Whenever you create a shape, you can save it as a custom shape. You can load the saved shape into the Custom Shape picker and use it in other areas of an image or even in different Photoshop projects without having to redraw the shape. This is especially useful when you have logos or other symbolic elements that you use repeatedly and that require multiple steps to create.

Placing a custom shape

A custom shape, representing a golf ball balanced on a tee, has been created for you. In this scenario, the tournament organizers intend to print this image on various types of collateral items—mailing letterheads, registration forms, advertisements, name tags, T-shirts, Web pages, and so forth—that may be printed in different sizes and colors.

You'll now load that shape into your Custom Shape picker and then use it in your poster for the golf tournament.

1 In the toolbox, select the custom shape tool (), hidden under the polygon tool ().

2 In the tool options bar, click the pop-up arrow for the Shape option to open the custom-shape picker. Then click the arrow button on the right side of the picker to open the palette menu, and choose Load Shapes.

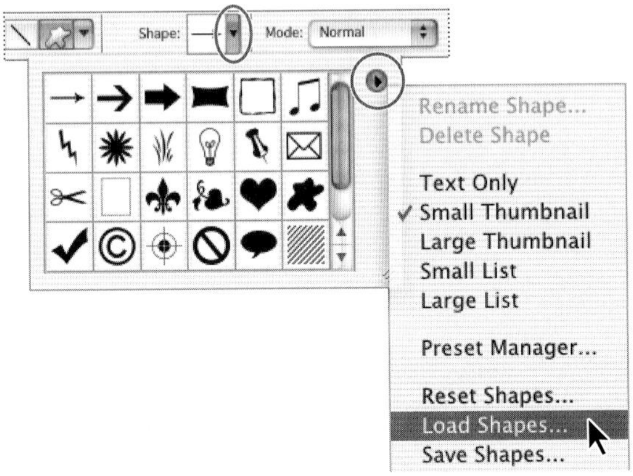

3 In the Load dialog box, go to the Lessons/Lesson10 folder on your hard disk and select Golfball.csh. Click Load.

4 Select the golf-ball shape at the bottom of the custom-shape picker (you may need to scroll or drag the corner of the picker to see the shape), and press Enter. Holding down Shift constrains the shape to its original proportions.

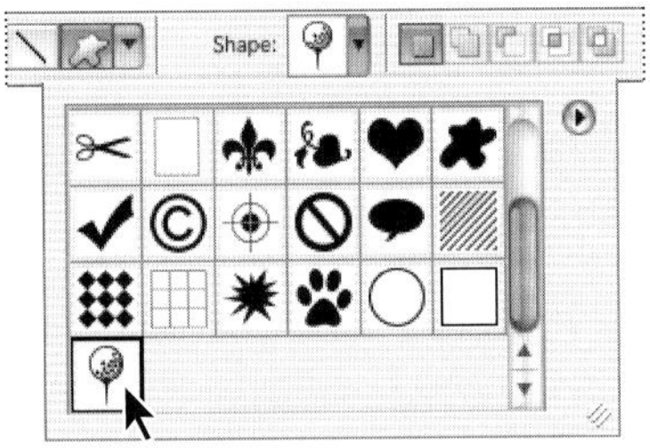

5 In the tool options bar, select the Shape Layers option (□)—the first of the three buttons on the left side of the tool options bar.

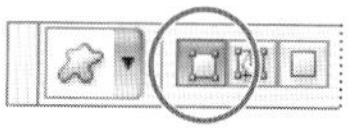

6 Make sure that the foreground color is white (or select white now), and then hold down Shift and drag diagonally in the image window to draw and size the shape.

A new layer, Shape 2, is automatically created.

7 Adjust the golf-ball shape as needed:

• To move the shape, select the path selection tool (↖) and drag it into position so that the bottom of the golf tee is just to the right of the word *moon*.

• To resize the shape, choose Edit > Free Transform, and Shift-drag one of the corner handles. The golf ball should be about half the height of the poster.

8 When you are satisfied with the golf-ball image, press Enter or click the Dismiss Target Path button (✔) on the tool options bar (if it is available).

Adding layer styles to a custom shape

You're almost finished with your poster project. Right now, your golf-ball shape is simply a composite, solid-white shape, unlike the golf ball you saw in the sample End file. You'll create the same results with very little effort by applying layer styles to the custom shape.

1 In the Layers palette, make sure that the Shape 2 layer is selected.

2 Click the Layer Style button () at the bottom of the Layers palette, and choose Bevel And Emboss on the pop-up menu that appears.

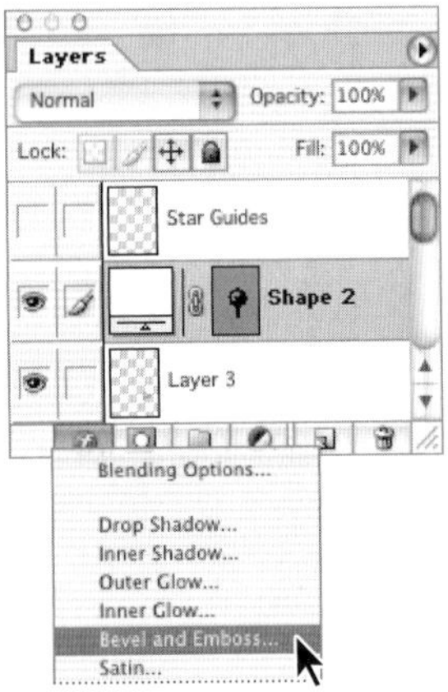

3 Make sure that the Preview check box is selected and then move the Layer Styles dialog box so that you can watch the changes to the golf-ball shape as you make style selections.

4 In the Structure area of the Layer Style dialog box, use the following settings:

- For Style, use Inner Bevel.
- For Technique, use Smooth.
- For Depth, type or drag the slider to set the value at about **150%**.
- For Direction, use Up.
- For Size, use **5** px.
- For Soften, type or drag the slider to set the value at **6** px.

Do not close the dialog box yet.

5 In the Shading area of the Layer Style dialog box, make sure that the following settings are selected:

- For Angle, use **–41º** (being careful to make the number negative).
- For Altitude, use **28º**.

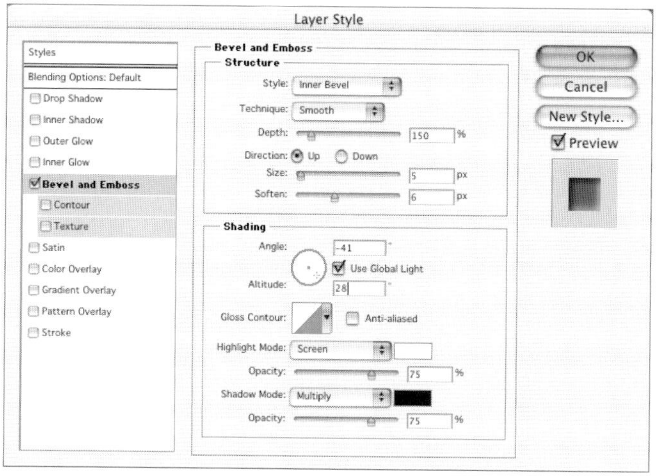

Leave the dialog box open for the next step.

6 In the Styles list on the left pane of the Layer Style dialog box, select the Gradient Overlay check box. Do not click OK yet.

7 In the Styles list, click the Outer Glow listing so that it is highlighted and its check box is automatically selected. Then select the following settings on the right side of the dialog box:

- In the Structure section, click the color swatch to open the color picker, and select a pale yellow color by setting the following values: R=**255**, G=**255**, B= **190**, and then click OK to close the color picker.
- In the Elements section, leave Technique set as Softer, enter **8%** for Spread, and enter **27** for Size.

8 Review the settings and then click OK to close the dialog box.

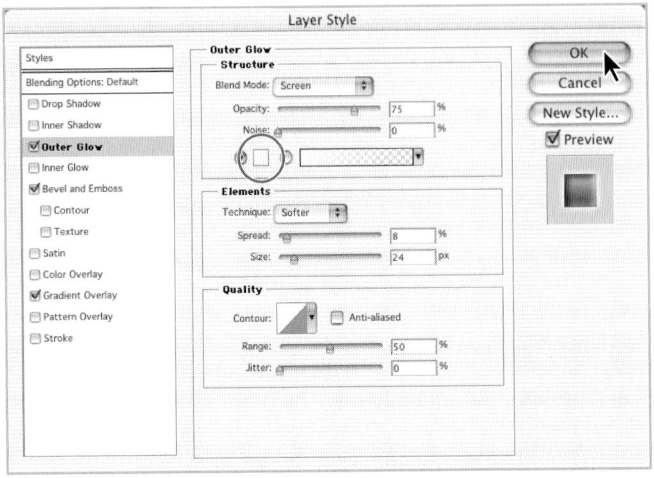

Although you opened the Layer Styles dialog box just once, you applied a total of three different layer styles: Bevel and Emboss, Gradient Overlay, and Outer Glow.

9 If necessary, click a blank area in the Paths palette to deselect the Shape 2 Vector Mask, and then save your work.

Congratulations! You've finished your work on the poster.

Review questions

1 What is the difference between a bitmap image and a vector graphic?

2 What does a layer shape do?

3 What tools are used to move and resize paths and shapes?

4 Does the type tool create vector shapes?

5 What is the purpose of merging layers?

Review answers

1 Bitmap or raster images are based on a grid of pixels and are appropriate for continuous-tone images such as photographs or artwork created in painting programs. Vector graphics are made up of shapes based on mathematical expressions and are appropriate for illustrations, type, and drawings that require clear, smooth lines.

2 A layer shape stores the outline of a shape in the Paths palette. You can change the outline of a shape by editing its path.

3 You use the path selection tool (➤) and the direct-selection tool (➤) to move, resize, and edit shapes. You can also modify and scale a shape or path by choosing Edit > Free Transform Path.

4 No, the type tool adds text, not vector shapes, to an image. If you want to work with the characters as vector shapes, you must create a work path from the type. A work path is a temporary path that appears in the Paths palette. Once you create a work path from a type layer, you can save and manipulate it like any other path. You cannot edit characters in the path as text. However, the original type layer remains intact and editable.

5 Merging combines several layers into one to keep your file size manageable. When you've finalized the characteristics and positioning of a layer's contents, you can merge the layer with one or more other layers to create partial versions of your composite image.

Lesson 11

Creating an adjustment layer

Adjustment layers can be added to an image to apply color and tonal adjustments without permanently changing the pixel values in the image. For example, if you add a Color Balance adjustment layer to an image, you can experiment with different colors repeatedly, because the change occurs only on the adjustment layer. If you decide to return to the original pixel values, you can hide or delete the adjustment layer.

Here you'll add a Curves adjustment layer to create a greater contrast between the grille and the rust layer behind it. You'll do this by darkening the entire rust image.
An adjustment layer affects all layers below it in the image's stacking order. Because you'll place the Curves adjustment layer below the Metal Grille layer, the adjustment will affect the Rust layer and the Background but not the metal grille.

1 Select the Rust layer in the Layers palette.

2 Click the Create New Fill Or Adjustment Layer button (◐) at the bottom of the Layers palette and choose Curves from the pop-up menu.

3 Click the middle of the diagonal line in the grid (the color curve) to add a control point on the curve that will adjust the midtones.

4 Drag the control point down and to the right or enter values in the Input and Output text boxes. (We moved the control point so that the value in the Input text box was **150%** and the value in the Output text box was **105%**.)

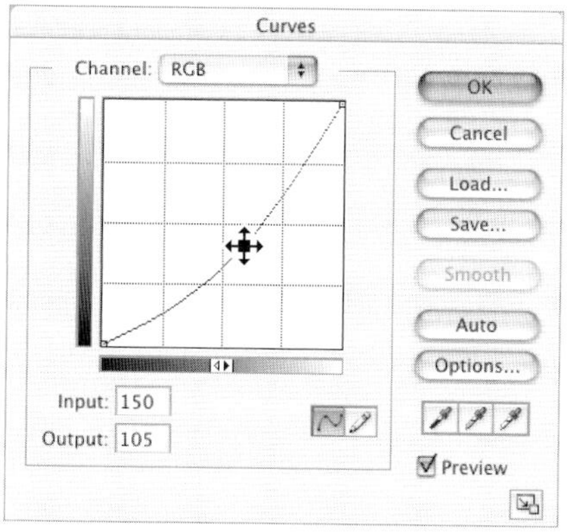

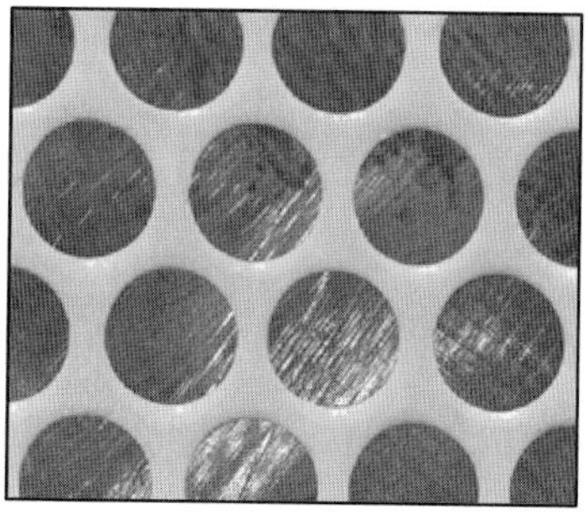

5 Click OK to close the dialog box.

An adjustment layer named Curves 1 appears in the Layers palette. The thumbnails for the new layer include one of the Curves 1 graph and one of the layer mask.

6 Choose File > Save.

You can experiment by clicking the eye icons for the Curves 1 and Rust layers off and on, to see the effect of the adjustment layer on the other layers. When you finish, be sure to return all layers to their visible state.

Creating a knockout gradient layer

Knockout layer options specify how one layer reveals other layers. In this section, you'll create a knockout gradient layer so that the lower third of the image reveals the Background layer.

You'll begin by creating a new layer in the Images layer set.

1 Select the Images layer set in the Layers palette and click the Create a New Layer button () at the bottom of the palette.

This creates a new layer (Layer 1) in the Images layer set, above the Metal Grille, Curves 1, and Rust layers.

2 Double-click the new Layer 1, and type **Knockout Gradient** to rename it. Keep the Knockout Gradient layer selected.

Now you'll create a gradient on this layer.

3 Select the gradient tool ().

4 If necessary, click the Default Foreground And Background Colors icon () in the toolbox to set the foreground color to black and the background color to white.

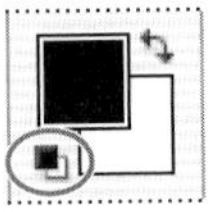

5 If necessary, click the Linear Gradient button () in the options bar to create a linear gradient.

6 Click the arrow (▾) to the right of the gradient display in the options bar to open the gradient picker.

7 Choose Small List from the gradient picker menu (opened by clicking the round arrow button in the upper right area of the gradient picker). Then choose Foreground to Transparent in the gradient picker, and close the gradient picker by clicking outside it.

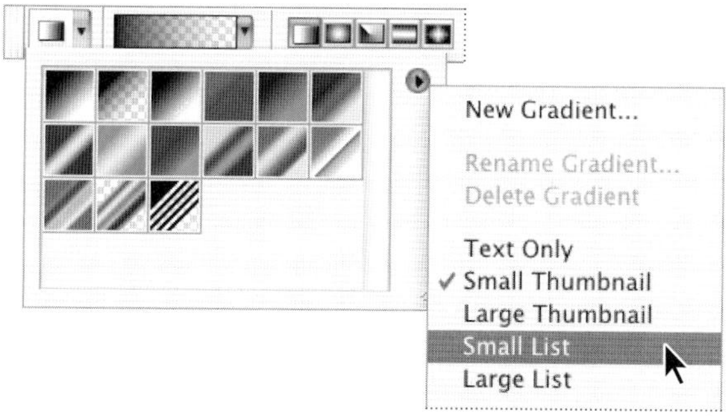

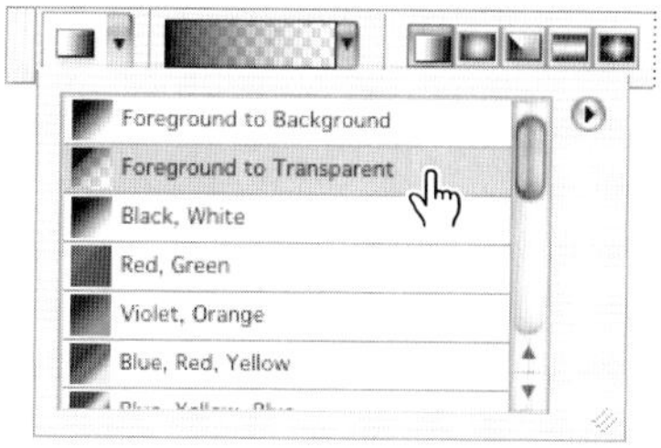

8 Shift-drag from the bottom of the image to slightly above the midpoint to create a gradient that goes from black at the bottom to transparent at the top.

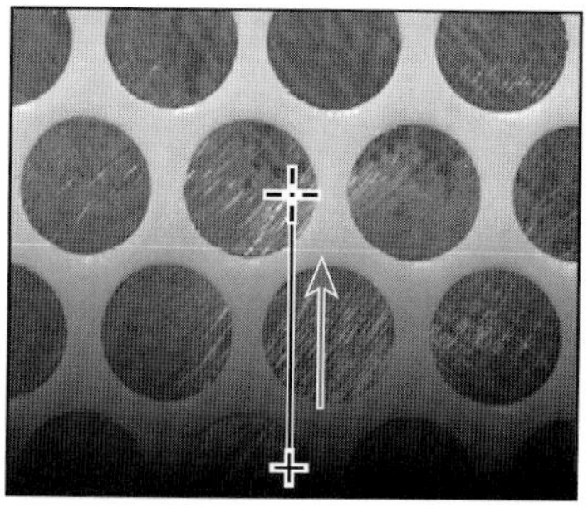

9 In the Layers palette, click the Layers Style button ( ) at the bottom of the palette and choose Blending Options from the pop-up menu.

10 In the Layer Style dialog box, do the following:

• Under Advanced Blending, drag the Fill Opacity slider or type to enter **0** as the value. (Be careful to adjust the Fill Opacity, not the Opacity option under General Blendings.)

• In the Knockout pop-up menu, select Deep.

• Click OK to close the dialog box.

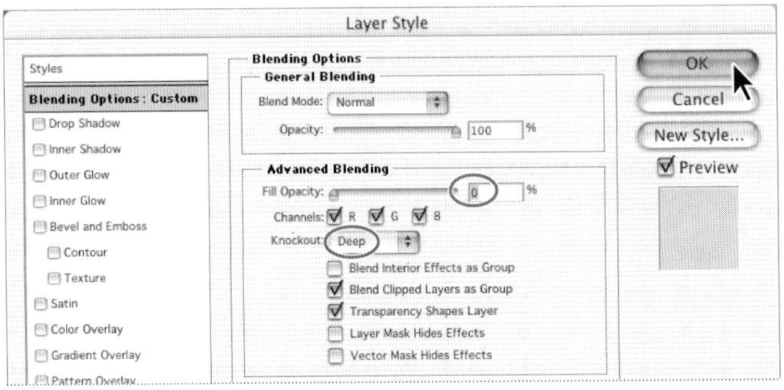

Now the horizontal stripes of gradient colors on the Background layer start to show through the layers in the Images layer set.

11 Choose File > Save.

Importing a layer from another file

In this part of the lesson, you'll import an existing layer from another file into your artwork. Although the imported layer contains the word *diesel* and was originally created with the type tool, the text has now been converted to a graphic. You can no longer edit it with the type tool, but the advantage here is that you also don't have to worry about whether or not your users or other people working on the file have the same font installed on their machines in order to see the image correctly.

1 Select the Words layer set in the Layers palette.

2 Choose File > Open, select Diesel.psd, and click Open.

3 With the Diesel.psd active, drag the Diesel layer from the Layers palette into the 11Start.psd image.

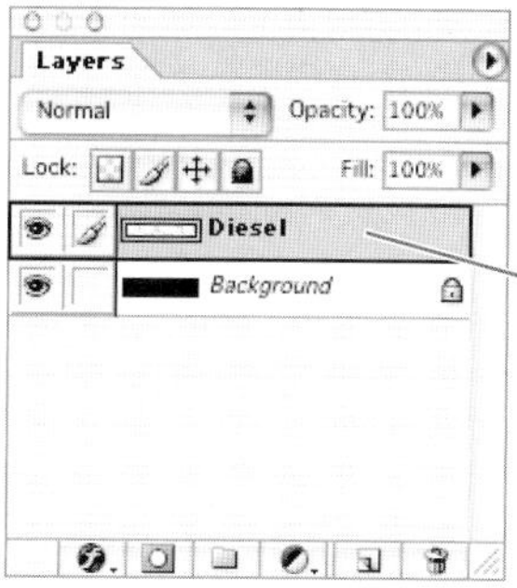

Because the Words layer set was selected in the 11Start.psd image, the Diesel layer is added to that set.

4 Select the move tool (▸✥) and drag the Diesel layer image into position so that it is in the center of the 11Start.psd image and near the bottom.

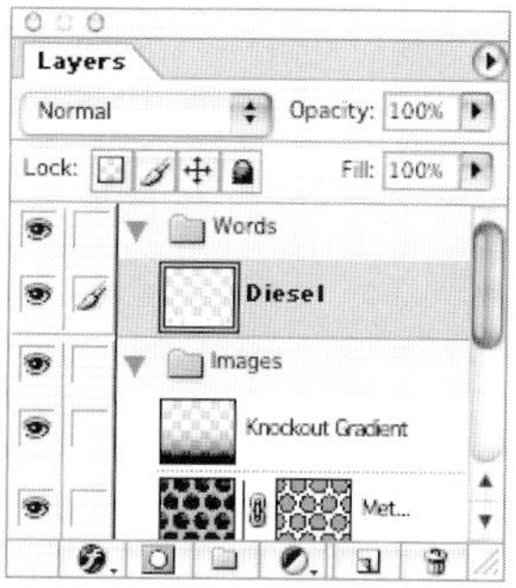

5 Choose File > Save to save your 11Start.psd file.

6 Choose Window > Documents > Diesel.psd, and then close that file without saving it.

Applying layer styles

Once you have the text arranged on the image, you can add layer styles to enhance the look of the type. Layer styles are automated special effects that you can apply to a layer. For more information on layer styles, see Lesson 5, "Layer Basics."

Now you'll add two different layer styles to the Diesel type layer.

1 With the Diesel layer selected in the Layers palette, click the Layer Styles icon (◉) at the bottom of the palette and select Drop Shadow from the pop-up menu.

2 In the Layer Style dialog box, select the Preview check box on the right side of the dialog box so you'll be able to see the changes as you work.

3 On the left side of the dialog box, click the words *Bevel and Emboss* so that they are highlighted and a checkmark appears in the Bevel and Emboss check box.

4 In the Structure area on the right side of the dialog box, adjust the sliders for Depth and Size until you achieve a fairly subtle beveled look in the Diesel image. (We used **2%** for Depth and **2** for Size, but you may think this is too subtle. Or, you can leave them set at the default values: 100% and 5.)

5 Click OK to close the dialog box.

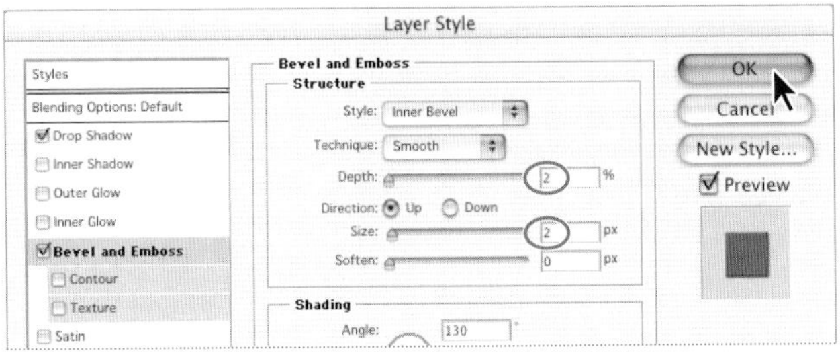

6 Choose File > Save.

Duplicating and clipping a layer

In this section, you'll learn how to copy the Rust layer and then use the compound shape of the Diesel layer to clip away some of the Rust layer.

First, you'll copy the Rust layer and move it above the Diesel layer.

1 Select the Rust layer in the Layers palette and drag it onto the Create a New Layer button ( ) at the bottom of the palette.

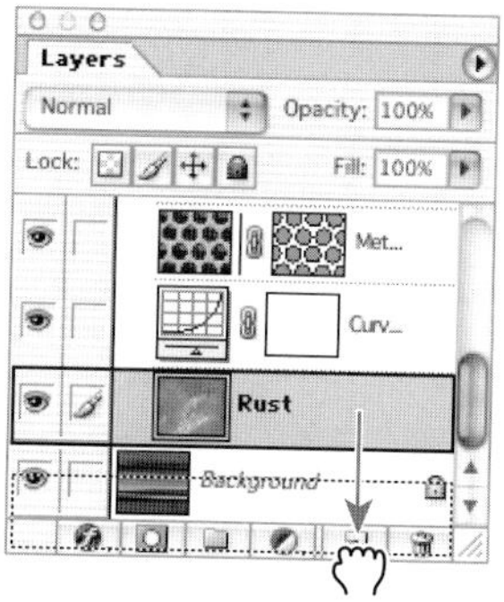

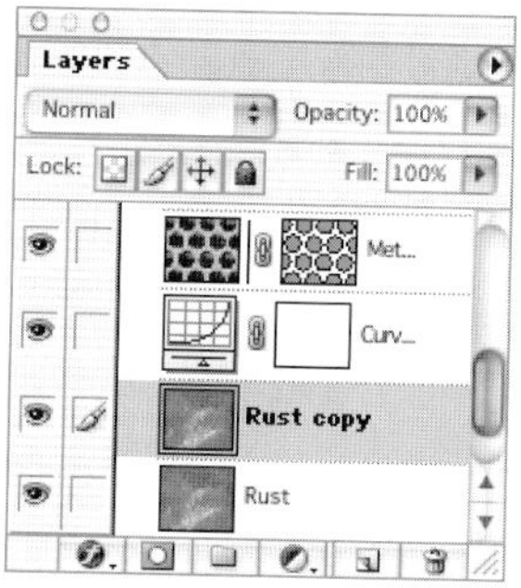

A new layer called "Rust copy" is created directly above the Rust layer in the palette.

2 In the Layers palette, drag Rust copy just above the Diesel layer inside the Words layer set.

Because Rust copy is the top layer, the rust image is all you can see.

3 Hold down Alt (Windows) or Option (Mac OS) and move the mouse pointer over the line dividing the Rust copy and Diesel layers in the Layers palette. When the pointer changes to two overlapping circles ( ), click the mouse button.

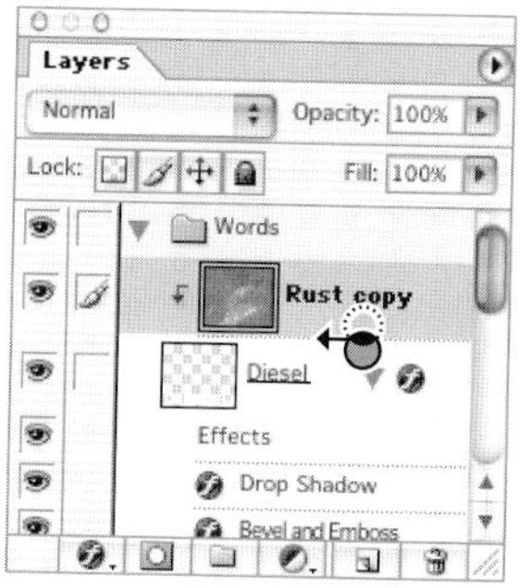

The Rust copy layer is clipped away so that it appears inside the Diesel shape and you can see the other layers in the other areas of the image.

4 Choose File > Save.

Liquifying a layer

The Liquify command lets you add a melted look to the image. In this part of the lesson, you'll make the metal grille look as if it has melted from one side to the other.

Note: *The Liquify filter in Photoshop 7.0 includes enhancements over previous versions. If you think you'll want to experiment with other Liquify effects after you finish the next procedure, save a copy of your 11Start.psd file now (choose File > Save As and give the copy a different name, such as 11Testing.psd), and then close it and reopen your 11Start.psd file to continue working.*

Rasterizing the mask

Before you can apply the Liquify feature to the metal grille, you must rasterize its vector mask and merge the mask and image to create just one image.

1 In the Layers palette, select the Metal Grille layer.

2 Choose Layer > Rasterize > Vector Mask. This converts the circles path, which is a vector graphic and resolution-independent, into a mask that is a raster image and resolution-dependent.

To view a mask by itself, Alt-click (Windows) or Option-click (Mac OS) the mask thumbnail in the Layers palette. You can then use the painting tools to add to or subtract from the mask. For more information, see Lesson 6, "Masks and Channels."

3 Choose Layer > Remove Layer Mask > Apply to merge the layer with its mask, creating a single rasterized image on that layer.

Using the Liquify command

The Liquify command lets you interactively push, pull, rotate, reflect, pucker, and bloat any area of an image. The distortions you create can be subtle or drastic, which makes the Liquify command a powerful tool for retouching images as well as creating artistic effects.

Note: *The Liquify command is available only for 8-bit images in RGB Color, CMYK Color, Lab Color, and Grayscale image modes.*

You can use tools or alpha channels to freeze areas of the preview image to protect them from further changes, or thaw the frozen areas.

Certain reconstruction modes change unfrozen areas in relation to the distortions in frozen areas. You can hide or show the mask for frozen areas, change the mask color, and use a Brush Pressure option to create partial freezes and thaws.

–From Adobe Photoshop 7.0 online Help

Applying the Liquify command

Now you'll warp the layer with the Liquify command and warp tool.

The Liquify filter works by applying a mesh warping. This distorts the image by dragging handles at the intersection of a hidden grid or *mesh*. Turning on the mesh visibility can help you understand more clearly how you're manipulating this grid and the different effects created by the various liquify tools.

1 With the Metal Grille layer selected in the Layers palette, chose Filter > Liquify.

2 In the Liquify dialog box, select the following options:

• In the upper left corner of the dialog box, make sure that the warp tool () is selected.

• On the upper right side of the dialog box under Tool Options, select a brush size that's the same size as the holes in the grille (we used 133). Then for Brush Pressure, select a moderate value (we used 20).

• (Optional) Under View Options on the lower right side of the dialog box, select the Backdrop check box, make sure that All Layers is selected on the Backdrop pop-up menu, and then drag the Opacity slider or type **100%**.

These view options make the layers under the Metal Grille layer visible. This can be visually confusing until you get used to it, especially because as you work you'll continue to see both the original metal grille and the liquified metal grille ghosted over it. To return to your original view, just deselect the Backdrop check box.

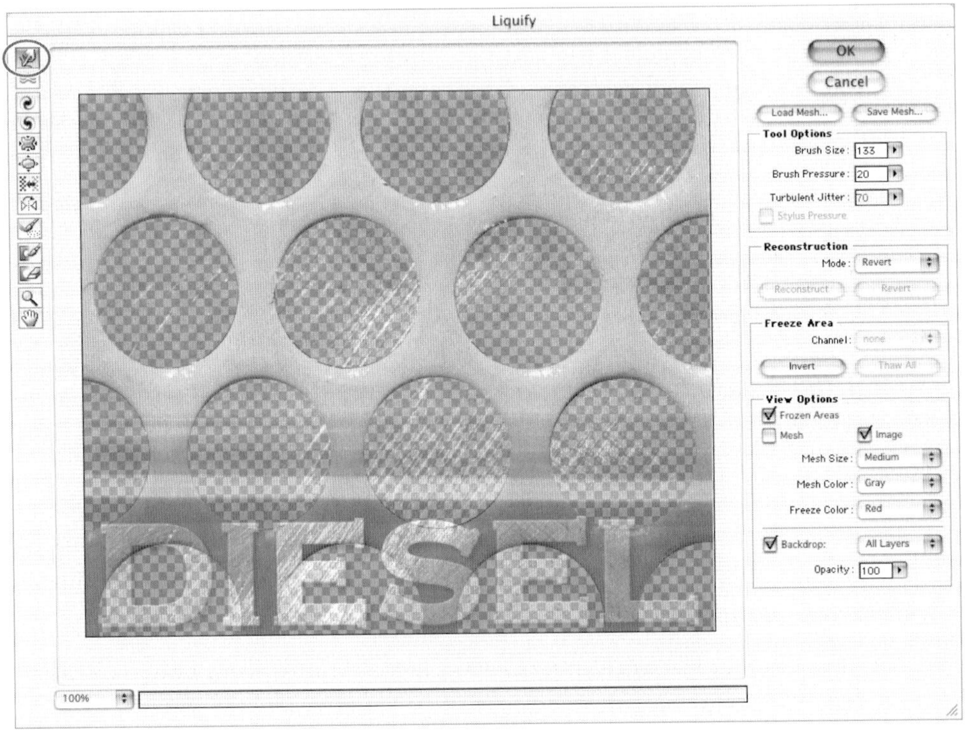

3 Still in the Liquify dialog box, drag the brush across and down the image once to start applying the Liquify filtering effect.

4 Under View Options in the Liquify dialog box, select the Mesh check box, and deselect the Backdrop check box, if necessary. Notice how the mesh has been distorted by the warp tool.

5 On the left side of the dialog box, select the turbulence tool (≋), and drag the brush across another area of the metal grille image.

Notice the differences between the results created with the warp tool and the results created by the turbulence brush: The warp tool simply pulled the mesh and image in one direction. The turbulence tool creates an additional random distortion.

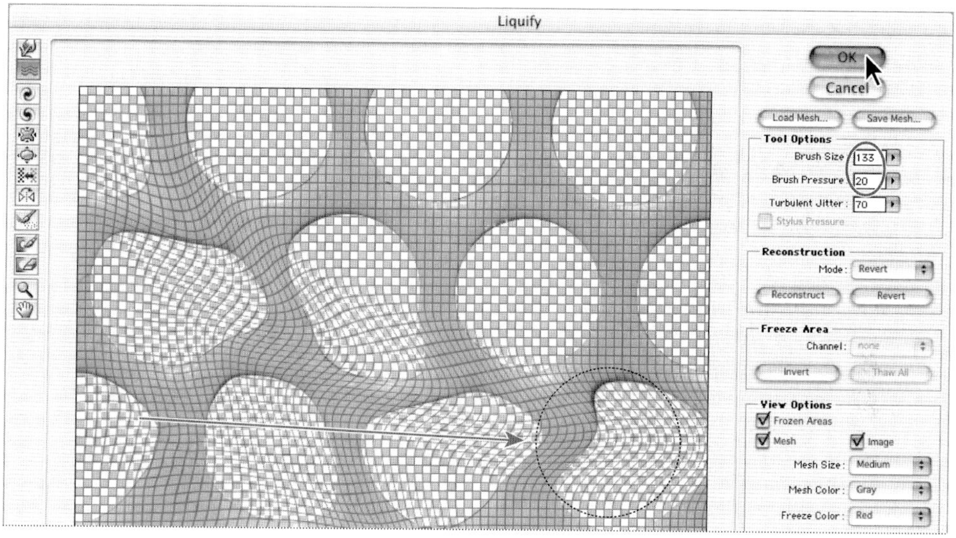

Note: *If you make mistakes or don't like one of the brush strokes you apply, press Ctrl+Z (Windows) or Command+Z (Mac OS) to undo that step. If you want to undo more than one step, click Cancel to close the Liquify dialog box, and then start the process again.*

6 Continue to apply different effects to the metal grille. When you are satisfied with the results, click OK to close the Liquify dialog box.

7 Choose File > Save.

Creating a border layer

To give the image a finished look, you'll add a border to it.

1 Click the Create a New Layer button (◻) in the Layers palette. (It doesn't matter which layer is currently selected because you're going to move the new layer a little later.)

2 Double-click the new Layer 1, and type **Image Border** to rename it.

3 Drag the Image Border layer to the top of the Layers palette stack, until a black line appears immediately above the Words layer set, and then release the mouse button.

The Image Border layer is now the top layer in the image.

4 Choose Select > All to select the entire image.

5 Choose Edit > Stroke. In the Stroke area, enter **5 px** for Width and click OK. (Or, for a more dramatic black border, enter a larger number, such as **10** or **15** pixels.)
A 5-pixel-wide black stroke now appears around the entire image.

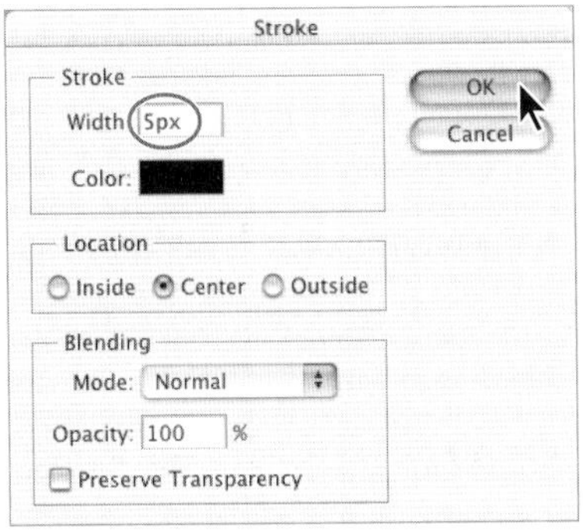

6 Choose Select > Deselect to deselect the entire image.

7 Choose File > Save.

Flattening a layered image

If you plan to send a file out for proofs, it's also a good idea to save two versions of the file—one containing all the layers so that you can edit the file if necessary, and one flattened version to send to the print shop. When you flatten a file, all layers are merged into a single background, greatly reducing the size of the file.

1 First, note the values in the lower-left corner of the application window (Windows) or the 11Start.psd image window (Mac OS). If the display does not show the file size (such as "Doc: 909K/6.4M"), click the arrow on the bottom of the window to open a pop-up menu, and choose Document Sizes.

The first number is the printing size of the image, which is about the size that the saved, flattened file would have in Adobe Photoshop format. The number on the right indicates the approximate document size of the file as it is now, including layers and channels.

2 Choose Image > Duplicate, name the duplicate file **11Final.psd**, and click OK.

3 On the Layers palette menu, choose Flatten Image. The layers for the 11Final.psd file are combined onto a single background layer.

4 Notice that the file size of the 11Final.psd image is significantly smaller than the 11Start.psd image, because it has been flattened onto the background.

5 Choose File > Save. In the Save As dialog box, click Save to save the file in Photoshop format.

You've completed the Advanced Layer Techniques lesson.

Review questions

1 Why would you use layer sets?

2 What are grouped layers? How could you use them in your work?

3 How do adjustment layers work, and what is the benefit of using an adjustment layer?

4 What are layer styles? Why would you use them?

Review answers

1 Layer sets help you organize and manage layers. For example, you can move all the layers in a layer set as a group and apply attributes or a mask to them as a group.

2 A layer group consists of at least two layers, where the artwork on the base layer is used as a mask for artwork on the layer or layers above.

3 Adjustment layers are a special type of Photoshop layer that works specifically with color and tonal adjustments. When you apply an adjustment layer, you can edit an image repeatedly without making a permanent change to the colors or tonal range in the image. You can view adjustment layers in ImageReady, but you can create or edit them only in Photoshop.

4 Layer styles are customizable effects that you can apply to layers. They enable you to apply changes to a layer that you can modify or remove at any time.

Lesson 12

12 Creating Special Effects

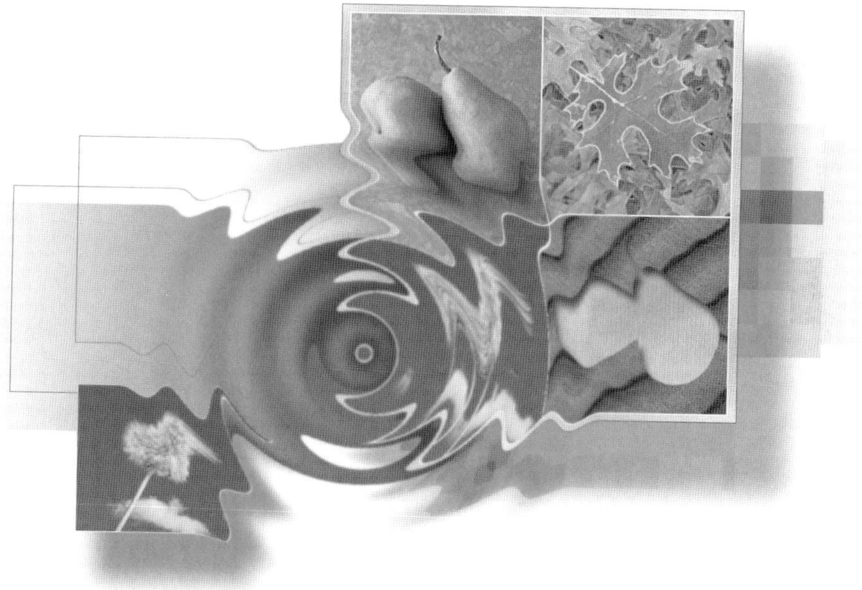

The huge assortment of filters available for Adobe Photoshop lets you transform ordinary images into extraordinary digital artwork. You can select filters that simulate a traditional artistic medium—a watercolor, pastel, or sketched effect—or you can choose from filters that blur, bend, wrap, sharpen, or fragment images. In addition to using filters to alter images, you can use adjustment layers and painting modes to vary the look of your artwork.

In this lesson, you'll learn how to do the following:

- Record and play back an action to automate a series of steps.
- Add guides to help you precisely place and align images.
- Save selections and load them as masks.
- Apply color effects only to unmasked areas of an image.
- Add an adjustment layer to make a color correction to a selection.
- Apply filters to selections to create various effects.
- Add layer styles to create editable special effects.

This lesson will take about 60 minutes to complete. The lesson is designed to be done in Adobe Photoshop, but information on using similar functionality in Adobe ImageReady is included where appropriate.

If needed, remove the previous lesson folder from your hard drive, and copy the Lesson12 folder onto it. As you work on this lesson, you'll overwrite the start files. If you need to restore the start files, copy them from the *Adobe Photoshop 7.0 Classroom in a Book* CD.

Note: *Windows users need to unlock the lesson files before using them. For more information, see "Copying the Classroom in a Book files" on page 4.*

Getting started

Before beginning this lesson, restore the default application settings for Adobe Photoshop. See "Restoring default preferences" on page 5.

You'll start the lesson by viewing the final Lesson file, to see what you'll accomplish.

1 Start Adobe Photoshop.

If a notice appears asking whether you want to customize your color settings, click No..

2 Choose File > Open, and open the 12End.psd file, located in the Lessons/Lesson12 folder.

An image containing a photo montage appears. The montage is comprised of four images, each of which has had a specific filter or effect applied to it.

3 When you have finished viewing the file, either leave it open for reference, or close it without saving changes.

Automating a multi-step task

An *action* is a set of one or more commands that you record and can play back to apply that series of commands to a single file or a batch of files. In this section of the lesson, you'll see how the Actions palette can help you save time by applying a multi-step process to the four images you'll use in this project.

Using actions is one of several ways that you can automate tasks in Adobe Photoshop and Adobe ImageReady. To learn more about recording actions, see Photoshop 7.0 online Help.

Opening and cropping the files

You'll start by opening and resizing four files. Since this part of the task involves aesthetic choices about where and how much of the image to crop, you'll do these steps manually rather than recording them with the Actions palette.

1 Choose File > Open, and select the 12Start.jpg file, which is in the Lesson12 folder on your hard disk.

2 In the toolbox, select the crop tool (⌗). Hold down Shift and drag a square selection marquee around the pears. (Holding down Shift constrains the selection to a square.)

3 If necessary, make any adjustments to the selection so that the pears are centered in the cropping marquee and fit fairly snugly inside it:

• To move the marquee, click inside it and drag until it is positioned properly.

• To resize the marquee, hold down Shift and drag one of the corners to make the marquee larger or smaller.

4 Press Enter to crop the image. Or, to start over without using this cropping marquee, click any tool in the toolbox and click Don't Crop when a message appears; then start the cropping process again.

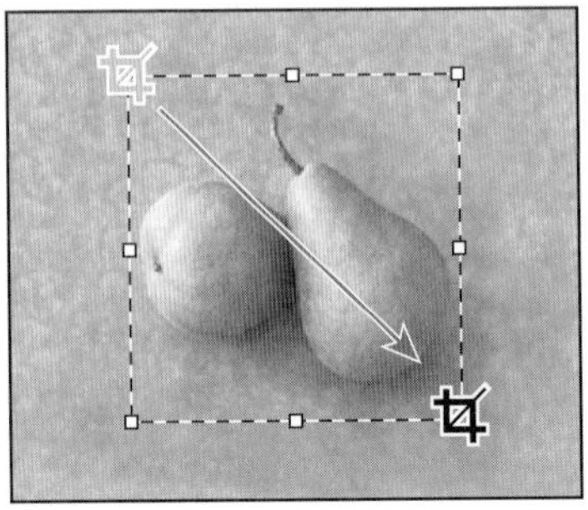

Dragging the cropping marquee

Cropped image

Because you're working with a number of files, you'll rename the 12Start.jpg file with a descriptive name so that it will be easy to identify.

5 Choose File > Save As, and save the cropped image as **Pears.jpg** in your Lesson12 folder. If a dialog box appears with options for image quality, click OK to accept the default settings.

6 Repeat steps 1 through 4 for each of the Leaves.jpg, Dandelion.jpg, and Sand.jpg images, all of which are in your Lesson12 folder.

Note: *It is not necessary to make all the cropped images the same size. You will adjust their sizes again later in this lesson.*

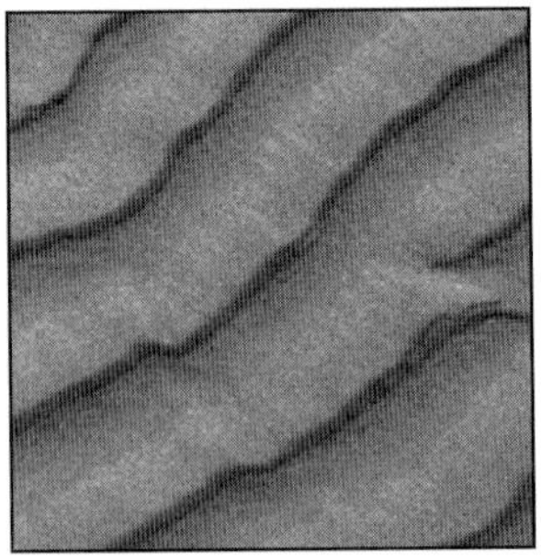

Cropped versions of the Leaves, Dandelion, and Sand JPEG files

Leave all the newly cropped files open for the next procedures.

Preparing to record an action

You use the Actions palette to record, play, edit, and delete individual actions. You also use the Actions palette to save and load action files. You'll start this task by opening a new document and preparing to record a new action in the Actions palette.

1 Choose Window > Actions to bring the Actions palette forward in its palette group.

2 In the Actions palette, click the New Layer Set button ( ) at the bottom of the palette. Or, you can create a new set by choosing New Set on the Actions palette menu (opened by clicking the arrow button ( ) in the upper right corner of the palette).

3 In the New Set dialog box, type **My Actions**, and click OK.

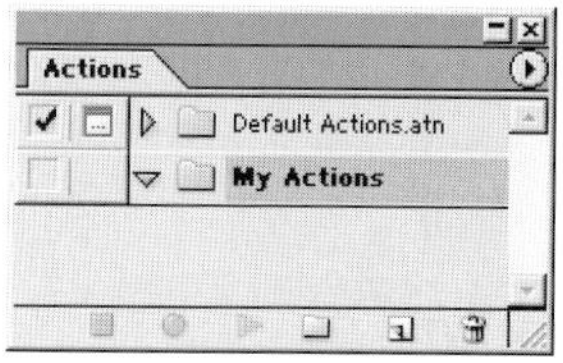

4 Choose Window > Documents > Dandelion.jpg to make that file active.

Recording a new action set

For this project, you want the images to be identical sizes and for each to be surrounded by a narrow white border. You're now ready to perform those tasks on the dandelion image, which you'll do by setting the image dimensions to a specific number of pixels and by setting a stroke and stroke properties that will surround the image. As you work, you'll set the Actions palette to record each step of the process.

***Note:** It is important that you finish all the steps in this procedure without interruption. If you become distracted and need to start over, skip ahead to step 9 to stop the recording. Then you can delete the action by dragging it into the Delete button ( ) in the Actions palette, and start again at step 1.*

1 In the Actions palette, click the New Action button ( ) or choose New Action on the Actions palette menu.

2 In the New Action dialog box, type **Size & Stroke** in the Name option and make sure that My Actions is selected in the Set pop-up menu. Then click Record.

Note: *Take all the time you need to do this procedure accurately. The speed at which you work has no influence on the amount of time required to play a recorded action.*

3 Choose Image > Image Size.

4 Make sure that both the Constrain Proportions and the Resample Image check boxes are selected at the bottom of the Image Size dialog box. Then, for the Width, type **275** and make sure that pixels is selected as the unit of measurement. Then click OK.

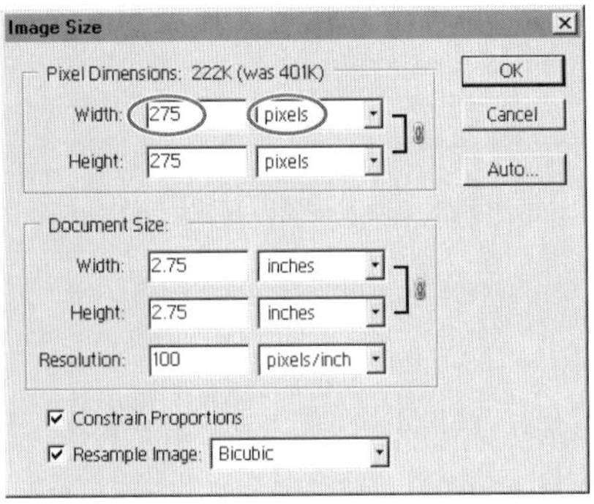

5 Choose Select > All.

6 Choose Edit > Stroke.

7 In the Stroke dialog box, make sure that the following options are selected, or select then now:

- In the Width option, leave the value at **1** pixel.
- In the Color swatch, use white, or select it by clicking the swatch to open the color picker, selecting white (C, M, Y, and K = 0), and clicking OK to close the color picker.
- Under Location, leave Center selected.
- Under Blending, leave Mode set to Normal and Opacity set at 100%.
- Then click OK to close the Stroke dialog box.

8 Choose Select > Deselect.

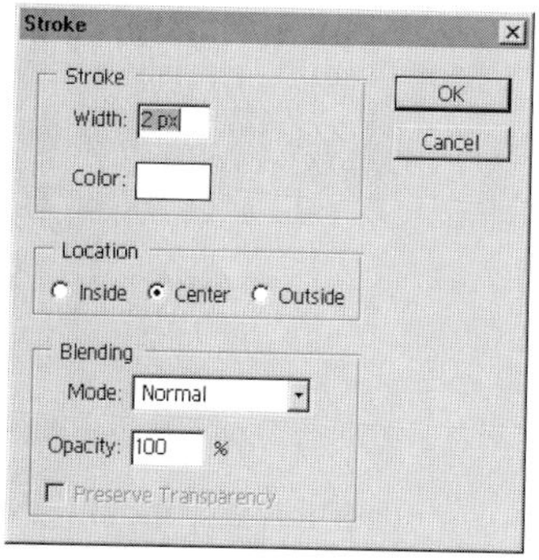

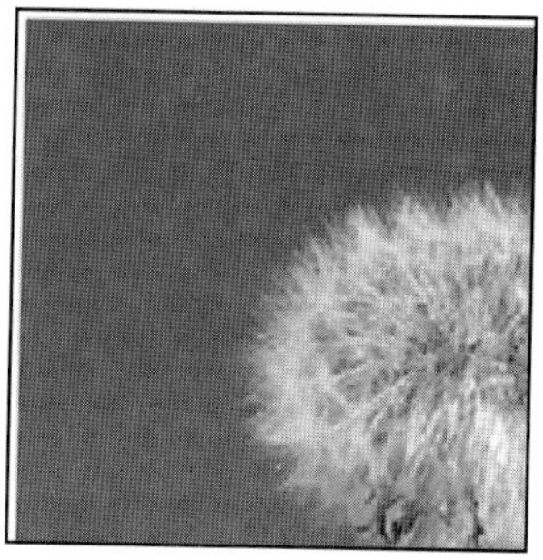

Stroke dialog box settings and close-up of resulting border on image

9 In the Actions palette, click the green Stop button (■) at the bottom of the palette to stop recording steps. Save your work.

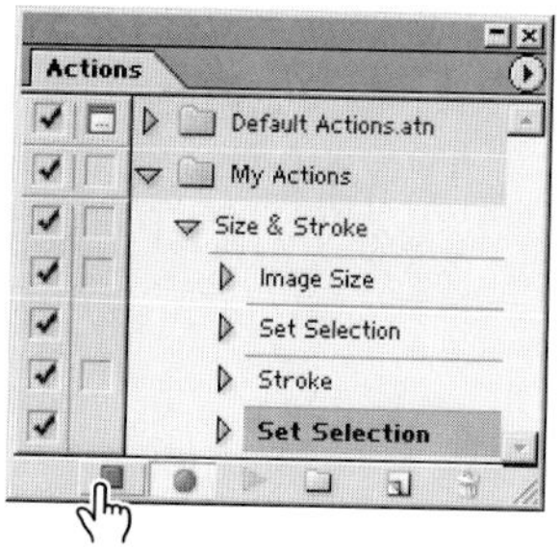

Your action is now saved in the Actions palette. You can click the arrows to the left of the My Actions set, the Size & Stroke action, and beside each step of that action to expand and collapse them at your convenience. With these expanded, you can examine each recorded step and the specific selections you made. When you finish reviewing the action, click the arrows to collapse the steps.

Playing an action on an individual file

Now that you've recorded the process of setting the image size and stroke characteristics for the dandelion image, you can use the action as an automated task. You'll apply the Stroke & Size action to one of the other three image files you cropped earlier in this section.

1 If the Leaves.jpg, Pears.jpg, and Sand.jpg files are not still open, choose File > Open and open them now.

2 Choose Window > Document > Sand.jpg to make that image active.

3 In the Actions palette, select the Size & Stroke action in the My Actions set, and then click the Play button (▶), or choose Play on the Actions palette menu.

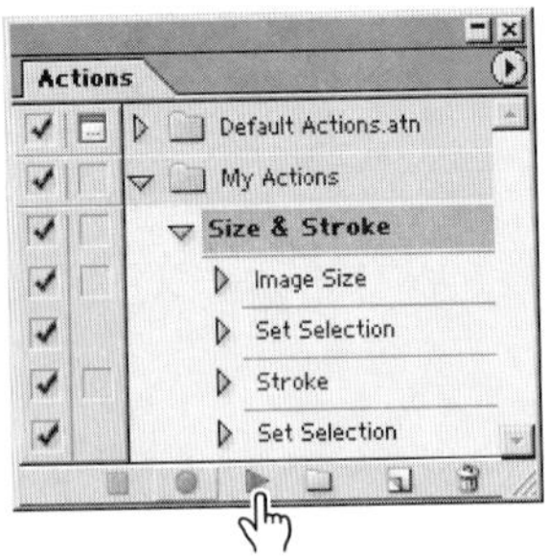

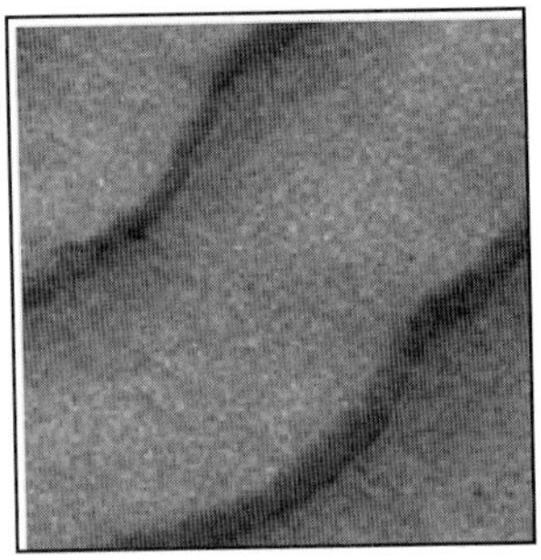

The Sand.jpg image is automatically resized and given a stroke so that it now matches the Dandelion.jpg image for these properties.

4 Choose File > Save.

Batch-playing an action

Applying actions is a time-saving process for performing routine tasks on files, but it can streamline your work even further by applying actions to all open files. You have two more files in this project that need to be resized and given strokes, so you'll apply your automated action to them simultaneously.

1 Close the Dandelion.jpg and Sand.jpg files. Make sure that only the Pears.jpg and Leaves.jpg files are open.

2 Choose File > Automate > Batch.

3 Under the Play section of the Batch dialog box, make sure that My Actions is selected for Set and that Size & Stroke is selected for Action.

4 In the Source pop-up menu, select Opened Files.

5 Leave Destination set as None, and click OK.

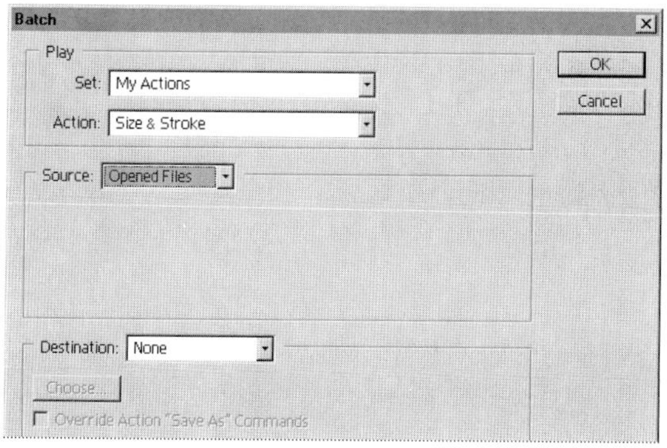

The action is applied to both the pears and leaves images, so that the files have identical dimensions and strokes surrounding them.

6 Choose File > Save and then File > Close for each of the two files.

In this exercise, you batch-processed only two files instead of making all the same changes in each of them; this was a mild convenience. But creating and applying actions can save significant amounts of time and tedium when you have dozens or even hundreds of files that require any routine, repetitive work.

Setting up a four-image montage

Now that you've finished preparing the four images, you'll place them together in a new composite image. Using guides, you'll be able to align the images precisely without a lot of effort.

Adding guides

Guides are non-printing lines that help you line up elements in your document, either horizontally or vertically. You can choose a Snap To command so that the guides behave like magnets: Objects you drag to positions that are close to a guide will snap into place along the guide when you release the mouse button.

1 Choose File > Open, and open the Montage.psd file in the Lesson12 folder.

2 Choose View > Rulers. A vertical ruler appears along the left side of the window and a horizontal ruler appears along the top of the window.

Note: *If the ruler units are not inches, choose Edit > Preferences > Units & Rulers (Windows, Mac OS 9) or Photoshop > Preferences > Units & Rulers (Mac OS 10), and select Inches from the Rulers pop-up menu; then click OK.*

3 Choose Window > Info to bring the Info palette forward in its palette group.

4 Drag from the horizontal ruler to the middle of the image window, watching the Info palette to see the Y coordinates as you drag. Release the mouse when Y = 3.000 inches. A blue guideline appears across the middle of the window.

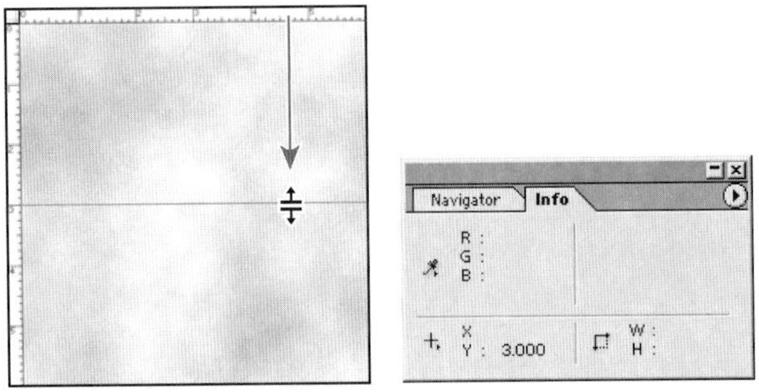

5 Drag another guide from the vertical ruler to the middle of the image and release the mouse when X = 3.000 inches.

6 Choose View > Snap To > and make sure that the Guides command is checked, or select it now.

7 Choose View > Rulers to hide the rulers again.

Snapping images into position

Your guides are in place, so now you're ready to arrange your four cropped images in the montage.

1 Choose File > Open Recent > Pears.jpg. The pears image opens in a separate image window.

2 In the toolbox, select the move tool (▶✛).

3 Click the move tool anywhere in the pear image and drag from that image window to the larger Montage.jpg window, and release the mouse button.

4 Still using the move tool, drag the pears image into the upper left quadrant of the image so that its lower right corner snaps into place against the intersection of the two guides at the center of the window.

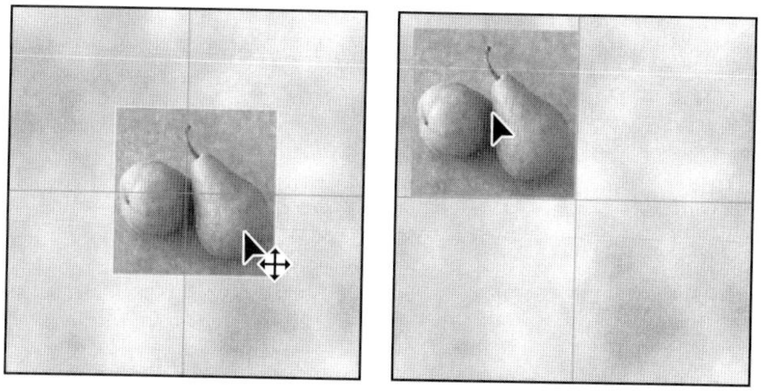

In the Layers palette, you'll notice that the pears image is on a new layer, Layer 1.

5 Choose Window > Documents > Pears.jpg to make it active again, and then close it, either by clicking the Close button or by choosing File > Close.

6 Repeat steps 1–5 for the three other cropped files, placing the leaves image in the upper right quadrant, the dandelion in the lower left quadrant, and the sand in the lower right quadrant. All the images should fit snugly against the intersection of the guides in the center of the window.

7 Choose View > Show > Guides to hide the guides.

Saving selections

Next, you'll select the two pears and save the selection itself. Later, you can reload the selection and use it as needed. Later in this lesson, you'll used your saved selection to colorize the pears and to add a special effect.

1 In the toolbox, select the zoom tool (🔍), and drag a marquee around the pears to magnify your view. Make sure that you can see all of both pears in the image window.

2 Hold down the mouse on the lasso tool (⌒) to open the hidden tools list, and select the magnetic lasso tool (⌒).

For best results when tracing the pear stem with the magnetic lasso tool, decrease the tool's lasso width and frequency values on the tool options bar. For example, try tracing the pear using a Lasso Width of **1** or **2** pixels and a Frequency of **40**.

Note: *ImageReady does not include the magnetic lasso tool.*

3 Click once to set a point on the edge of the pear on the right, and then move the pointer (you do not need to hold down the mouse button) around the pear to trace its outline.

As you move the pointer, the active segment snaps to the strongest edge in the image. Periodically, the magnetic lasso tool adds fastening points to the selection border to anchor previous sections. Try to make your selection a reasonably accurate outline of the pear, but don't worry if it's not perfect.

You can also click the magnetic lasso tool as you trace the outline to add your own fastening points. This might be especially helpful around the stem or where the highlights or shadows make the edge between the pear and the background less distinctive.

4 When you get back to your starting point, a small circle appears in the lower right area of the magnetic lasso pointer ( ), indicating that you can click to close the segment. Do that now.

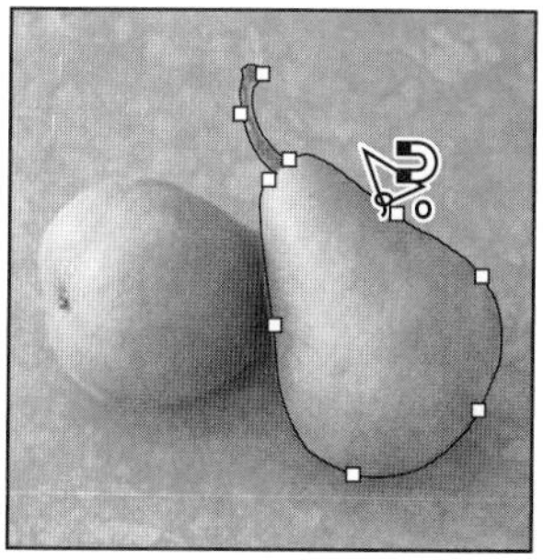

5 Choose Select > Save Selection, and then type **Right Pear** for Name, and click OK to save the selection in a new channel.

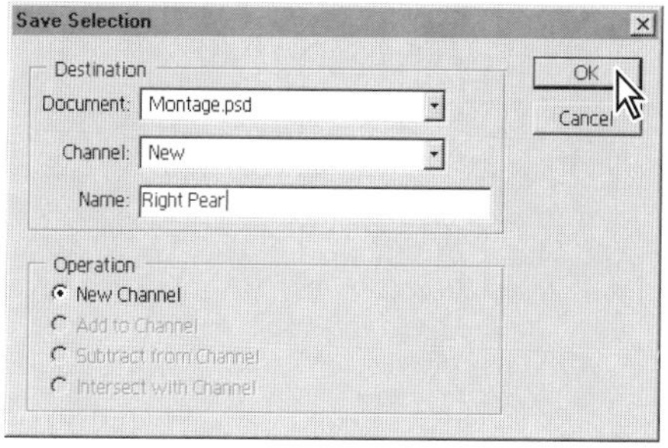

6 Choose Select > Deselect to deselect the right pear.

7 Repeat the process (steps 1–6), this time selecting the left pear and saving the selection as **Left Pear**.

You now have two selections saved. To see them, click the Channel palette tab to open it and scroll down, if necessary. Click each pear channel name in turn to make the channel masks appear in the image window.

When you are ready to continue working, scroll to the top of the Channels palette and click the RGB channel to select it. Click the tab for the Layers palette to bring it forward in the palette group so it will be ready for the next procedure.

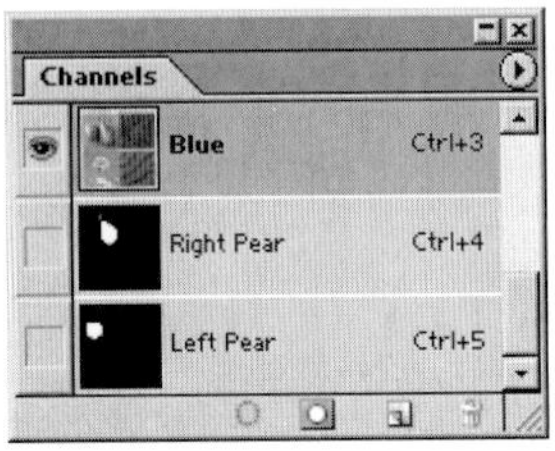

Hand-coloring selections on a layer

You'll start to add special effects to your montage by hand-coloring the pears, beginning with the pear on the right. To select it, you'll simply load the first selection you created in the previous procedure. Then, you'll remove the color from the selection so that you can color it by hand. Finally, after adding a layer above the pears, you'll be ready to apply new color by adding it to the new layer. In this way, you can simply erase the layer and start over if you don't like the results.

You could do most of the following tasks in ImageReady rather than Photoshop, but this is not recommended. ImageReady has the same Load Selection command and filters, and many of the same color-collection options, blending modes, and tools for applying and tracking color that you find in Photoshop. ImageReady uses a slightly different technique for creating gradients, as noted in that topic, "Adding a gradient" on page 372, and cannot create or edit an adjustment layer, as discussed in "Changing the color balance" on page 374. Because of this, it's better to do these procedures in Photoshop for this project.

Desaturating a selection

You'll use the Desaturate command to *desaturate*—that is, to remove the color from—the selected pear area. Saturation is the presence or absence of color in a selection. When you desaturate a selection within an image, you create a grayscale-like effect without affecting the colors in other parts of the image.

1 In the Layers palette, select Layer 1, the layer with the pears image.

2 Choose Select > Load Selection.

3 In the Load Selection dialog box, select Right Pear from the Channel pop-up menu, and click OK. A selection border appears around the right pear in your image.

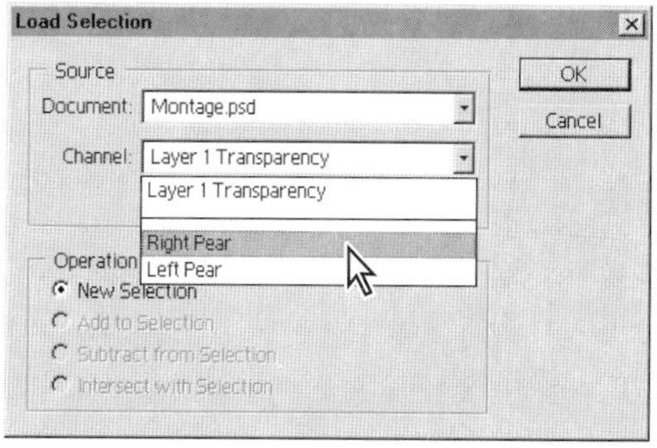

4 Choose Image > Adjustments > Desaturate. The color is removed from the selection.

5 Choose Select > Deselect.

6 Choose File > Save to save your work.

Creating a layer and choosing a blending mode

Now you'll add a layer and specify a layer blending mode for painting the desaturated pear image. By painting on a separate layer, you won't permanently alter the image. This makes it easy to start over if you aren't satisfied with the results.

You use layer blending modes to determine how the pixels in a layer blend with underlying pixels on other layers. By applying modes to individual layers, you can create myriad special effects.

1 In the Layers palette, click the New Layer button (◘) to add Layer 5 to the image, just above Layer 1 in the palette.

2 Double-click Layer 5 and type **Paint** to rename the layer.

3 In the Layers palette, choose Color from the pop-up mode menu to the left of the Opacity text box.

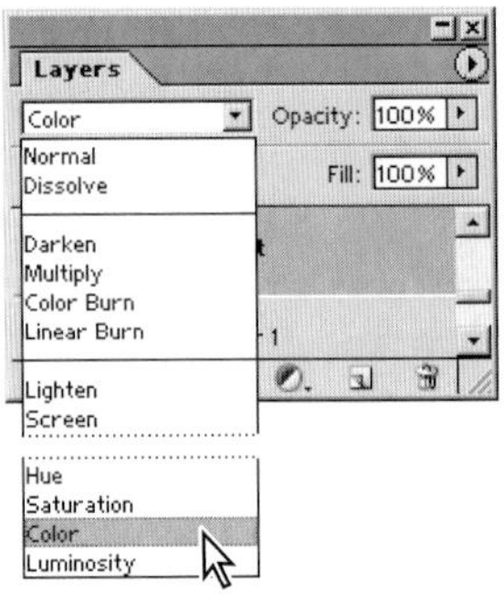

The Color mode option is a *blending mode*. These modes determine how the pixels in this layer blend with underlying pixels on the Background layer.

Note: *Next to the New Layer button, you'll see the Trash button. Any time you want to throw your Paint layer away, you can drag the layer to the trash in the Layers palette.*

You can use the Color mode to change the hue of a selection without affecting the highlights and shadows. This means that you can apply a variety of color tints without changing the original highlights and shadows of the pears.

Applying painting effects

To begin painting, you must again load the selection that you created earlier. By applying the Right Pear channel, you protect the unselected areas of the image as you apply colors, making it easy to paint within the lines.

For an illustration of hand-painting the pears, see figure 12-1 in the color section.

1 Choose Select > Load Selection > Right Pear.

Notice in the Load Selection dialog box that the color-mode change you just made also was saved as a selection, called *Paint Transparency.* Click OK to close the dialog box.

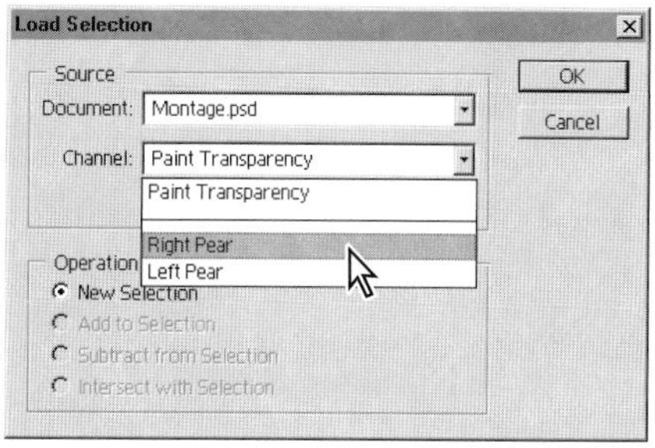

2 Select the brush tool ( ). Then, in the tool options bar, set the Opacity to about **50%**.

Change the brush opacity by pressing a number on the keypad from 0 to 9 (where 1 is 10%, 9 is 90%, and 0 is 100%).

3 In the Brush pop-up palette, select a large, soft-edged brush, such as the soft round 35-pixel brush.

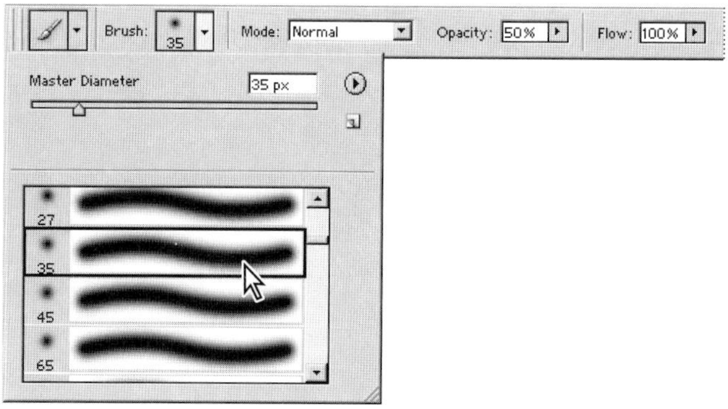

4 Choose Window > Swatches to bring the Swatches palette forward, and then select any yellow-green color that appeals to you as your foreground color.

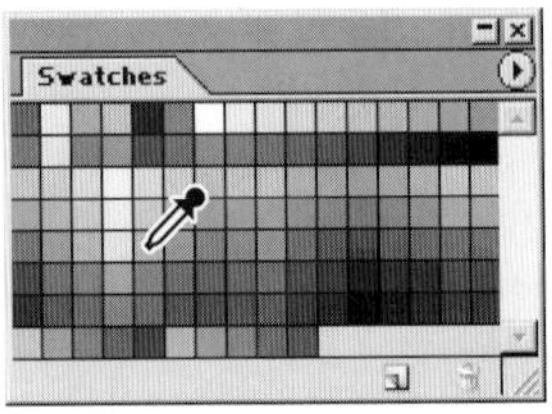

5 Drag the brush over the entire pear to apply the color.

Next, you'll use a darker and a lighter shade to add highlights and shadows.

6 Select a darker green from the Swatches palette. In the tool options bar, set the brush opacity to about 30%. Paint around the edges in the pear selection, avoiding the highlight area.

7 Select a rose color from the Swatches palette. In the tool options bar, select a smaller brush size and decrease the paint opacity to about 20%. Then paint highlights on the pear.

8 When you are satisfied with your results, choose Select > Deselect, and then choose File > Save.

Adding a gradient

Now you'll use the gradient tool to add a gradient to the other pear for a highlight effect. (ImageReady does not have a gradient tool. Instead, gradients are created as ImageReady layer effects.)

First, you'll need to load the selection that you made earlier of the left pear.

1 Choose Select > Load Selection, and select Left Pear. Click OK. A selection border appears around the left pear in your image.

2 Click the Color palette tab to bring it forward, and then select red as the foreground color by typing or dragging the R slider to **255** and the G and B sliders to **0**.

3 Click the Set Background Color icon in the upper left area of the Color palette and then select yellow as the background color by setting R and G at **255** and B at **0**.

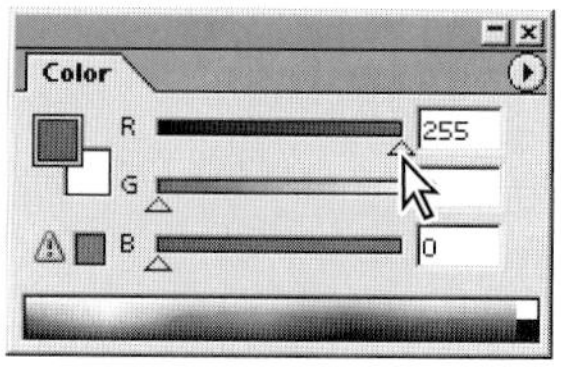

Foreground color

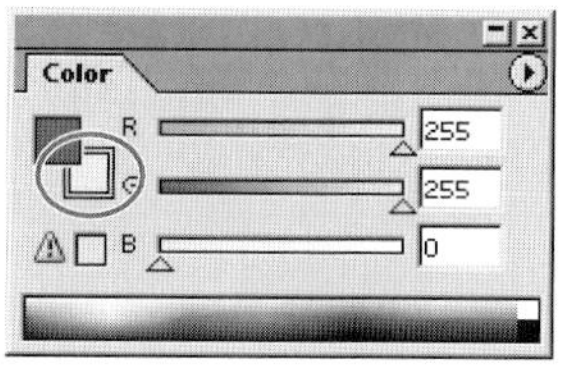

Background color

4 Select the gradient tool (■). On the tool options bar, select the following options:

• Select Radial Gradient.

• Open the gradient picker and make sure that Foreground to Background is selected, so that the color blends from the foreground color (red) to the background color (yellow).

• Set the opacity to **40%**.

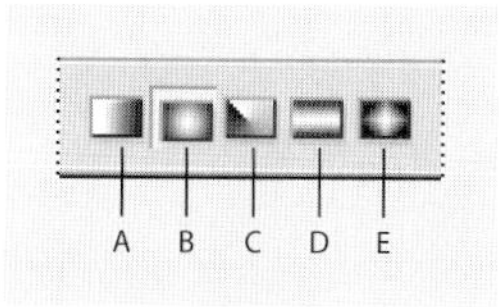

A. *Linear gradient*
B. *Radial gradient*
C. *Angle gradient*
D. *Reflected gradient*
E. *Diamond gradient*

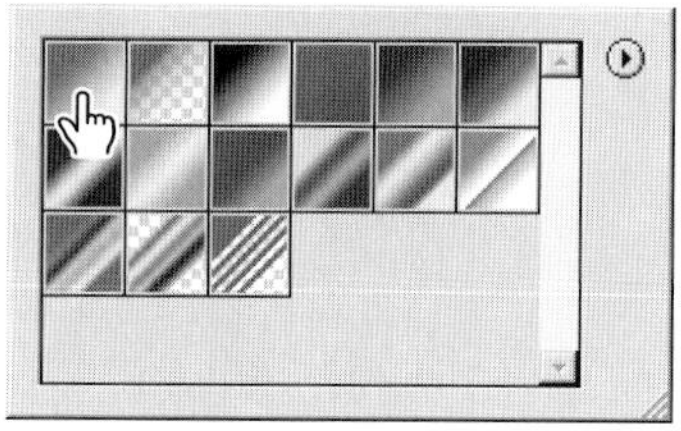

Selecting Foreground to Background

5 Position the gradient tool near the pear's highlight, and drag toward the stem end.

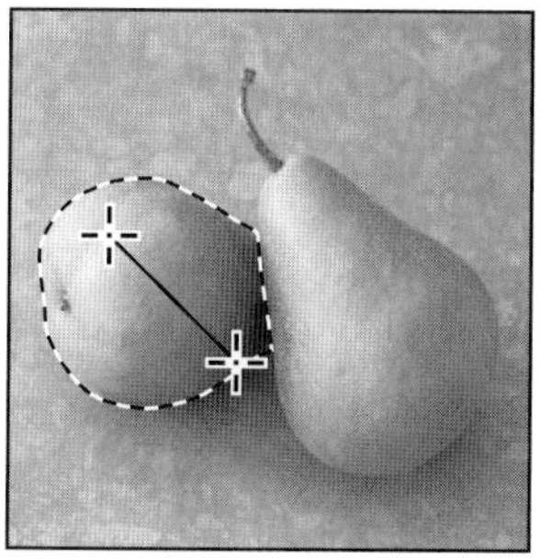

6 When you're satisfied with the results, choose Select > Deselect.

Merging layers

The next step, merging layers, helps you to keep the file size relatively small. However, after you merge, you cannot easily go back and restore the image or start the process over, so be sure that you are happy with your results before you choose a merge command.

1 In the Layers palette, make sure that the Paint layer is selected.

2 Choose Layer > Merge Down to merge the Paint layer with the pear image.

Now the two layers are fused as Layer 1.

3 Double-click the hand tool ( ) so that the entire image fits in the image window, or double-click the zoom tool ( ) to reduce the view to 100%.

4 Choose File > Save.

Changing the color balance

Now you'll use an adjustment layer to adjust the color balance on the leaves image. ImageReady has many of the same color-correction features as Photoshop, but they cannot be applied to adjustment layers or channels because you cannot create or edit adjustment layers or channels in ImageReady.

Altering the color for a channel or a regular layer permanently changes the pixels on that layer. However, with an adjustment layer, your color and tonal changes reside only within the adjustment layer and do not alter any pixels in the layers beneath it. The effect is as if you were viewing the visible layers through the adjustment layer above them. By using adjustment layers, you can try out color and tonal adjustments without permanently changing pixels in the image. You can also use adjustment layers to affect multiple layers at once.

1 In the Layers palette, select the layer containing the leaves (in the upper right quadrant of the montage).

In our example this is Layer 2, but it may be on another layer in your file if you originally placed the images in a different sequence.

2 Choose Layer > New Adjustment Layer > Color Balance.

3 In the New Layer dialog box, select the Group With Previous Layer check box, and then click OK. This ensures that your adjustment layer will affect only the leaves image, not the other three sections of the montage.

The Color Balance dialog box opens, where you can change the mixture of colors in a color image and make general color corrections. When you adjust the color balance, you can keep the same tonal balance, as you'll do here. You can also focus changes on the shadows, midtones, or highlights.

4 Move the dialog box so that you can see the leaves in the image window and make sure that the Preview check box is selected.

5 In the Color Balance dialog box, experiment with different Color Levels for the image. (The example uses +10, –20, and –20.)

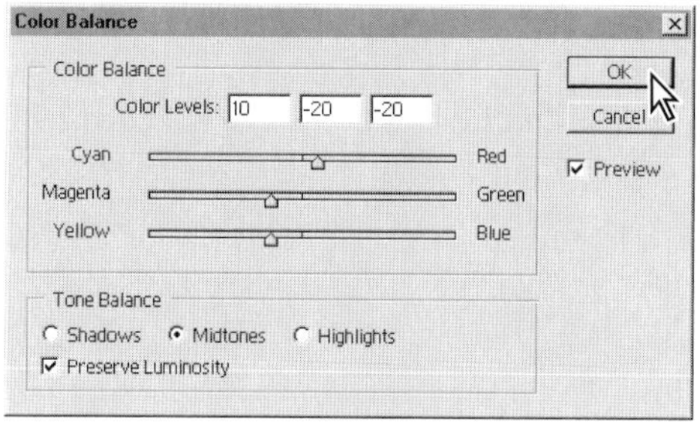

6 When you are happy with the result, click OK, and then save your work.

Adjustment layers act as layer masks, which can be edited repeatedly without permanently affecting the underlying image. You can double-click an adjustment layer to display the last settings used and adjust them as many times as you want. You can delete an adjustment layer by dragging it to the Trash button at the bottom of the Layers palette.

Applying filters

To conclude the project, you'll apply two different styles of filters to the leaves and dandelion images. Because there are so many different filters for creating special effects, the best way to learn about them is to try out different filters and filter options. ImageReady supports the same filters that areincluded with Photoshop.

To save time when trying various filters, experiment on a small, representative part of your image or on a low-resolution copy.

Improving performance with filters

Some filter effects can be memory-intensive, especially when applied to a high-resolution image. You can use these techniques to improve performance:

- *Try out filters and settings on a small portion of an image.*
- *Apply the effect to individual channels—for example, to each RGB channel—if the image is large and you're having problems with insufficient memory. (With some filters, effects vary if applied to the individual channel rather than the composite channel, especially if the filter randomly modifies pixels.)*
- *Free up memory before running the filter by using the Purge command. (See "Correcting mistakes" in Photoshop 7.0 online Help.)*
- *Allocate more RAM to Photoshop or ImageReady (Mac OS). You can also exit any other applications to make more memory available to Photoshop or ImageReady.*
- *Try changing settings to improve the speed of memory-intensive filters such as Lighting Effects, Cutout, Stained Glass, Chrome, Ripple, Spatter, Sprayed Strokes, and Glass filters. (For example, with the Stained Glass filter, increase cell size. With the Cutout filter, increase Edge Simplicity, decrease Edge Fidelity, or both.)*

If you plan to print to a grayscale printer, convert a copy of the image to grayscale before applying filters. However, applying a filter to a color image and then converting to grayscale may not have the same effect as applying the filter to a grayscale version of the image.

Applying and fading the Accented Edges filter

The Accented Edges filter exaggerates the margins between areas with different colors. You can adjust the extent of the exaggeration by changing the edge brightness control, but in this procedure, you'll use a Fade command to mute the results.

1 In the Layers palette, select theLeaves layer. Make sure that you select the layer itself and not the adjustment layer.

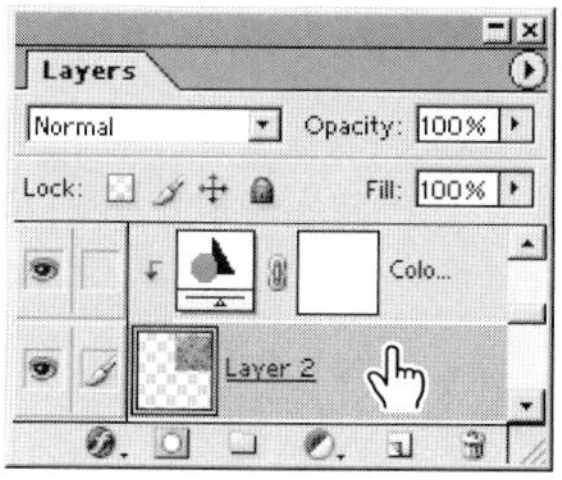

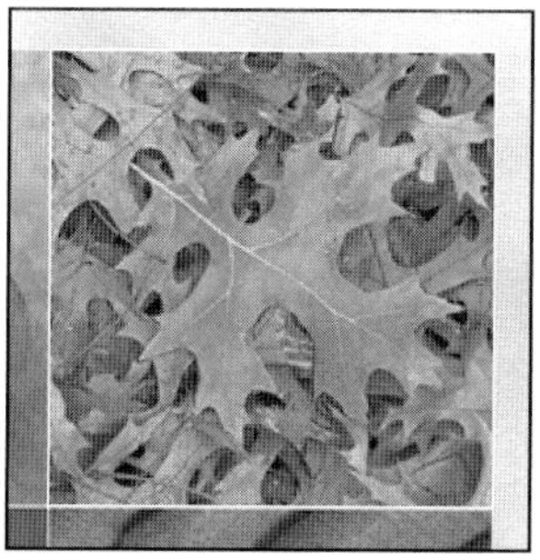

2 Choose Filter > Brush Strokes > Accented Edges. Click OK to accept the default settings in the Accented Edges dialog box.

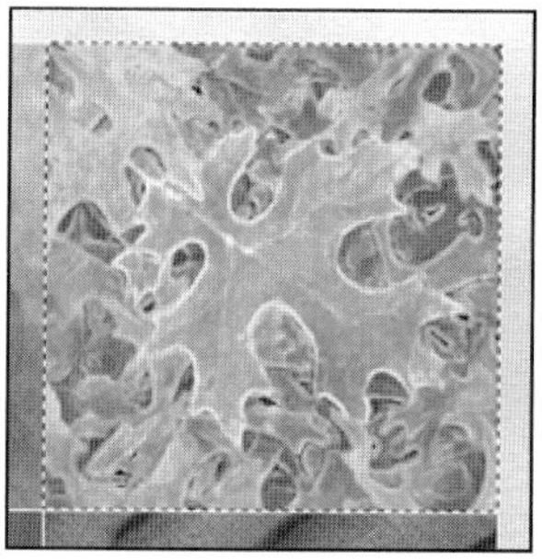

This image is somewhat too bright, so you'll tone it down slightly.

3 Choose Edit > Fade Accented Edges.

4 In the Fade dialog box, drag the Opacity slider to **60%**; then click OK.

5 Save your work.

Note: *The Fade command settings determine how the modified pixels in the selection appear in relation to the original pixels. The blending modes in the Fade dialog box are a subset of those available in the painting and editing tools Options palette.*

Using filters

To use a filter, choose the appropriate submenu command from the Filter menu. These guidelines can help you in choosing filters:

- *The last filter chosen appears at the top of the menu.*
- *Filters are applied to the active, visible layer.*
- *Filters cannot be applied to Bitmap-mode or indexed-color images.*
- *Some filters work only on RGB images.*
- *Some filters are processed entirely in RAM.*
- *Gaussian Blur, Add Noise, Median, Unsharp Mask, High Pass filters, and Dust & Scratches can be used with 16-bit-per-channel images, as well as 8-bit-per-channel images.*

–From Adobe Photoshop 7.0 online Help

Applying the ZigZag filter

Next, you'll use the ZigZag filter to create the impression that you're viewing the reflection of a dandelion on the surface of a rippled pool of water.

1 In the Layers palette, select the Dandelion layer.

2 Choose Filter > Distort > ZigZag.

13 Preparing Images for Two-Color Printing

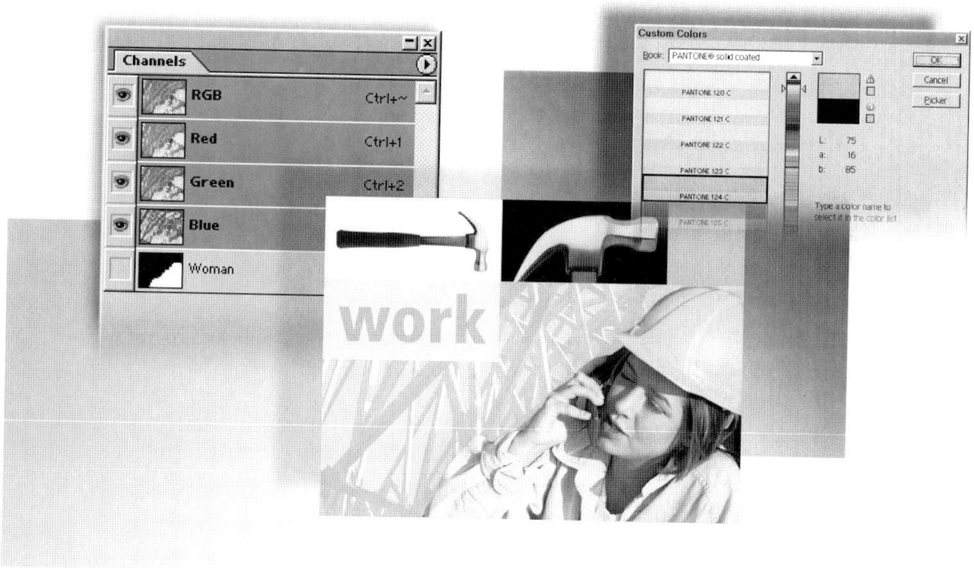

Not every commercially printed publication requires four-color reproduction. Printing in two colors using a grayscale image and spot color can be an effective and inexpensive alternative. In this lesson, you'll learn how to use Adobe Photoshop to prepare full-color images for two-color printing.

In this lesson, you'll learn how to do the following:

- Convert a color image to monochrome, and improve its overall quality.
- Adjust the tonal range of the image by assigning black and white points.
- Sharpen the image.
- Convert a color image to grayscale.
- Add spot color to selected areas of the image.

This lesson will take about 45 minutes to complete. The lesson is designed to be done in Adobe Photoshop. ImageReady does not support channels or spot color.

If needed, remove the previous lesson folder from your hard drive, and copy the Lesson13 folder onto it. As you work on this lesson, you'll overwrite the start files. If you need to restore the start files, copy them from the *Adobe Photoshop 7.0 Classroom in a Book* CD.

Note: *Windows users need to unlock the lesson files before using them. For more information, see "Copying the Classroom in a Book files" on page 4.*

Printing in color

Color publications are expensive to print commercially because they require four passes through the press—one for each of the four process colors used to create the full-color effect. The colors in the publication must be separated into cyan, magenta, yellow, and black plates for the press, which also adds to the expense.

Printing images in two colors can be a much less costly yet effective approach for many projects, even if they begin with an image in full color. With Photoshop, you can convert color to grayscale without sacrificing image quality. You can also add a second spot color for accent, and Photoshop will create the two-color separations needed for the printing process.

Note: *Spot color is intended for images that will be printed to film during the printing process. The spot-color techniques covered in this lesson are not appropriate for color images printed to desktop printers or for images designed for electronic distribution.*

Using channels and the Channels palette

Channels in Adobe Photoshop are used for storing information, and they play an important role in this lesson. *Color channels* store the color information for an image, and *alpha channels* store selections or masks that let you edit specific parts of an image. A third channel type, the *spot-color channel*, lets you specify color separations for printing an image with spot-color inks. For more information about channels, see Lesson ,6 "Masks and Channels."

In this lesson, you'll use all three types of channels. You'll learn to mix color channels to improve the quality of an image. You'll select areas of the image by loading a selection from an alpha channel. And you'll use a spot-color channel to add a second color to the image.

Getting started

Before beginning this lesson, restore the default application settings for Adobe Photoshop. See "Restoring default preferences" on page 5.

You'll start the lesson by viewing the final Lesson file to see the duotone image that you will create.

1 Start Adobe Photoshop.

2 Choose File > Open, and open the 13End.psd file, located in the Lessons/Lesson13 folder.

3 When you have finished viewing the file, either leave it open on your desktop for reference or close it without saving changes.

Now you'll open the start file for the lesson.

4 Choose File > Open, and open the 13Start.psd file in the Lessons/Lesson13 folder on your hard drive.

5 If guides are showing, choose View > Show > Guides to hide guides.

Using channels to change color to grayscale

Sometimes it's possible to improve the quality of an image by blending two or more color channels. For instance, one channel in an image may look particularly strong but would look even better if you could add some detail from another channel. In Photoshop, you can blend color channels with the Channel Mixer command in either RGB mode (for on-screen display) or CMYK mode (for printing). For more information on color modes, see Lesson 17, "Setting Up Your Monitor for Color Management."

In this lesson, you'll use the Channel Mixer command to improve the quality of an RGB image that you'll then convert to grayscale mode. But first, you'll use the Channels palette to view the different channels in the image.

1 Choose Window > Channels (or click the Channels tab) and drag the palette from group that also contains the Layers and Paths palettes. Place the Channels palette on your screen where you can easily access it.

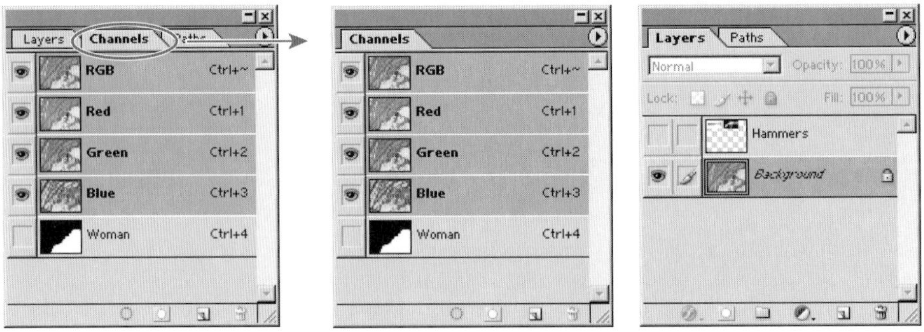

Drag the Channels palette from the Layers palette to make both palettes visible at the same time.

Because the image is in RGB mode, the Channels palette displays the image's red, green, and blue channels. Notice that all the color channels are currently visible, including the RGB channel, which is a composite of the separate red, green, and blue channels. To see the individual channels, you can use the palette's eye icons.

2 Click the eye icons (👁) to turn off all color channels in the Channels palette except the Red channel. The colors in the Start image change to shades of gray.

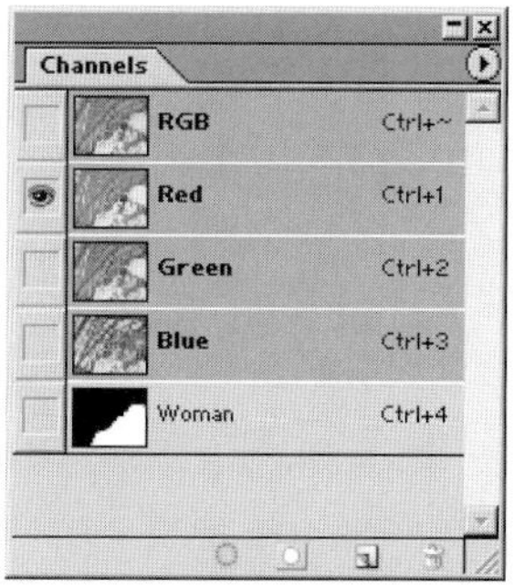

All channels off except red

Red channel

3 Drag the eye icon from the Red channel to the Green channel and then to the Blue channel. Notice how the monochrome image in the image window changes with each channel. The Green channel shows the best overall contrast and the best detail in the woman's face, while the Blue channel shows good contrast in the framework behind the woman.

Green channel

Blue channel

4 In the Channels palette, click the eye icon column for the composite RGB channel to display all the color channels in the image.

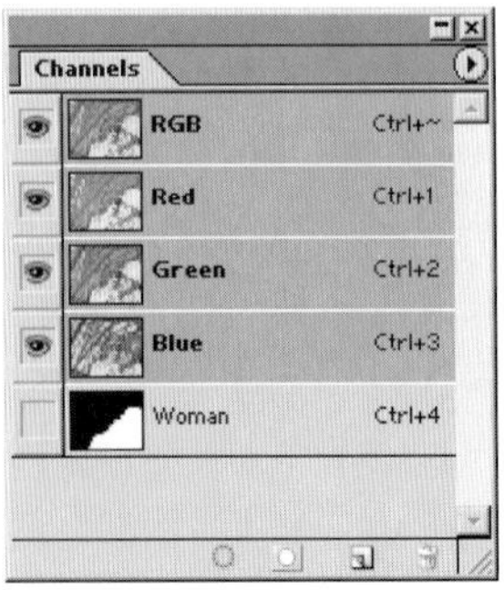

All channels displayed

RGB image

Now you'll use the Channel Mixer command to improve the image in this lesson. Specifically, you'll divide the image into two areas, the woman and the framework, and mix different amounts of source channels in each selection.

Mixing the woman's image

First, you'll select the woman's image by loading a premade selection.

1 In the Layers palette, make sure that the background is selected.

2 Choose Select > Load Selection. In the dialog box, select Woman from the Channel menu to load a selection that outlines the image of the woman. Click OK.

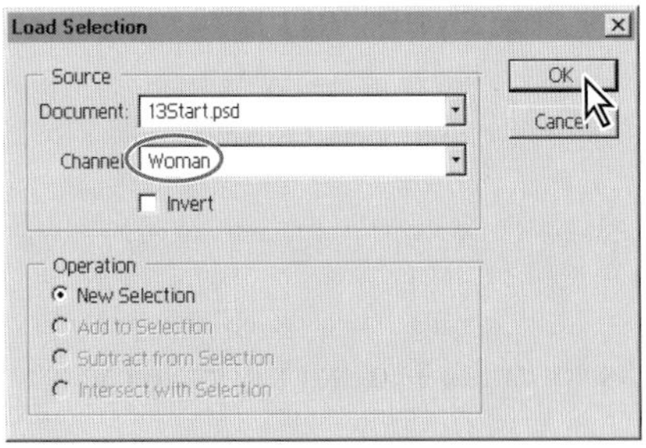

Now you'll mix the Green and Blue channels to improve the selection's contrast. You'll use Green as the base channel because it has the best overall contrast for the image.

3 Choose Image > Adjustments > Channel Mixer.

4 In the Channel Mixer dialog box, choose Green for the Output Channel. The Source Channel for Green changes to 100%.

5 Select the Monochrome check box to change the image to shades of gray. This option gives you an idea of how the selection will look in grayscale mode, so that you can more accurately adjust the selection's tonal range.

The resulting image is a little flat. You can bring out the contrast and improve the highlights by blending in some of the Blue channel.

6 Drag the slider for the Blue Source Channel to 10%. Click OK.

Selection loaded

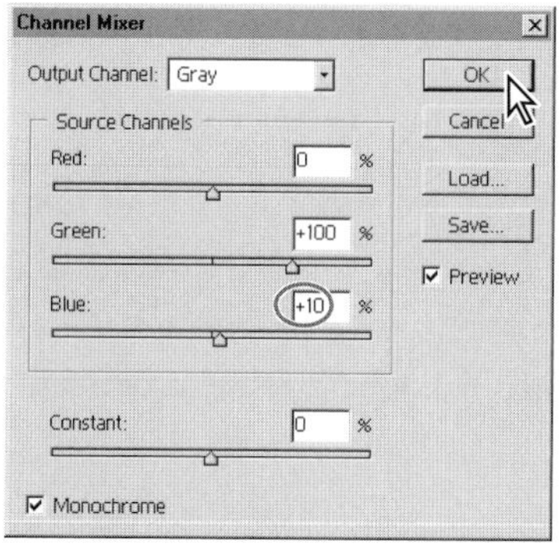

Channel Mixer dialog box with 10% blue

Mixing the framework's image

Next you'll select the framework, convert this part of the image to monochrome, and again mix channels to improve the contrast and detail.

1 Choose Select > Inverse to select the framework behind the woman.

2 Choose Image > Adjustments > Channel Mixer.

3 In the Channel Mixer dialog box, choose Green for the Output Channel, and select Monochrome.

This time the resulting image is dark and lacks contrast. You can improve the image again by blending in some of the Blue channel to increase the contrast.

4 Drag the slider for the Blue Source Channel to 26%. Click OK.

Inverse of selection

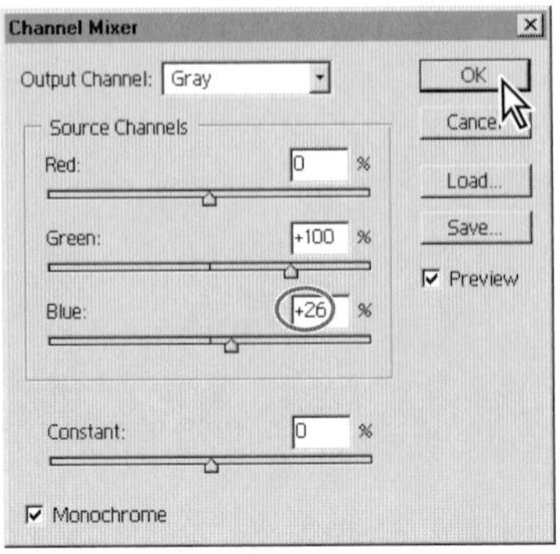

Channel Mixer dialog box with 26% blue

5 Choose Select > Deselect.

Both the woman and the framework now show better contrast and detail. But the image is still an RGB color image (one that contains only gray values). To convert the image to grayscale mode, you will use the Grayscale command.

6 Choose Image > Mode > Grayscale. When prompted, select Don't Flatten to keep the image's two layers intact. (You'll use the second layer later in this lesson.) The image converts to grayscale mode, and the color channels in the Channels palette are replaced by a single Gray channel.

7 Choose File > Save to save your work.

Now you can add a lighter block of spot color to the image.

3 Make a rectangular selection directly below the left hammer and bounded by the guides.

4 In the Color palette, drag the color slider to 20% to set the value for the new block of color.

5 Hold down Alt/Option and press Delete to fill the selection with a 20% screen of PANTONE 124.

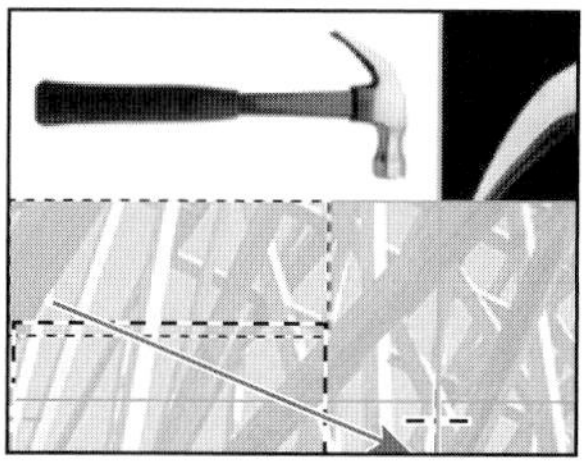

Making selection

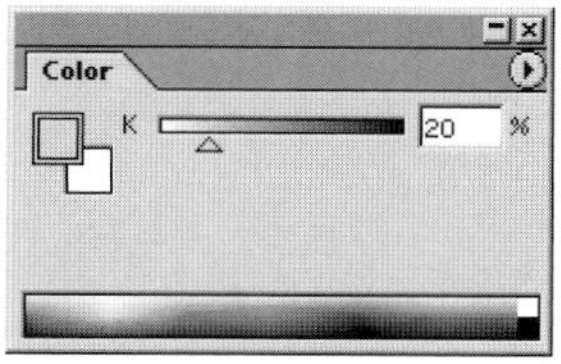

Color value set to 20%

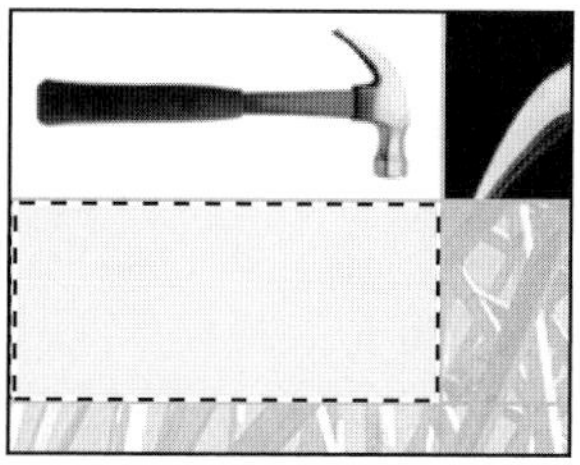

Selection filled with 20% color

6 Choose Select > Deselect.

7 Choose View > Show Extras or View > Show > Guides to hide guides.

8 Choose File > Save.

Adding spot color to text

Text in an image can also appear in spot color. There are different methods for creating this effect, but the most straightforward is to add the text directly to the spot-color channel. Note that text in a spot-color channel behaves differently from text created on a type layer. Spot-color–channel text is uneditable. Once you create the type, you cannot change its specifications, and once you deselect the type, you cannot reposition it.

Now you'll add text to the spot-color channel and place the text in the light block of spot color.

1 In the Color palette, return the color slider to 100%.

2 Select the type tool (T), and click the image in the light block of color. A red mask appears over the artwork, and an insertion point for the text flashes.

3 In the type tool options bar, choose a sans serif bold typeface from the Font menu (such as Myriad, which is included on the *Adobe Photoshop 7.0 Classroom in a Book* CD, or Arial), and enter **66** for the point size in the Size text box.

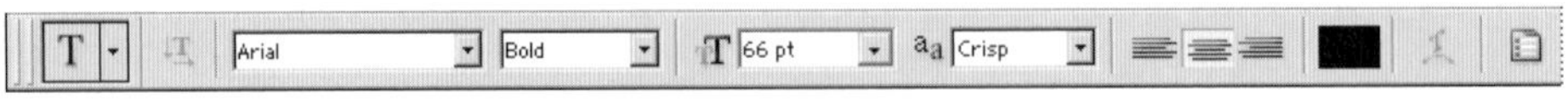

4 Type **work** in the image window.

5 Select the move tool (), and drag the text so that it is centered in the light block of color.

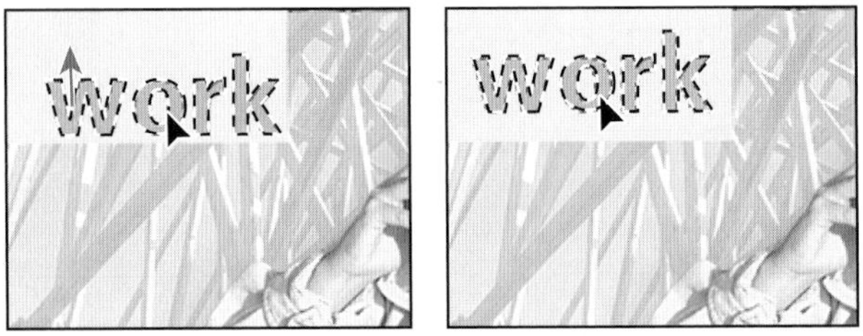

6 Choose Select > Deselect.

7 Choose File > Save.

You have finished preparing the image for two-color printing. To see how the color separations for the printed piece will look, try alternately hiding and displaying the two color channels in the Channels palette.

8 Click the eye icon () for the Gray channel in the Channels palette. The Gray channel is hidden, and the image window changes to just the areas of the image that will print in the spot color.

9 Redisplay the Gray channel by clicking its eye icon column. Then hide the PANTONE 124 C channel by clicking its eye icon. Just the grayscale areas of the image appear in the image window.

10 Click the eye icon column for the PANTONE 124 C channel to display both channels.

Final image

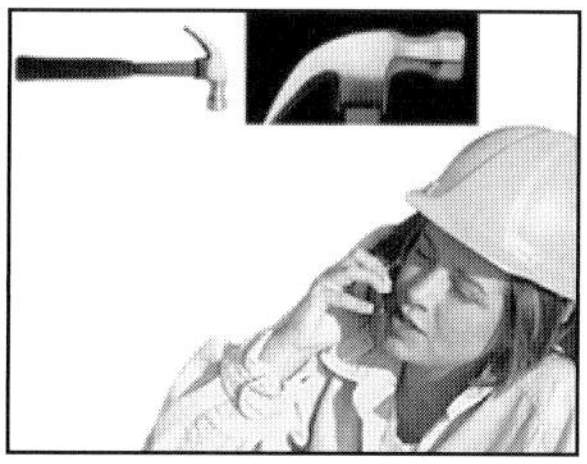

Black channel

PANTONE 124 C channel

If you have a printer available, you can also try printing the image. You'll find that it prints on two sheets of paper—one representing the color separation for the spot color and one representing the grayscale areas of the image.

For the Web: Creating two-color Web graphics

Two-color images are used in print to keep costs down and expand the tonal range of grayscale images. Even when printing costs aren't an issue, you can use two-color images for effect. Try this technique in ImageReady for creating effective two-color graphics for the Web that deliver maximum impact without increasing the file size. You can start with an image in Photoshop, or you can work exclusively in ImageReady.

1 For a duotone effect, start by creating a grayscale image in Photoshop or by desaturating an ImageReady image. To convert your color Photoshop image to grayscale, choose Image > Mode > Grayscale.

In ImageReady, it's not possible to create a grayscale image, but you can use the Image > Adjustments > Desaturate command. ImageReady supports only RGB files. Even an image that may appear to be grayscale in ImageReady is actually an RGB file.

2 In Photoshop, choose Image > Mode > RGB Color to convert your grayscale image to RGB mode.

3 In the Layers palette, click the New Layer button (icon) at the bottom of the palette to create a new layer. Then drag the new layer into position below the grayscale image layer.

In Photoshop, if the grayscale image is the Background, you must convert the Background to a layer by double-clicking the Background in the Layers palette and naming it in the New Layer dialog box.

4 In the image, fill the new layer with a second color, using a two-step process:

• In the Color palette, enter values for the color to set the foreground color. (Or, you can select a color swatch in the Swatches palette.)

• Press Alt+Delete (Windows) or Option+Delete (Mac OS).

The new foreground color fills the new layer.

Note: *There are several other ways to fill a new layer with the selected color, such as choosing Layer > New Fill Layer > Solid Color, or selecting the New Fill Or Adjustment Layer button at the bottom of the Layers palette and then selecting Solid Color on the pop-up menu.*

5 Select the top layer of the image and choose Multiply from the Layers palette mode menu.

Multiply mode looks at the color information in each layer and multiplies the base color by the blend color. The resulting color is always darker. Multiplying any color with another color produces progressively darker colors.

6 Duplicate the top layer by dragging it to the New Layer button at the bottom of the Layers palette.

Grayscale image with color layer beneath

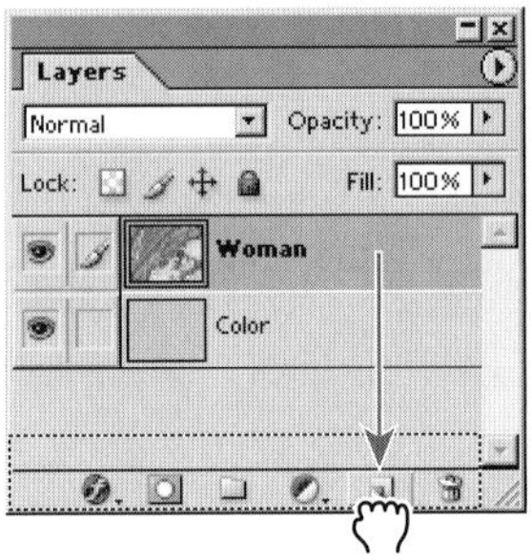

Duplicating the top layer

7 With the new layer selected, choose Hard Light from the Layers palette mode menu. This mode brings out the color underneath.

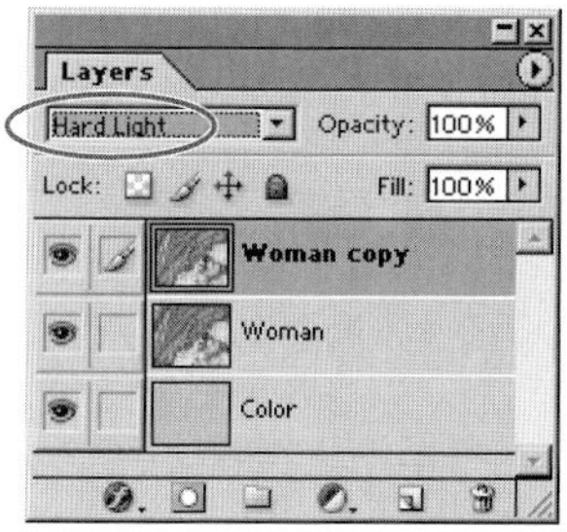

Hard Light filter applied

This technique works most effectively on the top layer of an image with the Hard Light mode applied. Hard Light mode multiplies or screens the colors, depending on the blend color. The effect is similar to shining a harsh spotlight on the image. If the blend color (light source) is lighter than 50% gray, the image is lightened as if it were screened. This is useful for adding highlights to an image. If the blend color is darker than 50% gray, the image is darkened as if it were multiplied. This is useful for adding shadows to an image.

8 Select the middle layer. Choose Image > Adjustments > Levels, and adjust the histogram using the sliders to let more or less color from the bottom layer show through.

9 If desired, decrease the opacity of the different layers and note the effect.

10 Save the file in the GIF file format for the Web, optimizing the file as needed.

As a variation, select the dodge or burn tool and adjust one detail or object in your image at a time.

Review questions

1 What are the three types of channels in Photoshop, and how are they used?

2 How can you improve the quality of a color image that has been converted to grayscale?

3 How do you assign specific values to the black and white points in an image?

4 How do you set up a spot-color channel?

5 How do you add spot color to a specific area in a grayscale image?

6 How can you apply spot color to text?

Review answers

1 Channels in Photoshop are used for storing information. Color channels store the color information for an image; alpha channels store selections or masks for editing specific parts of an image; and spot-color channels create color separations for printing an image with spot-color inks.

2 You can use the Color Mixer command to blend color channels to bring out the contrast and detail in an image. You can extend the tonal range of the image by adjusting its black and white points. You can also sharpen the image by applying the Unsharp Mask filter.

3 You assign specific values with the Levels command black and white eyedropper tools.

4 You set up a spot-color channel by choosing New Spot Channel from the pop-up menu on the Channels palette and by specifying a color from the Custom color picker in the New Spot Channel dialog box.

5 With the Gray channel active, you select the area, cut it from the Gray channel, and paste it into the spot-color channel.

6 You can add the text to the spot-color channel. However, text created in this way is not editable and cannot be repositioned once it is deselected.

Lesson 14

14 Optimizing Web Images and Image Maps

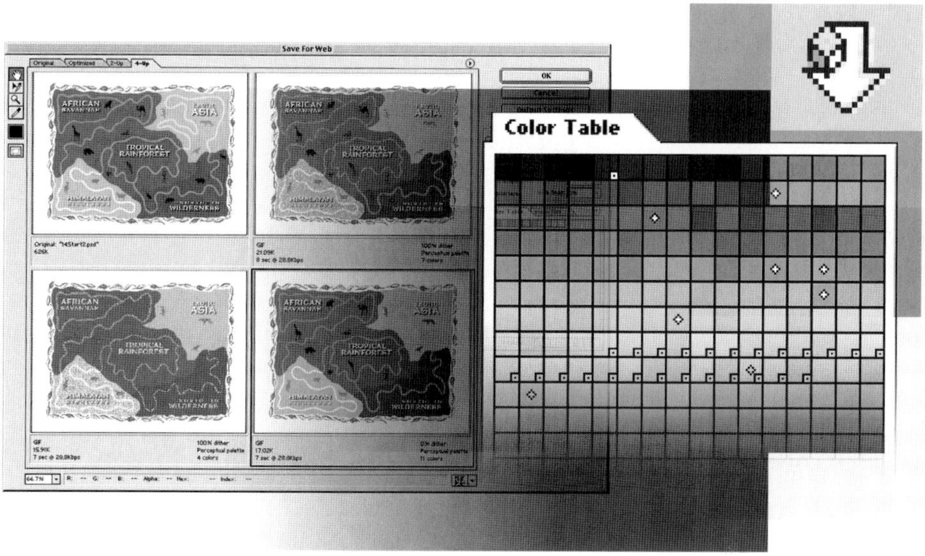

For effective Web publishing, your images must strike a good balance between file size and display quality. Using Adobe Photoshop and Adobe ImageReady, you can optimize your images so that they have reasonable download times from a Web server without losing essential details, colors, transparencies, or navigational elements such as image maps.

In this lesson, you'll learn how to do the following:

- Optimize JPEG and GIF files, and adjust the optimization settings to achieve the desired balance between file size and image quality.
- Adjust the amount of dithering applied to an image.
- Define a transparent background for an image.
- Create a hypertext image map.
- Batch-process files to automate the optimization process.

This lesson will take about one and a half hours to complete. The lesson is designed to be done in Adobe Photoshop and Adobe ImageReady.

If needed, remove the previous lesson folder from your hard drive, and copy the Lesson14 folder onto it. As you work on this lesson, you'll overwrite the start files. If you need to restore the start files, copy them from the *Adobe Photoshop 7.0 Classroom in a Book* CD.

Note: *Windows users need to unlock the lesson files before using them. For more information, see "Copying the Classroom in a Book files" on page 4.*

Optimizing images using Photoshop or ImageReady

Adobe Photoshop and Adobe ImageReady give you an effective range of controls for compressing the file size of an image while optimizing its on-screen display quality. Compression options vary according to the file format used to save the image.

- The JPEG format is designed to preserve the broad color range and subtle brightness variations of continuous-tone images (such as photographs or images with gradients). This format can represent images using millions of colors.
- The GIF format is effective at compressing solid-color images and images with areas of repetitive color (such as line art, logos, and illustrations with type). This format uses a palette of 256 colors to represent the image, and supports background transparency.
- The PNG format is effective at compressing solid-color images and preserving sharp detail. The PNG-8 format uses a 256-color palette to represent an image; the PNG-24 format supports 24-bit color (millions of colors). However, many older browser applications do not support PNG files.

In this lesson, you'll learn how to use Photoshop and ImageReady to optimize and save images in JPEG and GIF formats for distribution on the World Wide Web. You'll work with a set of images designed to be used on a fictitious Web site for a virtual zoo.

Photoshop (through its Save For Web dialog box) and ImageReady (through its Optimize palette) share many of the same capabilities for optimizing images so that your files are small and efficient but still look great. For example, you can use either application to select from a wide array of file formats and settings, to suit the goals for your project. You can also use either one to compare side-by-side views of different optimized versions of a file. Using optimization features and color palettes in either Photoshop or ImageReady, you can maximize color integrity while minimizing file size.

Getting started

Before beginning this lesson, restore the default application settings for Adobe Photoshop and Adobe ImageReady. See "Restoring default preferences" on page 5.

1 Start Adobe Photoshop.

If a notice appears asking whether you want to customize your color settings, click No.

2 Choose Open > Browse, or click the File Browser tab in the palette well to open it.

3 In the File Browser, use the upper left pane to navigate to the Lessons/Lesson14 folder, and select the Lesson14 folder.

Thumbnails of four different Start and End files appear in the right pane, many of which appear to be quite similar. You can also select the Photos folder in the Lesson14 folder to see the five photographs used to make up the background for the 14Start1.psd file, but then select the Lesson14 folder again.

4 Select the 14Start1.psd thumbnail, so that the thumbnail and metadata for that file appear in the left panes of the File Browser. If necessary, resize the File Browser panes to enlarge the thumbnail.

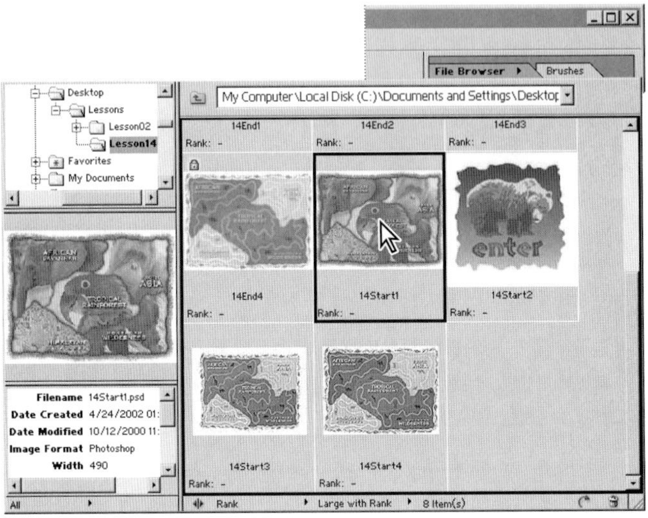

This file is a modified version of the zoo map that you will be using later in this lesson. This version of the map has been enhanced with scanned photographs of animals, which have been further manipulated in Photoshop. In the lower left pane of the File Browser, scroll down the metadata and notice that the file size is quite large.

5 Select the 14End1.psd thumbnail. Notice that the file size listed in the metadata is dramatically smaller but the image looks about the same as the 14Start1.psd.

6 One by one, select the other numbered Start and End files in the Lesson14 folder to preview them.

7 Double-click the file 14Start1.psd to open that file in Photoshop.

Optimizing a JPEG image

In this lesson, you will optimize files in both JPEG and GIF formats. You can use either Photoshop or ImageReady to compress files in either format.

Currently, the 14Start1.psd file size is too large for use on a Web page. You'll compare different file-compression formats to see which one gives you the most compression without sacrificing too much image quality.

Using the Save For Web dialog box

The Photoshop Save For Web dialog box has all of the optimization capabilities of ImageReady. You can compare two or more versions of a file as you work, so that you can adjust optimization settings until you have the best possible combination of file size and image quality.

1 With the 14Start1.psd file open and active in Photoshop, choose File > Save for Web.

2 In the Save For Web dialog box, click the 4-Up tab to view four versions of the image.

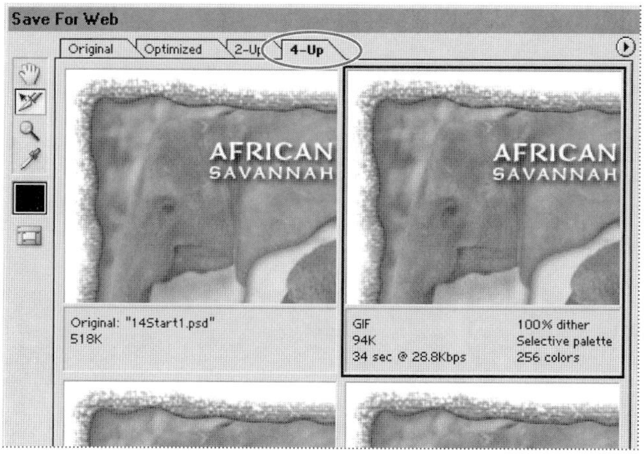

Photoshop automatically generates three different sets of optimization settings, besides the original image. Notice the information listed under each view of the image, including the file size and the number of seconds required to download the image. The first pane shows the original file. The second, third, and fourth panes show different combinations of optimization settings for the image, including the file format (such as GIF or JPEG) and color-reduction algorithm (such as Selective, Perceptual, or Web).

3 In the lower-left corner of the Save For Web dialog box, select 200% or higher from the Zoom Level pop-up menu so that you can see the details of the image, and then click the preview at the upper right to deactivate the zoom option.

Compare the preset views of the different optimization settings.

4 Hold down the spacebar, so that the pointer becomes a hand, and drag the image so that the Tropical Rainforest text (in the center of the image, over the green parrot) is visible in all four views of the image. Again, examine the details closely so that you can see the differences among the optimized views.

Comparing optimized GIF, JPEG, and PNG formats

You can customize any of the optimized views in the Save For Web dialog box. To do this, you select one of the optimized image previews, and then select settings for it on the right side of the dialog box. By experimenting with different combinations of settings, you can get a good idea of which settings will best suit your purpose.

Before you begin, make sure that the optimized preview at the upper right is selected.

1 In the Settings pop-up menu on the right side of the Save For Web dialog box, select GIF 128 Dithered (if it is not already selected).

The information listed below the selected image preview changes.

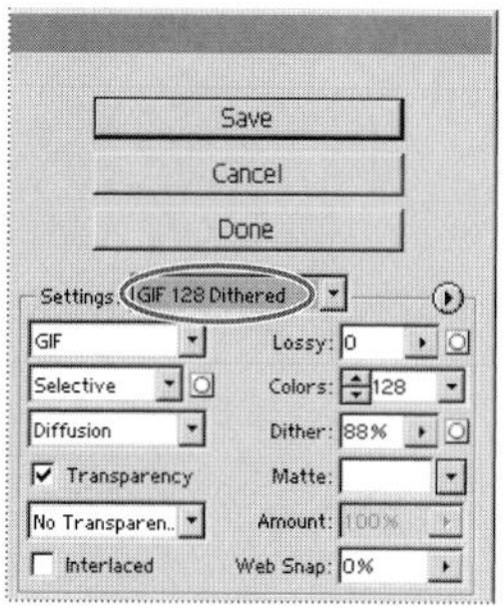

Notice the dark group of pixels around the text and on the parrot's beak. (You may need to hold down Shift and drag the image again to see the beak.)

You'll use the two bottom versions of the image to compare GIF 128 Dithered optimization with JPEG and PNG optimization.

2 Click the lower-left version of the image to select it, and select the following JPEG options, one at a time, on the Settings pop-up menu:

- JPEG Low. Notice that the image details and text are unacceptably choppy.
- JPEG High.The image quality improves, but the file size increases significantly.

JPEG Low

JPEG High

- JPEG Medium. At this setting, the image quality is acceptable and the file size is lower than either the JPEG High version or the GIF version.

Note: *You can select other intermediate levels of quality for JPEG files by typing or dragging the Quality slider option on the right side of the Save For Web dialog box.*

Now that you've tried different GIF and JPEG settings, you'll use the fourth image preview to try another format.

3 Select the lower-right version of the image, and then use the Settings menu to select PNG-8 128 Dithered.

Although this results in a smaller file size than the original image, the image quality is not as good as the JPEG Medium version, which also has a smaller file size. Furthermore, many older browsers cannot read the PNG format. To make this image compatible with older browsers, you will save this file for the Web using the JPEG Medium optimization.

4 Select your JPEG Medium version of the optimized image (in the lower-left corner of the dialog box), and then select the Progressive check box.

Note: *When Progressive is selected, any download of the image occurs in several passes, each of which increases the image quality.*

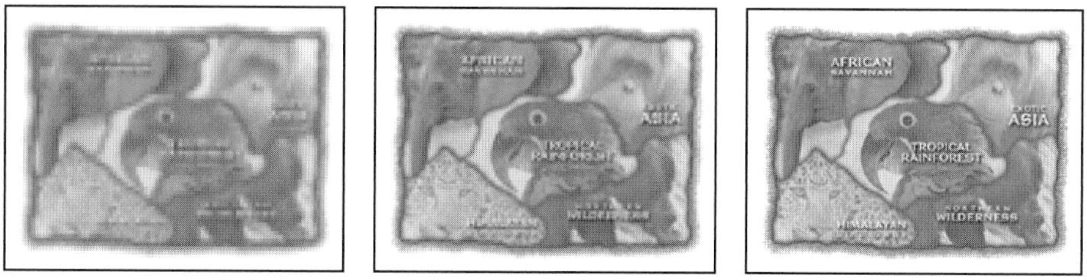

The Progressive JPEG download

5 Click Save. In the Save Optimized As dialog box, use the default name **14Start1.jpg**, and save the file in the same folder as the original Photoshop file.

6 Choose File > Close, and don't save your changes.

Optimizing a GIF image

Now you'll optimize a flat-color image in GIF format and compare the results of different palette and dither settings. Although you could do this entire section in Photoshop, you'll use ImageReady.

Photoshop and ImageReady share many features, but some tasks are more appropriately done in one application or the other, depending on your intended use of the image file. Certain tasks can be done only in Photoshop and others only in ImageReady. For these reasons, both applications include convenient ways to jump from one to the other.

If you have an open file when you jump from Photoshop to ImageReady or vice versa, the file opens in the application that you jump to. If you have more than one file open, only the active file opens in the other application when you jump. If no files are open, you can still jump back and forth from one application to the other.

Preparing an ImageReady workspace

Before you begin working on a new file, you'll jump from Photoshop to ImageReady and then define an ImageReady workspace for the tasks you'll do in this section.

1 In Photoshop, click the Jump To ImageReady button ( ) at the bottom of the toolbox to switch from Photoshop to ImageReady.

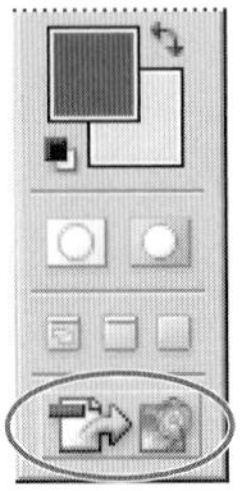

Note: *If you do not have enough memory to run both applications simultaneously, quit Photoshop and then start ImageReady.*

2 In ImageReady, choose Window > Workspace > Reset Palette Locations to make sure that all palettes are in their default positions.

3 Drag the tabs of the following palettes out of their palette groups to separate them as stand-alone palettes:

- The Info palette (from the Optimize palette group).
- The Color Table palette (from the Rollovers palette group).

4 Click the close boxes in the following palette groups to hide these palettes:

- The Color palette group (the Color, Swatches, and Styles palettes).
- The Info palette.
- The Rollovers palette group (the Rollovers and Layer Options palettes).

5 Drag the Optimize, Color Table, and Layers palette groups to rearrange them in your work area as needed, and resize them to take advantage of the available space.

6 Choose Window >Workspace > Save Workspace.

7 In the Save Workspace dialog box, type **Optimize_14**, and click OK.

The Optimize_14 workspace option now appears on the Window > Workspace menu, named to help you remember that you created this workspace in Lesson 14 for work with optimizing. You can reset your workspace to this configuration of palettes or go back to the default workspace at any time by choosing the one you want to use on the Workspace submenu.

Choosing basic optimization settings in ImageReady

Earlier in this lesson, you used Photoshop optimization settings that were integrated into the Save For Web dialog box. In ImageReady, the same options appear in the Optimize palette.

1 In ImageReady, choose File > Open, and open the file 14Start2.psd from the Lessons/Lesson14 folder.

This image was created in Adobe Illustrator, and then rasterized into Photoshop format. The image contains many areas of solid color.

2 Click the 2-Up tab in the image window.

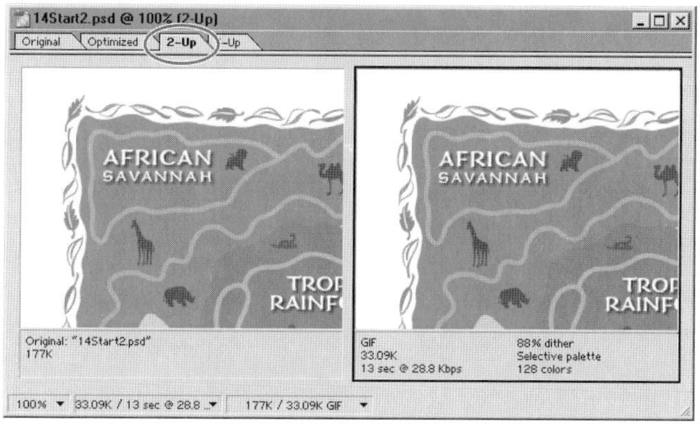

The optimized version of the image is selected on the right side of the window.

3 In the Settings pop-up menu on the Optimize palette, choose GIF 128 No Dither.

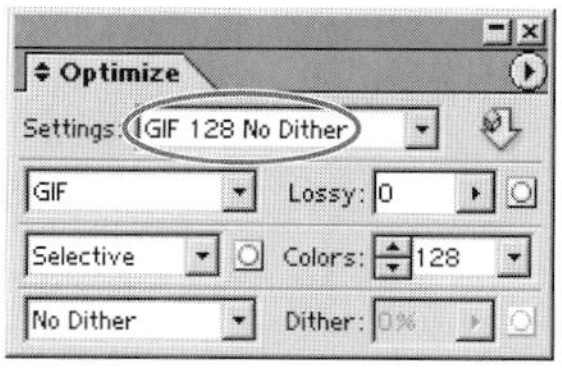

4 In the Color Reduction Algorithm menu, select Perceptual.

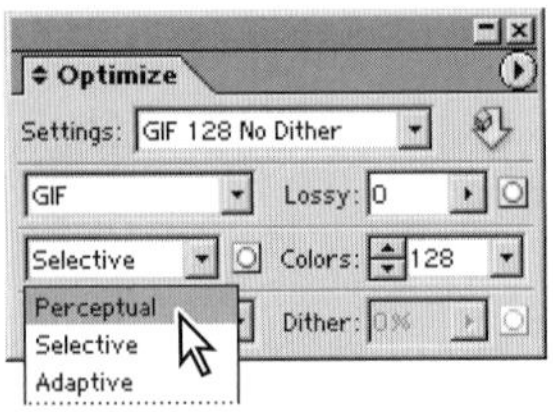

Selecting a color reduction algorithm

One of the ways to reduce image file size is to reduce the number of colors in the image. Photoshop can calculate the most needed colors for you, based on any of several available algorithms. You specify which algorithm is used by making a selection from the Color Reduction Algorithm menu, which includes the following options:

Perceptual *Creates a custom color table by giving priority to colors for which the human eye has greater sensitivity.*

Selective *Creates a color table similar to the Perceptual color table, but favors broad areas of color and the preservation of Web colors. This color table usually produces images with the greatest color integrity. Selective is the default option.*

Adaptive *Creates a custom color table by sampling colors from the spectrum appearing most commonly in the image. For example, an image with only the colors green and blue produces a color table made primarily of greens and blues. Most images concentrate colors in particular areas of the spectrum.*

Web *Uses the standard 216-color color table common to the Windows and Mac OS 8-bit (256-color) palettes. This system ensures that no browser dither is applied to colors when the image is displayed using 8-bit color. (This palette is also called the Web-safe palette.) If your image has fewer colors than the total specified in the color palette, unused colors are removed.*

Custom *Preserves the current color table as a fixed palette that does not update with changes to the image.*

Windows or Mac OS *Uses the system's default 8-bit (256-color) color table, which is based on a uniform sampling of RGB colors. If your image has fewer colors than the total number specified in the color palette, unused colors are removed.*

–From Adobe Photoshop 7.0 online Help

The status bar at the bottom of the image window displays the view magnification and other useful information about the original and optimized versions of the image.

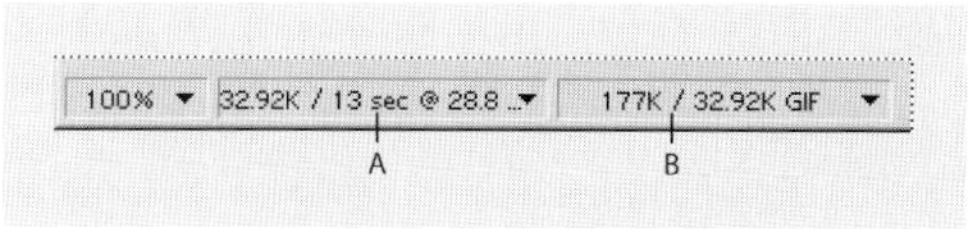

A. *File size and download time of optimized image*
B. *File sizes of original and optimized images*

You can customize the type of information that appears here.

5 In the status bar, choose Image Dimensions from the pop-up menu on the right.

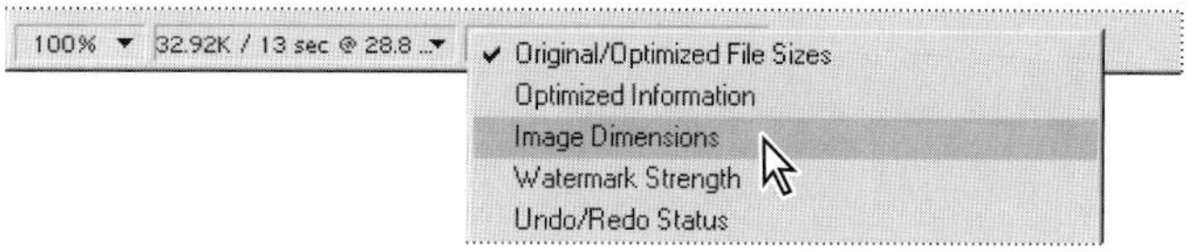

This option displays the size of the image in pixels, which is important when planning how to fit an image into a predesigned Web-page template.

Exploring the Color Table

The Color Table palette displays the colors that the currently selected color reduction algorithm uses for the currently active file—in this case, the colors that the Perceptual option selects for the zoo map image. The colors appear to be listed in random order in the palette.

The total number of colors is listed at the bottom of the palette. You can resize the palette or use the scroll bar to view all the colors. You can also change how the colors are arranged in the palette.

In the Color Table palette, a few of the colors have a tiny white diamond shape at the center of the swatch. These diamonds indicate that those colors are *Web-safe*.

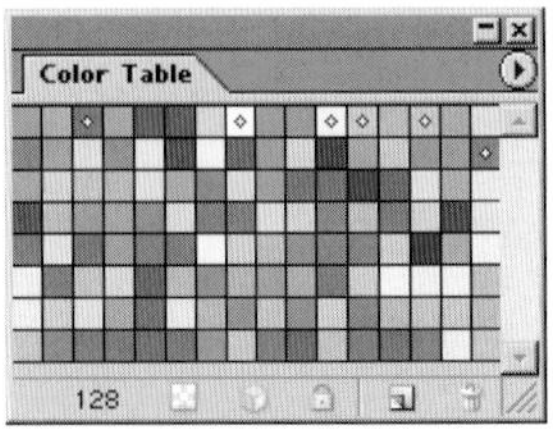

1 On the Color Table palette menu, choose Sort By Hue, and notice how the arrangement of the color swatches changes.

2 In the Optimize palette, choose Web from the Color Reduction Algorithm menu.

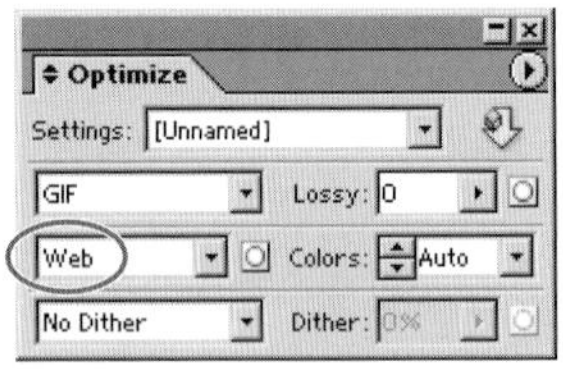

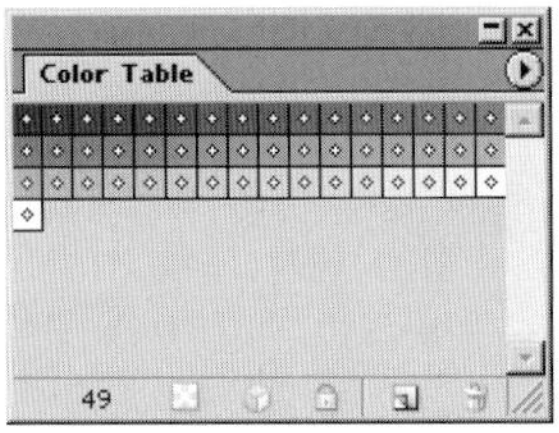

Notice that the color changes in the image and in the Color Table palette, which updates to reflect the Web palette.

3 Experiment by selecting different optimize options and notice the effects on the image and on the Color Table palette.

4 When you finish experimenting, re-enter the settings you had earlier: GIF 128 No Dither and Perceptual. (You can leave the colors sorted any way: unsorted, by hue, by luminance, or by popularity.)

3 Click the Web-shift button () at the bottom of the Color Table palette.

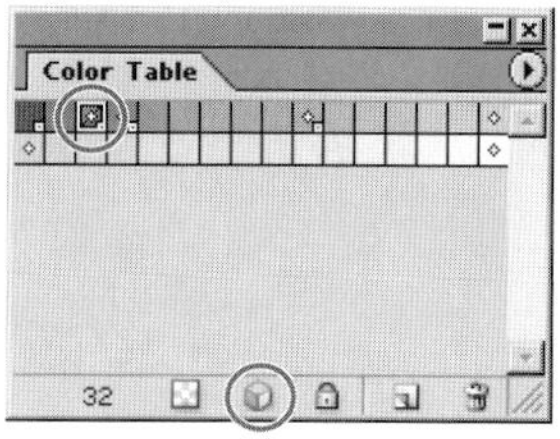

The swatch changes position in the palette and a small diamond appears in the center of the swatch, indicating that it has been shifted to its nearest Web-palette equivalent.

By Web-shifting the brown background, you change its color to one that can be displayed without dithering by a Web browser on a 256-color system.

4 Choose File > Save.

Note: *In Photoshop 7.0 and ImageReady 7.0, you can also quickly map one color to another color or to a transparency. This remapping reassigns all the pixels that appeared in the selected color to the new color or transparency. For more information, see Adobe Photoshop 7.0 online Help.*

Specifying background transparency

Background transparency lets you place a nonrectangular graphic object against the background of a Web page; the areas outside the borders of the object are defined as transparent, letting the Web-page background color show through. You can specify background transparency for GIF and PNG images.

Converting the Background into an ordinary layer

Before you can use the GIF file format's ability to preserve transparency, you must create some transparency in your image. You'll do that by removing the white backdrop surrounding the image map. To start this process, you'll first convert the Background layer to a regular layer.

1 Make sure that the 14Start2.psd file is open in ImageReady.

2 Select the Original tab at the top of the image window.

3 Choose Fit on Screen from the Zoom Level menu in the lower left corner of the image window.

4 On the Layers palette menu, choose Layer Options. Without changing the default settings (including the name, Layer 0), click OK. The layer now appears in the Layer palette as Layer 0.

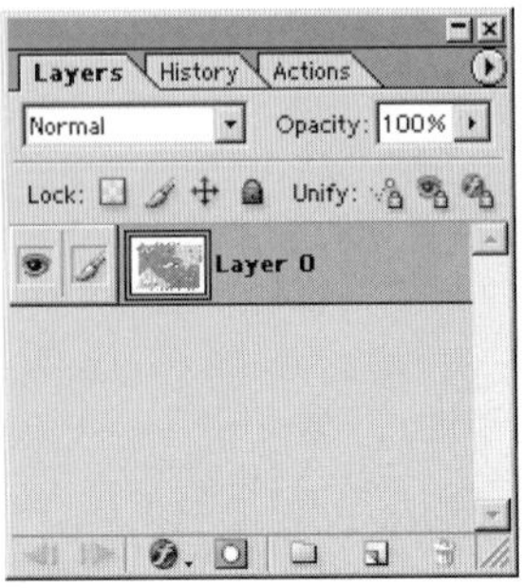

A Background layer cannot contain any transparency information because, by definition, there is nothing behind it to be seen. If you tried to use one of the techniques that usually can replace colored pixels with transparent ones, the results would be that the original pixels would be changed to the currently selected background color instead of becoming transparent pixels.

Using the magic wand tool to create transparency

In this part of the lesson, you'll use the magic eraser tool to quickly convert the backdrop color of the zoo map to transparent pixels.

The magic eraser tool erases all pixels of a particular color with a single click. You'll use this tool to erase all of the white pixels in the layer. However, you only want to erase the white pixels outside of the zoo map (not the white of the lettering), so you will first create a selection that excludes the interior portion of the image.

1 Select the rectangular marquee tool ( ).

2 Draw a rectangular selection marquee so that it includes all the text in the five colored regions of the zoo map, as shown in the illustration below.

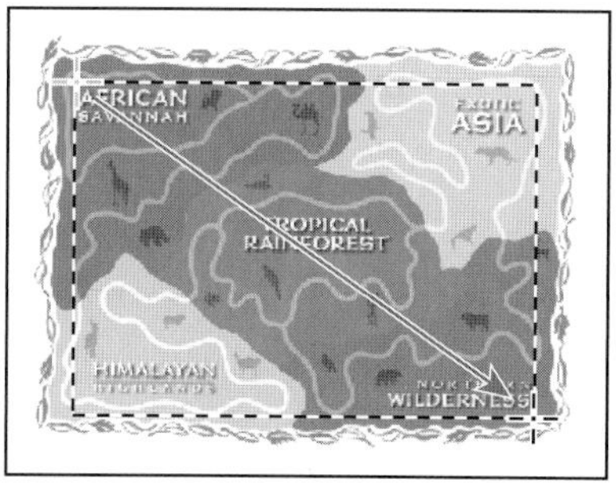

3 Choose Select > Inverse to select everything outside of the rectangular selection marquee.

4 Select the magic eraser tool ( ), hidden under the eraser tool ( ).

5 In the tool options bar, deselect the Contiguous option so that all white pixels in the selection will be erased, including each isolated white section within the leaves.

6 Click the white background outside of the zoo map.

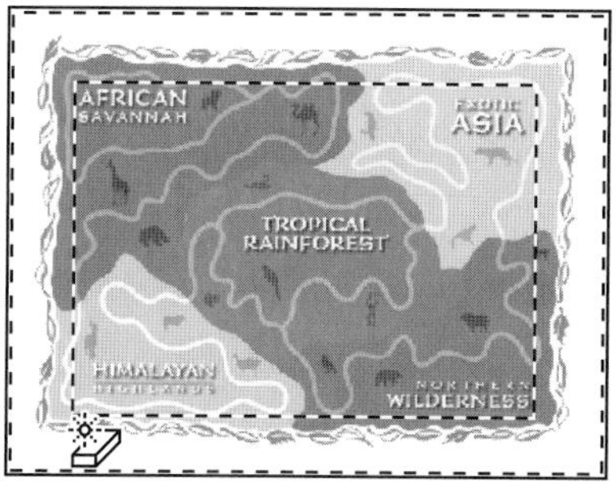

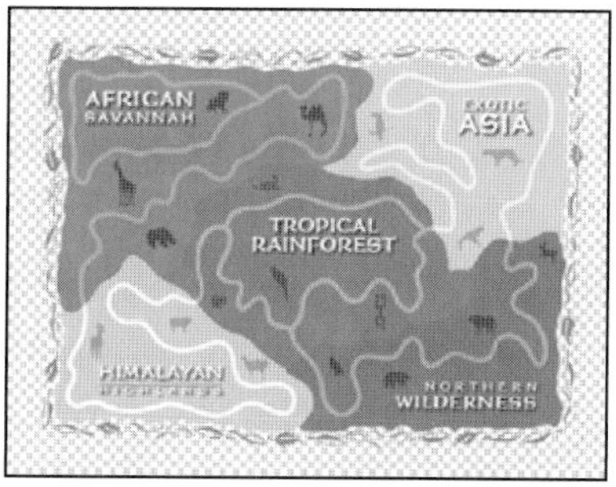

Now all the white backdrop is gone, replaced by transparency so that you can see the checkerboard pattern behind the image.

Preserving and previewing transparency

Now you will confirm that the transparent areas in the image will be included as transparent pixels in the optimized GIF file. Then, you'll preview the transparency in your browser.

Because the ImageReady preview feature displays the image on a Web page with a white background, you'll change the matte color of the image so that you can see the transparency.

1 On the Optimize palette, make sure that the Transparency check box is selected. (If you don't see that check box, choose Show Options on the Optimize palette menu.)

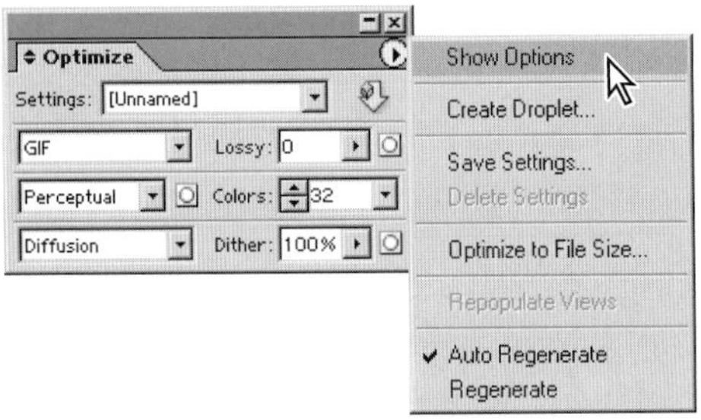

Selecting Transparency converts areas in the original image with less than 50% opacity to background transparency in the optimized image.

2 Choose Select > Deselect, and then choose File > Save.

3 Click the Matte swatch in the Optimize palette to open the color picker, and then select any color except white. Click OK to close the color picker.

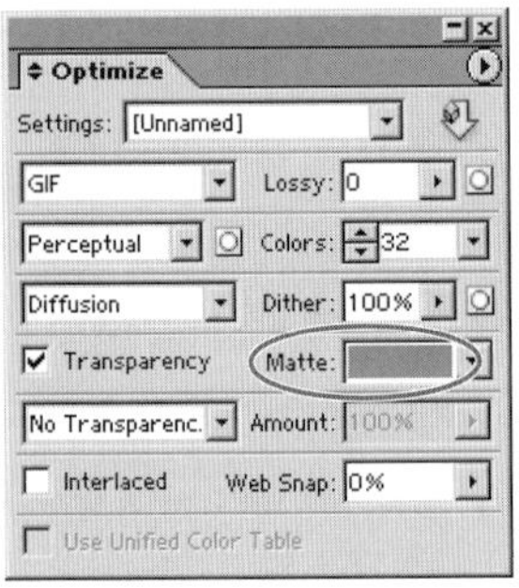

4 Choose File > Preview In, and choose a Web browser from the submenu.

Note: *To use the Preview In command, you must have a Web browser installed on your system.*

If it is not already open, the browser first starts and then displays the optimized image in the upper-left corner of the browser window. The browser also displays the pixel dimensions, file size, file format, and optimization settings for the image, along with the HTML code used to create the preview.

Transparency option selected

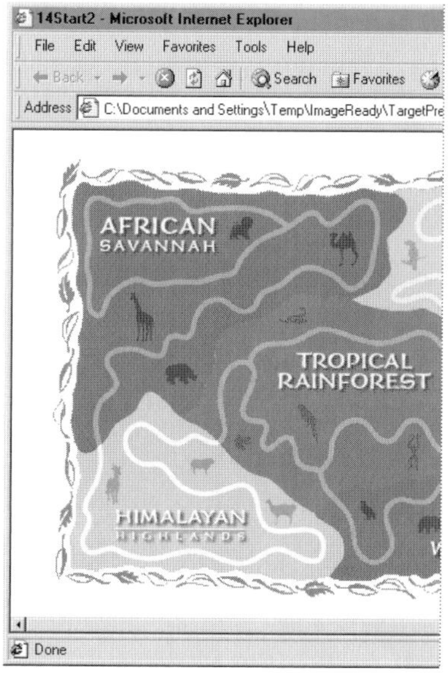

Transparency option deselected

5 Quit your browser when you're done previewing the image.

Trimming extra background areas

Although the background of the zoo-map image now contains transparent pixels that do not display, these pixels still take up file space, adding to the size of the image. You can trim away unneeded background areas to improve the layout of the image and optimize the file size.

1 In ImageReady, choose Image > Trim.

The Trim command lets you crop your image, according to the transparency or pixel color of the extra border area.

2 In the Trim dialog box, select Transparent Pixels if it is not already selected, and click OK.

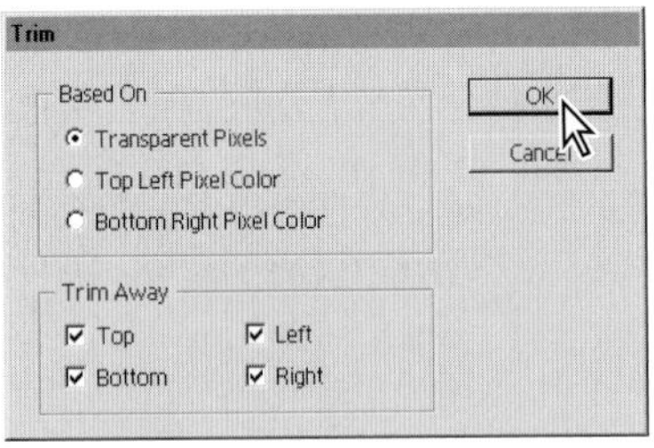

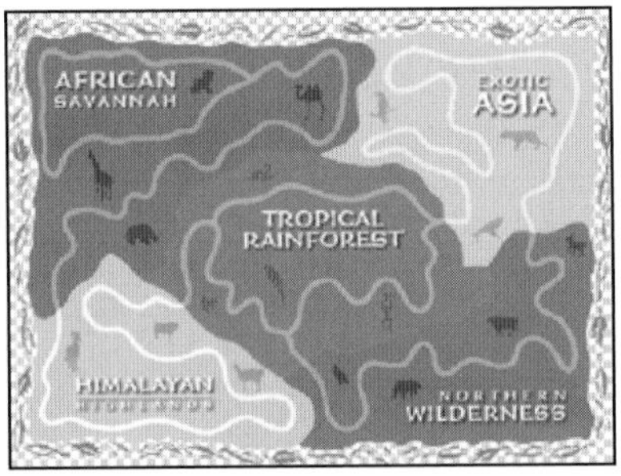

ImageReady trims the extra transparent areas from the image.

3 Choose File > Save Optimized As.

4 In the Save Optimized As dialog box, use the default name (**14Start2.gif**), and click Save.

5 In the Replace Files dialog box, click Replace (if it appears).

6 Choose File > Close.

You will be prompted to save the 14Start2.psd file before closing. Since you are finished with this file for the lesson, there is no need to save the last changes.

Creating a dithered transparency

In this section, you'll create a dithered transparency for a graphic that will serve as the entry point from another Web page to the zoo map. By creating a dither from an opaque drop shadow to transparency, you'll make it possible to create a smooth transition from the image to any color backdrop on the page without having to redo any work.

You'll do this in two procedures. First, you'll apply a drop shadow to the image. Then, you'll add dithering to the drop shadow so that it blends into a background color for the Web page.

You can do this procedure in Photoshop or do it in ImageReady using the same controls but in slightly different locations.

Adding a drop shadow

The file you'll be working on is intended to serve as the "entry" button on the portal page to the zoo Web site. You'll add a drop shadow to the button to make the image appear to float above the background, emphasizing that it is an interactive element of the page.

1 Choose File > Open, and select the 14Start3.psd file in the Lessons/Lesson14 folder.

2 In the Layers palette, click the Add A Layer Style button (icon) at the bottom of the palette, and then select Drop Shadow from the pop-up menu.

3 In the Layer Style dialog box (Photoshop) or the Drop Shadow palette (ImageReady), enter the following values:

- For Distance, drag the slider or type **15**.
- For Spread, drag the slider or type **7%**.
- For Size, drag the slider or type **15**.

4 (Photoshop only) Click OK to close the Drop Shadow dialog box.

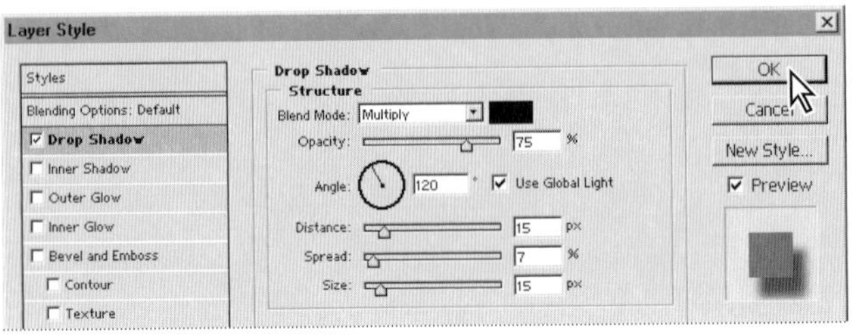

5 Choose File > Save.

Adding transparency dithering to the drop shadow

As you've already learned, dithering is a method of creating gradations of color with a limited color palette. This makes it useful for Web pages because you can simulate smoother gradations without sacrificing small file size and quick downloads.

1 With the 14Start3.psd active, choose File > Save for Web to open the Save for Web dialog box. (This step is not necessary in ImageReady.)

2 Click the Optimized tab in the Save for Web dialog box (Photoshop) or image window (ImageReady).

3 On the right side of the Save for Web dialog box (Photoshop) or in the Optimize palette (ImageReady), set the following options:

- In the Settings pop-up menu, select GIF 128 Dithered.
- Select the Transparency check box, if it is not already selected.

Note: *In ImageReady, if you do not see the Transparency check box, open the Optimize palette menu and choose Show Options, or click the double-arrows (⬍) on the Optimize tab to expand the palette so that you can see all the options.*

• In the pop-up menu below the Transparency check box, select Diffusion Transparency Dither.

• In the Amount option, use the pop-up slider or type **55%**.

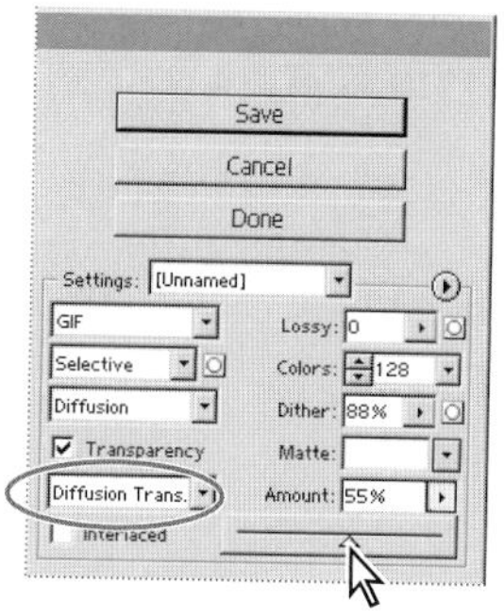

Save For Web dialog box (Photoshop)

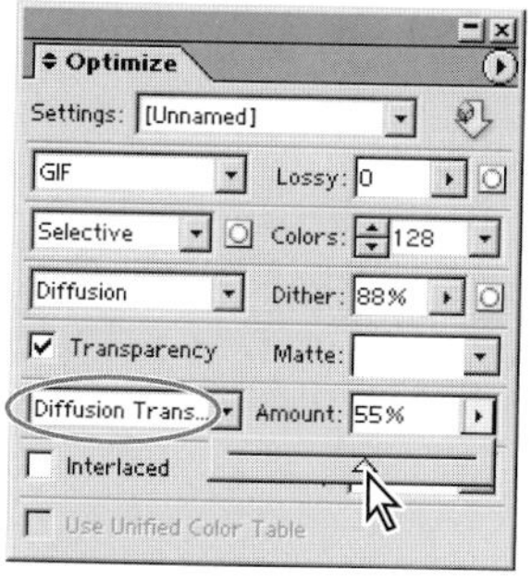

Optimize palette (ImageReady)

4 Click the Matte swatch to open the color picker. Select any color other than white, and click OK. (We selected a light brown: R=220, G=190, B=150.)

To see the effect of the matte setting, try zooming in so that you can see individual pixels in the dither—about 400% or higher. Notice that the pixels closest to the edge of the green area are black and that the others become increasing more blended with the matte color as they occur farther from the edge. Then zoom back to 100%.

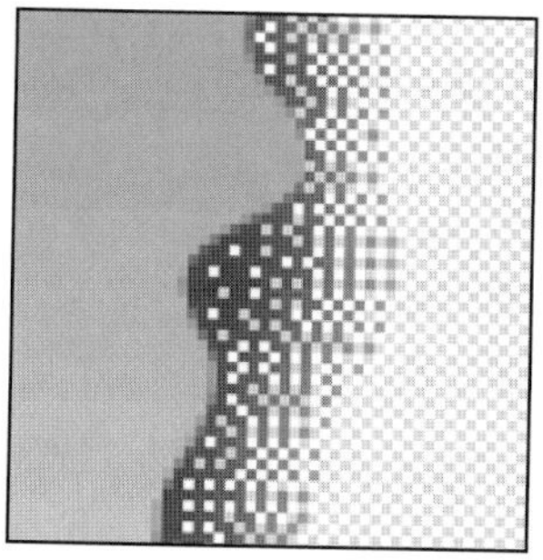

5 At the bottom of the Save For Web dialog box, click the button with the browser icon, or click the arrow to select your browser from the pop-up menu. (In ImageReady, use the Preview In Default Browser button in the toolbox to open the file in a browser.)

6 In the browser, notice how the drop shadow blends against the background matte color. When you finish viewing your document, close the browser or switch back to Photoshop (or ImageReady).

7 Click the Save button in the Save for Web dialog box. (In ImageReady, choose File > Save Optimized.)

8 In the Save Optimized As dialog box, accept the default settings and filename (14Start3.gif) and save the file in your Lessons/Lesson14 folder.

9 Choose File > Save to save the 14Start3.psd file, or close the file without saving.

Working with image maps (ImageReady)

An *image map* is an image that contains multiple hypertext links to other files on the Web. Different areas, or *hotspots*, of the image map link to different files. Adobe ImageReady creates client-side image maps and server-side image maps.

Creating image maps is one of the functions that you must do in Adobe ImageReady. You can use Photoshop to create slices, which share certain functionality with image maps, but you cannot create image maps with Photoshop.

Note: *For information about slicing an image into multiple image files and linking each slice to another Web page, see Lesson 15, "Adding Interactive Slices and Rollovers."*

Creating and viewing image maps (ImageReady)

Image maps enable you to link an area of an image to a URL. You can set up multiple linked areas—called image map areas*—in an image, with links to text files; other images; audio, video, or multimedia files; other pages in the Web site; or other Web sites. You can also create rollover effects in image map areas.*

The main difference between using image maps and using slices to create links is in how the source image is exported as a Web page. Using image maps keeps the exported image intact as a single file, while using slices causes the image to be exported as a separate file. Another difference between image maps and slices is that image maps enable you to link circular, polygonal, or rectangular areas in an image, while slices enable you to link only rectangular areas. If you need to link only rectangular areas, using slices may be preferable to using an image map.

Note: *To avoid unexpected results, do not create image map areas in slices that contain URL links—either the image map links or the slice links may be ignored in some browsers.*

–From Adobe Photoshop 7.0 online Help

Using layers to create image maps

In this procedure, you'll create an image map in an existing image. You define hotspots using layers or one of the image-map tools. Then you'll assign each hotspot to an URL, linking it to a site on either a local computer or the World Wide Web.

You'll use a version of the zoo-map image that places each colored region on its own layer. You'll convert each layer to an image-map hotspot. By using layers to define the hotspots, you easily gain control over the shapes of those areas.

1 In ImageReady, choose File > Open, and open the file 14Start4.psd from the Lessons/Lesson14 folder.

2 In the Settings menu on the Optimize palette, choose GIF 64 Dithered.

3 In the Layers palette, select the African Savannah layer.

4 Choose Layer > New Layer Based Image Map Area.

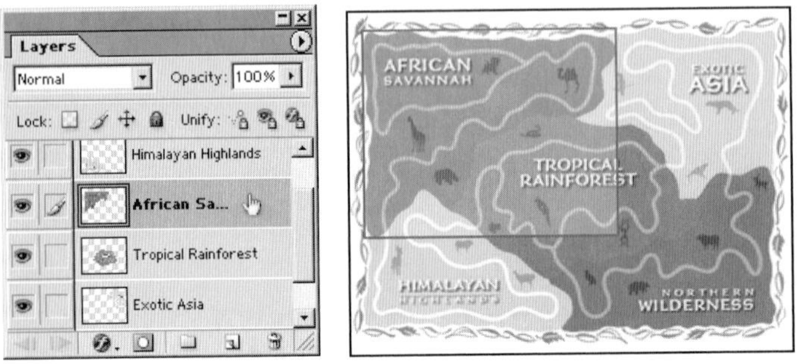

A ghosted rectangular area surrounded by a red line appears, enclosing the entire African Savannah portion of the image. This red line and ghosting define the hotspot area included in the image map.

5 In the Animation palette group, click the Image Map tab, and choose Polygon from the Shape pop-up menu. (You can also open the Image Map palette by choosing Window > Show Image Map.)

Now the red outline approximates the shape of the savannah area.

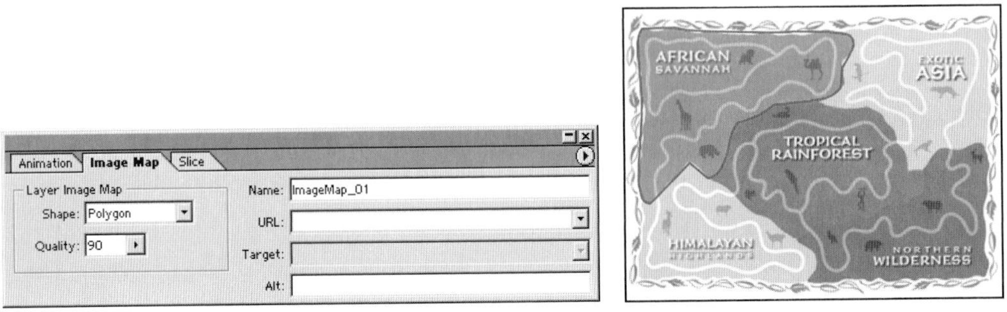

6 In the Quality option on the Image Map palette, drag the slider or type **90** to make the red line more closely conform to the savannah area shape.

Now that you've defined the hotspot area, you can link it to another file in your Web site or to a different location on the Web. For the purposes of this lesson, you'll link your hotspots to fictitious URLs for the zoo.

7 In the URL option in the Image Map palette, type the fictitious address of a Web site, **http://www.adobe.com/african_savannah.html,** in the URL text box.

In the Layers palette, a pointing-finger icon now appears on the African Savannah layer, indicating that the layer has a layer-based image map.

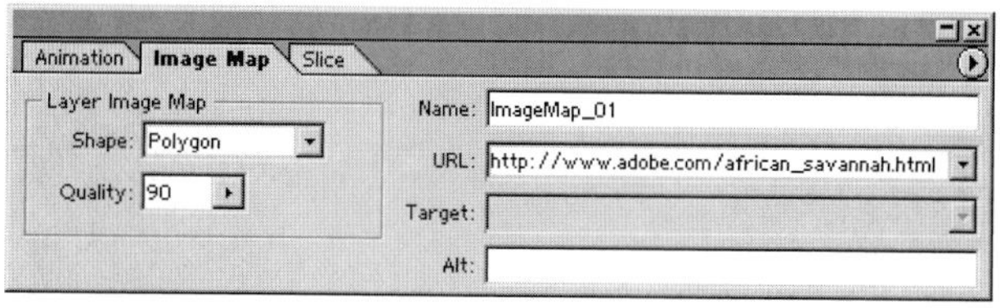

Note: *If you prefer, you can use other URLs for this exercise, linking the hotspots to your own local intranet pages or to some of your favorite sites on the World Wide Web.*

8 (Optional) For more practice with image maps, select the other four areas of the zoo map (Exotic Asia, Tropical Rainforest, Himalayan Highlands, and Northern Wilderness) and, one layer at a time, repeat steps 3 through 7 to create more layer-based image maps. Use the same settings, but change the "african_savannah" part of the URLs, replacing it with the name of the layer used to create the image map.

Don't worry now about any mistakes you might make when you type in your URLs. You'll learn how to edit image-map information later, in "Creating the HTML file and editing image-map information" on page 447.

9 Choose File > Save.

Adjusting the cross-platform gamma range

Before you take your final steps to publish your image-mapped illustration of the zoo image on your network or the Web, you'll verify whether or not the brightness of your image is compatible across monitors on different platforms. Machines running Windows generally display a darker midtone brightness, or *gamma*, than Macintosh machines.

Note: *Before starting this part of the lesson, be sure to calibrate your monitor so that it displays color accurately. For information, see Lesson 17, "Setting Up Your Monitor for Color Management."*

1 In the ImageReady toolbox, click the Toggle Image Maps Visibility button () to hide the polygon boundary lines of the image-map areas.

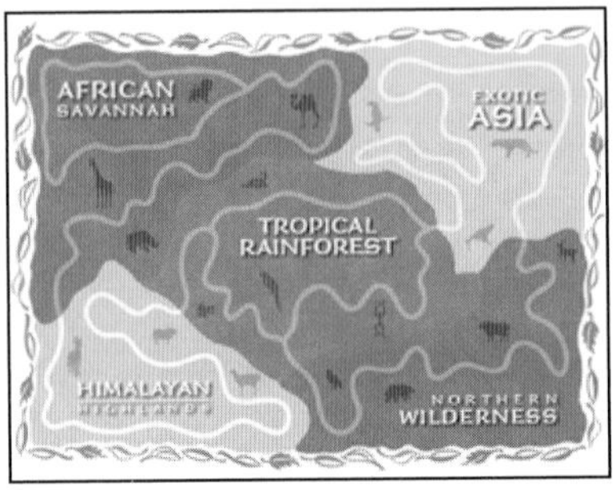

2 Choose View > Preview > and then choose a command as follows, to preview the image as it will appear on the platform you're *not* using:

- If you are working in Windows, choose Standard Macintosh Color.
- If you are working in Mac OS, choose Standard Windows Color.

3 Choose Image > Adjustments > Gamma.

4 Click the appropriate button:

- If you are working in Windows, click Windows to Macintosh, and then click OK.
- If you are working in Mac OS, click Macintosh to Windows, and then click OK.

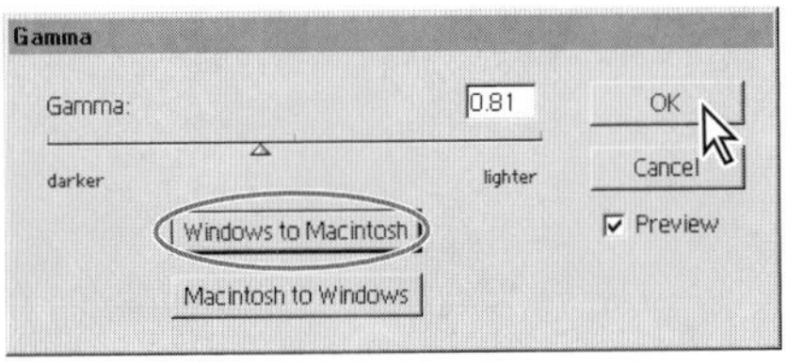

5 Choose File > Save Optimized As.

6 In the Save Optimized As dialog box, choose Images Only from the Format menu, use the default name **14Start4.gif**, and click Save.

Now you'll preview your image map in a Web browser.

7 Choose File > Preview In, and choose a browser application from the submenu.

8 In the browser window, move the pointer over the different zoo regions, and notice that these elements contain hypertext links. If you had a modem and an Internet connection and if these were authentic URLs, you could click the hotspots to jump to the specified page of the zoo site.

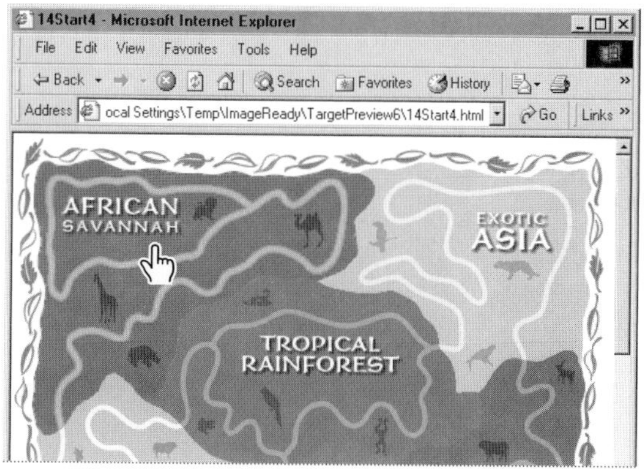

9 Quit your browser to return to Adobe ImageReady.

Creating the HTML file and editing image-map information

When you save an image map in an HTML file, the basic HTML tags needed to display the image on a Web page are generated automatically. The easiest way to do this is simply to choose the HTML and Images Format option when you save the optimized image.

Once you have created the HTML file, it can easily be updated to reflect any changes, such as new or modified image-map areas or URLs.

1 In ImageReady, choose File > Save Optimized As.

Note: *In Photoshop, you create an HTML file in the Save Optimized As dialog box that appears after optimizing the image and clicking OK in the Save For Web dialog box.*

2 In the Save Optimized As dialog box, select the HTML and Images option on the Save As Type pop-up menu (Windows) or the Format menu (Mac OS). Use the default name **14Start4.html**, and save the file in your Lessons/Lesson14 folder.

If the Replace Files dialog box appears, click Replace.

When you select the HTML and Images option, an HTML page containing the image is saved automatically, in addition to the graphic file. This HTML file will have the same name as the image, but with the .html extension.

Now you'll use ImageReady to change one of the URL links and update the HTML file.

3 In the toolbox, select the image map select tool (), hidden under the rectangle image map tool ().

4 In the image window, click to select the African Savannah image-map area.

5 In the Image Map palette, change the URL to **http://www.adobe.com/newafrica.html**.

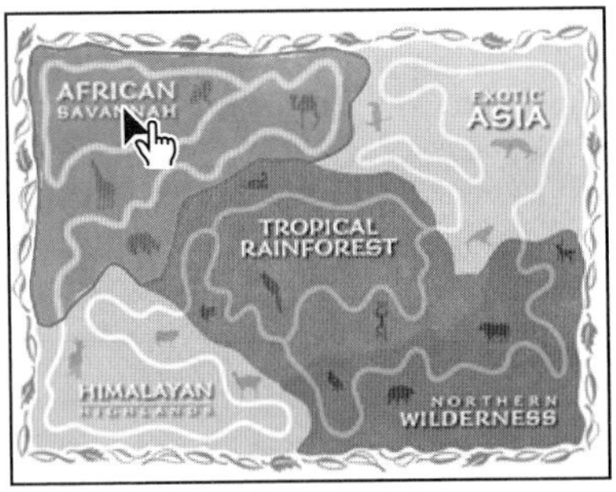

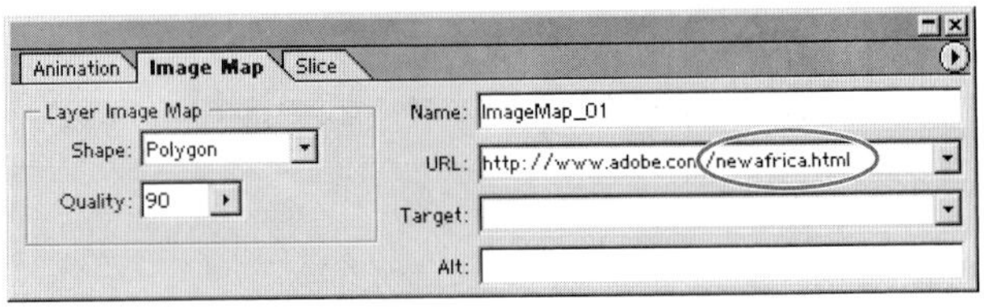

If you have other image-map information that you want to edit, use the image map select tool to select the image-map areas that you want to update, and then enter your changes in the Image Map palette options.

6 When you finish making changes, choose File > Update HTML.

7 In the Update HTML dialog box, select the 14Start4.html file, and click Open. Then click Replace when the Replace Files dialog box appears and click OK to dismiss the update message.

8 Choose File > Close to close the image. Don't save changes, if prompted.

You can use your Web browser to open and view 14Start4.html. You can also open the file in a text editor, or a word-processing or HTML editing program to make your own revisions to the HTML code.

For the Web: HTML File-Naming Conventions

Use the UNIX® file-naming convention, because many network programs truncate (shorten) long filenames. This convention requires a filename of up to eight characters, followed by an extension. Use the .html or .htm extension.

Do not use special characters such as question marks (?) or asterisks (*), or spaces between the letters in your filename—some browsers may not recognize the pathname. If you must use special characters or spaces in the filename, check with an HTML editing guide for the correct code to use. For example, to create spaces between letters you will need to replace the space with "%20".

Batch-processing file optimization

ImageReady supports batch-processing through the use of *droplets*—icons that contain actions for ImageReady to perform on one or more files. Droplets are easy to create and use. To create a droplet, you drag the droplet icon out of the Optimization palette and onto the desktop. To use a droplet, you drag a file or folder over the droplet icon on the desktop.

1 In ImageReady, choose File > Open, and open any file in the Lessons/Lesson14/Photos folder.

2 Experiment with different file formats and other settings in the Optimize palette as desired until you are satisfied with the result.

We used JPEG, High quality (60), and Progressive.

3 Drag the droplet icon (icon) out of the Optimize palette and drop it anywhere on your desktop. (If you are using Windows, you may have to resize the ImageReady window to make your desktop visible.)

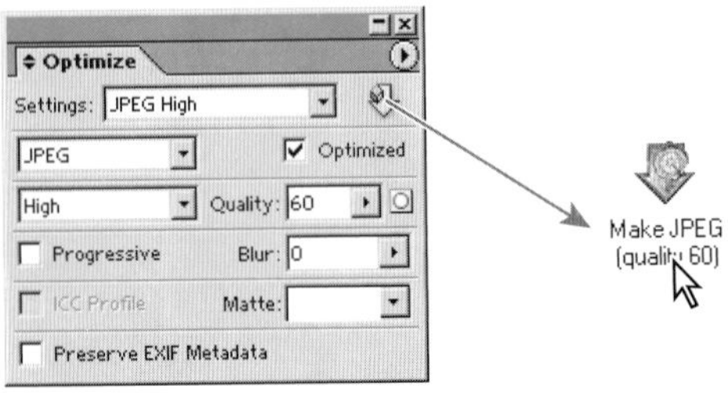

4 Close the file (without saving it).

5 From your desktop, drag the Photos folder from the Lessons/Lesson14 folder and drop it onto the droplet to batch-process the photographic images within the folder.

ImageReady optimizes each file and adds the Web image to the Photos folder.

6 Open any of the Web image files in the Photos folder.

Notice that they have all been optimized according to the settings specified when the droplet was created.

7 Quit ImageReady when you are done.

Review questions

1 For image optimization, what are the advantages of using ImageReady rather than Photoshop?

2 What is a color table?

3 When does browser dither occur, and how can you minimize the amount of browser dither in an image?

4 What is the purpose of assigning matte color to a GIF image?

5 Summarize the procedure for creating an image map.

Review answers

1 There aren't really any advantages to using one application over the other for optimization. Both Photoshop and ImageReady can perform a wide range of image-optimization tasks. ImageReady has many Web-specific features that you won't find in Photoshop, but image optimization is not one of them.

2 A color table is a table that contains the colors used in an 8-bit image. You can select a color table for GIF and PNG-8 images, and add, delete, and modify colors in the color table.

3 Browser dither occurs when a Web browser simulates colors that appear in the image's color palette but not in the browser's display system. To protect a color from browser dither, you can select the color in the Color Table palette, and then click the Web-shift button at the bottom of the palette to shift the color to its closest equivalent in the Web palette.

4 By specifying a matte color, you can blend partially transparent pixels in an image with the background color of your Web page. Matting lets you create GIF images with feathered or anti-aliased edges that blend smoothly into the background color of your Web page. But, with ImageReady 7.0, you can also specify a dither to transparency.

5 To create an image map, you define hotspot areas of the image using the image-map tools or by selecting layers and choosing Layer > New Layer Based Image Map Area. Then you use the Image Map palette to define the shape of the hotspot and link each hotspot to a URL address.

Lesson 15

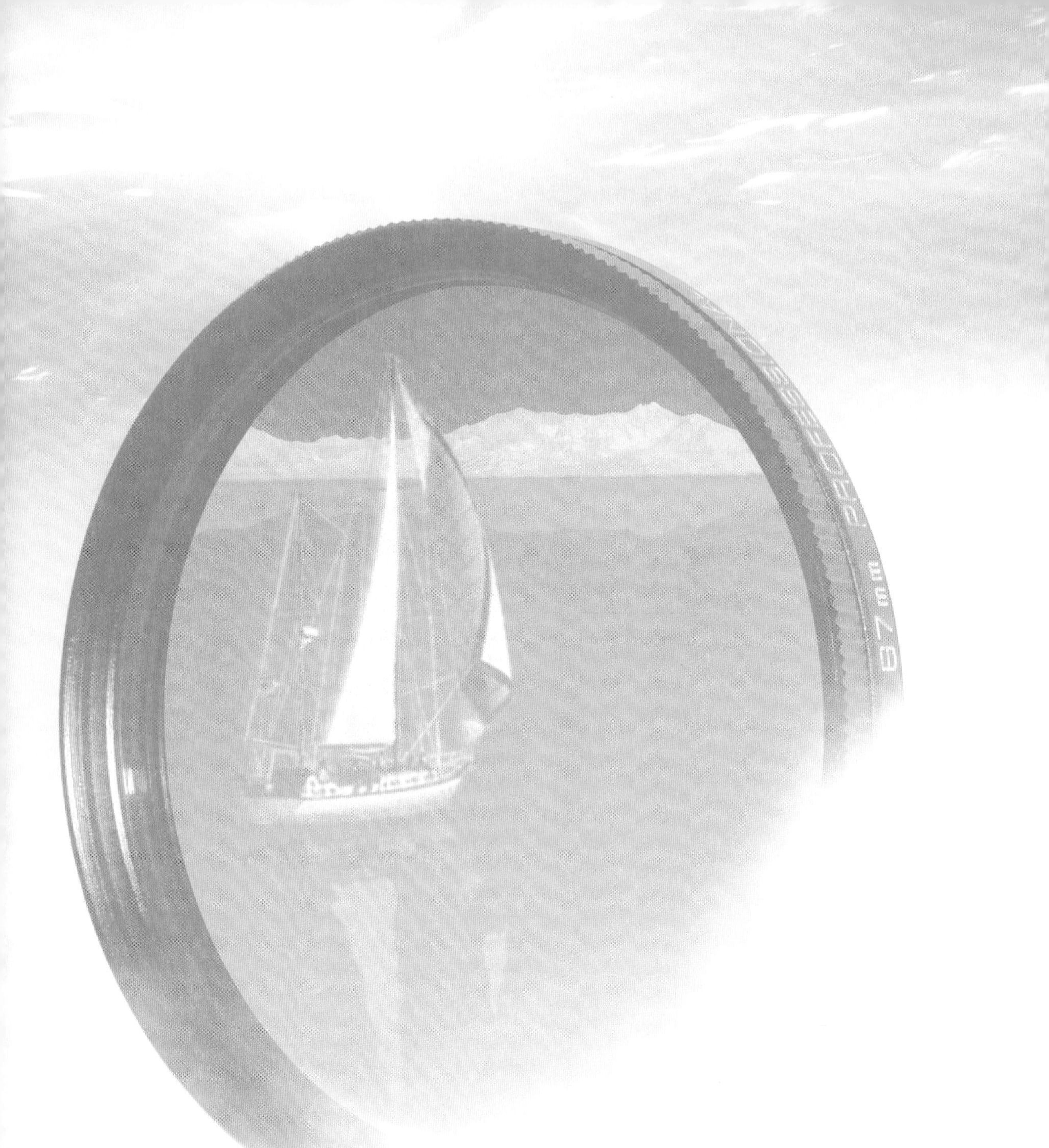

15 Adding Interactive Slices and Rollovers

Slices are divisions of an image area that you can define using Adobe Photoshop or Adobe ImageReady. You can animate your slices, link them to URL addresses, and use them for rollover buttons. Another practical use of slices is to optimize them individually in different Web image formats to maximize the effectiveness of your Web images while minimizing download times.

In this lesson, you'll learn how to do the following:

- Create image slices, using four different methods.
- Optimize individual image slices using various settings and file formats.
- Create "no image" slices to contain text and HTML.
- Create rollover buttons.
- Apply a warped text style to a text layer.
- Create Over, Down, and Selected rollover states for slices.
- Specify different combinations of hidden and visible layers as the designated conditions of various rollover states.
- Generate an HTML page that contains the sliced image in a table.

This lesson will take about 90 minutes to complete. The lesson is designed to be done in Adobe Photoshop and Adobe ImageReady. Some sections must be done in ImageReady.

If needed, remove the previous lesson folder from your hard drive, and copy the Lesson15 folder onto it. As you work on this lesson, you'll overwrite the start files. If you need to restore the start files, copy them from the *Adobe Photoshop 7.0 Classroom in a Book* CD.

Note: *Windows users need to unlock the lesson files before using them. For more information, see "Copying the Classroom in a Book files" on page 4.*

Getting started

Before beginning this lesson, restore the default application settings for Adobe Photoshop and Adobe ImageReady. See "Restoring default preferences" on page 5.

You'll start the lesson by viewing an example of the finished HTML banner that you'll create. The banner graphics react to your actions with the mouse. For example the image changes appearance when the pointer "rolls over" some areas or you click those areas.

1 Start a Web browser, and open the end file Banner.html from the Lessons/Lesson15/15End/Architech Pages folder.

The file contains an HTML table that links to several Web images all created from Photoshop and ImageReady slices.

2 Move the mouse pointer over the "designs," "structures," "art," and "contact" buttons in the banner.

Notice the small graphics that appear to the left of the buttons when you move the pointer over the first three buttons. Also notice the change in the word *Architech* when you move the pointer over the last button.

3 Hold down the mouse button and drag the pointer over the first three buttons, noticing how the word *Architech* changes this time. Release the mouse button.

4 Move the pointer over the large blue circle near the center of the image and let it hover until you see a pop-up text box with additional information. Then click the blue circle to go to the Team page.

5 On the Team page, try rolling the pointer over the three different buttons and notice the changes. Try clicking each button, and then click the Team button. Notice the changes.

If you want to go back to the banner page, use the Back button on your browser.

6 When you're done viewing the end file, close it and quit the browser.

About slices

Slices are areas in an image that you define based on layers, guides, or precise selections in the image, or by using the slice tool. When you define slices in an image, Photoshop or ImageReady creates an HTML table or cascading style sheet to contain and align the slices. If you want, you can generate an HTML file that contains the sliced image along with the table or cascading style sheet.

You can optimize slices as individual Web images, add HTML and text to slices, and link slices to URL addresses. In ImageReady, you can animate slices and create rollovers with them.

In this lesson, you'll explore different ways to slice an image in Photoshop and ImageReady, optimize the slices, and create four rollover buttons for the banner.

To learn how to animate slices, see Lesson 16, "Creating Animated Images for the Web."

Slicing an image in Photoshop

Adobe Photoshop lets you define slices using the slice tool or by converting layers into slices. You'll begin the lesson by slicing parts of a banner image for buttons using the slice tool in Photoshop. You'll name the slices and link them to URL addresses, and then optimize the slices. Then you'll continue slicing the banner image in ImageReady and create rollovers for the button slices.

About designing Web pages with Photoshop and ImageReady

When designing Web pages using Adobe Photoshop and Adobe ImageReady, keep in mind the tools and features that are available in each application.

- *Photoshop provides tools for creating and manipulating static images for use on the Web. You can divide an image into slices, add links and HTML text, optimize the slices, and save the image as a Web page.*
- *ImageReady provides many of the same image-editing tools as Photoshop. In addition, it includes tools and palettes for advanced Web processing and creating dynamic Web images such as animations and rollovers.*

–From Adobe Photoshop 7.0 online Help

Experimenting with slices in Photoshop

In this procedure, you'll learn not only some of the ways you can create slices, but also the difference between *use slices* and *auto slices*. User slices and auto slices also have different capabilities, which is the reason that it is important to understand the distinctions between them.

- User slices are areas that you actively designate as slices.
- Auto slices are the rectangular divisions of the remainder of the image—all the areas that are outside of a user slice. Photoshop and ImageReady create these slices for you.

1 Start Adobe Photoshop.

If a notice appears asking whether you want to customize your color settings, click No.

2 Choose File > New, and then click OK to accept the default settings.

3 Choose View > Show > Slices so that a checkmark appears on the Slices command.

4 In the toolbox, select the slice tool ( ), and then drag a small rectangle anywhere inside the image window. You have just created a user slice.

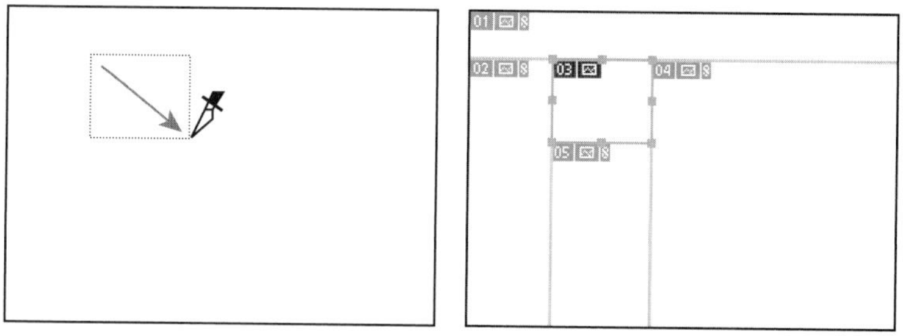

Notice that the rectangle is selected (borders are highlighted and handles are visible). Also, notice that there are other slices, which are identified by a differently colored label. These other slices are the auto slices. Each slice is numbered.

5 Create another user slice by dragging the slice tool in another area of the image window.

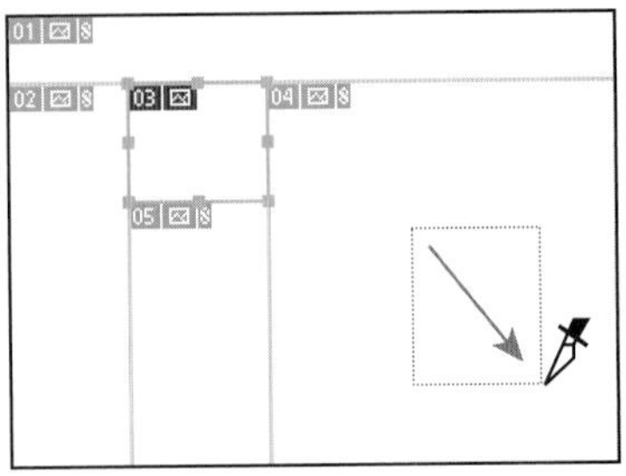

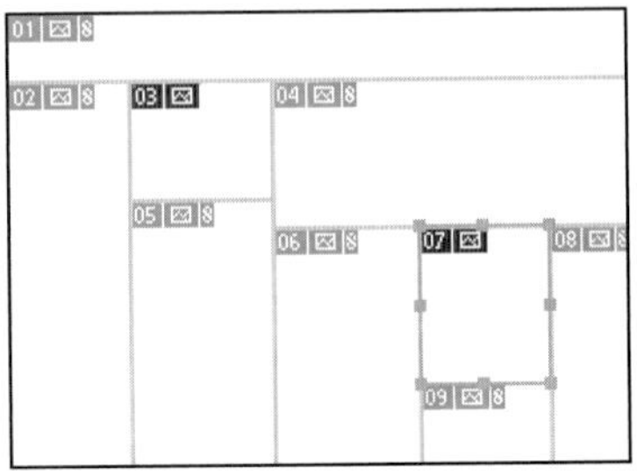

Slices are numbered sequentially, moving from top to bottom and left to right across the image. When you define a new user slice, all the slices in the image are renumbered.

6 In the toolbox, select the slice select tool () hidden under the slice tool, and try the following:

- Select one of the user slices you drew. Drag it to another position. Then drag one of the anchor points to resize the slice.

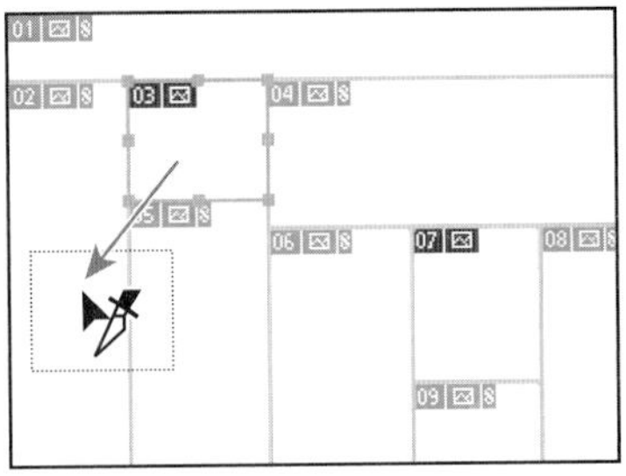

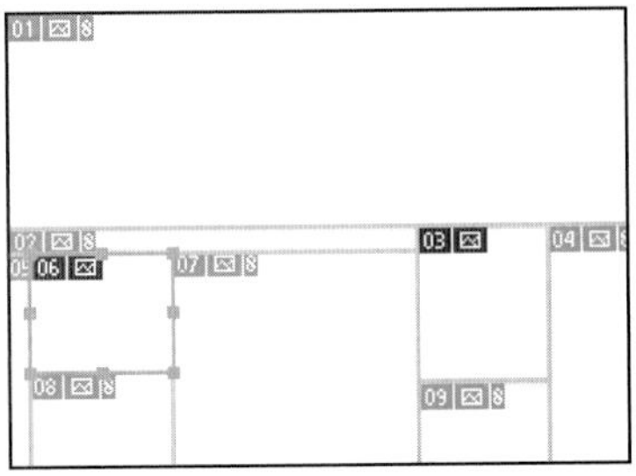

- Select one of the auto slices. Then try dragging or resizing it.

Although you can select both user slices and auto slices, you can drag and resize only user slices. Auto slices do not have selection handles.

7 Select one of the larger slices (either a user slice or an auto slice), and then go to the tool options bar and try the following actions:

- Click the Hide Auto Slices button. Then click it again (as the Show Auto Slices button).

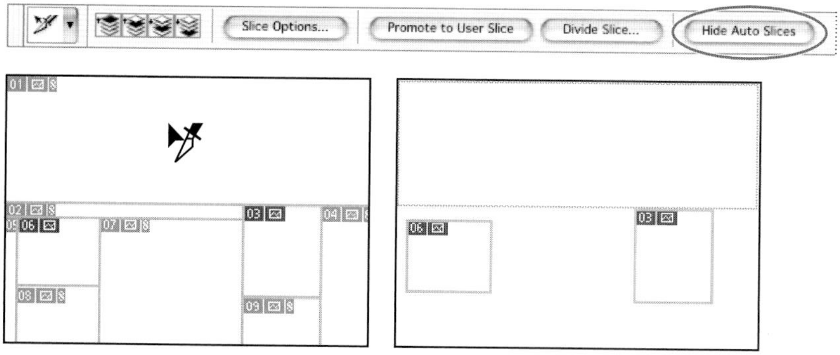

- Click the Slice Options button and examine the options available in the Slice Options dialog box. Click Cancel to close the dialog box. You'll do more work with this shortly.

- Click the Divide Slice button, and then make sure that the Preview button is selected in the dialog box and that you can see the entire selected slice in the image window. Then, in the dialog box, select the Divide Horizontally Into check box and enter a number greater than one for the number of evenly spaced slices you want to create. Notice the results. Repeat for the Divide Vertically Into option. When you finish experimenting, close the dialog box.

***Note:** In ImageReady, choose Slices > Divide Slice to do this procedure.*

8 Choose File > Close, and do not save your changes.

Types of slices

Slices you create using the slice tool are called user slices; *slices you create from a layer are called* layer-based slices. *When you create a new user slice or layer-based slice, additional auto slices are generated to account for the remaining areas of the image. In other words, auto slices fill the space in the image that is not defined by user slices or layer-based slices. Auto slices are regenerated every time you add or edit user slices or layer-based slices.*

User slices, layer-based slices, and auto slices look different—user slices and layer-based slices are defined by a solid line, while auto slices are defined by a dotted line. In addition, each type of slice displays a distinct icon. You can choose to show or hide auto slices, which makes your work with user and layer-based slices easier to view.

A subslice *is a type of auto slice that is generated when you create overlapping slices. Subslices indicate how the image will be divided when you save the optimized file. Although subslices are numbered and display a slice symbol, you cannot select or edit them separately from the underlying slice. Subslices are regenerated every time you rearrange the stacking order of slices.*

–From Adobe Photoshop 7.0 online Help

Using the slice tool to create slices

Now that you've had a taste of how slices work, you'll start making changes to the sample project for this lesson. Using the slice tool, you'll define four user slices for buttons in the banner.

1 Choose File > Open, and open the file 15Start.psd from the Lessons/Lesson15/15Start folder.

If a notice appears asking whether you want to update the text layers for vector-based output, click Update.

The lesson file includes blue horizontal and vertical guide lines. You'll use the guides and the snap-to commands when you draw marquees, so that they are tightly aligned.

2 Choose View > Show > and make sure that both Guides and Slices are selected (checked).

3 Choose View > Snap To > Guides, and then choose View > Snap To > Slices to select (place checkmarks on) both of these commands.

4 Select the slice tool ( ), and draw a marquee around the rectangular area containing the word *designs.*

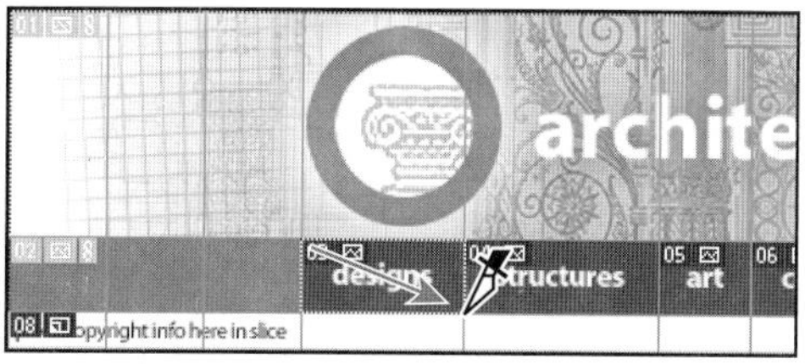

5 One at a time, draw slice marquees around each of the other words in the same row: around the words *structures, art,* and *contact* to create slices for three more buttons.

Make sure that there are no gaps between the slices, because gaps would become auto slices. (If necessary, use the zoom tool ( ) to get a closer view, and then double-click the zoom tool to return to 100%.)

You can change the way the pointer appears on-screen for the slice tool by changing your Photoshop preferences. To change the slice tool's standard pointer ( ) to the precise pointer (-¦-), choose Edit > Preferences > Display & Cursors (Windows, Mac OS 9) or Photoshop > Preferences > Display & Cursors (Mac OS 10), select Precise for Other Cursors, and click OK.

If you need to resize a slice, select the slice select tool ( ) hidden behind the slice tool, select the slice, and drag the selection handles.

6 Choose File > Save to save your work.

Setting options for slices in Photoshop

Before optimizing slices as Web images, you can set options for them, such as naming the slices or assigning URL links to them. The names you assign to the slices determine the filenames of the optimized images.

For the four user slices that you defined earlier, you'll name them, link them to other Web pages, and specify target frames.

Note: *Setting options for an auto slice automatically promotes it to a user slice.*

1 Select the slice select tool (), and use it to select the Designs slice.

2 In the tool options bar, click the Slice Options button.

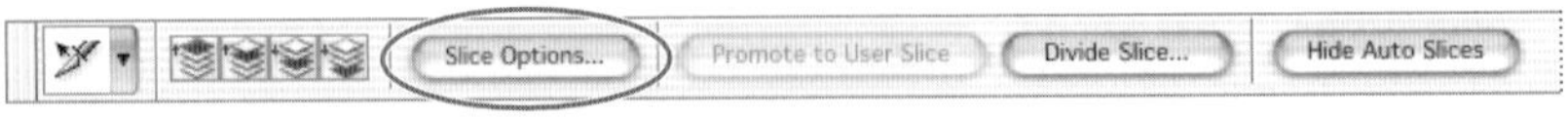

By default, Photoshop names each slice based on the filename and the slice number, so the current filename appears as "15Start_03," representing slice number three in the 15Start.psd file.

3 In the Slice Options dialog box, enter the following information: In Name, type **Designs_button**; in URL, type **Designs.html**; and in Target, type **_blank**. Then click OK.

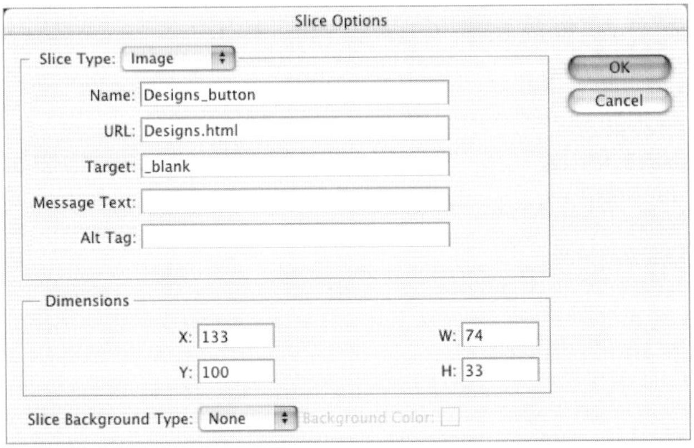

Note: *The Target option controls how a linked file opens when you click the link, such as whether the file opens in a new browser window or replaces the currently displayed file in the open browser. For more information, see Adobe Photoshop 7.0 online Help or an HTML reference (either printed or available on the Web).*

4 Enter information for the other three user slices you created:

• Select the Structures slice and type **Structures_button** in Name, **Structures.html** in URL, and **_blank** in Target.

• Select the Art slice, and type **Art_button** in Name, **Art.html** in URL, and **_blank** in Target.

• Select the Contact slice and type **Contact_button** in Name, **Contact.html** in URL, and **_blank** in Target.

5 Choose File > Save.

In the Slice Options dialog box, you can also enter message text to appear in the browser's status area, enter alternate text to appear in place of the images if they don't appear in the browser, specify dimensions to move or resize a slice, and change the slice to a No Image slice that contains HTML and text. Additional output settings for changing the background color of a slice are available when you open the Slice Options dialog box from the Save For Web dialog box or Save Optimized dialog box.

Optimizing slices in Photoshop

You can use Photoshop slices to optimize individual areas of the image, which is useful when some areas of the image require greater resolution or settings than the rest of the image. You optimize one or more slices by selecting them in the Save For Web dialog box, choosing optimization settings, and saving optimized files for either the selected slices or all slices. Photoshop creates an Images folder to contain the optimized files.

Next, you'll optimize the four user slices you defined.

1 Choose File > Save for Web.

2 On the left side of the Save For Web dialog box, select the slice select tool ( ).

3 In the optimized version of the image, Shift-click to select the four slices you created.

4 On the Settings pop-up menu, choose GIF Web Palette, and then click Save.

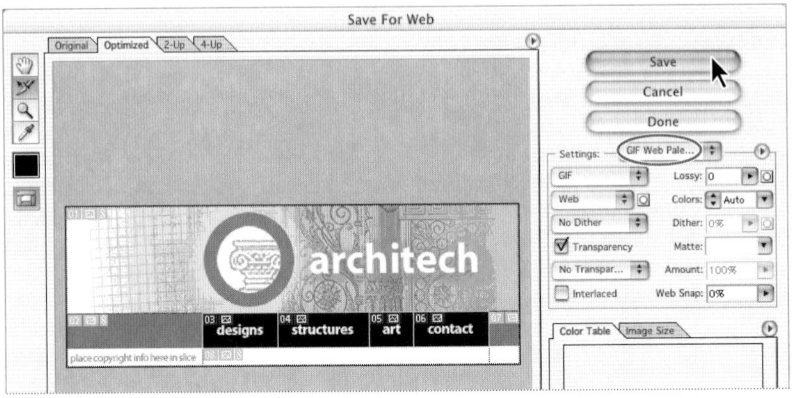

5 In the Save Optimized As dialog box, do the following:

- On the Format pop-up menu, choose Images Only.
- On the Slices pop-up menu, choose Selected Slices.
- Select the Lessons/Lesson15/15Start/Architech Pages folder as the location for the saved file.
- Leave the name setting as it is (15Start.gif), and click Save.

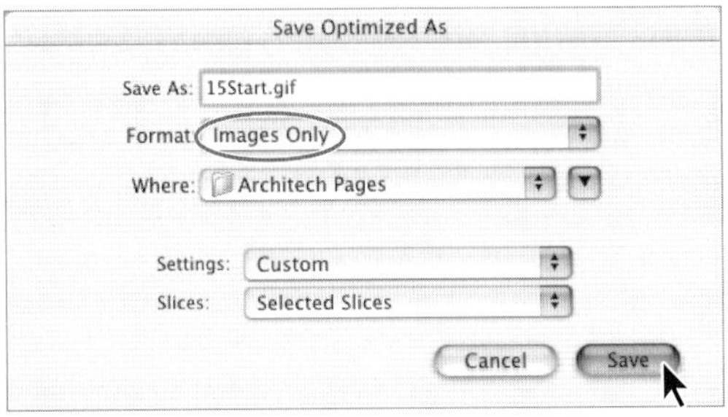

Photoshop saves the optimized images in an Images folder within the Architech Pages folder and uses the names you specified in the Slice Options dialog box for the filenames. If there are any gaps in the table, Photoshop creates a Spacer.gif file.

6 Choose File > Save.

Slicing the image in ImageReady

You've already learned several ways to create and work with slices in Photoshop, all of which can also be done in ImageReady. Although the options sometimes appear in different locations in the two applications, you can also use either Photoshop or ImageReady to create slices from guides or layers and to optimize individual slices.

In this part of the lesson, you'll use ImageReady to convert a layer into a slice, create a No Image slice, and create a precisely shaped slice from a selection. Later in the lesson, you'll work with the Rollovers palette—a feature unique to ImageReady—to build interactivity into your images.

You'll start by jumping directly from Photoshop to ImageReady. When you use the Jump To feature to go back and forth between Photoshop and ImageReady, the currently active file also jumps with you, opening in the target application.

1 In the Photoshop toolbox, click the Jump to ImageReady button ( ).

The 15Start.psd file opens in ImageReady.

2 Choose Window > Workspace > Reset Palette Locations to make sure that the palettes are in their default positions.

Notice that the ImageReady menu bar includes a Slices menu, and that a Slice palette tab appears in the Animations palette group in the lower left area of the workspace. This menu and palette group appear only in ImageReady, not in Photoshop.

Creating a custom workspace in ImageReady

To prepare for your ImageReady work with slices and rollovers, you'll streamline the work area by closing the palettes you won't need for these tasks and then resizing and arranging the ones you do need. By removing the clutter of unneeded palettes, you maximize your efficiency for these types of tasks. You'll save this arrangement as a custom workspace that you can reuse later.

To get a sense of the workspace arrangement you're aiming for, see the illustration with the final steps of this procedure.

1 Separate the palettes from their default palette groups as follows:

• Drag the Slice palette out of the Animation palette group.

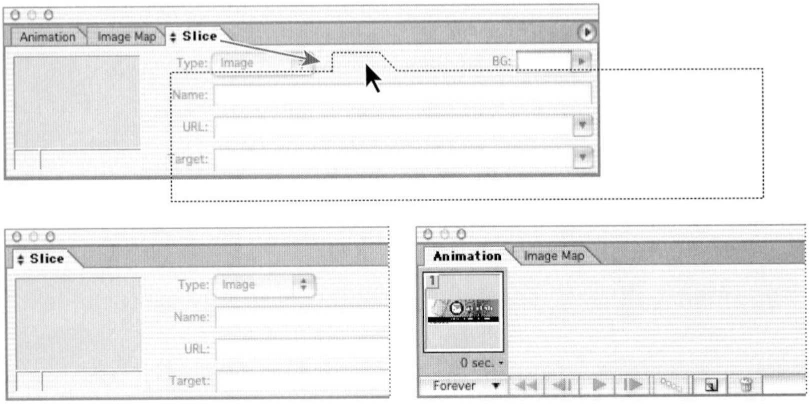

• Drag the Info palette out of the Optimize palette group.

• Drag the Rollovers palette out of its palette group (leaving the Color Table and Layer Options palettes together).

• Drag the Layers palette out its palette group (leaving the History and Actions palettes together).

2 You won't be using the following palettes in this lesson, so close them by clicking the close button on the palette title bar: the Animation palette group, the Info palette, the Color palette group, the Color Table palette group, and the History palette group.

Now just four palettes remain open: the Slice, Rollovers, Layers, and Optimize palettes.

3 Drag the Optimize palette to the upper right corner of your work area, and then open the Optimize palette menu and choose Show Options to expand the palette.

4 Drag the Layers palette just below the Optimize palette, and then drag the lower right corner of the Layers palette down to increase its height to take advantage of the available space.

5 Drag the Rollovers palette to the left of the Optimize palette. Drag its corner so that it is as tall as possible.

6 On the Slice palette menu, choose Show Options to expand the palette, and then drag it to the lower left corner of the work area.

Your workspace now includes all the palettes you'll need to see in this lesson, each expanded to the best size for the job.

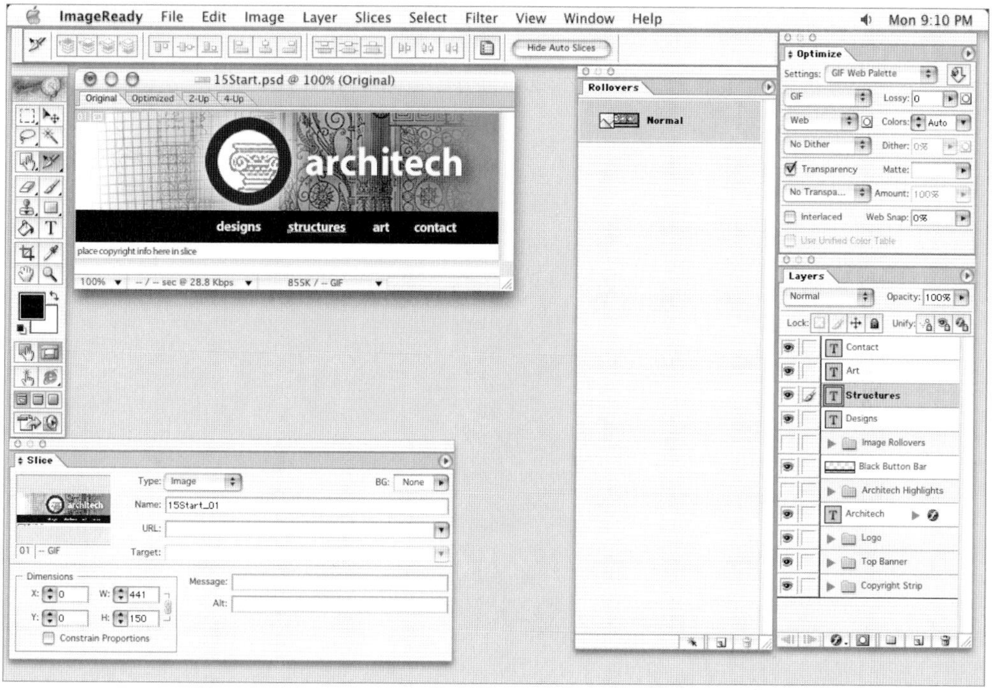

7 Choose Window > Workspace > Save Workspace. Then, in the Save Workspace dialog box, type **Rollovers_15**, and click OK.

You can now select the Rollovers_15 workspace on the Window > Workspace menu whenever you need to use it, such as if your ImageReady session is interrupted before you finish this lesson.

Note: *The custom workspaces you create and save for either ImageReady or Photoshop are not lost when you reset the default preferences for the application.*

Experimenting with slices created from guides

In Photoshop and ImageReady, you can convert all the areas between guides into user slices. When you convert guides into slices, the entire image is sliced and you lose any preexisting slices.

1 Choose File > Save, and then choose View > Show > and make sure that checkmarks appear by both Slices, Autoslices, and Guides commands. If not, select those commands now, as needed.

2 In the toolbox, select the slice select tool (), and then select the Designs_button slice in the image window.

In the Slice palette, notice that the slice name, URL, Target, and Alt text that you entered in Photoshop appear in this ImageReady palette.

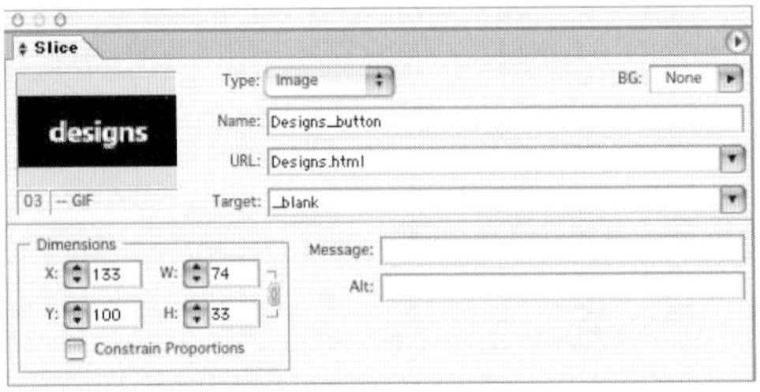

3 Choose Slices > Create Slices From Guides.

This is a quick method for creating slices for every rectangular area between the guides.

4 Use the slice select tool to select the Designs_button slice again.

Notice that the options in the Slice palette for the Designs_button slice have changed to a default name based on the filename and slice number, and you've lost the options you set in Photoshop. Because that isn't what you want to happen, you'll undo this process.

5 Choose Edit > Undo Create Slices From Guides.

6 Choose View > Show > Guides to deselect the Guides command and hide the guides.

In Photoshop, you can perform this same task by selecting the slice tool ( ) in the toolbox, and then clicking the Slices From Guides button on the tool options bar.

Creating a layer-based slice

Another method for defining slices in Photoshop and ImageReady is to convert layers into slices. A layer-based slice includes all the pixel data in the layer. When you edit the layer, move it, or apply a layer effect to it, the layer-based slice adjusts to encompass the new pixels. To unlink a layer-based slice from its layer, you can convert it to a user slice.

You'll create a slice based on the Copyright Strip layer, and then apply a layer effect to it so you can see how the slice adjusts to the new effect.

1 In the Layers palette, expand the Copyright Strip layer set and select the Strip Background layer.

The Strip Background layer contains the white strip that goes across the bottom of the banner.

2 Choose Layer > New Layer Based Slice.

ImageReady replaces the auto slices with one layer-based slice for the entire layer. Notice the icon ( ) in the upper left corner of the slice that indicates that the slice is layer-based.

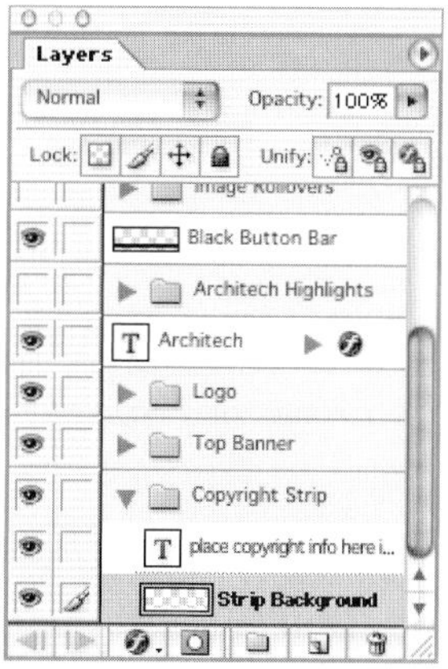

__Note:__ You can still apply layer styles to the layer that you used to create the layer-based slice. The dimensions of the slice automatically increase to accommodate any extra space required to show the effect.

3 Choose File > Save to save your work in ImageReady.

Creating No Image slices

In ImageReady and Photoshop, you can create *No Image* slices and add text or HTML source code to them. No Image slices can have a background color and are saved as part of the HTML file.

The primary advantage of using No Image slices for text is that the text can be edited in any HTML editor, saving you the trouble of having to go back to Photoshop or ImageReady to edit it. The disadvantage is that if the text grows too large for the slice, it will break the HTML table and introduce unwanted gaps.

Now you'll convert the Copyright Strip slice into a No Image slice and add text to it.

1 Make sure that the layer-based slice that you created for the copyright information is selected in the image window.

2 In the Slice palette, choose No Image from the Type pop-up menu.

3 Enter some copyright information for your banner in the Text box. (We used **©2003 architech art and structure**.)

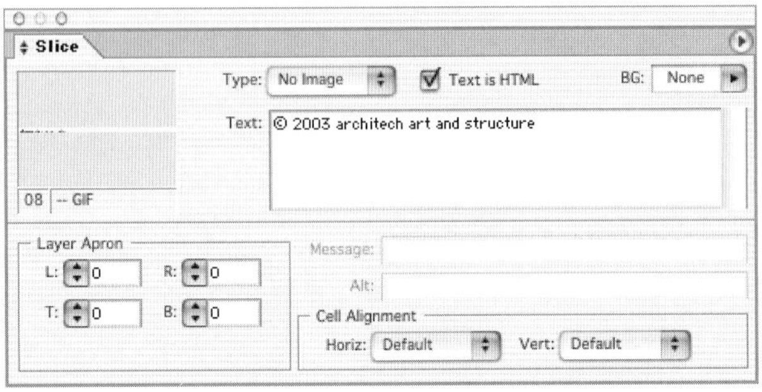

You can add a copyright symbol by pressing Alt+0169 on the numeric keypad (Windows) or Option+G (Mac OS).

Because you chose No Image for the slice type, the layer of placeholder text ("place copyright info here in slice") that you do see in ImageReady will not appear in the Web page. The text that you typed will appear in the Web page; however, it does not appear in your sliced image in ImageReady or Photoshop.

4 In the Layers palette, click the arrow to collapse the Copyright Strip layer set.

5 Choose File > Save.

Previewing in a Web browser

To make sure that the text you type will fit in the table cell, you'll preview the image in a Web browser.

Note: *(Mac OS 10 only) Make sure that you have a Mac OS 10 browser alias in place so that the browser doesn't open in classic mode.*

1 In the toolbox, click the Preview In Default Browser button (or) or choose a browser from the button's pop-up menu.

The image appears in the browser window, and the HTML source for the preview appears in a table below the image. Without pressing the mouse button, move the pointer over the buttons.

Note: *To add your browser to the Preview In Default Browser button, drag its shortcut (Windows) or alias (Mac OS) into the Preview In folder located inside the Helpers folder in the Photoshop 7.0 folder.*

2 When you're done previewing the copyright text, quit the browser to return to ImageReady.

Creating slices from selections

In ImageReady, the easiest way to create a slice for a small or unusually shaped graphic element is to select the element and use the selection as the basis for the slice. This is also a useful technique for slicing objects that are crowded closely together. For graphic elements that are distinctly colored, the magic wand tool () may be a good choice for making the initial selection. In this procedure, you'll use a keyboard shortcut to select a graphic element that is on its own layer.

1 In the Layers palette, expand the Logo layer set.

2 Hold down Ctrl (Windows) or Command (Mac OS) and select the Big Circle layer. The blue circle shape is now selected in the image window.

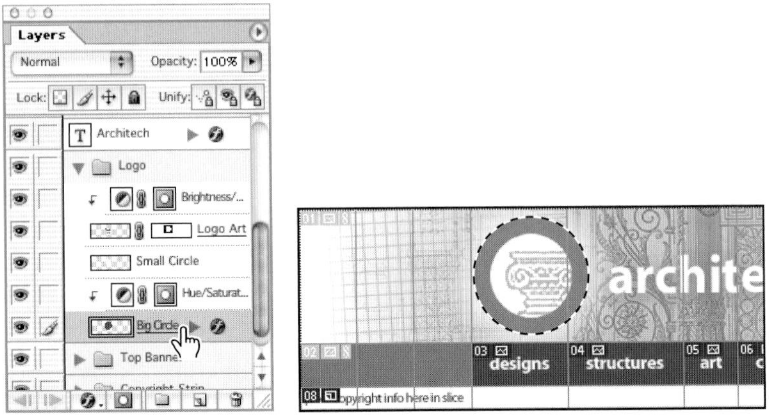

3 Choose Select > Create Slice from Selection.

Notice the additional auto slices that are created around the logo to complete the table.

4 In the Slice palette, enter the following: In Name, type **Logo**; in URL, type **Team.html**; and in Alt, type **Read about the team**. Enter **_blank** in the Target text box by choosing it from the Target pop-up menu.

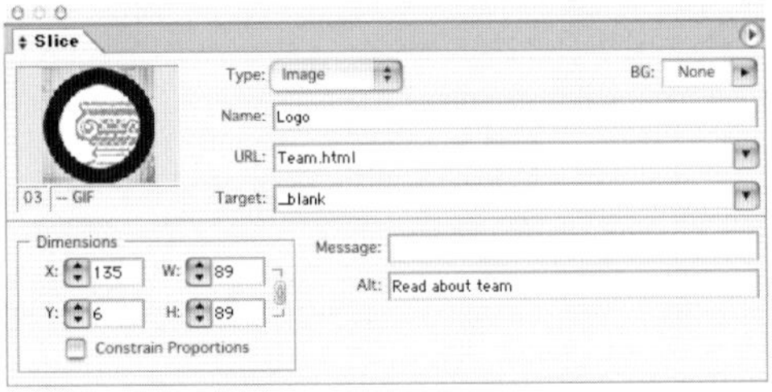

5 In the toolbar, make sure that the slice tool or slice selection tool is not selected, or select any other tool.

6 Choose Select > Deselect to remove selection lines from the logo. The slice selection border and handles remain selected.

If the slice tool or slice select tool is currently active, the Deselect Slices command appears on the Select menu instead of the Deselect command.

7 Choose File > Save.

You can choose URLs that you've already entered previously from the URL pop-up menu in the Slice palette.

Optimizing slices in ImageReady

ImageReady records separate optimization settings for every slice in the image. You specify optimization settings for a slice by selecting it and entering values in the Optimize palette. Then, you can save an optimized image file for the selected slice.

In this part of the lesson, you'll explore how to set the optimization for slices in ImageReady, and then you'll link the slices together to share the optimization settings.

Setting the optimization for selected slices

Slices use the optimization settings of the entire image until you select them and specify new settings.

1 In the toolbox, select the slice select tool (), and then select the number 02 auto slice in the image.

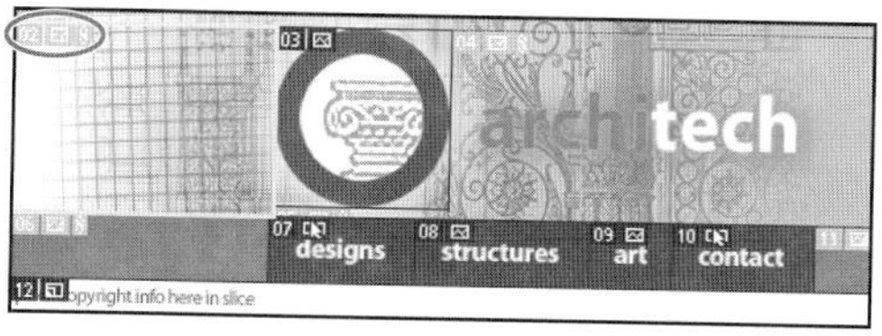

2 Click the 2-UP tab in the image window to display the original image next to the optimized image.

3 Choose 200% from the Zoom Level menu in the lower left corner of the image window.

Notice that the quality of the optimized image at its default setting (GIF Web Palette) is poor compared to the original image.

4 In the Optimize palette, choose GIF 32 Dithered from the Settings menu.

Now the quality of the selected slice is better than at the default GIF Web Palette setting.

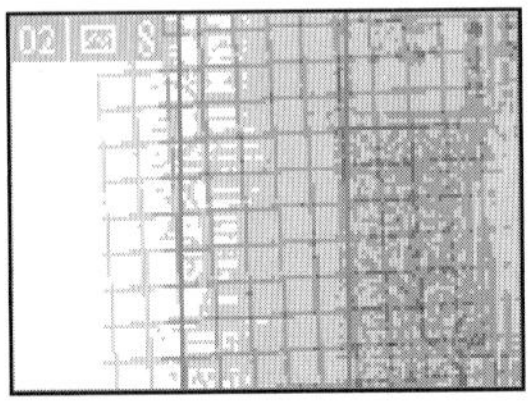

GIF Web Palette setting

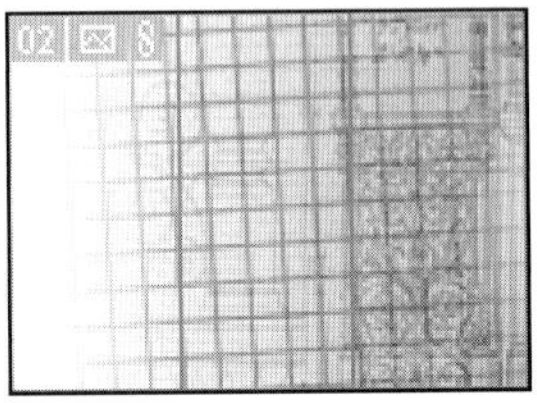

GIF 32 Dithered setting

5 Examine the optimized image at actual size by choosing 100% from the Zoom Level menu. You can click the Toggle Slices Visibility button ( ) in the toolbox to hide the slice numbers while you're viewing the optimized image.

6 In the image, select another auto slice.

In the Optimize palette, notice that the selected slice has the same GIF 32 Dithered setting. This is because all auto slices are linked together, and any optimization setting that you choose for one auto slice is automatically applied to the others.

7 Choose File > Save.

You'll save the optimized slices later, after you create some rollovers. For information about the optimization settings and available Web formats for your image slices, see Lesson 14, "Optimizing Web Images and Image Maps."

In ImageReady, you can link slices together to share the same optimization settings. Then, in ImageReady or Photoshop, you can change the settings for a linked slice and the new settings are instantly applied to the entire set of linked slices. Linked sets are color-coded to help identify slices in a set.

Creating rollovers

Rollovers are familiar Web effects. For example, many or even most Web pages feature some change in the appearance of a button or hotspot when you move the mouse over it, even though you don't click. This is a typical rollover state.

A rollover state is defined by the event that triggers the rollover behavior, such as a click, holding down the mouse (but not clicking), or just moving the pointer over that area of the image. For a description of the different rollover states available in ImageReady, see the sidebar "Rollover states in ImageReady," following below.

Secondary rollovers affect the appearance or behavior of other areas of the image when you perform the mouse action on the rollover button.

Only user slices can have rollover states. However, you can promote an auto slice to a user slice using the Slices > Promote to user slice command, and then assign rollover states to the slice.

Rollover states in ImageReady

When you create a rollover state, ImageReady assigns the type of state by default; however, you can easily change the state. You can also use the Rollovers palette to target the image content of a state for editing.

Over *Activates the image when the user rolls over the slice or image-map area with the mouse while the mouse button is not pressed. (Over is automatically selected for the second rollover state.)*

Down *Activates the image when the user presses the mouse button on the slice or image-map area. The state appears as long as the viewer keeps the mouse button pressed down on the area.*

Click *Activates the image when the user clicks the mouse on the slice or image-map area. The state appears until the user moves the mouse out of the rollover area.*

Note: *Different Web browsers, or different versions of a browser, may process clicks and double-clicks differently. For example, some browsers leave the slice in the Click state after a click, and in the Up state after a double-click; other browsers use the Up state only as a transition into the Click state, regardless of single- or double-clicking. To ensure your Web page will function correctly, be sure to preview rollovers in various Web browsers.*

Custom *Activates the image of the specified name when the user performs the action defined in the corresponding JavaScript code. (You must create JavaScript code and add it to the HTML file for the Web page in order for the Custom rollover option to function. See a JavaScript manual for more information.)*

None Preserves the current state of the image for later use, but does not output an image when the file is saved as a Web page.

Selected Activates the rollover state when the user clicks the mouse on the slice or image-map area. The state appears until the viewer activates another selected rollover state, and other rollover effects can occur while the selected state is active.

Out Activates the image when the user rolls the mouse out of the slice or image-map area. (The Normal state usually serves this purpose.)

Up Activates the image when the user releases the mouse button over the slice or image-map area.

–From Adobe Photoshop 7.0 online Help

Displaying warped text in the Over state

In the following topics in this lesson, you'll create several primary and secondary rollover effects for various rollover actions. You'll begin with a rollover for the Over state of the Contact button. Your goal is to make the text layer *architech* appear warped when the pointer moves over the Contact button. Because you'll create this rollover for the Contact button and the result will be a change in an area that is outside that slice, it fits the definition of a secondary rollover.

1 Click the Original tab in the image window.

2 Using the slice select tool (), select the Contact_button slice in the image window. Or, select it in the Rollovers palette. In either case, selecting it in one place also selects it in the other.

3 In the Rollover palette, click the Create Rollover State button (). A new Over State rollover appears nested below the Contact_button slice in the palette.

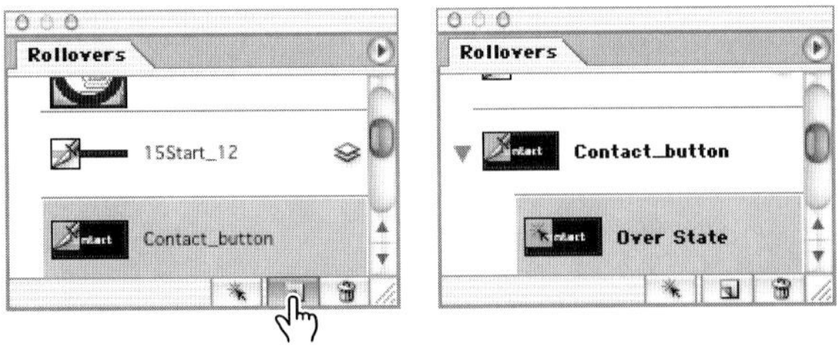

4 In the Layers palette, select the Architech type layer.

5 Select the type tool (T) to display the text options in the tool options bar, and click the Create Warped Text button ().

6 In the Style pop-up menu in the Warp Text dialog box, choose Bulge. Select Preview and wait a moment to see the effect applied to the type. (You may need to move the dialog box so you can see the type in the image.) You can try out various values for the different Bulge style settings or choose other styles to find a combination that appeals to you. When you're satisfied with a style and settings, make sure they are selected, and click OK.

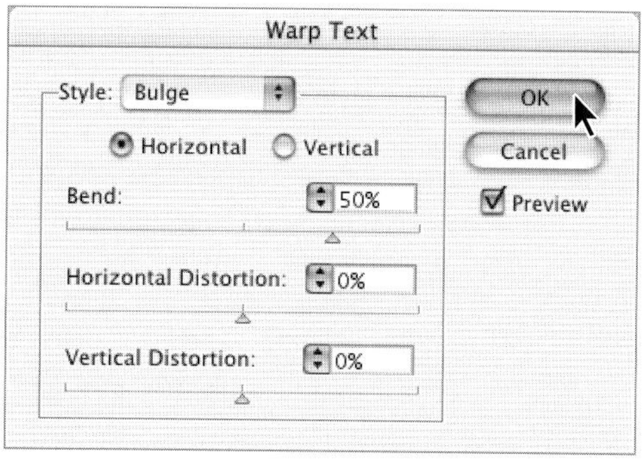

The Warped Text effect is applied only to the Over state of the button.

Normal state of the Contact button

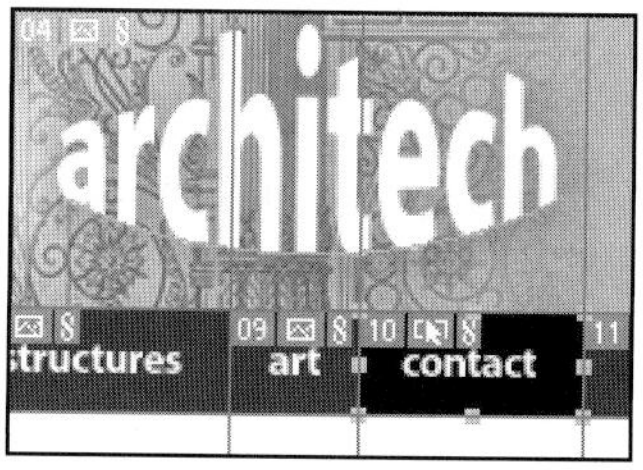

Over state of the Contact button

7 In the Rollover palette, click the Normal state. The word now appears in its undistorted condition.

8 Choose File > Save.

Previewing rollovers in ImageReady

ImageReady provides a quick way to preview rollovers in the image window without opening a Web browser. This rollover preview mode in ImageReady is consistent with Internet Explorer 5.0 (or later) for Windows.

1 In the toolbox, select the Toggle Slices Visibility button ( ) to hide the slice boundaries.

2 Also in the toolbox, select the Preview Document button ( ).

3 Move the pointer over the Contact button in the image and notice how the Architech text changes. Also notice how the selection in the Rollovers palette switches from Normal to the Over State below the Contact_button as you move the pointer.

4 Click the Preview Document button again to deselect it.

5 Click the Toggles Slices Visibility button to show the slice boundaries.

Showing and hiding layers in an Over rollover state

When you previewed the sample finished file in your browser at the beginning of this lesson, you saw images that appeared at the left side of the button bar when you moved the mouse over those buttons. These are also examples of secondary rollovers for the Over state, but this time the change in appearance is caused by tying the visibility of different layers to the OverStates of the slices.

1 Using the slice select tool ( ), select the Designs_button slice in the image window.

2 In the Rollover palette, click the Creates Rollover State button ( ) to create an Over State for the Designs_button slice.

3 In the Layers palette, select and expand the Image Rollovers layer set. If necessary, click to set an eye icon ( ) for the layer set to make it visible.

4 In the Image Rollovers layer set, click to remove the eye icons (👁) from the For Structures and For Art layers, as needed, so that the For Designs layer is the only visible layer in that layer set.

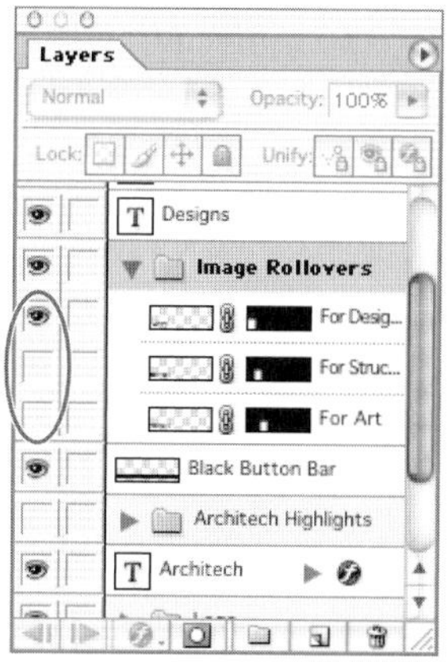

5 Using the slice select tool, select the Structures_button slice, and repeat steps 3 and 4, except this time make the For Structures layer visible and hide the For Designs and For Art layers.

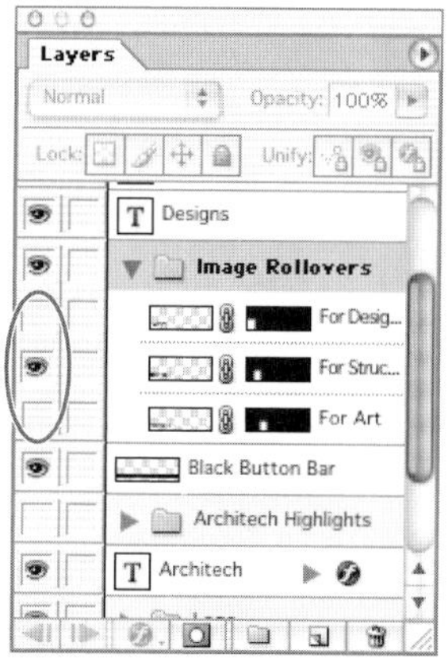

6 Select the Art_button slice and repeat steps 3 and 4 again, but make the For Art layer the only visible layer in the Image Rollovers layer set.

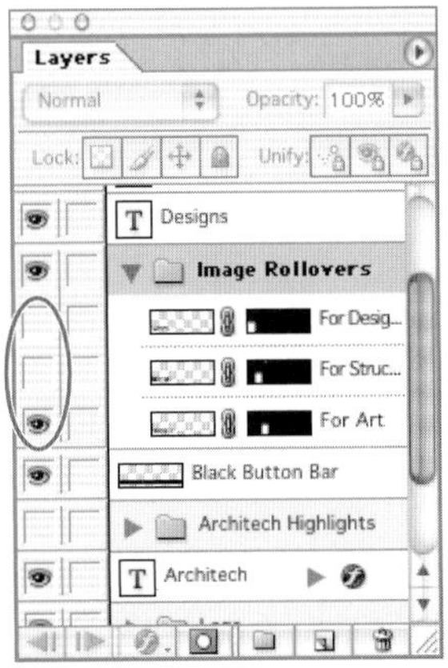

7 In the toolbox, select the Toggle Slices Visibility button (▭) and the Preview Document button (☝), and move the pointer back and forth across the buttons to see the results. Then click those two toolbox buttons again to deactivate them.

8 In the Layers palette, click the small arrow to collapse the Image Rollovers layer set. Then choose File > Save.

Showing and hiding layers in a Down rollover state

Next, you'll create a Down state for three of the buttons. A Down state is activated when the user holds down (but does not release) the mouse button over the slice.

1 Using the slice select tool (✂), select the Designs_button slice in the image window.

2 In the Rollover palette, click the Creates Rollover State button (▣). This time, ImageReady automatically creates a Down State for the Designs_button slice.

3 In the Layers palette, select the Architech Highlights layer set, and then click the small arrow to expand the layer set. If necessary, click the eye icon (👁) for the layer set to make all the layers in it visible in the image window.

Notice the blue text that appears over the word *Architech* in the image. You'll hide parts of the blue text to draw attention to other parts of the word.

4 Click the eye icons (👁) next to the bottom four layers to hide the blue highlighting for the letters "t-e-c-h."

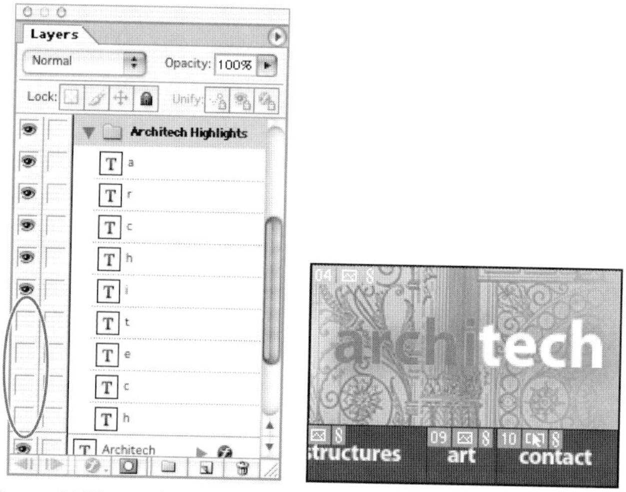

Layers hidden in the Down state of the Designs button

The Down state of the Designs button now shows the letters "a-r-c-h-i" in blue and "t-e-c-h" in white.

5 In the Rollovers palette, select the Structures_button slice and then click the New Rollover State button (▣) at the bottom of the palette. Then, in the Layers palette, click the eye icons in the Architech Highlights layer set so that the letters "a-r-c-h" are hidden and the letters "i-t-e-c-h" are visible.

6 Repeat step 5 for the Art_button slice, but this time hide the letters "a-r" and "t" and leave all the other layers in the Architech Highlights layer set visible.

7 In the Rollovers palette, click the Normal rollover state.

8 In the toolbox, select the Toggle Slices Visibility button (▭) and the Preview Document button (☝). In the image window, hold down the mouse button as you drag the pointer over the three slices.

9 When you finish previewing, deselect the Toggle Slices visibility and Preview Document buttons, and choose File > Save.

Working with more rollover states

You can improve the usability of your Web pages by adding appropriate navigational hints for your readers. In this section, you'll work on one of the auxiliary pages for the Architech Web site and create three different kinds of visual clues to help readers find information.

Creating a primary rollover state

So far, all the rollovers you've created have been secondary rollovers because the change appears outside the slice itself. This time, you'll create an Over rollover state that directly affects the appearance of the slice itself.

1 Choose File > Open, and select the team.psd file in the Lessons/Lesson15/15Start/Architech folder.

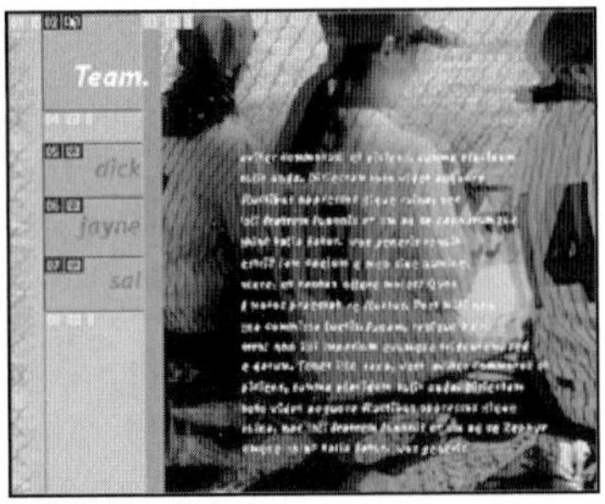

The new file is a page describing the Architech team. Some work has already been done for you, including the creation of some slices.

2 In the Layers palette, select the Names Glowing layer set, and click the arrow to expand it so that you can see the dick glo, jayne glo, and sal glo layers nested in the layer set.

3 In the Rollovers palette, select the dick_button slice and then click the Create Rollover State button ( ) at the bottom of the palette.

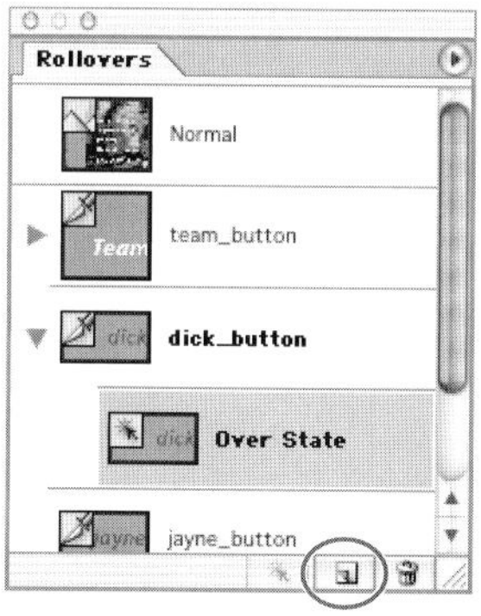

ImageReady creates and selects an Over State rollover under the dick_button slice.

4 In the Layers palette, under the Names Glowing layer set, click to set an eye icon for the dick glo layer so that it is visible. (Leave the jayne glo and sal glo layers hidden.)

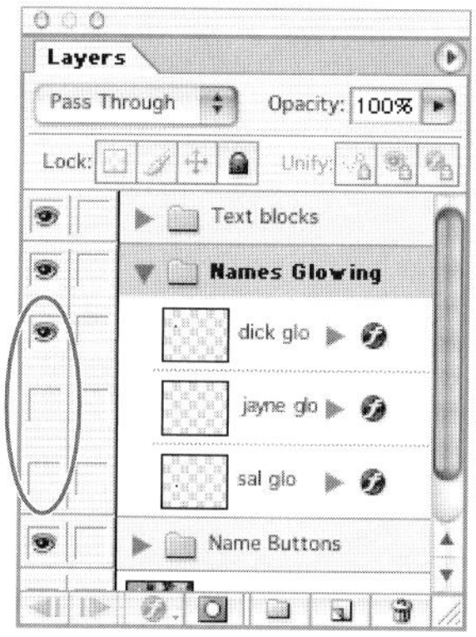

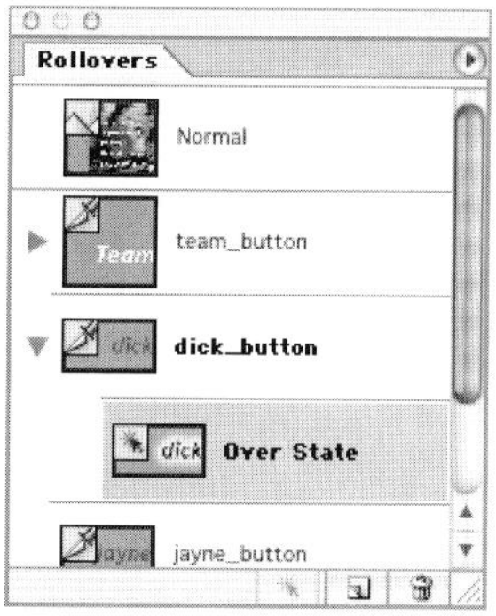

5 Repeat steps 3 and 4 for the jayne_button slice, but click an eye icon ( ) in only the jayne glo layer, leaving dick glo and sal glo hidden.

6 Again repeat steps 3 and 4 for the sal_button slice, making only the sal glo layer visible in the Names Glowing layer set.

7 Verify your results by selecting the Toggle Slices Visibility button ( ) and the Preview Document button ( ) in the toolbar, and then moving the pointer over the three names. If you've done this procedure correctly, each name glows when the pointer is over it and returns to normal view when the pointer moves away from the slice.

8 In the toolbox, click the Toggle Slices Visibility button (▭) and the Preview Document button (☝) again to deselect them.

9 Click the small arrow to collapse the Names Glowing layer set, and choose File > Save.

Creating a Selected rollover state

Ordinarily, users might expect that clicking a hotspot would jump the browser to a linked Web page. The Selected rollover state is especially useful when clicking the slice is not associated with a different URL.

1 In the Rollovers palette, select the dick_button slice, and click the Create Rollover State button (▫) at the bottom of the palette.

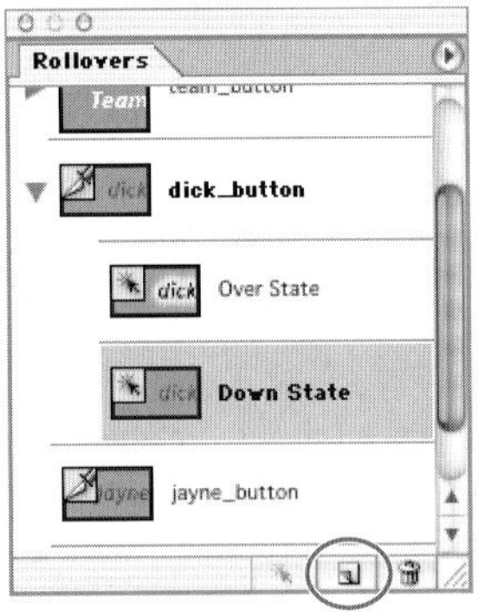

ImageReady creates a Down State rollover for the slice.

2 Double-click the new Down State rollover to open the Rollover State Options dialog box.

3 In the dialog box, select the Selected option, and click OK.

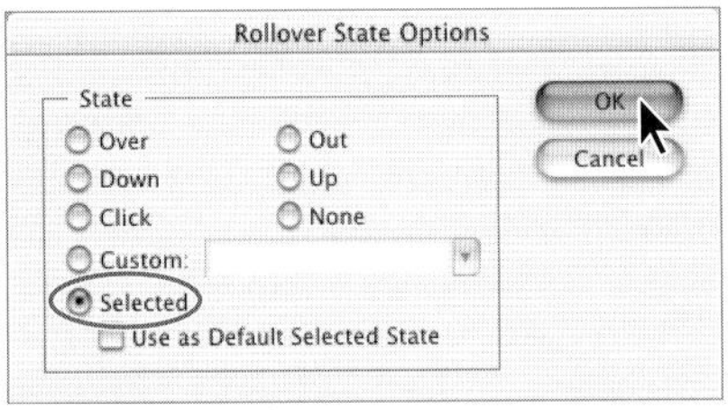

Now the new rollover shows that it is a Selected State rollover.

4 In the Layers palette, click the small arrow to expand the Text Blocks layer set. Notice the eye icons: The Text Blocks layer set and the Team layer are visible. The other three layers are currently hidden.

Note: *Although the thumbnails of the layers in the Text Blocks layer set look like identical transparent layers, they're not. Each one contains white text, which is virtually impossible to see in these tiny images.*

5 Click the eye icon (👁) to hide the Team_text layer, and then click the visibility option for the dick_text layer so that an eye icon appears there.

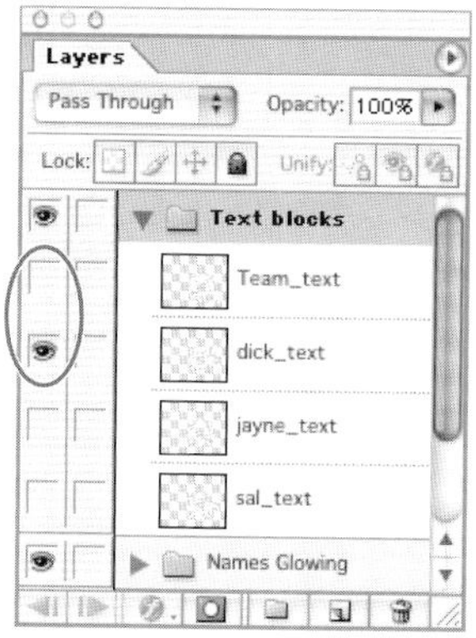

Now the large text block on the right side of the image changes, showing placeholder text for a short biography about Dick.

6 Repeat steps 1 through 5 for the jayne_button slice, but make only the jayne_text layer visible in the Text Blocks layer set.

7 Again, repeat steps 1 through 5 for the sal_button slice, but make only the sal_text layer visible in the Text Blocks layer set.

8 Verify your results by selecting the Toggle Slices Visibility button (▭) and the Preview Document button (☝) in the toolbar, and then clicking each of the three name slices. Then deselect those two toolbox buttons.

9 Click the small arrow to collapse the Text Blocks layer set, and choose File > Save.

Adding alternate text

Alternate text appears under two different circumstances: when an image is not shown in the browser window, or when the user allows the pointer to hover over a hotspot. Either way, taking the trouble to add alternate text adds to the usability of your Web pages. You'll add some alternate text to four slices in the Team.psd image.

1 In the Rollovers palette, select the dick_button slice.

2 In the Alt option in the Slice palette, type **Read about Dick, our Chairman**.

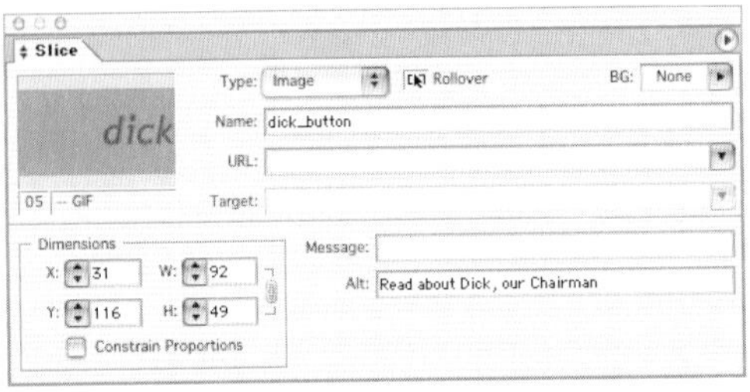

3 In the Rollovers palette, select the jayne_button slice, and then go to the Alt option in the Slice palette and type **Read about Jayne, our President**.

4 In the Rollovers palette, select the sal_button slice, and then go to the Alt option in the Slice palette and type **Read about Sal, our Founder**.

5 In the Rollovers palette, select the Team_button slice, and then go to the Alt option in the Slice palette and type **Read about our expert team**.

6 Verify your results by selecting the Toggle Slices Visibility button ( ) and the Preview Document button ( ) in the toolbar, and then letting the pointer hover for a few seconds over each of the four slices. Then deselect those two toolbox buttons.

7 Choose File > Save.

Previewing the completed pages in a browser

Before you save the optimized image slices, you'll preview the completed rollovers for the banner and team pages in a Web browser. However, the fictitious URL links that you assigned to the slices won't work in Preview In Browser mode, so you'll test them later when you generate the final HTML file and open the file from the browser.

1 Choose Window > Documents > 15Start.psd to switch back to the banner image.

2 In the toolbox, click the Preview In Default Browser button ( ) ( ) or choose a browser from the button's pop-up menu.

3 When the page opens in the browser window, move the pointer over each rollover button in the banner.

A different image appears for each of the first three buttons, and the warped text effect appears for the last button.

4 Hold the mouse button down when the pointer is over each button.

When you hold down the mouse button: On the Designs button, the white letters "tech" are visible; on the Structures button, the white letters "arch" are visible; and on the Art button, the white letters "art" are visible.

5 Click the blue circle in the middle of the image to open the Team.html page.

6 Move the pointer over the dick, jayne, and sal names to verify that the glowing Over State is functioning properly.

7 Click each of the four buttons (sal, jayne, dick, and Team) to verify that the Selected state is also functioning properly.

8 When you're finished previewing the rollovers, quit the browser and return to ImageReady.

Saving the sliced images in ImageReady

Now that the banner and team pages are complete, you'll save the optimized image slices and generate an HTML file that contains an HTML table of the sliced image.

ImageReady also lets you save slices in a cascading style sheet rather than a table. To set up the file for cascading style sheets, choose File > Output Settings > HTML. For Slice Output, select Generate CSS, and click OK. You can also change the output settings from the Save Optimized dialog box.

1 With the 15Start.psd file active, choose File > Save Optimized.

2 In the Save Optimized dialog box, enter **Banner.html** as the name. On the Format pop-up menu, choose HTML and Images, and choose All Slices from the Slices pop-up menu. Designate the Lesson/Lesson15/15Start/Architech Pages folder as the location, and click Save.

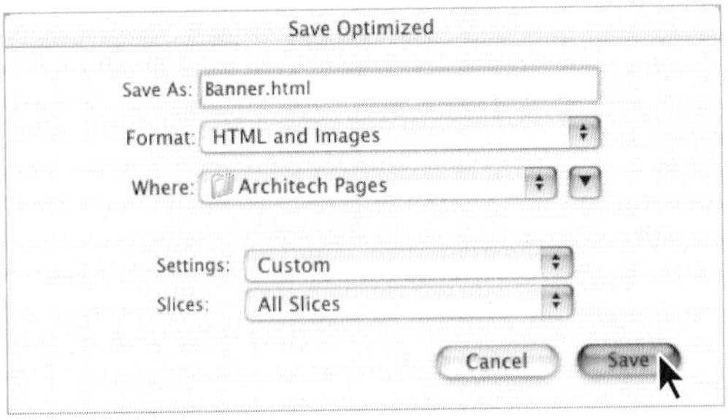

The Replace Files dialog box appears for the four button images you saved earlier in Photoshop.

3 Click Replace to save the new versions of the images.

ImageReady saves the HTML table of the entire sliced image in an HTML file and saves the optimized images for all of the auto slices, user slices, layer-based slices, and rollover states inside the Images folder. The filenames of the images are based on either the names you specified for the slices or the default names and numbers of the slices.

4 Choose Window > Documents > Team.psd to switch to the Team.psd file, and repeat steps 1 and 2, but this time enter **Team.html** as the filename for the saved optimized version.

5 To test the URL links that you assigned to the slices, start a Web browser and use it to open the Banner.html file. Again verify the behaviors of the rollover states of the various slices, including clicking the blue circle to open the linked Team page and testing the behaviors of those rollovers.

6 Close the browser, and then close the files and exit ImageReady and Photoshop.

You have finished your work on Lesson 15. To learn more about using animations with your slices and rollovers, see Lesson 16, "Creating Animated Images for the Web."

Review questions

1 What are slices?

2 Describe the five ways that image slices are created.

3 What is the advantage of linking slices together?

4 Describe the method for creating a slice with boundaries that exactly encompass a small or unusually shaped object.

5 How do you create a slice that contains no image? What purpose would such a slice serve?

6 Name two common rollover states and the mouse actions that trigger them. How many states can a slice have?

7 Describe a simple way to create rollover states for an image.

Review answers

1 Slices are rectangular areas of an image that you can define in Photoshop or ImageReady for individual Web optimization. With slices, you can create animated GIFs, URL links, and rollovers.

2 Image slices are created when you define areas in the image using the slice tool, or when you convert guides, layers, or selections into slices. They are also created automatically for areas in the sliced image that you leave undefined.

3 The advantage of linking slices together is that they'll share optimization settings—if you change the settings for one linked slice, the optimization settings automatically change for the other slices in the set.

4 Using the magic wand tool (or another appropriate selection tool) in ImageReady, select the object, and choose Slices > Create Slice from Selection.

5 Select the slice with the slice selection tool. In the Slice Options dialog box (Photoshop) or Slice palette (ImageReady), choose No Image from the Type menu. No Image slices can contain a background color, text, and HTML source code, or they can serve as a placeholder for graphics to be added later.

6 Normal and Over. Normal is active in the absence of any mouse action, and Over is triggered by moving the pointer over the slice. Selected is another state, which is triggered by clicking a slice. There are eight predefined states, counting Custom and None. But because you can create your own Custom states, there really is no limit to the number of states a slice can have.

7 Using a multilayer image, hide and reveal layers to create different versions of the image for each rollover state.

Lesson 16

16 Creating Animated Images for the Web

To add dynamic content to your Web page, use Adobe ImageReady to create animated GIF images from a single image. Compact in file size, animated GIFs display and play in most Web browsers. ImageReady provides an easy and convenient way to create imaginative animations.

In this lesson, you'll learn how to do the following:

- Open a multilayered image to use as the basis for the animation.
- Use the Layers palette and Animation palette together to create animation sequences.
- Make changes to single frames, multiple frames, and an entire animation.
- Use the Tween command to create smooth transitions between different settings for layer opacity and position.
- Preview animations in Adobe ImageReady and in a Web browser.
- Optimize the animation using the Optimize palette.

This lesson will take about 60 minutes to complete. The lesson must be done in Adobe ImageReady, not Adobe Photoshop.

If needed, remove the previous lesson folder from your hard drive, and copy the Lesson16 folder onto it. As you work on this lesson, you'll overwrite the start files. If you need to restore the start files, copy them from the *Adobe Photoshop 7.0 Classroom in a Book* CD.

Note: *Windows users need to unlock the lesson files before using them. For more information, see "Copying the Classroom in a Book files" on page 4.*

Creating animations in Adobe ImageReady

In Adobe ImageReady, you create animation from a single image using animated GIF files. An *animated GIF* is a sequence of images, or frames. Each frame varies slightly from the preceding frame, creating the illusion of movement when the frames are viewed in quick succession. You can create animation in several ways:

- By using the Duplicate Current Frame button in the Animation palette to create animation frames, and then using the Layers palette to define the image state associated with each frame.
- By using the Tween feature to quickly create new frames that warp text or vary a layer's opacity, position, or effects, to create the illusion of an element in a frame moving or fading in and out.
- By opening a multilayer Adobe Photoshop or Adobe Illustrator file for an animation, with each layer becoming a frame.

When creating an animation sequence, it's best to remain in Original image view—this saves ImageReady from having to reoptimize the image as you edit the frame contents. Animation files are output as either GIF files or QuickTime movies. You cannot create a JPEG or PNG animation.

For the Web: About working with layers in animations

Working with layers is an essential part of creating animations in ImageReady. Placing each element of an animation on its own layer enables you to change the position and appearance of the element across a series of frames.

Frame-specific changes *Some changes you make to layers affect only the active animation frame. By default, changes you make to layers using Layer palette commands and options—including layer opacity, blending mode, visibility, position, and style—are frame-specific. However, you can apply layer changes to all frames in an animation by using the unity buttons in the Layers palette.*

Global changes *Some changes affect every frame in which the layers are included. Changes you make to layer pixel values, using painting and editing tools, color- and tone-adjustment commands, filters, type, and other image-editing commands, are global.*

Each new frame starts out as a duplicate of the preceding frame—you edit the frame by adjusting its layers. You can apply layer changes to a single frame, a group of frames, or the entire animation.

–From Adobe Photoshop 7.0 online Help

Getting started

Before beginning this lesson, restore the default application settings for Adobe Photoshop and Adobe ImageReady. See "Restoring default preferences" on page 5.

In this lesson, you'll work with a set of images designed to appear on the Web page of a fresh-juice company. If you have a browser application installed on your computer, you can preview the finished animations.

Then, before you start working on the file, you'll define a new workspace especially for animation work.

1 Start your browser application.

2 From your browser, choose File > Open, and open the file Jus.html from the Lessons/Lesson16/Jus folder.

3 When you have finished viewing the file, quit the browser and start ImageReady.

4 In the ImageReady work area, close both the Color palette group and the Rollovers palette group.

5 Resize the Layers palette so that it is large enough to show at least five layers, and move it below the Optimize palette, leaving a gap between the two palettes of a half inch or so. (You'll need the space later, when you expand the Optimize palette.)

6 Choose Window > Workspace > Save Workspace, and then type **Animation_16** in the Save Workspace dialog box, and click OK.

Now you can quickly restore these palette sizes and positions by choosing Window > Workspace > Animation_16 at any time.

Animating by hiding and showing layers

In the Layers palette, any visible layer appears with an eye icon (👁) beside it.

Perhaps the simplest way to create a two-step animation is by toggling the visibility of two layers. For example, you can make an animated character alternate between different expressions or make an object move back and forth in a simple pattern.

To define an animation, you use the Layers palette in conjunction with the Animation palette. On the Animation palette, you add new frames, update existing frames, change the order of frames, and preview the animation.

Creating a simple animation

In this part of the lesson, you'll animate the shaking of a cartoon juice blender. The blender image is built in several layers. You'll create animation frames that alternate between hiding and showing two of those layers, representing different positions of the blender pitcher.

1 Choose File > Open, and open the file Blender.psd from the Lessons/Lesson16 folder on your hard drive.

In the Animation palette, a single default frame appears, showing the current state of the image. The frame is selected (outlined with a border), indicating that you can change its content by editing the image.

In the Layers palette, an eye icon (👁) appears next to Layer 1, indicating that this is the only visible layer in the image.

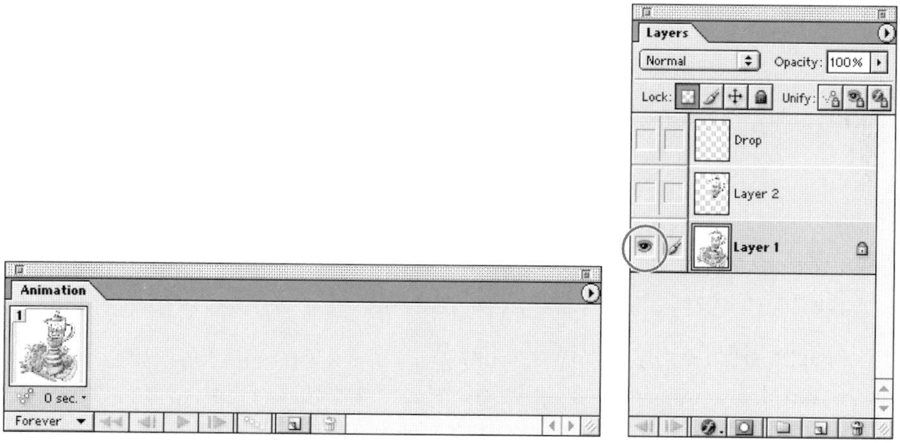

2 In the Animation palette, click the Duplicate Current Frame button (▣) to create frame 2.

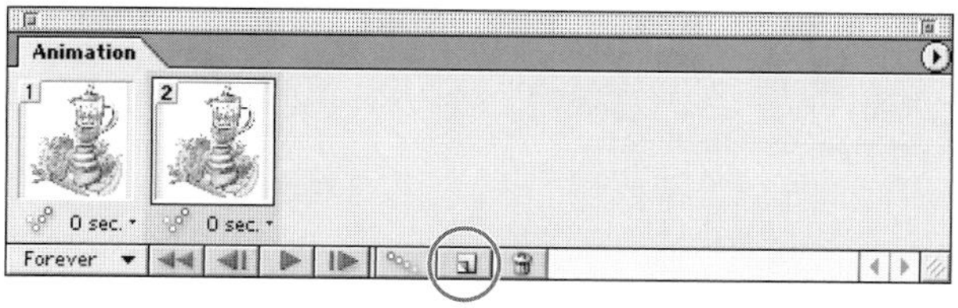

3 In the Layers palette, click the box for the Layer 2 eye icon to display this layer in the image. (Because Layer 2 sits above Layer 1 in the stacking order, it completely blocks the view of Layer 1.)

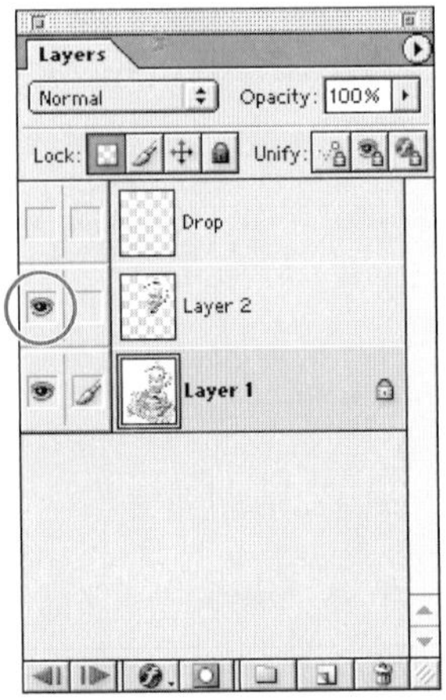

4 In the Animation palette, make sure that Forever is selected in the Looping pop-up menu in the lower left corner of the palette.

Navigating animation frames and previewing the animation

You can use a number of techniques to preview and scroll through your animation frames. Understanding the controls available on the Animation and Layers palettes is essential to mastery of the animation process.

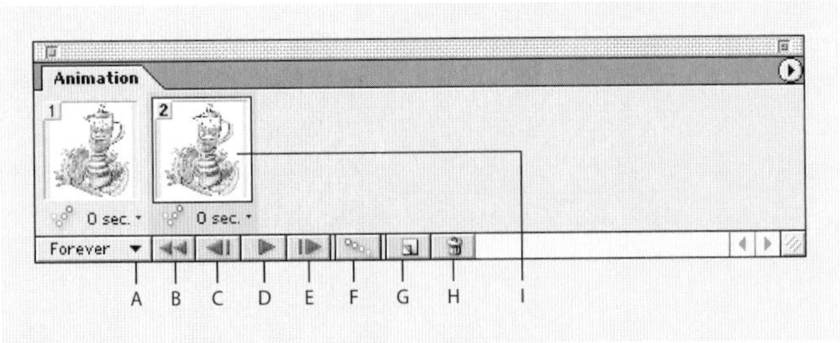

A. Looping pop-up menu B. First Frame button C. Backward button D. Play button E. Forward button F. Tween button G. Duplicate Current Frame button H. Trash I. Selected frame

1 In the Animation palette, click the first thumbnail to select that frame. In the image window and the Layers palette, only Layer 1 is visible.

2 Click the second thumbnail. Now Layer 2 is also visible.

3 In the Animation palette, click the Backward button ( ) to move to the other frame. (Try clicking the button repeatedly in quick succession, and watch the manual playback of the animation in the image window.)

4 In the Layers palette, click the Backward or Forward button in the lower left corner of the palette, and notice results similar to the previous step.

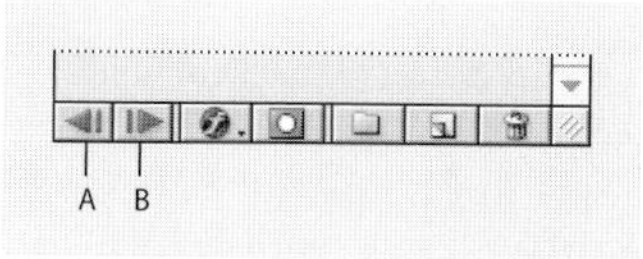

A. *Layers palette Backward button*
B. *Layers palette Forward button*

5 Click the Play button ( ) in the Animation palette to preview the animation. The Play button becomes the Stop button ( ) , which you can click to stop the playback.

Now you'll preview the animation in a Web browser.

6 Choose File > Preview In > and choose a browser application on the Preview In submenu.

You can also do this step by pressing Ctrl+Alt+P (Windows) or Command+Option+P (Mac OS) to launch a browser preview quickly, or clicking the browser button on the toolbox.

Note: *To use the Preview In command, you must have a browser application installed on your system. For more information, see "Previewing an image in a browser" in Photoshop 7.0 online Help (in ImageReady, choose Help > ImageReady Help).*

7 When you have finished previewing the animation, quit the browser window, and return to Adobe ImageReady.

8 Choose File > Save Optimized As, name the image **Blender.gif**, and click Save.

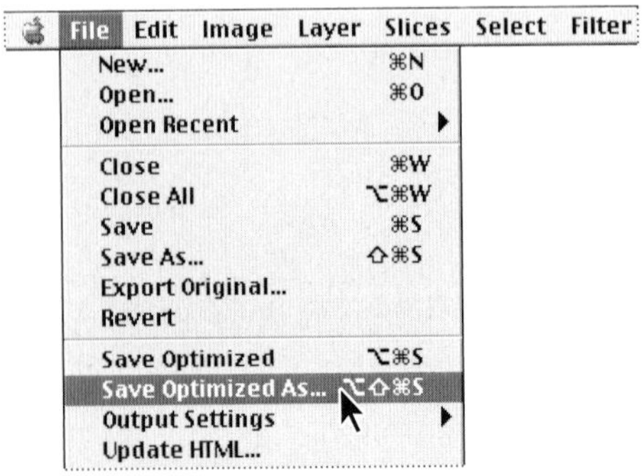

Preparing layer copies for an animation

Now you'll begin to animate a different element in the blender image, adding to the existing animation. In this procedure, you'll use the same basic technique—hiding and showing layers in different frames—to create your animation, but this time, you'll also create the different layers by copying and transforming a single layer.

Before adding layers to an image that already contains an animation, it's a good idea to create a new frame. This step helps protect your existing frames from unwanted changes.

1 In the Animation palette, select frame 2 and click the Duplicate Current Frame button (▣) to create a new frame (frame 3) that is identical to frame 2. Leave frame 3 selected.

2 In the Layers palette, make the Drop layer visible.

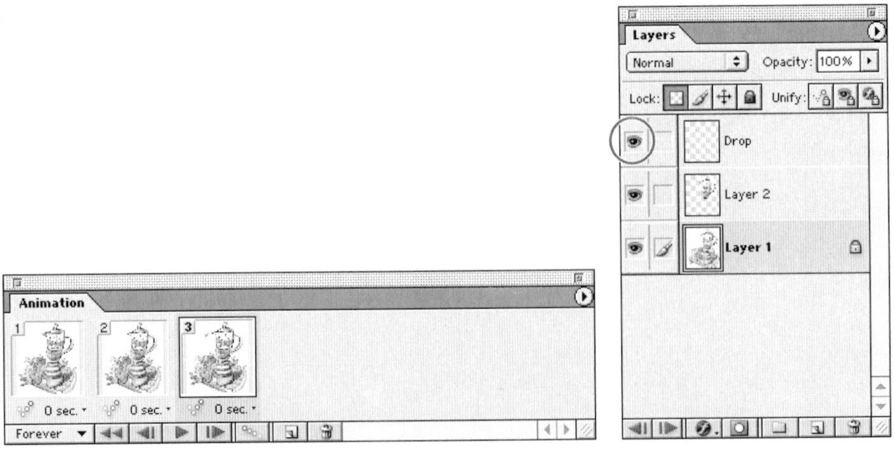

For the Web: Setting the frame disposal method

The frame disposal method specifies whether to discard the current frame before displaying the next frame. You select a disposal method when working with animations that include background transparency in order to specify whether the current frame will appear through the transparent areas of the next frame.

The Disposal Method icon indicates whether the frame is set to Do Not Dispose or Restore to Background. (No icon appears when the disposal method is set to Automatic.)

- *Choose the Automatic option to determine a disposal method for the current frame automatically, discarding the current frame if the next frame contains layer transparency. For most animations, the Automatic option yields the desired results and is, therefore, the default option.*

***Note:** Choose the Automatic disposal option when using the Redundant Pixel Removal optimization option, to enable ImageReady to preserve frames that include transparency.*

- *Choose the Do Not Dispose option to preserve the current frame as the next frame is added to the display. The current frame (and preceding frames) may show through transparent areas of the next frame. To accurately preview an animation using the Do Not Dispose option, preview the animation in a browser.*
- *Choose the Restore to Background option to discard the current frame from the display before the next frame is displayed. Only a single frame is displayed at any time (and the current frame will not appear through the transparent areas of the next frame).*

–From Adobe Photoshop 7.0 online Help

The disposal options—Restore to Background ( ) and Automatic—clear the selected frame before the next frame is played, eliminating the danger of displaying remnant pixels from the previous frame. The Do Not Dispose ( ) option retains the frames. The Automatic option is suitable for most animations. This option selects a disposal method based on the presence or absence of transparency in the next frame and discards the selected frame if the next frame contains layer transparency.

In addition to the optimization tasks applied to standard GIF files, several other tasks are performed for animated GIF files. If you optimize the animated GIF using an adaptive, perceptual, or selective palette, ImageReady generates a palette for the file based on all of the frames in the animation. A special dithering technique is applied to ensure that dither patterns are consistent across all frames, to prevent flickering during playback. Also, frames are optimized so that only areas that change from frame to frame are included, greatly reducing the file size of the animated GIF. As a result, ImageReady requires more time to optimize an animated GIF than to optimize a standard GIF.

The Bounding Box option directs ImageReady to crop each frame to preserve only the area that has changed from the preceding frame. Animation files created using this option are smaller but are incompatible with GIF editors, which do not support the option.

The Optimize by Redundant Pixel Removal option makes all pixels in a frame that are unchanged from the preceding frame transparent. When you choose the Redundant Pixel Removal option, the Disposal Method must be set to Automatic, as in step 5.

For more information, see "Optimizing Images for the Web" in Photoshop 7.0 online Help.

Using advanced layer features to create animations

In this part of the lesson, you'll learn some animation tricks that can be created through the use of advanced layer features, such as layer masks, clipping paths, and clipping groups.

Using layer masks to create animations

First, you'll use a clipping path to create the illusion of juice filling slowly to the top of the "U" in the logo text.

1 Choose File > Open, and open the file Logo2.psd from the Lessons/Lesson16 folder.

2 In the Layers palette, hide the Photo layer, and leave the Text layer and the Juice layer visible.

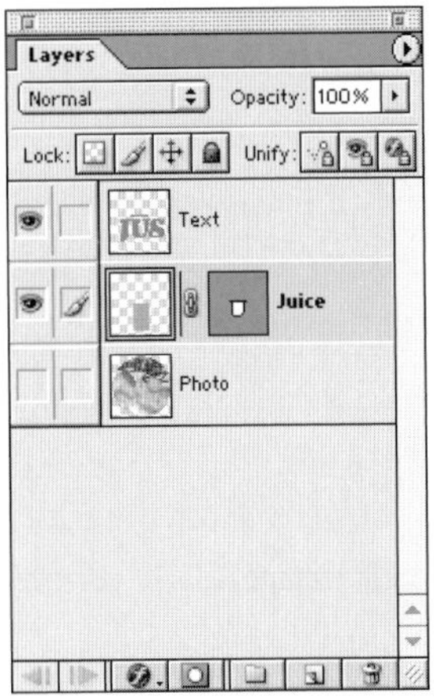

The Juice layer contains a layer mask, as indicated by the grayscale thumbnail that appears to the right of the layer thumbnail in the palette. The layer mask is U-shaped, restricting the orange juice to appearing only in the middle of the "U" in the logo text.

The orange juice currently fills to the brim of the "U." You'll move the Juice layer to define another frame that shows the "U" empty of juice.

3 In the Animation palette, click the Duplicate Current Frame button (▣) to create a second frame.

4 In the Layers palette, click the link icon (⛓) between the layer and layer mask thumbnails to turn it off.

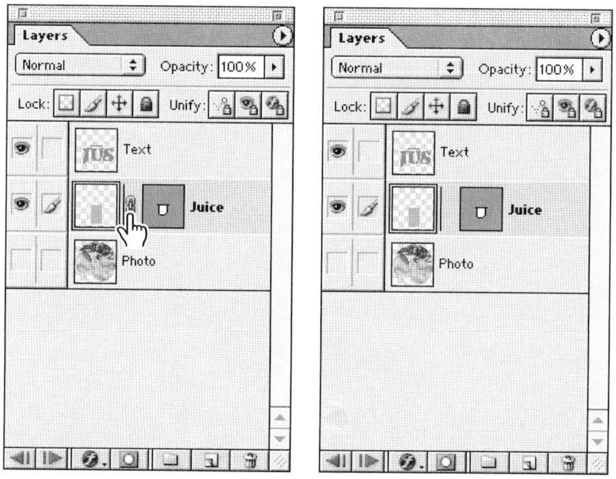

Turning off the link icon makes it possible to move the layer independently of its layer mask.

5 Select the move tool (▸✥).

6 In the Layers palette, click the layer thumbnail (on the left) for the juice layer to select it.

7 In the image, position the move tool over the orange color, and drag down to reposition the layer below the curve of the "U" so that the orange color is completely hidden.

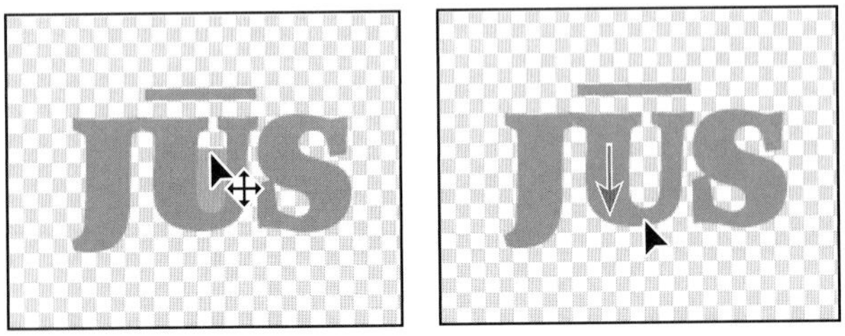

8 In the Animation palette, drag to reverse the order of frames 1 and 2.

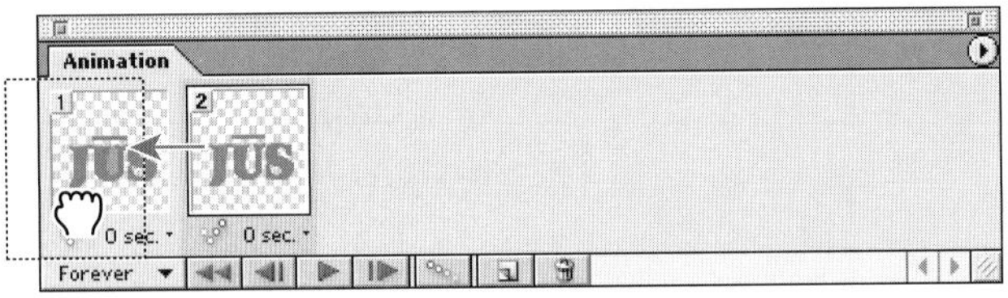

Because you have defined the two frames by repositioning a single layer, you can generate intermediate frames automatically using the Tween command.

9 Choose Tween from the Animation palette menu, and select the following options in the Tween dialog box:

- For Tween With, select Next Frame.
- For Frames to Add, enter 5.
- Under Layers, select All Layers.
- Under Parameters, select the Position check box, and then deselect the other two check boxes (Opacity and Effects).

• Click OK to close the dialog box.

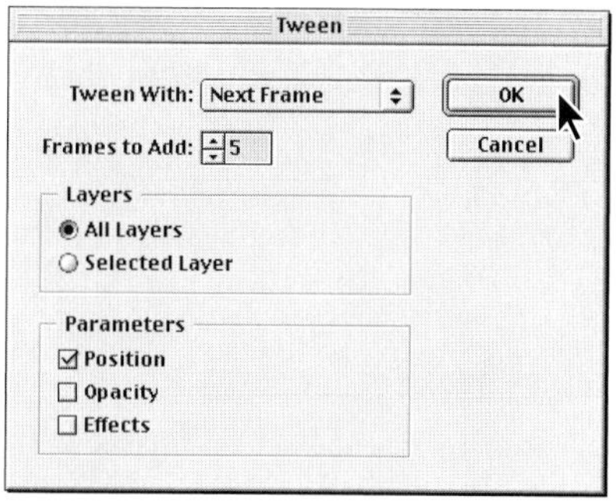

10 In the Animation palette, select frame 1; in the Layers palette, select the Photo layer and show it.

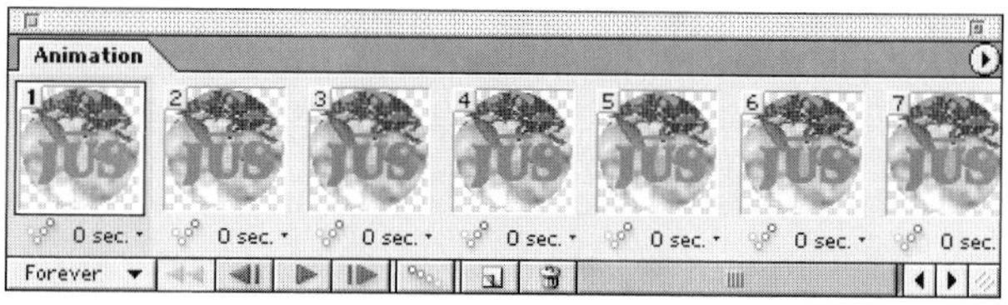

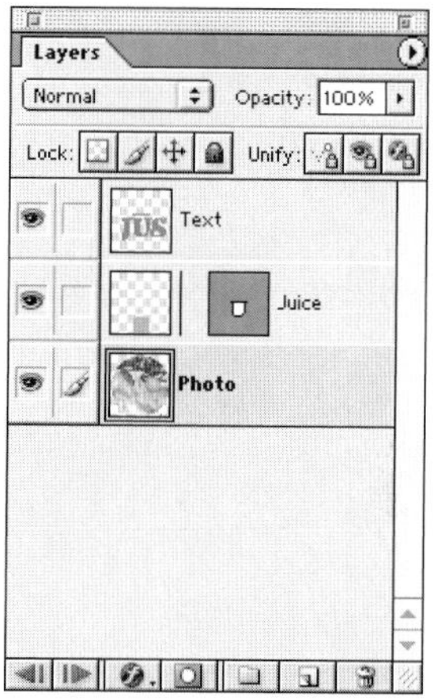

11 Click the Play button (▶) to play the animation. Click the Stop button (■) to stop the animation.

You can also choose File > Preview In, and choose a browser to play the animation, or select Preview In Default Browser in the toolbox. When you finish, return to ImageReady.

12 Choose File > Save Optimized As, name the file **Logo2.gif**, and click Save.

You are finished with your work on Logo2, so you can choose File > Close to close the original file without saving changes.

Using vector masks to create animations

Now you'll create the effect of strawberries shaking inside the logo text.

1 Choose File > Open, and open the file Logo3.psd from the Lessons/Lesson16 folder.

2 In the Layers palette, make sure that both the Strawberries and Text layers are visible.

To make the strawberries appear only through the shape of the logo text, you'll create a vector mask.

3 In the Layers palette, select the Strawberries layer. Hold down Alt (Windows) or Option (Mac OS), position the pointer over the solid line dividing two layers in the Layers palette until the pointer changes to two overlapping circles (), and click the dividing line between the layers. Or, you can do the same thing by choosing Layer > Group with Previous.

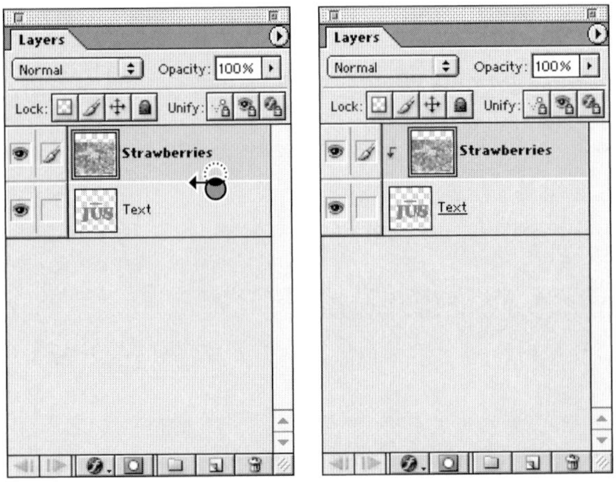

Notice that the strawberries now appear masked by the logo text. The thumbnail for the Strawberries layer is indented with a downward-pointing arrow (), indicating that the layer is grouped with the layer that precedes it.

4 In the Animation palette, click the Duplicate Current Frame button.

For the second animation frame, you'll reposition the Strawberries layer.

5 In the Layers palette, make sure that the Strawberries layer is selected. Then in the toolbox, select the move tool ().

6 In the image window, drag the Strawberries layer slightly to the right, or use the arrow keys to move the layer.

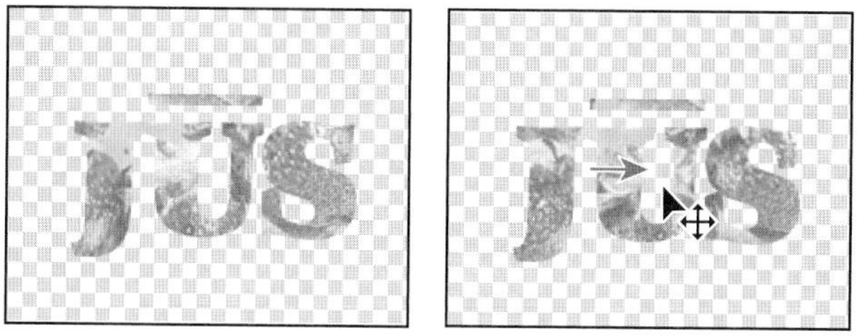

7 Click the Play button (▶) to play the animation. The strawberries move from side to side inside the logo. Click the Stop button (■) to stop the animation.

8 Choose File > Save Optimized As, name the file **Logo3.gif**, and click Save. ImageReady saves the animation as a GIF file using the current settings in the Optimize palette.

You can also preview the animation in the browser, using the methods you've already learned in this lesson. When you finish, return to ImageReady.

9 Choose File > Close to close the original file without saving changes.

You are now finished with your work on Lesson 16.

On your own: Creating the remaining animations

You've already learned all the essentials you need to know for creating the other parts of the JUS home-page animations.

Use the six-layered Fruit.psd file in your Lessons/Lesson16 folder to create a montage sequence in which six different images of fruit appear and replace each other.

- The simplest way to create the frames you need is to use the Animation palette menu and choose Make Frames From Layers. This creates your six basic frames with the eye icons for each layer set just the way you want them to be.
- You can smooth out the transitions between frames by changing the Frame Time Delay value in the pop-up menu below the frames.
- You can smooth the transitions out further by adding duplicate frames between the existing frames, reducing the opacity, and adding Tween frames.

- You can create another transformation animation by duplicating one of the images repeatedly and then using the Edit > Transform > Numeric command to change the scale of each duplicate layer by a specific amount, such as multiples of 20%.

Use the Logo4.psd file to practice creating a transition between image states. In this file, you'll make the photograph of the orange branch (the Photo layer) dissolve into the painting of the same branch (the Illustration layer).

- Click the appropriate boxes in the Layers palette to define a starting state in which the Photo and the (blocked) Illustration layers are visible.
- Create a duplicate frame and hide the Photo layer by removing its eye icon in the Layers palette.
- Use the Tween command on the Animation palette menu to create a 4-frame transition for All Layers between the selected frame and the Previous Frame.
- Use the Looping pop-up in the Animation palette to change the looping from Forever to Once.
- Use the File > Save Optimized As command to save the image in GIF format.

Review questions

1 Describe a simple way to create animation.

2 In what instances can you tween animation frames? When can't you tween frames?

3 How do you optimize an animation?

4 What does optimizing an animation accomplish?

5 What is frame disposal? Which frame-disposal method should you generally use?

6 How do you edit an existing animation frame?

7 What file formats can you use for animations?

Review answers

1 A simple way to create animation is to start with a layered Photoshop file. Use the Duplicate Current Frame button in the Animation palette to create a new frame, and then use the Layers palette to alter the position, opacity, or effects of one of the selected frames. Then, create intermediate frames between the selection and the new frame either manually, by using the Duplicate Current Frame button or automatically, by using the Tween command.

2 You can instruct Adobe ImageReady to tween intermediate frames between any two frames, to change layer opacity or position between two frames, or to add new layers to a sequence of frames. You cannot tween discontiguous frames.

3 Click the Show Options button in the Optimize palette, and then choose File > Save Optimized to optimize animations. Choose Optimize Animation from the Animation palette menu to perform optimization tasks specific to animation files, including removing redundant pixels and cropping frames according to the bounding box.

4 In addition to the optimization tasks applied to standard GIF files, ImageReady generates an adaptive, perceptual, or selective palette for the file based on all frames in the animation if you selected one of those palettes. ImageReady applies a special dithering technique to ensure that dither patterns are consistent across all frames, to prevent flickering during playback. The application also optimizes frames so that only areas that change from frame to frame are included, greatly reducing the file size of the animated GIF.

5 A frame-disposal method specifies whether to discard the selected frame before displaying the next frame when an animation includes background transparency. This option determines whether the selected frame will appear through the transparent areas of the next frame. Generally, the Automatic option is suitable for most animations. This option selects a disposal method based on the presence or absence of transparency in the next frame, and discards the selected frame if the next frame contains layer transparency.

6 To edit an existing animation frame, you first select the frame, either by clicking the frame thumbnail in the Animation palette or by navigating to the desired frame using the First Frame, Backward, or Forward buttons in the Animation palette or Layers palette. Then edit the layers in the image to update the contents of the selected frame.

7 Files for animations must be saved in GIF format or as a QuickTime movie. You cannot create animations as JPEG or PNG files.

Lesson 17

17 Setting Up Your Monitor for Color Management

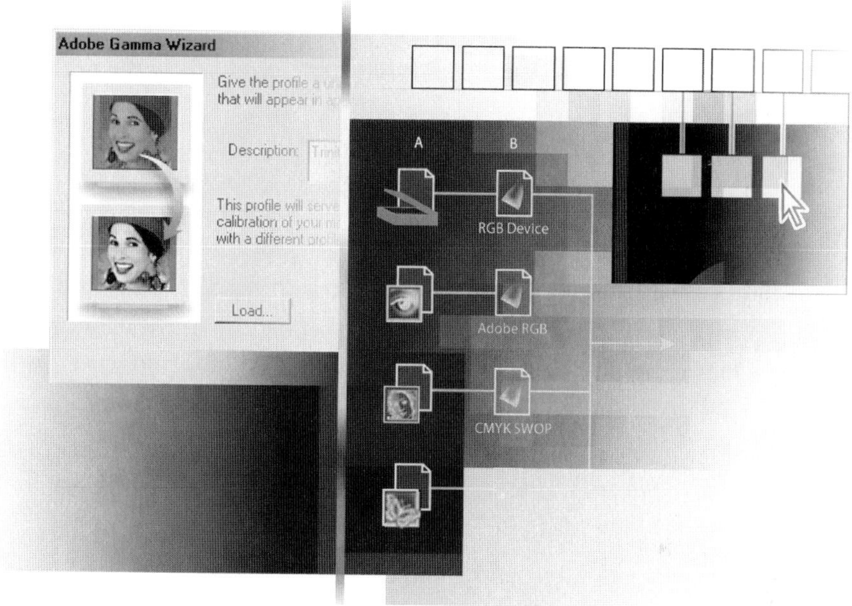

The most basic requirement for color management is to calibrate your monitor and create an ICC profile for it. Applications that support color management will use your monitor's ICC profile to display color graphics consistently. If you don't have a hardware-based calibration and profiling utility, you can get reasonably accurate results using Adobe Gamma.

In this lesson, you'll learn how to do the following:

- Examine the principles associated with color management.
- Calibrate your monitor using Adobe Gamma.
- Create an ICC profile for your monitor using Adobe Gamma.

This lesson will take about 45 minutes to complete.

Note: *You can skip this lesson if you have already calibrated your monitor using a hardware-based tool or an ICC-compliant calibration tool , and if you haven't changed your video card or monitor settings.*

Getting started

In this lesson, you'll learn some basic color-management concepts and terminology. In addition, you'll calibrate your monitor to a known color condition, and then create an ICC profile that describes your monitor's specific color characteristics. For information about setting up RGB and CMYK color spaces in Photoshop, see Lesson 18, "Producing and Printing Consistent Color."

Color management: An overview

Although all color gamuts overlap, they don't match exactly, which is why some colors on your monitor can't be reproduced in print. The colors that can't be reproduced in print are called *out-of-gamut* colors, because they are outside the spectrum of printable colors. For example, you can create a large percentage of colors in the visible spectrum using programs such as Photoshop, Illustrator, and InDesign, but you can reproduce only a subset of those colors on a desktop printer. The printer has a smaller *color space* or *gamut* (the range of colors that can be displayed or printed) than the application that created the color.

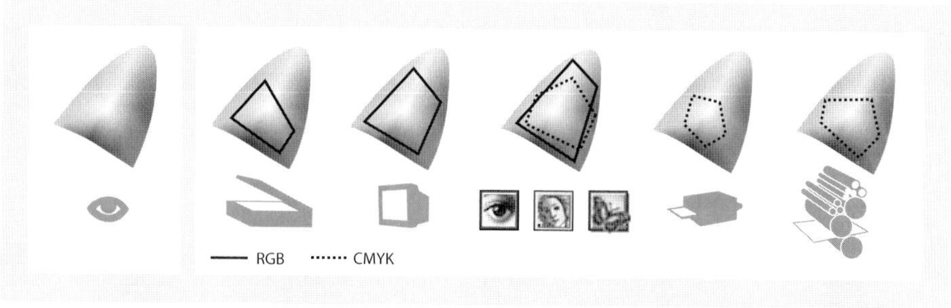

Visible spectrum containing millions of colors (far left) compared with color gamuts of various devices and documents

To compensate for these differences and to ensure the closest match between on-screen colors and printed colors, applications use a color management system (CMS). Using a color management engine, the CMS translates colors from the color space of one device into a device-independent color space, such as CIE (Commission Internationale d'Eclairage) LAB. From the device-independent color space, the CMS fits that color information to another device's color space by a process called *color mapping*, or *gamut mapping*. The CMS makes any adjustments necessary to represent the color consistently among devices.

A CMS uses three components to map colors across devices:

- A device-independent (or reference) color space.
- ICC profiles that define the color characteristics of particular devices and documents.
- A color management engine that translates colors from one device's color space to another according to a *rendering intent*, or translation method.

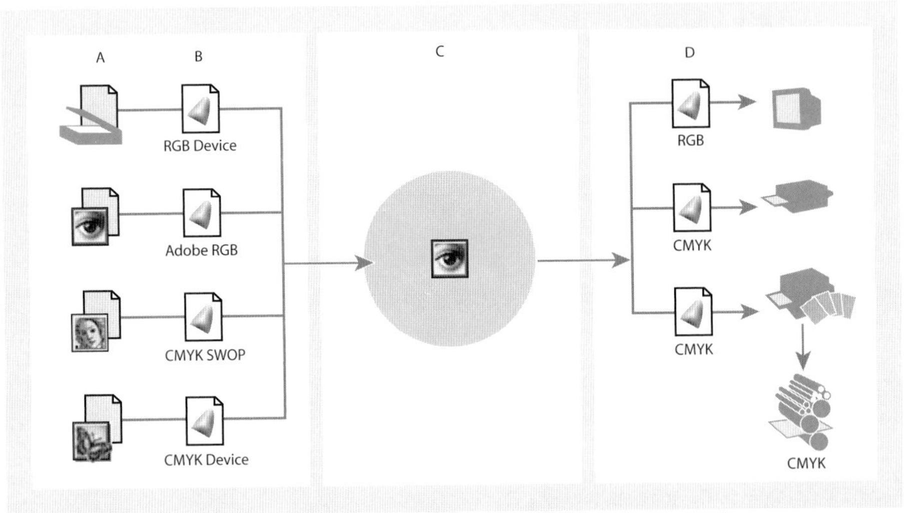

***A.** Scanners and software applications create color documents. Users choose document's working color space.* ***B.** ICC source profiles describe document color spaces.* ***C.** A color management engine uses ICC source profiles to map document colors to a device-independent color space through supporting applications.* ***D.** The color management engine maps document colors from the device-independent color space to output-device color spaces using destination profiles.*

About the device-independent color space

To successfully compare gamuts and make adjustments, a color management system must use a reference color space—an objective way of defining color. Most CMSs use the CIE LAB color model, which exists independently of any device and is big enough to reproduce any color visible to the human eye. For this reason, CIE LAB is considered *device-independent*.

About ICC profiles

An *ICC profile* describes how a particular device or standard reproduces color using a cross-platform standard defined by the International Color Consortium (ICC). ICC profiles ensure that images appear correctly in any ICC-compliant applications and on color devices. This is accomplished by embedding the profile information in the original file or assigning the profile in your application.

At a minimum, you must have one *source profile* for the device (scanner or digital camera, for example) or standard (SWOP or Adobe RGB, for example) used to create the color, and one *destination profile* for the device (monitor or contract proofing, for example) or standard (SWOP or TOYO, for example) that you will use to reproduce the color.

About color management engines

Sometimes called the color matching module (CMM), the color management engine interprets ICC profiles. Acting as a translator, the color management engine converts the out-of-gamut colors from the source device to the range of colors that can be produced by the destination device. The color management engine may be included with the CMS or may be a separate part of the operating system.

Translating to a gamut—particularly a smaller gamut—usually involves a compromise, so multiple translation methods are available. For example, a color translation method that preserves correct relationships among colors in a photograph will usually alter the colors in a logo. Color management engines provide a choice of translation methods, known as *rendering intents*, so that you can apply a method appropriate to the intended use of a color graphic. Examples of common rendering intents include *Perceptual (Images)* for preserving color relationships the way the eye does, *Saturation (Graphics)* for preserving vivid colors at the expense of color accuracy, and *Relative* and *Absolute Colorimetric* for preserving color accuracy at the expense of color relationships.

Color management resources

You can find additional information on color management on the Web and in print. Here are a few resources:

• On the Adobe Web site (www.adobe.com), search for **color management** or go directly to http://www.adobe.com/support/techguides/color/.

• On the Apple® Web site (www.apple.com), search for **ColorSync**.

• On the LinoColor Web site (www.linocolor.com), open the *Color Manager Manual.*

• On the Agfa Web site (www.agfa.com), search for the publication *The Secrets of Color Management.*

• On the ColorBlind Web site (www.color.com), click Color Resources.

• At your local library or bookstore, look for *GATF Practical Guide to Color Management*, by Richard Adams and Joshua Weisberg (May 1998); ISBN 0883622025.

For information about setting up color management in Photoshop, see Photoshop 7.0 online Help.

Calibrating and characterizing your monitor

The first requirement for color management is to calibrate your monitor and create an accurate ICC profile for it. Although this doesn't address your entire workflow, at least it ensures that your monitor displays colors as precisely as it can. *Calibration* is the process of setting your monitor, or any device, to known color conditions. *Characterization*, or profiling, is the process of creating an ICC profile that describes the unique color characteristics of your device or standard. Always calibrate your monitor, or any device, before creating a profile for it; otherwise, the profile is only valid for the current state of the device.

Monitor adjustment for Mac OS

Mac OS 8.x and Mac OS 9.x users can get good results from the Monitor Calibration Assistant built into their systems in the Monitors control panel. In Mac OS 10, use the Display Calibration Assistant in the System Preferences. The resulting ICC profile uses the calibration settings to describe precisely how your monitor reproduces color.

Before you begin calibrating your monitor, be sure to remove any old Adobe Gamma control panels from your system. Then, simply follow the on-screen instructions, and you're finished with this lesson.

Monitor adjustment on Windows

Although monitor calibration and characterization are best done with specialized software and hardware, you can get reasonably accurate results with the newest version of the Adobe Gamma utility for Windows, included with your Adobe product. If you are satisfied with your existing monitor profile, you do not need to use Adobe Gamma because Adobe Gamma will overwrite those settings.

You may find it helpful to have your monitor's user guide handy while using Adobe Gamma.

Preparing to calibrate your monitor

Before you begin to make monitor adjustments, it's important that the conditions be right for the procedure and that your computer is cleared of settings or old utilities that might conflict with the process.

1 If you have any older versions of Adobe Gamma, delete them because they are obsolete. Use the latest Adobe Gamma utility instead. (Windows only): If the Monitor Setup Utility (included with PageMaker 6.x) is on your system, delete it because it, too, is now obsolete.

2 Make sure your monitor has been turned on for at least a half hour. This gives it sufficient time to warm up for a more accurate color reading.

3 Set the room lighting to the level you plan to maintain consistently.

4 Remove colorful background patterns on your monitor desktop. Busy or bright patterns surrounding a document interfere with accurate color perception. Set your desktop to display neutral grays only, using RGB values of 128. For more information, see the manual for your operating system.

5 If your monitor has digital controls for choosing the white point of your monitor from a range of preset values, set those controls before starting. If you set them after you begin the calibration process, you'll need to begin the process again. Later, you'll set the white point to match your monitor's current setting.

6 On the Windows desktop, choose Start > Settings > Control Panel.

7 Double-click Display, and then click the Settings tab and make sure that your monitor is displaying thousands of colors or more.

Calibrating the monitor

On Windows, you'll use the Adobe Gamma utility to calibrate and characterize your monitor. The resulting ICC profile uses the calibration settings to describe precisely how your monitor reproduces color. In this section, you'll load an existing monitor profile as a starting point for calibrating your monitor.

Note: *Adobe Gamma can characterize, but not calibrate, monitors used with Windows NT®. Its ability to calibrate settings in Windows 98 depends on the video card and video-driver software. In such cases, some calibration options documented here may not be available. For example, if you're only characterizing your monitor, you'll choose the default white point and gamma, but not the target calibration settings.*

1 If the Control Panel is not open, choose Start > Settings > Control Panel. Then double-click Adobe Gamma.

Note: *If you are running Windows XP and do not see the Adobe Gamma icon in the Control Panel, try changing the View menu selection to Classic View.*

You can use either the control panel or a step-by-step wizard to make all the adjustments necessary for calibrating your monitor. In this lesson, you will use the Adobe Gamma control panel. At any time while working in the Adobe Gamma control panel, you can click the Wizard (Windows) or Assistant (Mac OS) button to switch to the wizard for instructions that guide you through the same settings as in the control panel, one option at a time.

2 In the Adobe Gamma wizard, click the Control Panel option, and click Next.

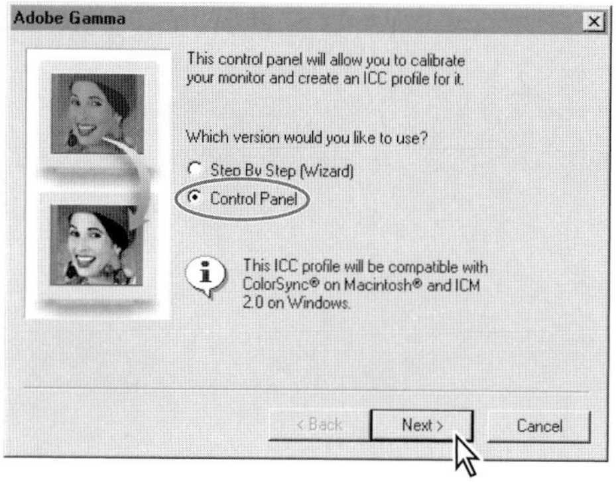

The next step is to load an ICC monitor profile that describes your monitor. This profile serves as a starting point for the calibration process by supplying some preset values. You'll adjust these values in Adobe Gamma to characterize the profile to match your monitor's particular characteristics.

3 Do one of the following:

- If your monitor is listed in the Description area at the top of the control panel, select it.
- Click the Load button for a list of other available profiles, and then locate and open the monitor ICC profile that most closely matches your monitor. To see the full name of an ICC profile at the bottom of the Open Monitor Profile dialog box, select a file. (Windows profile filenames have the .icm extension, which you may not see if the extension display is off.) Make your choice, and click Open.

- Leave the generic Adobe monitor profile selected in the Description area.

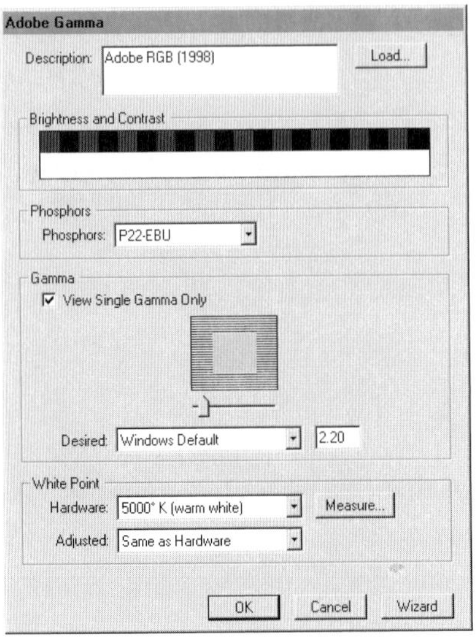

Adobe Gamma utility control panel

Setting the optimal brightness and contrast

Now you'll adjust the monitor's overall level and range of display intensity. These controls work just as they do on a television. Adjusting the monitor's brightness and contrast enables the most accurate screen representation for the gamma adjustment that follows.

1 With Adobe Gamma running, set the contrast control on your monitor to its highest setting. On many monitors, this control is shown next to a contrast icon (◐).

2 Adjust the brightness control on your monitor—located next to a brightness icon (☼) on many monitors—as you watch the alternating pattern of black and gray squares across the top half of the Brightness and Contrast rectangle in Adobe Gamma. Make the gray squares in the top bar as dark as possible without matching the black squares, while keeping the bottom area a bright white. (If you can't see a difference between the black and gray squares while keeping the bottom area white, your monitor's screen phosphors may be fading.)

***A.** Gray squares too light **B.** Gray squares too dark and white area too gray **C.** Gray squares and white area correctly adjusted*

Do not adjust the brightness and contrast controls on your monitor again unless you are about to update the monitor profile. Adjusting the controls invalidates the monitor profile. You can tape the hardware controls in place if necessary.

Selecting phosphor data

The chemical phosphors in your monitor determine the range of colors you see on your screen.

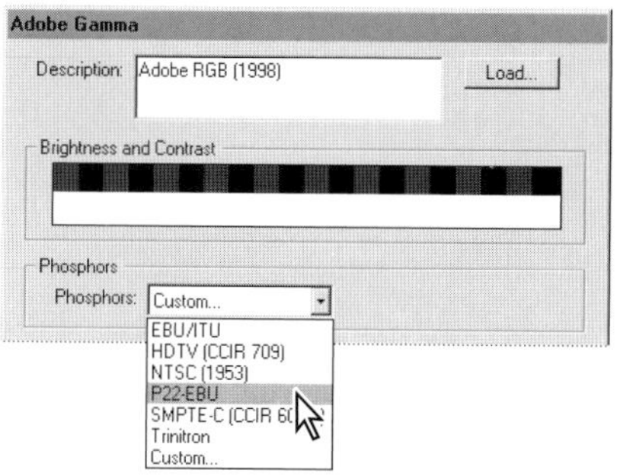

Do one of the following from the Phosphors menu:

• Choose the exact phosphor type used by the monitor you are calibrating. The two most common phosphor types are EBU/ITU and Trinitron.

• If the correct type is not listed but you were provided with chromaticity coordinates with your monitor, choose Custom, and enter the red, green, and blue chromaticity coordinates of the monitor's phosphors.

• If you're not sure which phosphors your monitor uses, see the monitor's documentation; contact the manufacturer; or use a color-measuring instrument such as a colorimeter or spectrophotometer to determine them.

Setting the midtones

The gamma setting defines midtone brightness. You can adjust the gamma based on a single combined gamma reading (the View Single Gamma Only option). Or you can adjust the midtones individually for red, green, and blue. The second method produces a more accurate setting, so you will use that method here.

For the Gamma option in the Adobe Gamma utility, deselect the View Single Gamma Only option. Drag the slider under each box until the shape in the center blends in with the background as much as possible. It may help to squint or move back from the monitor.

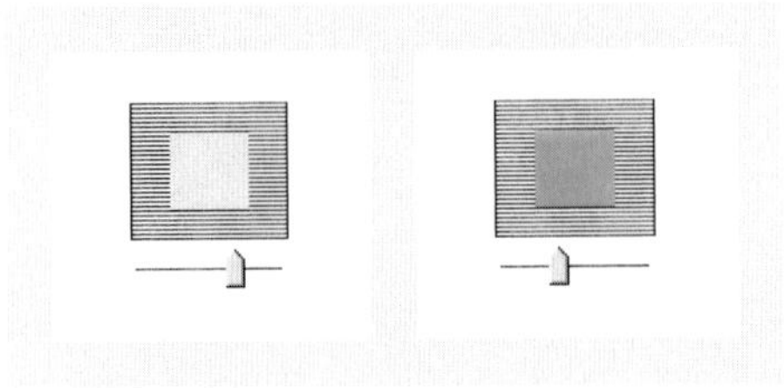

Single gamma not calibrated (left), and calibrated (right)

Make adjustments carefully and in small increments; imprecise adjustments can result in a color cast not visible until you print.

Selecting a target gamma

You may also have an option for specifying a separate gamma for viewing graphics.

Note: *This option is not available in Windows NT, due to its hardware protection shield that prevents Adobe Gamma from communicating with the computer's video card.*

If you have this option, choose one of the following from the Desired menu:

- Windows Default for Windows systems. Leave the setting at 2.2.
- Macintosh Default for Mac OS computers. Leave the setting at 1.8.

Setting the monitor's white point

Now you'll adjust the hardware *white point*, the whitest white that a monitor is capable of displaying. The white point is a measurement of color temperature in Kelvin and determines whether you are using a warm or cool white.

First, you'll make sure that the white-point setting matches the white point of your monitor. Do one of the following:

- If you know the white point of your monitor in its current state, you can select it from the Hardware menu in the White Point section. If your monitor is new, select 9300 Kelvin, the default white point of most monitors and televisions.

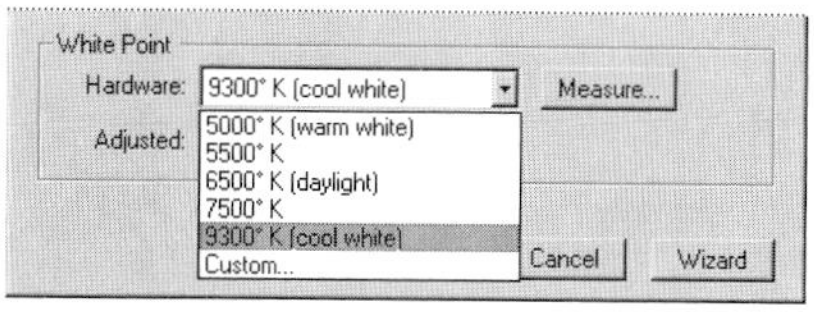

- If you started from a manufacturer's profile for your monitor, you can use the default value. However, the older your monitor, the less likely it is that its white point still matches the manufacturer's profile.
- If your monitor is equipped with digital controls for setting the white point, and you already set those controls before starting Adobe Gamma, make sure that the Hardware menu matches your monitor's current setting. Remember, though, that if you adjust these hardware controls at this point in the calibration process, you'll need to start over, beginning with the procedure in "Setting the optimal brightness and contrast" on page 538.

- If you don't know the white point and don't know the appropriate values, you can use the Measure option to visually estimate it. If you choose this option, continue to step 1.

To get a precise value, you need to measure the white point with a desktop colorimeter or spectrophotometer and enter that value directly using the Custom option.

If you were unable to choose a hardware setting as described, try the following experiment:

1 For best results, turn off all lights in the room.

2 Click Measure, and then click OK (Windows) or Next (Mac OS). Three squares appear.

The goal here is to make the center square as neutral gray as possible. You'll train your eyes to see the contrasts between the extreme cooler (blue) white and warmer (yellow) white, and then adjust the colors in the squares to find the most neutral gray between them.

3 Click the left square several times until it disappears, leaving the middle and right squares. Study the contrast between the bluish square on the right and the center square.

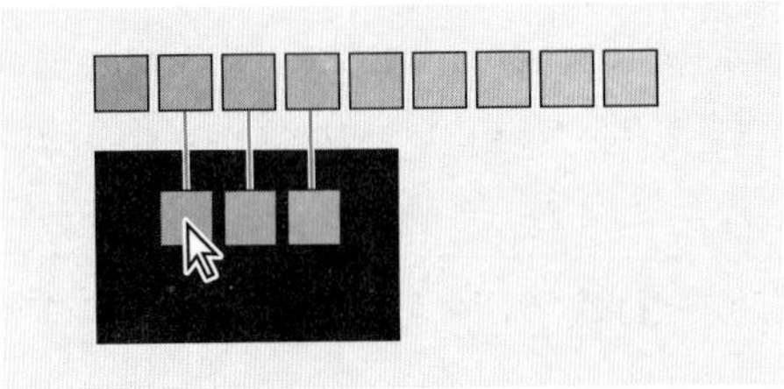

Clicking on the left square will reset all the squares a shade cooler.

4 Click the right square several times until it disappears, and study the contrast between the yellowish square on the left and the center square.

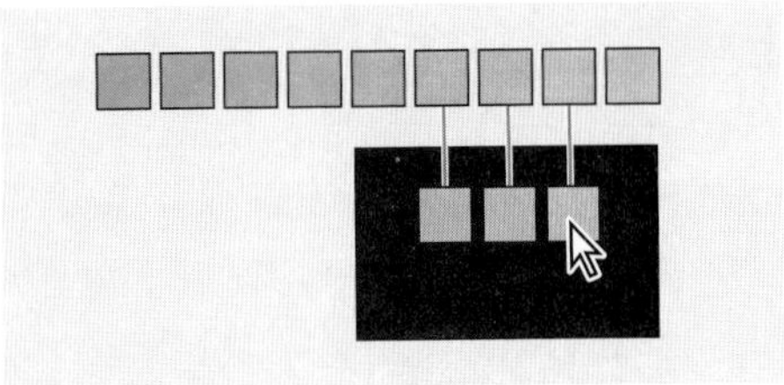

Clicking on the right square will reset all the squares a shade warmer.

5 Click the left or right square until the center square is a neutral gray. When complete, commit the changes by clicking the center square.

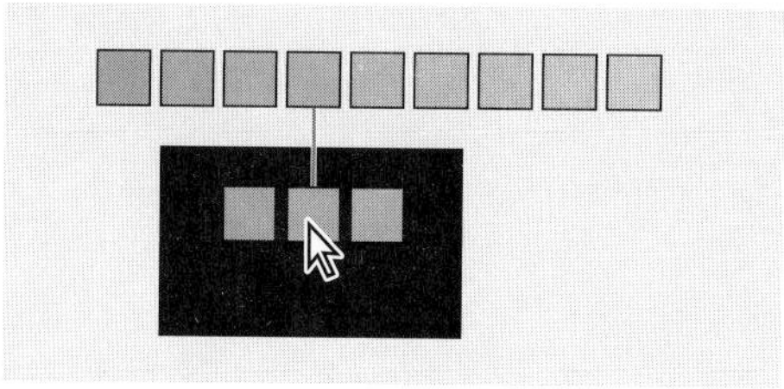

For a color illustration of adjusting the white point, see figure 17-1 of the color section.

Setting an adjusted white point

This option, when available, sets a working white point for monitor display, if that value differs from the hardware white point. For example, if your hardware white point is 6500 Kelvin (daylight), but you want to edit an image at 5000 Kelvin (warm white) because that most closely represents the environment in which the image will be viewed, you can set your adjusted white point to 5000 Kelvin. Adobe Gamma will change the monitor display accordingly.

Do one of the following to specify a separate white point for viewing graphics:

- To use the current white point of your monitor, choose Same as Hardware from the Adjusted menu.
- To specify your monitor's white point to a target value other than the Hardware value, choose the gamma setting you want from the Adjusted menu

Saving the monitor profile

Now that you have adjusted all the settings for your monitor, you will save the ICC profile you have created. Applications that support color management will use this monitor profile to display color graphics.

1 In Adobe Gamma, rename the monitor profile by editing the text in the Description text box. (We named the profile **My Monitor**.) When you name the monitor here, it appears by default when you start Adobe Gamma.

2 Click OK.

3 In the Save As dialog box, type the filename again, and save the file in the Color folder.

Adobe Gamma makes the new monitor profile the default. You can use this profile in any application that supports ICC-compliant color management.

Review questions

1 What does the color management engine do?

2 What is calibration?

3 What is characterization?

Review answers

1 The color management engine translates colors from the color space of one device to another device's color space by a process called color mapping.

2 Calibration is the process of setting a device to known color conditions.

3 Characterization, or profiling, is the process of creating an ICC profile that describes the unique color characteristics of a particular device. You should always calibrate a device before creating a profile for it.

Lesson 18

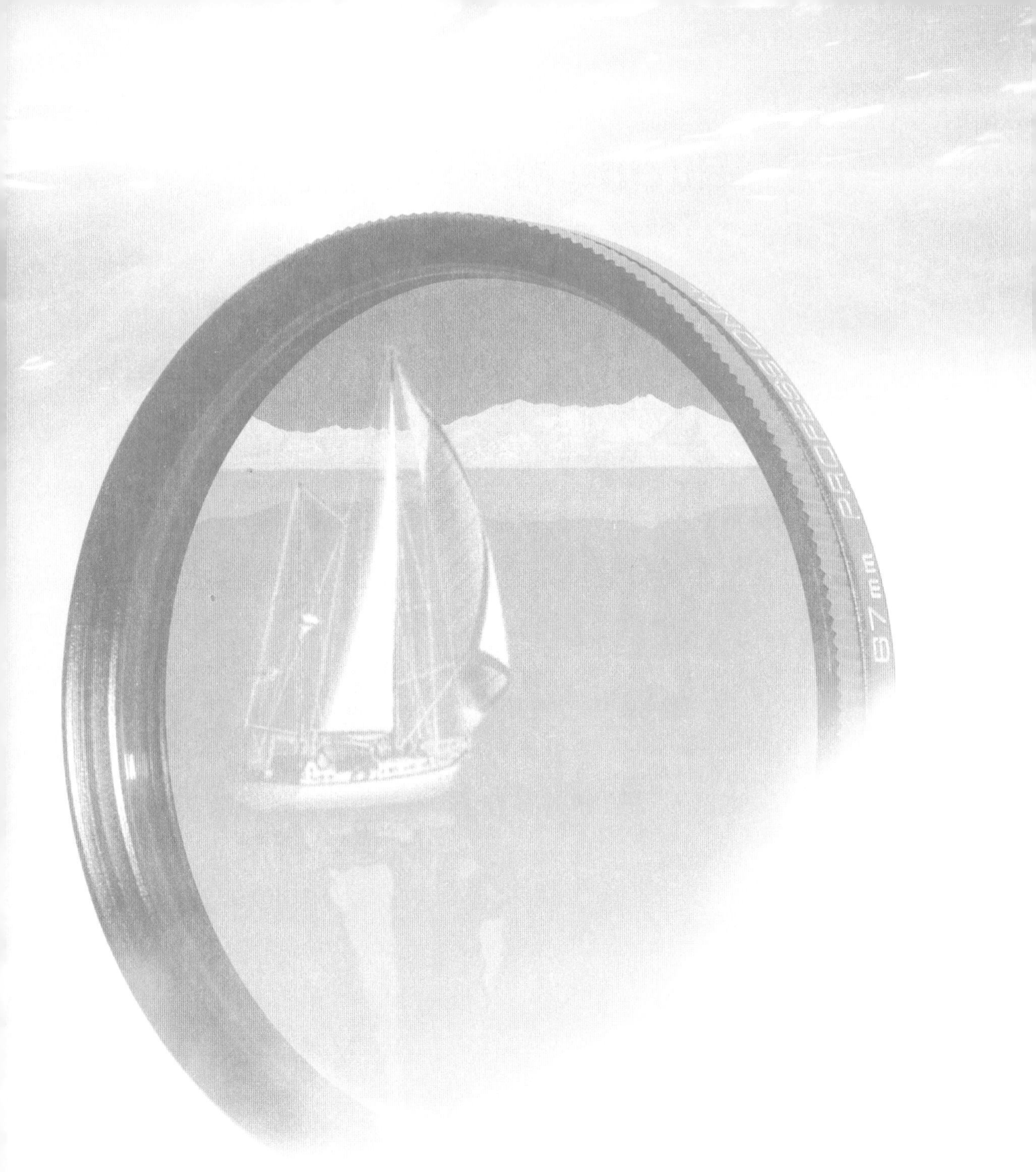
67mm

18 Producing and Printing Consistent Color

To produce consistent color, you define the color space in which to edit and display RGB images, and in which to edit, display, and print CMYK images. This helps ensure a close match between on-screen and printed colors.

In this lesson, you'll learn how to do the following:

- Define RGB, grayscale, and CMYK color spaces for displaying, editing, and printing images.
- Prepare an image for printing on a PostScript® CMYK printer.
- Proof an image for printing.
- Create a color separation, the process by which the colors in an RGB image are distributed to the four process-ink colors: cyan, magenta, yellow, and black.
- Understand how images are prepared for printing on presses.

This lesson will take about 60 minutes to complete. The lesson is designed to be done in Adobe Photoshop.

If needed, remove the previous lesson folder from your hard drive, and copy the Lesson18 folder onto it. As you work on this lesson, you'll overwrite the start files. If you need to restore the start files, copy them from the *Adobe Photoshop 7.0 Classroom in a Book* CD.

Note: *Windows users need to unlock the lesson files before using them. For more information, see "Copying the Classroom in a Book files" on page 4.*

Reproducing colors

Colors on a monitor are displayed using combinations of red, green, and blue light (called RGB), while printed colors are typically created using a combination of four ink colors—cyan, magenta, yellow, and black (called CMYK). These four inks are called *process colors* because they are the standard inks used in the four-color printing process.

RGB image with red, green, and blue channels

CMYK image with cyan, magenta, yellow, and black channels

For color samples of channels in both RGB and CMYK images, see figure 18-1 and figure 18-2 in the color section.

Because the RGB and CMYK color models use very different methods to display colors, they each reproduce a different *gamut*, or range of colors. For example, because RGB uses light to produce color, its gamut includes neon colors, such as those you'd see in a neon sign. In contrast, printing inks excel at reproducing certain colors that can lie outside of the RGB gamut, such as some pastels and pure black. For an illustration of the RGB and CMYK gamuts and color models, see figure 18-3, 18-4, and 18-5 in the color section.

But not all RGB and CMYK gamuts are alike. Each model of monitor and printer is different, and so each displays a slightly different gamut. For example, one brand of monitor may produce slightly brighter blues than another. The *color space* for a device is defined by the gamut it can reproduce.

RGB model

A large percentage of the visible spectrum can be represented by mixing red, green, and blue (RGB) colored light in various proportions and intensities. Where the colors overlap, they create cyan, magenta, yellow, and white.

Because the RGB colors combine to create white, they are also called additive colors. *Adding all colors together creates white—that is, all light is transmitted back to the eye. Additive colors are used for lighting, video, and monitors. Your monitor, for example, creates color by emitting light through red, green, and blue phosphors.*

CMYK model

The CMYK model is based on the light-absorbing quality of ink printed on paper. As white light strikes translucent inks, part of the spectrum is absorbed while other parts are reflected back to your eyes.

In theory, pure cyan (C), magenta (M), and yellow (Y) pigments should combine to absorb all color and produce black. For this reason these colors are called subtractive colors. *Because all printing inks contain some impurities, these three inks actually produce a muddy brown and must be combined with black (K) ink to produce a true black. (K is used instead of B to avoid confusion with blue.) Combining these inks to reproduce color is called* four-color process printing.

–From Adobe Photoshop 7.0 online Help

An ICC profile is a description of a device's color space, such as the CMYK color space of a particular printer. In this lesson, you'll choose which RGB and CMYK ICC profiles to use. Once you specify the profiles, Photoshop can embed them into your image files. Photoshop (and any other application that can use ICC profiles) can then interpret the ICC profile in the image file to automatically manage color for that image. For general information about color management and about preparing your monitor, see Lesson 17, "Setting Up Your Monitor for Color Management".

For information on embedding ICC profiles, see Photoshop 7.0 online Help.

Getting started

Before beginning this lesson, restore the default application settings for Adobe Photoshop. See "Restoring default preferences" on page 5.

You also need to make sure that you have calibrated your monitor as described in Lesson 17. If your monitor does not display colors accurately, the color adjustments you make to an image displayed on that monitor may be wrong.

Specifying color management settings

In the first part of this lesson, you'll learn how to set up a color-managed workflow. To help you with this, the Color Settings dialog box in Photoshop contains most of the color management controls you need. (This dialog box appears the first time you start Photoshop.)

For instance, Photoshop is set up for RGB as part of a Web/online workflow by default. However, if you're preparing artwork for print production, you would likely change the settings to be more appropriate for images that will be printed on paper rather than displayed on a screen.

You'll begin this lesson by starting Photoshop and creating customized color settings.

1 Start Adobe Photoshop.

If you used another application to modify and save the current color-settings file, a dialog box appears, prompting you to synchronize the common color settings when you start Photoshop or reopen the Color Settings dialog box in Photoshop.

Synchronizing the color settings helps to ensure that color is reproduced consistently among Adobe applications that use the Color Settings dialog box. You can also share custom color settings by saving and loading the settings file in the desired applications and providing the settings file to other users. For more information, see Photoshop 7.0 online Help.

2 Choose Edit > Color Settings (Windows, Mac OS 9) or Photoshop > Color Settings (Mac OS 10) to display the Color Settings dialog box.

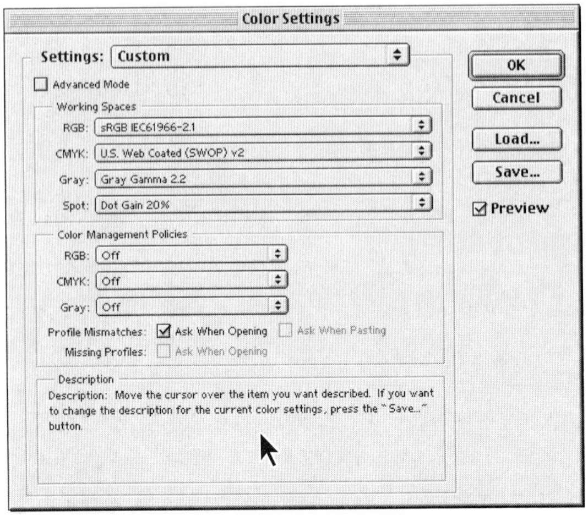

The bottom of the dialog box contains information about the various color-management options in it, which you'll now review.

3 Move the mouse pointer over each part of the dialog box, including the names of areas (such as Working Spaces) and the options you can choose (such as the different menu options), returning the options to their defaults when you're done. As you move the mouse, view the information that appears at the bottom of the dialog box.

Now you'll choose a general set of options that will specify the individual options for you. In this case, you'll pick one designed for a print workflow, rather than an online workflow.

4 Select a prepress default from the Settings menu at the top of the dialog box (we used U.S. Prepress Defaults) and click OK.

Proofing an image

In this part of the lesson, you'll begin working with a typical file of the kind you might scan in from a printed original. You'll open it, convert its color profile, and set it up so that you can see on-screen a close representation of what it will look like when printed. This will enable you to proof the printed image on your screen for printed output.

You'll begin by opening the file.

1 Choose File > Open, and open the file 18Start.tif from the Lessons/Lesson18 folder.

Because 18Start.tif contains a color profile that indicates that the image was created in a different color space than the one you set up for Photoshop, the Embedded Profile Mismatch notice appears, asking you to resolve this difference.

There are three options in the notice. Selecting Use the Embedded Profile changes the color settings from the ones you defined for Photoshop in the previous section to the ones represented by the profile in the image. Selecting Discard the Embedded Profile displays the document as though it had no profile and can result in inaccurate colors being displayed. Rather than choose either of these, you'll select another option instead.

2 Select the Convert Document's Colors to the Working Space option, and click OK.

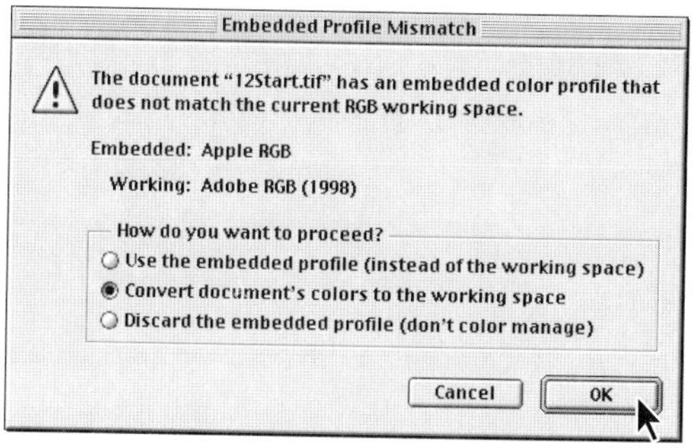

An RGB image of a scanned postcard is displayed.

The Convert Document's Color to the Working Space option makes Photoshop compare the color space in 18Start.tif's embedded color profile with the color space you defined in the Color Settings dialog box. Photoshop then converts 18Start.tif's colors as necessary to display the image on-screen as accurately as possible.

Note: *Depending on what you've specified in the Color Settings dialog box, if the image did not have a color profile already, the Missing Profile notice would have appeared. This notice lets you choose whether to leave the image without a profile (that is, without color management); apply the current color profile that you specified in the Color Settings dialog box; or assign a profile from a list of possible profiles. Applying the current color profile is generally a good choice.*

Before soft-proofing—that is, proofing on-screen—or printing this image, you'll set up a proof profile. A proof profile (also called a *proof setup*) defines how the document is going to be printed, and adds those visual properties to the on-screen version for more accurate soft-proofing. Photoshop provides a variety of settings that can help you proof images for different uses, including print and display on the Web. For this lesson, you'll create a custom proof setup. You can then save the settings for use on other images that will be output the same way.

3 Choose View > Proof Setup > Custom.

4 Make sure that the Preview check box is selected.

5 On the Profile pop-up menu in the Proof Setup dialog box, choose a profile that represents a final output source color profile, such as that for the printer you'll use to print the image. If you don't have a specific printer, the profile Working CMYK - U.S. Web Coated (SWOP) v2 is generally a good choice.

6 Make sure Preserve Color Numbers is not selected. Leaving this option off simulates how the image will appear if colors are converted from the document space to their nearest equivalents in the proof profile space.

Note: *This option is not available on all operating systems. Continue to the next steps.*

7 From the Intent menu, choose a rendering intent for the conversion (we chose Relative Colorimetric, a good choice for preserving color relationships without sacrificing color accuracy).

8 If it's available for the profile you chose, select Ink Black. Then choose Paper White.

Notice that the image appears to lose contrast. Ink Black simulates the dynamic range defined by an image's profile. Paper White simulates the specific shade of white for the print medium defined by an image's profile. That is, the whites shown in the image are now simulating the white of paper.

Normal image

Image with Ink Black and Paper White options

9 Click OK.

To turn the proof settings off and on, choose View > Proof Colors.

Identifying out-of-gamut colors

Most scanned photographs contain RGB colors within the CMYK gamut, and changing the image to CMYK mode (which you'll do later in order to print the file) converts all the colors with relatively little substitution. Images that are created or altered digitally, however, often contain RGB colors that are outside the CMYK gamut—for example, neon-colored logos and lights.

Note: *Out-of-gamut colors are identified by an exclamation point next to the color swatch in the Color palette, the color picker, and the Info palette.*

Before you convert an image from RGB to CMYK, you can preview the CMYK color values while still in RGB mode.

1 Choose View > Gamut Warning to see out-of-gamut colors. Adobe Photoshop builds a color- conversion table and displays a neutral gray where the colors are out-of-gamut.

Because the gray can be hard to spot in the image, you'll now convert it to a stronger gamut-warning color.

2 Choose Edit > Preferences > Transparency & Gamut (Windows, Mac OS 9) or Photoshop > Preferences > Transparency & Gamut (Mac OS 10). Then click the Color sample at the bottom of the dialog box.

3 Choose a vivid color, such as pink or a saturated clear blue, and click OK.

4 Click OK again to close the Transparency & Gamut dialog box. The gray is replaced by the new color you chose.

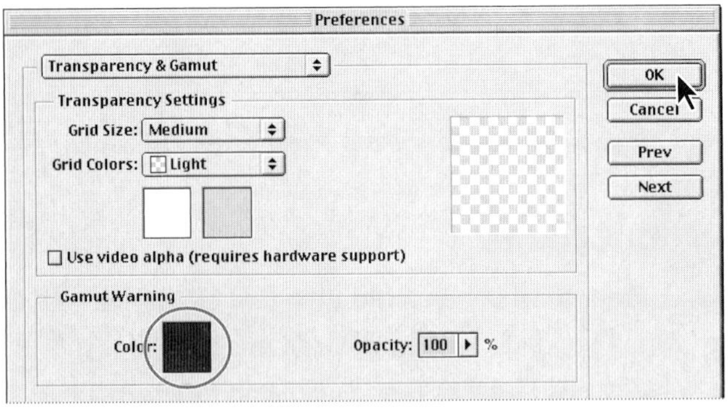

5 Choose View > Gamut Warning to turn off the preview of out-of-gamut colors.

Photoshop will automatically correct these out-of-gamut colors when you save the file in Photoshop EPS format later in this lesson. Photoshop EPS format changes the RGB image to CMYK, adjusting the RGB colors as needed to bring them into the CMYK color gamut.

Adjusting an image and printing a proof

The next step in preparing an image for output is to make any color and tonal adjustments to the image. In this part of the lesson, you'll add some tonal and color adjustments to correct an off-color scan of the original postcard.

So that you can compare the image before and after making corrections, you'll start by making a copy.

1 Choose Image > Duplicate and click OK to duplicate the image.

2 Arrange the two image windows in your workspace so that you can compare them as you work.

Here you'll adjust the hue and saturation of the image. There are various ways to adjust color, including using the Levels and Curves commands. In this lesson, you'll use the Hue/Saturation command to adjust the artwork.

3 Select 18Start.tif (the original image) and choose Image > Adjustments > Hue/Saturation.

4 Drag the Hue/Saturation dialog box aside so that you can still see the 18Start.tif image, and then select the following settings:

- Drag the Hue slider until the colors, especially the flesh tones, look more natural. (We used +20.)
- Drag the Saturation slider until the intensity of the colors looks normal (we used –17).
- Leave the Lightness setting at the default value (0), and click OK.

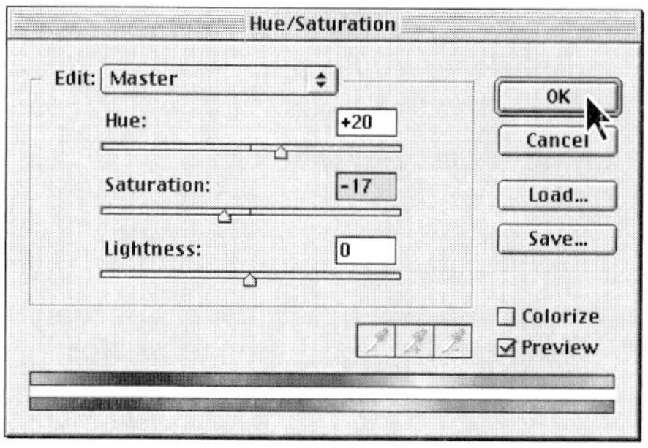

5 With 18Start.tif still selected, choose File > Print With Preview.

6 In the Print dialog box, make sure that the Show More Options check box is selected, or select it now. Then select the following options:

• In the pop-up menu immediately below the Show More Options check box, choose Color Management.

• Under Source Space, select Proof Setup.

• Under Print Space, use the Profile and the Intent pop-up menus to select the profile for the color printer on which you plan to print the image for proofing. If your specific printer isn't listed, choose Working CMYK.

• Click Done.

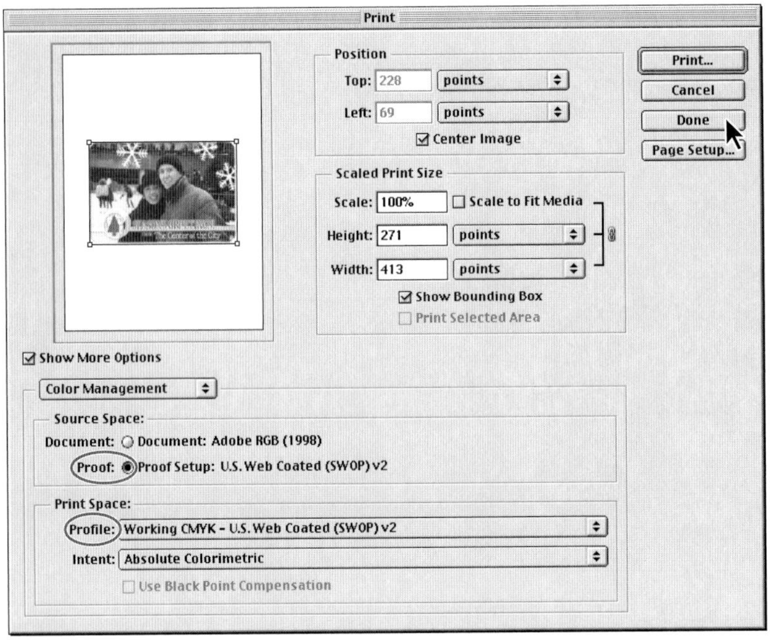

7 Choose File > Save to save your work.

8 Print a copy of the image to a color printer and compare it to the on-screen version.

Saving the image as a separation

In this part of the lesson, you'll learn how to save the image as a separation, so that it can print out on separate cyan, magenta, yellow, and black plates.

1 With 18Start.tif still selected, choose File > Save As.

2 In the Save As dialog box, select the following options:

- On the Format pop-up menu, select Photoshop EPS.
- Under Save Options, for Color, select the Use Proof Setup: Working CMYK check box.

***Note:** These settings cause the image to be automatically converted from RGB to CMYK when it is saved in the Photoshop Encapsulated PostScript (EPS) format.*

3 Name the file **18Start.eps** and click Save.

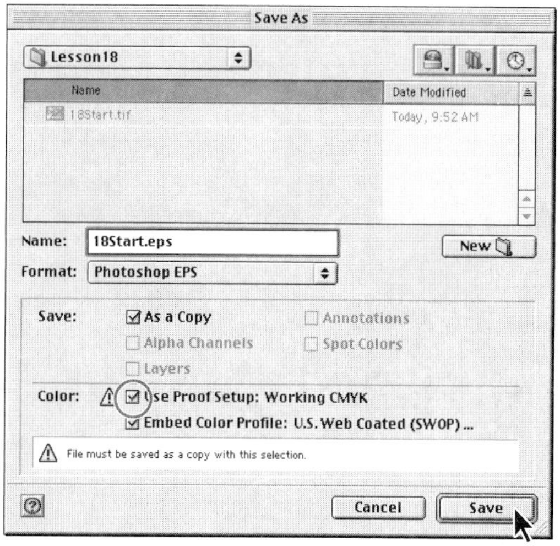

4 Click OK on the EPS Options dialog box that appears.

5 Choose File > Open, and open the 18Start.eps file, located in the Lessons/Lesson18 folder.

Notice that 18Start.eps is now a CMYK file.

6 Choose File > Save and then close the 18Start.tif and 18Start copy.tif.

Now only the 18Start.eps file is open in Photoshop.

Selecting print options

To select printing options, you make choices in the File Info and Print With Preview dialog boxes and then choose Options from the Print dialog box. The next sections introduce you to some of the printing options.

For information on all the print options, see Photoshop 7.0 online Help.

Entering file information

Photoshop supports the information standard developed by the Newspaper Association of America and the International Press Telecommunications Council to identify transmitted text and images.

1 Select the 18Start.eps image and choose File > File Info. The File Info dialog box opens with General selected in the Section option.

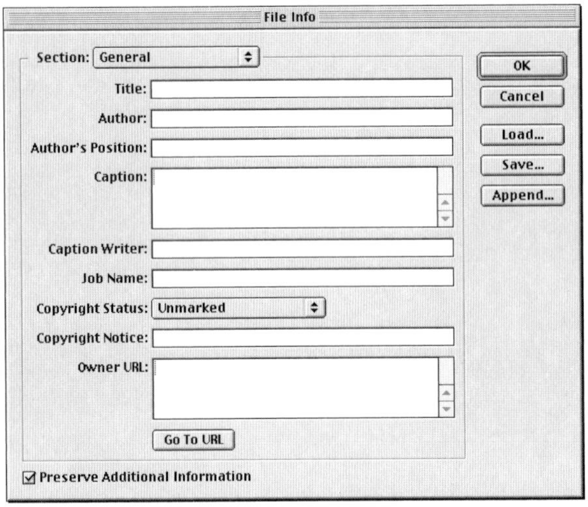

2 Type information in any of the options available, such as a title for the image, a caption, and so forth.

Note: *To print a caption when you print an image, choose File > Print With Preview, and click the Caption option.*

3 In the Section pop-up menu, select Keywords.

4 Type a keyword (such as **skating** or **winter**) in the text box, and then click the Add button. You can type and enter as many other keywords as you want.

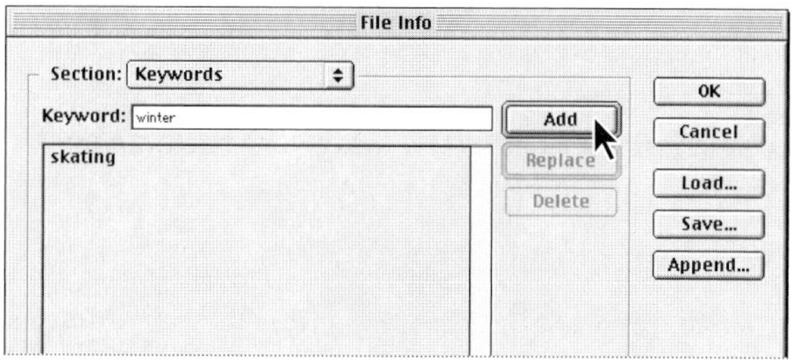

5 In the Section pop-up menu, select Origin.

6 Click the Today button to enter today's date in the Date Created text box. Then type any other information you want to enter in the other options.

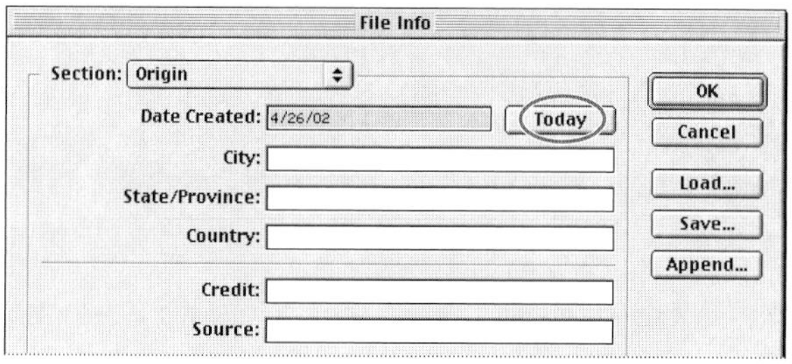

Note: *There are two more choices on the Section pop-up menu: Categories and EXIF. You can use the Categories option with the Associated Press regional registry. The EXIF option displays summarized information, some of which is imported data from a digital camera and some of which represents a few of the entries you make elsewhere in the File Info dialog box.*

7 Click OK to close the File Info dialog box, and then choose File > Save.

For complete information about all the File Info sections, see Photoshop 7.0 online Help.

Printing

When you're ready to print your image, use the following guidelines for best results:

- Set the parameters for the halftone screen.
- Print a *color composite*, often called a *color comp*. A color composite is a single print that combines the red, green, and blue channels of an RGB image (or the cyan, magenta, yellow, and black channels of a CMYK image). This indicates what the final printed image will look like.
- Print separations to make sure the image separates correctly.
- Print to film.

Printing a halftone

To specify the halftone screen when you print an image, you use the Screen option in the Print With Preview dialog box. The results of using a halftone screen appear only in the printed copy; you cannot see the halftone screen on-screen.

You use one halftone screen to print a grayscale image. You use four halftone screens (one for each process color) to print color separations. In this example, you'll be adjusting the screen frequency and dot shape to produce a halftone screen for a grayscale image.

The *screen frequency* controls the density of dots on the screen. Since the dots are arranged in lines on the screen, the common measurement for screen frequency is lines per inch (lpi). The higher the screen frequency, the finer the image produced (depending on the line-screen capability of the printer). Magazines, for example, tend to use fine screens of 133 lpi and higher because they are usually printed on coated paper stock and on high-quality presses. Newspapers, which are usually printed on lower-quality paper stock, tend to use lower screen frequencies, such as 85 lpi.

The *screen angle* used to create halftones of grayscale images is generally 45°. For best results with color separations, select the Auto option in the Halftone Screens dialog box (choose Page Setup > Screens > Halftone Screens). You can also specify an angle for each of the color screens. Setting the screens at different angles ensures that the dots placed by the four screens blend to look like continuous color and do not produce moiré patterns.

Diamond-shaped dots are the most commonly used in halftone screens. In Adobe Photoshop, however, you can also choose round, elliptical, linear, square, and cross-shaped dots.

Note: *By default, an image will use the halftone screen settings of the output device or of the software from which you output the image, such as a page-layout program. You usually don't need to specify halftone screen settings in the following way unless you want to override the default settings.*

1 Make sure that the 18Start.eps image window is active.

2 Choose Image > Mode > Grayscale; then click OK to discard the color information.

3 Choose File > Print With Preview, and make sure that the Show More Options check box is selected.

4 Immediately under the Show More Options check box, select Output from the pop-up menu.

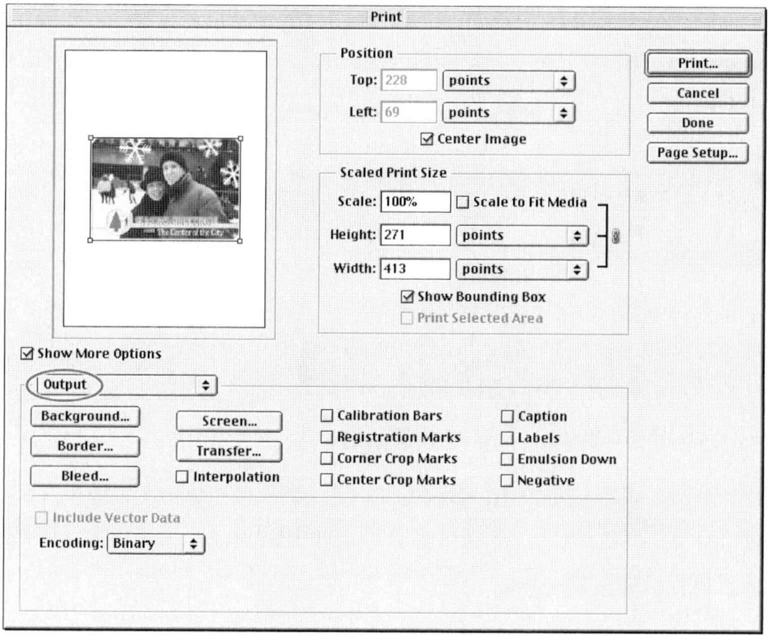

5 Click Screen to open the Halftone Screen dialog box, and enter the following options:

- Deselect the Use Printer's Default Screen check box.
- In Frequency, type **133**, and make sure that Lines/Inch is selected.
- For Angle, type **45°**.
- For Shape, choose Ellipse.
- Click OK to close the Halftone Screen dialog box.

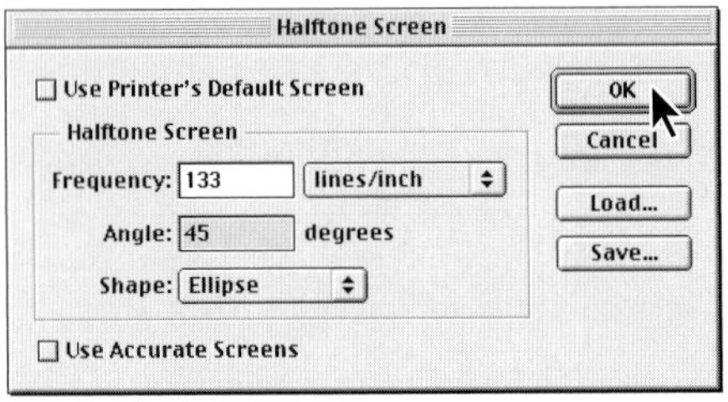

6 Click Done to close the Print With Preview dialog box.

7 To print the image, choose File > Print. (If you don't have a printer, skip this step.)

8 Choose File > Close, and don't save your changes.

For more information about printing halftones, see Photoshop 7.0 online help.

Printing separations

By default, a CMYK image prints as a single document. To print the file as four separations, you need to select the Separations option in the Print With Preview dialog box. Otherwise, the CMYK image prints as a single, composite image.

In this optional part of the lesson, you can print the file as separations.

1 Choose File > Open, and open the18Start.eps file in the Lessons/Lesson18 folder on your hard drive.

2 Choose File > Print With Preview.

3 In the Print dialog box, make sure that the Show More Options check box is selected, and then set the following options:

- In the pop-up menu immediately below the Show More Options check box, select Color Management.
- For Source Space, select Document.
- On the Profile pop-up menu, select Separations.

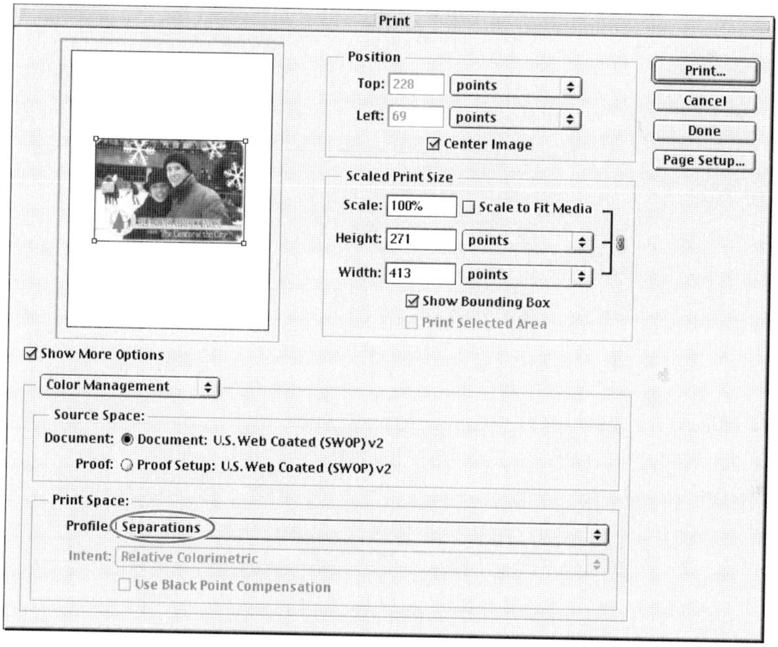

4 Click Print. (If you don't have a printer, skip this step.)

5 Choose File > Close, and don't save the changes.

This completes your introduction to producing color separations and printing using Adobe Photoshop.

For information about all color management and printing options, see Photoshop 7.0 online Help.

Review questions

1 What steps should you follow to reproduce color accurately?

2 What is a gamut?

3 What is an ICC profile?

4 What is a color separation? How does a CMYK image differ from an RGB image?

5 What steps should you follow when preparing an image for color separations?

Review answers

1 Calibrate your monitor, and then use the Color Settings dialog box to specify which color spaces to use. For example, you can specify which RGB color space to use for online images and which CMYK color space to use for images that will be printed. You can then proof the image, check for out-of-gamut colors, adjust colors as needed, and—for printed images—create color separations.

2 A gamut is the range of colors that can be reproduced by a color model or device. For example, the RGB and CMYK color models have different gamuts, as do any two RGB scanners.

3 An ICC profile is a description of a device's color space, such as the CMYK color space of a particular printer. Applications such as Photoshop can interpret ICC profiles in an image to maintain consistent color across different applications, platforms, and devices.

4 A color separation is created when an image is converted to CMYK mode. The colors in the CMYK image are separated into the four process-color channels: cyan, magenta, yellow, and black. An RGB image has three color channels: red, green, and blue.

5 You prepare an image for print by following the steps for reproducing color accurately, and then converting the image from RGB mode to CMYK mode to build a color separation.

Index

T

Z